Praise for *Sams Teach Yourself jQuery Mobile in 24 Hours*

"Phil does a great job taking you through the mobile ecosystem and how jQuery Mobile makes it dead simple to break into it. Going from the fundamentals of web and mobile to advanced topics like video and themes, anyone looking to gain greater knowledge in mobile development will profit from this book."

—**Brett Child**, Software Consultant, Software Technology Group

"*Sams Teach Yourself jQuery Mobile in 24 Hours* by Phil Dutson is full of rock-solid real-world examples that can be easily built upon to create a functional, rich, custom, completely usable mobile website.

The book reads incredibly easy; you find that the learning comes almost effortlessly as you read and work through the tutorials. In addition to learning the elements you need to build your own website, you'll also learn how to extend and fill your mobile website with elements such as video and the creation and scanning of QR and Microsoft Tag codes. It even covers the introduction of jQuery Mobile into WordPress and the development of Android-based applications using jQuery Mobile and PhoneGap. I highly recommend a read if you're doing any type of mobile web development."

—**Drew Harvey**, Solution Architect, CrossView, Inc.

"This book is an excellent resource for any developer looking to integrate jQuery mobile into their next project. Phil covers the fundamentals of jQuery mobile while also providing best practices for mobile development."

—**Jim Hathaway**, Web Developer

"This book is an excellent read for beginners and web veterans alike. Phil Dutson does an excellent job of highlighting the jQuery Mobile framework's semantics and syntax while also providing an introduction to mobile web development best practices in general."

—**Greg Lavallee**, Software Engineer, The Washington Post Company

"Well-written, detail-oriented, and documented with plenty of hands-on examples makes *Sams Teach Yourself jQuery Mobile in 24 Hours* flow and easily comprehensible. This book is a must-have library addition for the software developer beginning down the mobile application development path."

—**Tamara Urry**, Sr. Software Engineer & Owner, JET Technical

"In my years of learning, training, and teaching programming, I have rarely come across an individual with Phil Dutson's ability to explain code. Whether you are a beginner, novice, or experienced programmer, *Sams Teach Yourself jQuery Mobile in 24 Hours* is written for you. Developers who want to take advantage of the vast mobile market will want to add this book to their arsenal."

—**Dale Wallentine**, Associate Dean, School of Technology Stevens-Henager College, Logan Utah Campus

Phil Dutson

Sams **Teach Yourself**

jQuery Mobile

in **24** **Hours**

SAMS   800 East 96th Street, Indianapolis, Indiana, 46240 USA

Sams Teach Yourself jQuery Mobile in 24 Hours

ISBN-13: 978-0-672-33594-5
ISBN-10: 0-672-33594-8

Library of Congress Cataloging-in-Publication Data:

Dutson, Phil, 1981-
    Sams teach yourself jQuery mobile in 24 hours / Phil Dutson.
        p. cm.
    ISBN 978-0-672-33594-5 (pbk. : alk. paper)
    1. JavaScript (Computer program language)–Programmed instruction. 2. Web site development-
-Programmed instruction. I. Title.
    QA76.73.J38D88 2013
    005.2'762–dc23

                                                2012015341

Printed in the United States of America

First Printing July 2012

Trademarks

All terms mentioned in this book that are known to be trademarks or service marks have been appropriately capitalized. Sams Publishing cannot attest to the accuracy of this information. Use of a term in this book should not be regarded as affecting the validity of any trademark or service mark.

Warning and Disclaimer

Every effort has been made to make this book as complete and as accurate as possible, but no warranty or fitness is implied. The information provided is on an "as is" basis. The author and the publisher shall have neither liability nor responsibility to any person or entity with respect to any loss or damages arising from the information contained in this book.

Bulk Sales

Sams Publishing offers excellent discounts on this book when ordered in quantity for bulk purchases or special sales. For more information, please contact

> U.S. Corporate and Government Sales
> 1-800-382-3419
> corpsales@pearsontechgroup.com

For sales outside of the U.S., please contact

> International Sales
> international@pearsoned.com

Editor-in-Chief
Mark Taub

Executive Editor
Laura Lewin

Development Editor
Songlin Qiu

Managing Editor
Kristy Hart

Senior Project Editor
Lori Lyons

Copy Editor
Geneil Breeze

Indexer
Tim Wright

Proofreader
Kathy Ruiz

Technical Editors
Jim Hathaway
Greg Lavallee

Publishing Coordinator
Olivia Basegio

Multimedia Developer
Dan Scherf

Interior Designer
Gary Adair

Cover Designer
Anne Jones

Compositor
Nonie Ratcliff

Contents at a Glance

Part IV: Extending the Mobile Experience

Table of Contents

About the Author

Phil Dutson is the lead front-end developer for ICON Health and Fitness. He has worked on projects and solutions for NordicTrack, ProForm, Freemotion, Sears, Costco, Sam's Club, and others. He was an original team member of the iFit team that integrated Google Maps into personalized workout n and playback. Phil co-founded and currently manages The E-Com DevBlog, a development blog focused on web development and solutions. To learn more visit http://dev.tonic1394.com.

Dedication

To my patient and exceptionally loving family. Thank you for the support and encouragement.

Acknowledgments

A huge thanks to all of the wonderful people at Sams for working with me on this project. In no particular order I'd like to single out my project editors, Trina MacDonald and Laura Lewin, for making sure I hit or at least came close to my deadlines; Olivia Basegio for helping me get things turned in; my awesome development editor, Songlin Qiu, who not only made sure that I always spelled "lets" as "let's" but also made sure that everything flowed nicely together; and my outstandingly brilliant technical editors, Jim Hathaway and Greg Lavallee, who not only tested every bit of code I threw at them, but pointed out when more explanation was necessary for the reader to really understand the concepts presented. I would also like to thank the production team, who put this book into your hands: Lori Lyons, Geneil Breeze, Nonie Ratcliff, and Kathy Ruiz.

As a personal thanks, I'd like to tell Dave "Davidicus" Brown thank you for being indirectly and yet directly responsible for this endeavor. Another special thanks goes to my designer friends in UltraCube for always telling anyone who would listen (including me) to "believe in your dreams," as well as my current eCommerce crew (Tracy, Casey, Sid, Remo, Brett, Eric, Chris, and Kim) and my previous crew (Berticus, Drewbie, Matt, Branden, and Stretch) for the support, praise, slight criticism, and sanity checks.

We Want to Hear from You!

As the reader of this book, you are our most important critic and commentator. We value your opinion and want to know what we're doing right, what we could do better, what areas you'd like to see us publish in, and any other words of wisdom you're willing to pass our way.

You can email or write me directly to let me know what you did or didn't like about this book—as well as what we can do to make our books stronger.

Please note that I cannot help you with technical problems related to the topic of this book, and that due to the high volume of mail I receive, I might not be able to reply to every message.

When you write, please be sure to include this book's title and author as well as your name and phone or email address. I will carefully review your comments and share them with the author and editors who worked on the book.

E-mail: consumer@samspublishing.com

Mail: Sams Publishing
            ATTN: Reader Feedback
            800 East 96th Street
            Indianapolis, IN 46240 USA

Reader Services

Visit our website and register this book at informit.com/register for convenient access to any updates, downloads, or errata that might be available for this book.

Introduction

There is little doubt that the way we currently access, use, and share the things we find online is going to continue to become more and more mobile. Every month thousands of new smartphones are activated and accompany their owners everywhere from trips to the grocery store to mountain hiking. As our thirst for connectivity expands into areas not possible a few years ago we need sites that deliver information quickly and easily, and that will work no matter what device we are u sing for access. This can be done with jQuery Mobile.

Built on the popular and stable jQuery framework, jQuery Mobile can be utilized to transform existing sites into mobile-friendly ones. If you do not have a site yet, don't worry because starting out with a blank slate is a great way to see how simple and easy using jQuery Mobile is. Shortly you will have a site that handles as well on a mobile device as it does on a desktop.

Getting into mobile site development is no longer an option; it's a necessity. Even though the landscape is morphing as much for the mobile web as for the current desktop websites, using a framework like jQuery Mobile helps bridge the gaps between hardware and software platforms. This gives you the peace of mind that users can still use your site, even if they are on a legacy device that may fail to support many other sites today.

Key Features of This Book

You're not only going to learn how to use jQuery Mobile, you're going to put it to work with scannable codes, videos, and CMS integration. Starting out with the basics we build a simple web page to display information about you. You'll then kick it up a notch and learn how to customize your page by including a responsive layout so that small screen devices are shown content made just for them while tablet users get an optimized experience that takes advantage of the increased screen space. You also learn how to detect mobile devices and route them to special directories or sections of your site based on the User Agent.

Mobile users also enjoy the use of rich site content, including videos that improve the user experience by providing a visual guide to a product or service. You learn about embedding videos as well as encoding video so that they play back on mobile devices as well as the pros and cons for each method.

If you are in marketing looking into the viability of a mobile project or endeavor, you'll enjoy learning about the use of scannable codes to help track and direct mobile users to specific sites, videos, or text messages. These codes can be printed in magazines, manuals, and on product packaging to help users learn more about your product or to sign up for updates.

As you progress hour by hour, you get a great foundation for mobile site development as well as gain valuable insight through the tricks, tips, and warnings scattered throughout. Twenty-four hours from now you'll have a greater understanding of mobile site development and what needs to be done to get your next project mobilized and into the hands of millions.

How to Use This Book

This book is straightforward. It starts here in the introduction, and then moves on into the first hour. There are 24 lessons, each of which should take about an hour to complete. I tried to set up the book not only as a lesson guide, but also as a handy reference guide that you can keep around once you are finished. As each hour covers a portion of the jQuery Mobile framework along with examples, this book should prove useful even if you use it only for reference. While it is possible to quaff an energy drink or two and have this entire book finished in one go, I'd honestly recommend you give your subconscious some time to process the concepts you learn in each hour.

How This Book Is Organized

This book has been carved into four parts to help you focus or reference the section that best suits your level of learning or interest. They are

- ▶ Part I, "Beginning jQuery Mobile," covers the basics, everything from HTML, CSS, and JavaScript to building a page using jQuery Mobile. If you are entirely new to the game, start right here, and you'll be up to speed in no time.

- ▶ Part II, "Creating the User Interface," teaches you about the user interface and how it is styled with jQuery Mobile. This is anything the user is going to see, touch, and use. This part even covers the use of events to help create custom functionality for gestures as well as adjusting the built-in theme manually.

- ▶ Part III, "Customizing Your Content," takes you beyond the jQuery Mobile defaults and looks at adding plug-ins, themes, responsive design, and device detection.

- ▶ Part IV, "Extending the Mobile Experience," is all about taking it to the next level. Video integration, device emulation, minified code, creating an Android app using PhoneGap, and even adding jQuery Mobile to a WordPress theme are all covered here.

▶ Q&A, Quiz, and Exercises

At the end of each hour you find a section that contains some questions and answers for the topic covered during the hour. While some of these questions may offer a deeper explanation or insight into what was covered, others explain the reasons for covering some solutions while overlooking others. The Quiz section can be used to help you test what you learned in the hour while the Exercises help you put it all into practice.

Conventions Used in This Book

This book contains special elements as described here:

TIP

This Is a Tip

These are tips and tricks that you can use to help make your site or experience a little better.

NOTE

This Is Important Information

When you see these you get important information about a topic that was mentioned or covered.

CAUTION

This Is a Warning!

When you see these be careful; the information posted here usually saves you from doing something that might break your code, or lets you know about a result that would otherwise be unexpected.

This book uses a special `monospace` font on code/progamming-related terms/text such as `id="home"`

Code listings contain numbered lines for better understanding.

Sample Code for This Book

Throughout the book various files are referenced to help you learn jQuery Mobile as occasional starting points and for comparison with code you have written yourself. These files can be downloaded in a compressed format by visiting www.informit.com/title/9780672335945. Go to the Downloads tab and click on the "Sample Code" link.

NOTE

The Author's Websites

Anything web related moves fast. Sometimes there are small gaps of time between versions in a framework or browser, but when a community is driving new functionality and more and more devices are released into the market, things are quickly changed. The author of this book, Phil Dutson, maintains two websites that can be useful as you learn about jQuery Mobile and web development. The first is http://www.jquerymobilein24.com/ where you can find blog entries and updates to the world of jQuery Mobile. The second is the eCom DevBlog, which can be found by visiting http://dev.tonic1394.com/.

Each site hosts a blog with a searchable index to help you find what you are looking for, as well as a comments section that you can use to leave feedback or ask questions.

PART I

Beginning jQuery Mobile

Getting to Know jQuery Mobile

What You'll Learn in This Hour:

▶ Why you should use jQuery Mobile

▶ What devices support jQuery Mobile

▶ The tools that will help you develop your site

I am excited that you are intrigued enough with jQuery Mobile to start learning it. To kick things off, we start with a short discussion on why you should be thinking about diving into mobile design and why jQuery Mobile is the perfect solution.

Then we learn about the different types of devices that jQuery Mobile works with as well as a quick look at some supported operating systems.

Finally we discover what software is available to help you get started developing on whatever platform you are currently using.

Why You Should Use jQuery Mobile

The world is going mobile. It is predicted that mobile web traffic will overtake desktop web traffic within the next few years. Even now people everywhere use their mobile devices to learn, shop, compare, or even as a distraction while they wait for an appointment. Mobile devices are convenient and easily taken anywhere.

Think about how you use your current mobile device. Even if you have only an iPod Touch, I'm betting you still check email, look up the forecast, and do some light web surfing on it. Think about the apps you have installed; a few of them probably could be or already are cleverly designed web applications.

While browsing on your mobile, you have probably noticed that more and more websites provide a mobile experience or version of their site. You may wonder how they created the site, or whether they used a complicated in-house system or framework to make the site.

Of course maybe that's not it at all. Maybe you have a tablet or smartphone and have noticed that when you load a site in your mobile browser the device buckles under the weight of all the assets it has to try to load.

You know there has to be a way to make a mobile site responsive, flexible, and simple, but where do you start? An abundance of mobile development kits and tools are available, but what about support for those kits or their reliability?

The answer to your questions is easy: You should be using jQuery Mobile.

Responsive

Many things make a site responsive: how a page looks when it transitions, what happens when you tap on a button, even how content loads.

Did you know that there is a difference between a "click" event and a "touch" event? More importantly, did you know that there is around a 300ms difference between the two events? Sure 300ms may not sound like much, but when was the last time you pressed a button that had a one-third of a second delay on it? Did you press the button again because it felt "laggy"? This is one of the problems that jQuery Mobile helps you remedy. Using touch events decreases the lag, increases the perceived speed of your website, and greatly increases user happiness.

Another problem with normal sites on mobile devices is how long they take to load. Sometimes you see the backgrounds render and then some image boxes and finally some text. I have even been on websites that load the background and then nothing else because large image elements or a video needed to load, leaving the whole page in an ugly unfinished state. I didn't hang around long enough to see whether they ever finished loading. An unresponsive site where you can't even see the page or navigate around it does not make a good mobile experience.

jQuery Mobile solves loading problems by using deferred loading techniques mixed with a healthy dose of Ajax to load images, content, and more. This means that the site loads what is important to the user first and adds extra content while the user is absorbing the information they came to see in the first place.

Flexible

When developing, few things are worse than committing to a framework and finding out that you cannot customize any of it. What if you don't like one of the widgets provided in the framework? What if the styles are ugly or do not match your brand? What if the framework lets you customize the style but doesn't let you add in your own custom widget? These are all real problems, and each of them is easy to overcome with jQuery Mobile.

If you don't like the included themes you can use ThemeRoller and make your own. What if you like the main theme styles but need a different colored header style? Easy, you can include a second style sheet and overwrite the existing styles. For the ultimate in flexible style changes, you can actually replace one of the included themes with your own. This allows you to fine-tune everything to fit your needs or branding.

As for widgets, you are free to build whatever you want. Because jQuery Mobile is built on the jQuery framework you can build and use widgets and plug-ins just as you would on nonmobile websites. While you need to plan ahead for differences in the mobile environment (no hover states or events, size constraints, less computing power, and so on), you have the freedom to build whatever you want and use it within your mobile site using standard JavaScript or by leveraging the jQuery framework.

Simple

By leveraging some of the new HTML5 proposed standards along with using the jQuery framework, setting up a site is easy. There are no framework-only tags to learn, just modification attributes used in the existing tags that you are already using today.

Support and Reliability

jQuery Mobile is built on the amazing jQuery library. jQuery has been proven to be a fast, efficient, and dependable JavaScript library. jQuery has taken the Web by storm and changed the way developers implement and use JavaScript on websites and web applications.

The jQuery team is dedicated to making the jQuery library the number one choice in JavaScript development. Having this as the foundation for jQuery Mobile ensures a fully supported and reliable solution for years to come. jQuery was even chosen by Microsoft as a preferred JavaScript framework, and Microsoft has included full auto-completion support for jQuery inside Visual Studio.

Contacting the jQuery Mobile team is easy; they have a dedicated blog, forum, and Twitter account with continuing posts about updates, features, and helpful hints and how-to's. The community is rapidly growing, and now is a great time to jump in and get involved with the project.

Supported Devices

What can jQuery Mobile be used on? Almost any device that has a browser can run jQuery Mobile (including desktops). You will, however, get a different experience based on what browser you use and on the hardware that is pushing the browser. Of course it goes a little deeper than that; it also depends on what operating system your device has. The following sections start with larger hardware devices and work down through smaller ones.

Desktop, Laptops, and All-in-One Systems

On your PC, Mac, or Linux computer jQuery Mobile sites run in any modern browser (note that by "modern" I mean browsers that have support for HTML5 tags and some CSS3 support). Running your mobile site in Firefox, Chrome, Safari, or Opera should yield a good result as they all have some support for HTML5. You may see an occasional rounded corner that isn't round, but for the most part the site looks good and behaves as expected. Even Chrome Desktop displays and works well with jQuery Mobile.

Tablets

The experience that you get using jQuery Mobile is determined not only by the supported browsers of the device but also by the processing power of the tablet.

Most tablets have a large screen, and it can take a considerable amount of processing power to drive that screen. This means that while your site still loads quickly and renders correctly, some page transitions and dialog pop-ups may appear to be skipping frames. This doesn't necessarily mean that your site is actually any slower, but on some tablets it may appear to stutter.

To clarify, when I was testing with an iPad and iPad 2 I found that all special effects and page transitions were as fluid and as smooth as I expected. When testing with a Galaxy Tab 10.1 things were still smooth, but I noticed some stutter or a complete lack of animation while the screen was being transitioned from page to page.

While I have not personally tested the TouchPad, ZiiO, Playbook, or the newer Archos tablets, they are reported to handle jQuery Mobile fairly smoothly.

Smartphones

There are way too many phones to list them all, so instead this section talks about the OS support on various phones. Let me also restate that jQuery Mobile works on just about every platform, but some of the advanced features and Ajax loading may not be supported. This is another reason why using jQuery Mobile is a wise decision. The ability to fall back to support older devices and still have a functioning site is a must-have.

Android

If you are using the built-in browser on Android all the advanced features will work and you will be treated to the full array of visual splendor in transitions. Note that if you are using Fennec, Firefox, or Opera mobile you may run into some styling issues and some lack of full support on animations, but your overall experience should be rather pleasant.

iOS

The way jQuery Mobile handles on the iPhone is actually impressive. Transitions are smooth, animations are fluid, and the dialog boxes pop in and out perfectly. Support is definitely not lacking for mobile Safari on iOS.

A warning about third-party browsers: Using a browser app may degrade some performance, and in some cases actually cause Ajax navigation to fail. This doesn't mean that the site is not usable, it just means that instead of a nice seamless transition between pages the site loads more like a standard site, using page refreshes in response to taps or clicks.

BlackBerry

The BlackBerry operating system has several versions released, and your experience will vary based on what version you are running. Version 6.0+ has all the bells and whistles that Android and iOS have. Version 5.0 still looks good but loses Ajax navigation. Any of the version 4 devices get a standard fallback version of the site. This means that instead of nice CSS3 styling and transitions you get a simple styled site that uses page refreshes to move to new content.

The Playbook runs an independent operating system and provides an experience similar to version 6.0 and 7.0 of the BlackBerry operating system.

webOS

With the future of webOS itself looking continually grim, and hardware support already at an end, I will just say that versions 1.4 to 3.0 all handle jQuery Mobile with full functionality.

The slower your webOS device is, the more chance you will see some frame skipping, but you still get full Ajax support, styles, and transitions.

Windows Mobile

Windows Phone 7 handles jQuery Mobile without a problem. It looks good, runs smoothly, and all features are enabled. This is due to the included web browser being based on Internet Explorer 9, giving users access to some HTML5 and CSS3 features.

Windows Mobile 6.5, however, is a different story. Windows Mobile 6.5 uses an older version of the Internet Explorer browser and suffers from a lack of feature support. While the Windows Mobile team is hard at work making new releases of Internet Explorer more developer and standard friendly, those using an older version of the browser will miss out on AJAX navigation and some styling. Any mobile device running Windows Mobile prior to version 6.5 displays the basic fallback version of the site.

eReader Devices

This is actually a tough one to nail down because there are many eReader devices on the market.

What I can tell you is that jQuery Mobile supports Kindle devices that include the experimental WebKit-based browser. Other eReader devices, such as the Nook Color, that run a modified version of Android also have full support for jQuery Mobile.

Keep in mind that with eReader devices, the ones that use current E-Ink technology are required to redraw the entire screen when a page is loaded, so performance on these devices may suffer.

The Developer's Arsenal

Now that we know that jQuery Mobile runs on just about any connected device, you may have a few questions, such as:

▶ What programming languages do I use to create my mobile site in?

▶ What, if any, IDEs are available to work with?

▶ Do I need to have web server installed to write mobile sites?

▶ What platform should I be on to write a mobile site?

▶ Can I develop for free, or is there a cost associated with the software?

These are real and important questions, and one should always know what tools are available. Let's answer each of these questions and expand on them so you know exactly what is available in the developer arsenal.

Programming Languages

If you have already created a website and are looking to make a mobile version or convert your existing site into a mobile one, I have some great news for you. You already have the entire basic skill set needed to use jQuery Mobile.

Knowledge of HTML, CSS, and JavaScript are what you need to get started. You can also get crazy with it and mix in some scripting languages too. If you want you can run with a PHP backbone without a problem. If you need some Ruby in there to help keep things flowing your way, go ahead and use it. While being skilled with other programming languages is helpful, it is not required.

Integrated Development Environment (IDE), Platforms, and Cost

While there are the hard-core, die-hard, do-it-yourself types of developers who need nothing more than notepad, textedit, or vi to get their coding done, there are also plenty of developers who enjoy a little help with auto-complete, auto-close, and snippet libraries to dig through. If you enjoy a little help from your programmatic friends, then you are likely going to want to develop inside an IDE.

Whether you run with the Windows crowd, stand confidently with OSX, or love to get up to your elbows in Linux, you can use whatever platform you want. Remember, jQuery Mobile is just a JavaScript framework so whatever platform you are already using to develop your current site with will most likely work with jQuery Mobile.

Cost is a funny thing. Some people gladly pay for support, features, and usability. Others sacrifice one or even all three of these if they can get the program for free or at a discounted price.

Let's talk about some of the available development applications for your OS and whether you should expect to pay for it, or pick it up for free.

Development Applications for Windows

The applications are programs that run on the Windows platform. This includes both the XP and 7 versions of Windows.

Aptana Studio

Aptana bills itself as the world's most powerful open-source web development IDE. It comes with an included web server for debugging and has support for server-side JavaScript.

For a development IDE, I have personally found Aptana to be a great starting point for those unfamiliar with web development who could use a library of snippets and who do not want to mess around with figuring out how to install a web server to make their project run.

Aptana was also purchased by Appcelerator and has included support for Titanium. With Titanium you can create a web application and then package it as a native application for most mobile devices and mobile operating systems.

Eclipse

If you looked at Aptana Studio and thought it looked strikingly similar to Eclipse, you would be correct. Eclipse is one of my favorite IDEs. I've used it for projects built in PHP, Java, and a few projects in-between.

There are many different flavors of Eclipse, but all have support for plug-ins and software add-ons, allowing it to be modular and customizable. A vanilla version of Eclipse will set you back nothing, as it is open-source.

You are encouraged to donate to the Eclipse project to keep it free and for continued development and support.

Dreamweaver

Back in the emerging days of web development Macromedia had a great little IDE named Dreamweaver that took a WYSIWYG approach to web development. Macromedia was later acquired by Adobe, and Dreamweaver has since been integrated with several other web technologies for rapid web development and deployment.

The latest version of Dreamweaver sports built-in support for jQuery Mobile and includes several prebuilt mobile templates to get you going.

The pricing varies somewhat on Dreamweaver because different versions are available, but you may download a 30-day trial to give it a spin and see whether it matches your personal flow and development needs.

Visual Web Developer Express

Microsoft puts out this specialized version of Visual Studio for developers who are new or who want to learn a new technology. There are stipulations with using this free version of Visual Studio. For personal or education use you are unlimited, but if you want to profit from your project or release it commercially, you need to step up to the full version of Visual Studio.

Visual Web Developer Express features full jQuery code-completion and can be integrated with .NET and IIS.

Notepad++

The last program I will mention as an IDE for use in Windows is the one I actually use the most. Notepad++ is a free program that is similar to the notepad application that comes with Windows.

It is similar to notepad in that it can process a file with an extension of .txt. Then it takes a massive leap forward by adding support for multiple open files sorted into tabs, syntax highlighting, a plug-in architecture, scripting support, and more.

Whether I am editing XML, PHP, HTML, CSS, JavaScript, or various other files, Notepad++ is my favorite tool to use. It does not feature an integrated server, but you can use plug-ins with it and set up remote connections to upload files through FTP to your site for use with testing.

Komodo IDE/Edit

Those looking for another option for an IDE can use Komodo by ActiveState. Komodo IDE is the flagship product with many excellent features including code collaboration, a debugger, and a database explorer. Those on a budget can appreciate Komodo Edit. This is the freeware offering from ActiveState that features the base toolkit without the extra features. This means you get an editor that has auto-complete as well as a toolbox for storing code snippets. Both versions run on Windows, Linux, and OSX.

Development Applications for OSX

The following applications run on the Apple OSX platform. The applications listed should run on the Snow Leopard and Lion versions of OSX.

Kod

I used Kod briefly and found it to be a sufficient IDE for development. It is a free application and integrates itself into the file system, becoming the default application to edit most of your web files.

Coda

This is a much talked about IDE that can be purchased in the App Store. It is one of the most popular web development applications available for OSX. It also comes with some useful tools such as a built-in SVN client and various file transfer protocols. Dreamweaver users will feel fairly comfortable in the layout and use of the program.

TextWrangler

Whenever I am doing a quick edit, or just need to look at files I tend to use TextWrangler. This is a free program by the makers of BBEdit and has syntax highlighting with support for most web languages.

You definitely cannot beat the price, and if you need more features you can always step up to the more fully featured BBEdit.

TextWrangler is not built for the HTML newbie. It does not come with the comprehensive tools or snippets that BBEdit comes with, so those who are just embarking on website development would probably feel more comfortable using another IDE.

Espresso

Espresso is a web IDE from the makers of CSSEdit. This great little IDE has all the features of the other big players—code completion, live preview, file transfer protocol support, extensions—and includes a 15-day free trial to help you decide whether you want to purchase it.

Eclipse

Eclipse is a multiplatform application, and as such is available for use on OSX. It generally rolls with the same amount of plug-ins and extensions as the versions found on other platforms.

Aptana Studio

Yep that's right, Aptana Studio is also available for the Mac. There are no feature differences between Windows and Mac, so if you are constantly switching platforms you will already be at home and familiar with Aptana Studio.

Komodo IDE/Edit

When developers move from Windows to OSX something that becomes annoying quickly is that the Home and End keys no longer move you to the beginning or end of a line but rather to the beginning or end of the document. Komodo IDE and Komodo Edit have both remapped the functionality of these keys to have the same behavior as found in Windows. While this may be a small feature, for some developers this is actually a big deal.

Development Applications for Linux

The following applications can be used on most versions or flavors of Linux. You need to either build from source or check repositories for versions of these apps for your Linux environment.

GNU Emacs

Featuring syntax highlighting and customization support, Emacs is a great way to just jump in and get going. Note that there are not many bells or whistles so be prepared to just jump in and get coding.

Emacs does have extensive search and replace tools as well as support for regular expressions. It also allows you to edit remote files, or even files owned by another user when given credentials and connection information.

gedit

Those familiar with gnome already use gedit. It is the default text editor of the gnome desktop and has syntax highlighting and a code snippet library available. For most Linux users, this is more than enough to get them going in the right direction.

Aptana Studio

Small world isn't it? Turns out that Aptana Studio works in your Linux environment too. All the features of the Windows and OSX versions are also available in Linux.

Eclipse

As mentioned in the OSX section, Eclipse is multiplatform, so, yes, it works on Linux, both 32- and 64-bit versions. It has all the same features as the other platform versions, making transitioning between platforms a snap.

Komodo IDE/Edit

As mentioned before, the Komodo IDE and Komodo Edit are available for Linux as well. This is a good solution if you are using multiple platforms and would prefer to have the same experience between them.

Web Servers

As a general disclaimer I will say that developing jQuery Mobile applications does not necessarily require running a web server, or even require you to have Internet access. You can load and reference all the required files locally and test them in a modern HTML5 and CSS3 supporting browser.

Of course without running your code on a server you will not get to see the effects of compression, possible server issues, network latency, user permissions, .htaccess file changes, or even complete testing from an actual mobile device. Here is the short list of available web servers. You may also run into problems with file locations and permissions.

While many different types of web servers are available, they do not all run on the same platform. The following descriptions list what platform the web server runs on.

Nginx

This is an all-in-one server that boasts the most connections with the smallest memory footprint. Versions are available for Linux, a buildable version for OSX, and some compiled binaries for Windows.

Note that the Windows binaries use some Cygwin files, so I strongly recommend against using the Windows version as a production server.

Apache

It is safe to say that most web developers have had experience in dealing with or having their site hosted on an Apache server.

It is probably the most popular open-source HTTP server available. It has many features and is fairly easy to maintain and operate. Versions are available for download for Unix/Linux and Windows.

If you are using OSX, you already have Apache installed. To see which version, open a terminal and type `httpd -v`.

Lighttpd

Pronounced "lighty," this up-and-comer in the server world is focused on speed. It is a Linux-only server and seems fairly straightforward (both in use and installation).

IIS

Our .NET loving friends already know about IIS, and it is the preferred web server of choice for them. It comes with most versions of the Windows OS and can be integrated with PHP. It features a GUI configuration and management system and has downloadable extensions to help you get the most out of it.

XAMPP

XAMPP is a package of applications used for web serving. It contains Apache, MySQL, PHP, and Perl. It runs on Linux, Windows, OSX, and Solaris. With its easy setup and configuration, this is the stack that I commonly use when developing.

Summary

You have learned why it is important to start developing mobile sites, and why you should be using jQuery Mobile to do it.

You now have a basic understanding of what devices support jQuery Mobile and gained an overview into planning for these devices.

Finally you learned about the different tools available for development, including programming languages, IDEs, and server software.

Using this knowledge you should now have a foothold on getting started with mobile development and be able to find the tools that are comfortable to use.

Q&A

Q. Is a web server absolutely necessary for mobile development?

A. That is a great question, and a little difficult to answer. If your mobile site is static and does not use any dynamic code, you can develop without a server. That being said, unless you develop a single page site, you will receive error messages when you attempt to load separate pages. Using a server gives you better results, allows AJAX, and allows you to test your site cross-device using emulators or with devices attached to the same network you are on.

Q. Do I have to use an IDE to develop? Some of the suggested IDEs are too expensive or don't offer me incentive to use them.

A. No, if you are a notepad, textedit, or vi kind of developer, you are already good to go. The listed IDEs are just suggestions to help you get started if you are new to development and need a little help with structure and/or file management.

Q. I have been using a WYSIWYG IDE for years and it has never let me down or been excessively difficult to use. Why does it seem to get "knocked" by developers on the Internet?

A. While a lot of "die-hard" developers make fun of WYSIWYG development programs, there is nothing wrong with them per se. The stigma comes from computer-generated code. When developing with a WYSIWYG editor you will find that there are few things worse than computer-generated code. While it may be optimized, it may not match the design or the flow that you would expect. Naming conventions are often not very descriptive and end up as a series of letters. These editors may also include hundreds of lines of CSS hacks and CSS evaluations (both may be looked upon unfavorably by the developer community).

Workshop

The workshop contains a quiz and some activities to help you check your comprehension and understanding.

Quiz

1. True or False: jQuery Mobile works only with mobile versions of Webkit-based browsers.

2. True or False: jQuery Mobile is based on plain JavaScript and does not require the use of any other JavaScript libraries or frameworks.

3. True or False: jQuery is a well-known and strongly supported framework.

Answers

1. False. Not only does jQuery Mobile work with mobile versions of Webkit-based browsers, but it works with mobile versions of Opera, Firefox, and BlackBerry. It also works with all modern desktop browsers.

2. False. jQuery Mobile is based on jQuery, which is a JavaScript framework. However, since it is a framework, it is not considered plain JavaScript. The jQuery Mobile framework uses more of an HTML attribute-based approach to development and leverages the power of the jQuery framework for DOM manipulation giving a fairly seamless cross-browser experience.

3. True. jQuery is very well-known and included in more websites and development programs than you would originally think. Dreamweaver, Aptana Studio, and even Expression Web come with built-in support for jQuery.

Exercises

1. Download a few of the programs mentioned previously and install them. Get a feel for which one fits your personal development style the best, and which one meets your personal and/or corporate budget.

2. Perform a search on mobile usage in your country and region for adoption rates and impact. Get familiar with the statistics for your area to get a better understanding of whether you will be setting the bar or playing catch-up in your niche.

3. Take a few minutes to surf the Web on a mobile device. Take notes on what you like and what features you wish the sites you view had available. Write down how many sites offered you a mobile site automatically and which ones ignored your mobile device. Add another note on whether the websites you visit offer a native app for your device.

HOUR 2
Working with HTML, CSS, and JavaScript

What You'll Learn in This Hour:

▶ The current role of HTML

▶ Different ways to add styles to a web page

▶ What JavaScript is and how you can use it

This hour reviews the concepts and current trends of using HTML, CSS, and JavaScript. This is important as it plays a major role in development with jQuery Mobile. Sites that use jQuery Mobile are built with HTML, and while they are styled by a default theme, you may want to change the styles to something a little more custom. Doing this requires knowledge of how to read and edit CSS. Understanding JavaScript comes into play when you want to bind events to button presses or screen taps. Understanding standard JavaScript is also useful when learning to use the jQuery Mobile framework.

While it would be fun to cover everything there is to know about HTML, CSS, and JavaScript, it's just not possible in an hour. However, if you have ever developed a website, toyed with HTML, or just been away for a few years, this should be an informative hour that gets you back up to speed.

Building Content with HTML

HTML is the basic building block of the Web. It is the frame that holds your site together and the foundation that allows you to extend your site into whatever you want it to be. HTML has come a long way from its inception and is continuing to grow and develop.

The Role of HTML

Before Cascading Style Sheets (CSS) were introduced, everything was handled with HTML tags. Images, text, layout, scrolling text, just about everything was put in place with HTML tags. You may remember viewing the source code on your browser and seeing lots of   character entities being used for layout purposes.

Things continued to get more complex as developers were eager to explore new territory and push the language further. Layouts based on tables emerged, and this allowed new flexibility and control in regards to how a site was displayed. Table layouts were immensely popular. This allowed new flexible or self-resizing sections and a more dynamic site flow. CSS was new, and when it was supported in browsers it was limited. This made styling containers and forms difficult. Some light CSS was starting to be thrown in, but it did not fully replace table layout containers, use of the <font> tag, and some other style-only tags.

Web developers continued to mold, push, and hack the way HTML was being rendered by browsers. This progression and community adopted standards helped to drive advancements in the various Internet browsers that were available. Soon most browsers had at least rudimentary support for CSS2. That soon moved into a fair amount of arguing over how HTML should really be used in site development.

The DOCTYPE

Continuing through the evolution of HTML brings us to talking about the DOCTYPE. This is an interesting tag that was added to let browsers know how to render the page.

While this is not actually an HTML tag per se, it is a necessary component for the correct rendering and handling of your website.

Developers who are still happily using deprecated HTML tags but want to move on to HTML 4 can use the Transitional DOCTYPE.

```
<!DOCTYPE HTML PUBLIC "-//W3C//DTD HTML 4.01 Transitional//EN"
"http://www.w3.org/TR/html4/loose.dtd">
```

The Transitional DOCTYPE allows the browser to parse through deprecated tags and displays them without throwing any errors.

Developers who do not want to include support for deprecated tags and the possible formatting errors that may ensue when using a "compatibility" mode can use the strict DOCTYPE.

```
<!DOCTYPE HTML PUBLIC "-//W3C//DTD HTML 4.01//EN"
"http://www.w3.org/TR/html4/strict.dtd">
```

Using the strict DOCTYPE tells the browser to throw errors when deprecated tags are included in the HTML file it is trying to load. This can be useful as it guarantees your work is at least up to the HTML 4 standard.

CAUTION

JavaScript Library Plug-ins and DOCTYPEs

Some JavaScript library plug-ins are a bit picky about the use of the Transitional and strict DOCTYPE used on a site. If you are using a JavaScript library or plug-in that does not work the same way for you as it does on a demo site, try changing your DOCTYPE and see whether it magically starts working as intended.

For current developers who want to cater to modern and mobile browsers, the HTML5 DOCTYPE is definitely the way to go.

Using the HTML5 DOCTYPE works on almost all legacy browsers and is already in use on many websites today.

To use the HTML5 DOCTYPE in your HTML file, use the following snippet:

```
<!DOCTYPE html>
```

Yep, that is really all there is to using the HTML5 DOCTYPE on your site. There is nothing crazy, long, or complicated to it.

What is even more impressive is that legacy browsers have rudimentary support for it. Rather than throw the browser into a complete quirks mode, it uses more of a semi-quirks mode that generally does not break the formatting of the site.

The Basic Structure

After the DOCTYPE has been added to the page, we can begin to assemble the basic structure of an HTML document. Listing 2.1 shows the required elements of an HTML file using the HTML5 DOCTYPE.

LISTING 2.1   Required Elements of an HTML File Using the HTML5 DOCTYPE

```
1:   <!DOCTYPE html>
2:   <html>
3:     <head><title></title></head>
4:     <body></body>
5:   </html>
```

As shown in Listing 2.1, the basic structure of an HTML document is exactly that, basic. On line 1 we declare the HTML5 DOCTYPE allowing the browser viewing this file to know how to parse the rest of the document. On line 2 we start the html element. All valid HTML tags that we want to use must be contained within this element. Line 3 contains both the opening and closing tags of the head element. Generally the head element contains the title element, meta tags, links to CSS files, links to JavaScript files, as well as a few other custom or specialty tags. Line 4 contains the opening and closing body tags. The body element contains all the structure, or the skeleton of your site. Along with standard HTML elements such as p, div, and ul, the body element may also contain inline JavaScript as well as links to external JavaScript files. Line 5 closes the html element and completes our HTML file.

TIP

Loading Files in the Head

Your site will stop loading until all files called in the head element have been downloaded and placed into memory. If you have large files or slow loading scripts included in your head element it can give the impression of a slow-loading or broken site. Unless these files are necessary to page functionality, it is best to put large JavaScript files just before the closing body tag.

Separation of Content and Presentation

The current view of correctly using HTML and CSS is to use it as the separation of content and presentation. This is a good idea as you can easily create themes and then change the entire look of your site just by changing the styles instead of the content. Some websites follow this model and have several different style sheets that allow you to switch the "theme" of the website.

Content is handled purely (or as close to purely as possible) by HTML while anything that affects the way the data is displayed or rendered to an end user is handled with CSS.

HTML tags that were once dedicated to changing the way fonts and text were displayed to the user were deprecated in HTML 4 and replaced with newer tags that attempted to describe the content being placed within them.

A short list of elements that had been deprecated but are again valid in HTML5:

▶ <b> is used to grab attention.

▶ <i> is used to declare an alternate voice or mood.

▶ <s> is used to display information no longer valid or relevant.

Sections of code are generally divided using div tags. Inside these tags are subsections that usually contain your text. The text is generally grouped into paragraphs and contained in p tags. HTML5 also introduces several new tags such as article and section elements that behave similarly to div elements. Sections can also be divided using the new header and footer elements.

If you have items that you want to list in your code, you can put them into an ordered list by using an ol tag, or you can use an unordered list by using the ul tag. The items you want displayed in the list are added as list items with <li> tags.

A trend with HTML 4 has been to use unordered lists to create navigation sections. While this is still in use today, the built-in navigation tags included with HTML5 will shortly make this practice obsolete.

Let's review what we've just learned about HTML and put some content into the basic HTML structure. Listing 2.2 shows an HTML file that contains content without any styling.

LISTING 2.2   The Full Text of nostyles.html

```
 1:  <!DOCTYPE html>
 2:  <html>
 3:    <head>
 4:      <title>Titles should be short descriptions of the page</title>
 5:        <meta charset="utf-8">
 6:    </head>
 7:    <body>
 8:      <div>
 9:      <h1>h1 tags should contain the most important information on your site </h1>
10:        <p>Paragraph tags should be where most of your text content lives,
or used as a separation between sections.</p>
11:        <ul>
12:         <li>This is a list element</li>
13:         <li>This is another element, notice the bullets and indentation </li>
14:        </ul>
15:        <p>You probably noticed that I used a "div" tag to wrap these other
 tags in. I'm using it as a container.</p>
16:      </div>
17:    </body>
18:  </html>
```

You can see that we added some content to our page; let's walk through the additions.

On line 4 we added a title element; the value we placed in it describes exactly what a title element should contain.

The next addition is on line 8 where we added an opening div tag. Often you find div tags used to contain various sections of the site as we are doing here.

On line 9 we put in an h1 element. This element is used to denote the most important thing on the page. Because of this, any text placed in an h1 element is generally 200% larger than the standard font size.

On line 10 we set up some text in a p element. This displays the text with some default margins and padding. Every browser applies a default margin and padding size, so if you are going for identical cross-browser display you may want to overwrite the default styles in your CSS.

Line 11 shows the beginning of an unordered list by use of an opening ul tag. Line 12 shows an li element. The li element stands for list item and is a child element of the ul element. This means that without a ul element surrounding it, the li element is invalid.

Line 15 shows another p element example, and line 16 closes out our div element.

We know what the code does, but let's take a look at what it actually looks like. Figure 2.1 shows what the rendered HTML looks like.

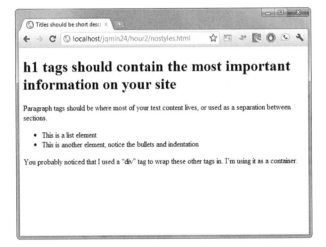

FIGURE 2.1
An HTML file using the HTML5 DOCTYPE without any CSS

CAUTION

Browser Defaults

You may have heard of browser-resets or CSS-resets styles. These are popular because every browser has a default rule or style that is applied to each HTML element. A quick example of this is to view an H1 tag in multiple browsers. You should notice that each browser renders this tag with a slightly different font size, and may or may not be styled bold.

We now have content and our page looks somewhat presentable; however, even though we now have substance, we are definitely missing style. Having substance without style is like holding onto an uncut gem; it is still valuable, but it is difficult to see the real value without some add-ing some design and polish.

Presenting CSS

Cascading Style Sheets are used to transform what would otherwise be boring content into an exciting and captivating experience. You can add styles to your site in a few different ways.

When adding CSS in style tags or with an external file, you can write your CSS all in a single line, or you can break it into a paragraph format.

Developers new to CSS generally prefer the paragraph format, while experienced developers may use a single line with spaces or tabs to show the style and layout hierarchy.

While I do favor one formatting style over the other, when it all comes down to it I minify my CSS for use on production, so keeping my CSS in one format over another really only matters for maintenance. We talk about minification and how it can benefit you in Hour 21, "Learning to Minify Everything."

Listing 2.3 shows a snippet of CSS written out using the paragraph format. Each style property is set on a separate line indented from the root element. You can see how this is an easy-to-read format that requires no horizontal scrolling. The drawbacks on this method are vertically long files (and subsequently larger files due to numerous line returns), and no visible means of hierarchy.

LISTING 2.3   CSS Code Using the Paragraph Style of Formatting

```
 1:  body {
 2:     background: #333333;
 3:     font-family: Helvetica, Arial, sans-serif;
 4:     font-size: 0.75em;
 5:  }
 6:
 7:  h1 {
 8:     font-size: 200%
 9:  }
10:
11:   p {
12:     margin: 5px 0;
13:     padding: 0 3px;
14:   }
15:
16:   .small {
17:     font-size: 80%;
18:   }
```

The CSS code in Listing 2.3 probably looks familiar. The paragraphs are easy to read, and each CSS property is listed on a line by itself to increase readability. As you can see on lines 6, 10, and 15, I included an empty line. This was intentional. Even with the tabs sometimes when scrolling through large CSS files it is possible to get confused, so the spaces help break up the sections.

Listing 2.4 contains the same styles as the previous snippet but is an example of the single-line hierarchy style of coding with CSS.

LISTING 2.4   CSS Code Using the Single-Line Hierarchy Style of Formatting

```
1:  body {background: #333333;font-family: Helvetica, Arial, sans-serif;
font-size: 0.75em;}
2:    h1 {font-size: 200%;}
3:    p {margin: 5px 0;padding: 0 3px;}
4:      .small {font-size: 80%;}
```

You can see how this takes up much less vertical space in your styles. This formatting style decreased the exact same code from 18 lines down to 4.

You can also see that by using tabs or spaces, the hierarchy of elements is shown. This is apparent by looking at line 1 and line 2. On line 1 the body element is not tabbed while the h1 element on line 2 has been tabbed showing that it is contained within the body element.

The drawbacks to using this method are that there is usually plenty of horizontal scrolling (especially with browser-specific styles and when incorporating CSS3 tags). This method can also be challenging to debug if you are not used to seeing CSS written in this format as the only character separating properties is a semicolon.

No matter which style you format your CSS code in, you can implement styles into your HTML files. Let's discuss how.

Style Tags

One thing that HTML 4 has support for is the use of a style tag. This is generally included in the head element and contains all the styles that you want to apply to the document. Using a style element in your HTML file is good for when you have a few specific styles you want to apply to the current document.

Listing 2.5 shows an example of applying styles with a style element being included in the head element of an HTML file.

LISTING 2.5   An Excerpt of headstyles.html

```
1: <head>
2:   <title>Titles should be short descriptions of the page</title>
3:     <meta charset="utf-8">
```

```
 4:    <style type="text/css">
 5:       body {
 6:          background: #e7e7e7;
 7:          font-family: Helvetica, Arial, sans-serif;
 8:          font-size: 0.75em;
 9:       }
10:       h1 {
11:          font-size: 200%;
12:       }
13:       p {
14:          margin: 5px 0;
15:          padding: 0 3px;
16:       }
17:       .small {
18:          font-size: 80%;
19:       }
20:       ul {
21:          list-style-type: none;
22:          font-weight: bold;
23:       }
24:    </style>
25: </head>
```

Looking at line 1, you can see that we are starting in the head element. Line 2 is the title element. While this doesn't have anything to do with styles, it does belong in the head element. Line 4 shows the opening style element. The style element includes type="text/css" to let the browser know how to process the data within this element. Lines 5 through 23 show CSS written in a paragraph format that does not have spaces between each element. Line 24 contains the closing style tag. That leaves line 25 showing the closing head element.

Figure 2.2 shows the file headstyles.html being rendered with the styles applied.

By comparing Figure 2.1 and 2.2, you can see that styles can have quite the effect on presentation. Styles do not always need to be included in the style element. They may also be included through external CSS files.

Using External CSS Files

With various methods of content delivery and compression, the most popular choice for using CSS is to include it in a separate file. This is done by creating a file with a file extension of .css and then calling that file in the head element with a link element.

Here is an example of calling or linking to an external css file:

```
<link rel="stylesheet" type="text/css" href="styles.css" />
```

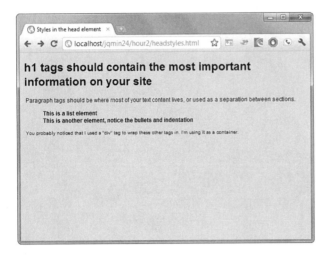

FIGURE 2.2
An HTML file that has been styled with the `style` element

In the preceding snippet we have a file named styles.css in the same folder as the HTML file calling it. Any styles that have been coded and placed in the file `styles.css` will be pulled into the document and used.

It is worth noting that you can store your CSS in subfolders, and even load it from offsite.

You are not limited to using one CSS file in your HTML file, either; you can actually use multiple files. Using multiple external CSS files has the advantage of separating styles that are not needed until a certain portion of your site has been entered and has the possibility of making your code easier to maintain.

Another use of separating styles is to create browser-specific styles that are included only when a certain browser is detected.

CAUTION

Using Multiple CSS Files

Using multiple CSS files can have a few somewhat serious drawbacks. If you are calling them all on the same page you could create HTTP request blocking, and inadvertently create a slower loading web page while all of the files are downloaded and parsed into memory. If you are using separate files based on browser detection, you will most likely run into maintaining different files for different versions. Your site may also have an increased loading time as your detection scripts need to load and include files based on what they find.

Inline Styles

Inline styles are available to use, but I will throw in a strong recommendation that they be used only for quick prototyping or for when there is absolutely no other way to get what you want done.

Inline styles overwrite browser-preset styles and styles that have been included. They are useful when debugging because you can pinpoint exact elements and adjust them.

The reason why I am against using inline styles is because they break the line between content and presentation. If you are "hard-coding" a style on a content piece, that style will stay unless steps are taken to remove that specific style or element. Although it is possible to use other means to remove hard-coded styles, it is much easier to just avoid it and save yourself the headache of chasing down bad code inside your HTML files.

Listing 2.6 shows an example of using inline styles within different HTML elements.

LISTING 2.6   The Full Text of inlinestyles.html

```
 1: <!DOCTYPE html>
 2: <html>
 3:   <head>
 4:     <title>Inline Styles</title>
 5:     <meta charset="utf-8">
 6:   </head>
 7:   <body>
 8:     <div style="margin:0 auto;width: 460px;border: 1px solid #000;
padding: 3px;">
 9:       <p>The parent container is hard-coded</p>
10:       <p style="font-weight: bold;">I probably should have used a class
instead.</p>
11:     </div>
12:   </body>
13: </html>
```

The preceding code is perfectly valid, in fact the inline styles applied on line 8 will center the div element when viewed in a browser as well as apply a border and some padding. The inline style is applied to the div element by including a style attribute within the opening div element. On line 10 you can see that we added a style attribute to the opening p element. The style that is being applied to the p element will make the text bold.

Figure 2.3 shows what inlinestyles.html looks like when rendered with the applied inline styles.

Now that we've seen different ways to present our page using CSS, it is time to look at making it function.

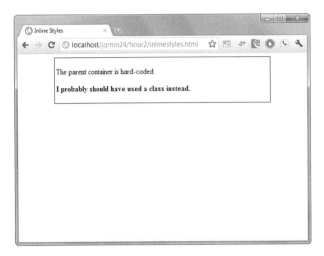

FIGURE 2.3
An HTML file that has been rendered with inline styles

Functioning with JavaScript

We now know how to style the content on a site—it might be nice if we could make something happen when a visitor comes to view the site. This is where JavaScript comes into play.

JavaScript originally picked up a bad reputation when it was first introduced. People did not understand what it was, or even what it was for. I remember a friend of mine was convinced that he had picked up a virus because every time he visited a certain website words would follow his mouse around the screen.

To many people, JavaScript became a nuisance and at best a practical joke language. At the time it was not realized what JavaScript could do or how it could enrich websites by adding animation, data collection, and event binding that can change the way a user interacts with a website. While I'm at it let me dispel one more myth, JavaScript is not Java.

Whether you realize it or not, today JavaScript does more heavy lifting and manipulation of the Document Object Model than ever before. Websites that could only do things with precompiled files and special playback plug-ins can now be displayed natively in a browser. JavaScript helps websites feel more interactive, or even more like a native application.

Where Scripts Can Be Added

You can include JavaScript by placing the code inside `script` tags. While these tags can be placed anywhere inside your document, you should take some time to consider where your script will be most effective.

The `Head` **Element**

Placing your `script` element inside the `head` element may cause blocking, but will make sure your code is ready or already executing before the rest of your page is loaded. Those that have experience with third-party "pixel" or tracking providers know that they want their pixel as high as they can get it. Placing a script in the `head` element ensures that it will be loaded, as the rest of the page must wait until the script has been downloaded before it can continue loading.

Loading scripts into the `head` element this way does have some drawbacks. If the script you are calling is remote you may end up waiting for it to load. Since some browsers let you have only two requests for URL data at a time, this can block one of your requests causing the rest of the elements on your site to load considerably slower.

The Middle

You could try loading scripts inside the `body` element. I've seen this done by developers who were debugging and never cleaned up their test scripts. I have also seen this used by those who thought it was a good idea to include the script right below the place where they needed it to execute.

While it seems like a good idea to keep the scripts close to where you are working or calling the methods, this can make site and page maintenance a nightmare. Trying to figure out where the code is that is breaking your site or web application is not a fun way to spend an afternoon (especially in compiled code where line numbers do not necessarily reflect the actual line numbers in your precompiled files).

The End of the Body

The last place you could include your scripts is just above the closing `body` tag. Putting your scripts here enables the rest of your page to start building before any included JavaScript files can drag the URL requests down with slowly loading remote JavaScript files. This gives users the feeling of a fast and responsive website because they can see the page starting to render even before the page has requested and loaded the functions that it needs to work.

The drawback to this method is the fact that if you are depending on extra functionality to be applied to the page on load and a user clicks on something that should trigger an event that uses events set up in your JavaScript file, the event may not be bound yet, so the click action will be wasted or will appear as an error.

A summary of placing JavaScript tags in your document:

- ► Loading scripts in the `head` element makes them load first but can adversely affect the perceived load time.

- ► Loading scripts inside the `body` may seem like a good idea but creates issues with maintenance and throws possible loading delays.

▶ Loading scripts just before the closing body tag makes your site appear to load quickly but may have an unintended consequence of missing site functionality for up to the first few seconds.

Loading Scripts

You can include JavaScript using a reference to an external .js file or include your code inside a script element. These references should be included in either the head element or inside the body element.

Script tags that reference an external file can be included like so:

```
<script src="http://code.jquery.com/jquery-1.6.4.min.js"></script>
```

Note that you can include more than one JavaScript file this way, and they can be included from both local and remote locations.

If you have JavaScript code that you want to include directly on the page, you may include it inside script tags.

Setting the Type

If you have looked at the source code of various websites you have probably noticed that some are missing the declaration "type=text/javascript" in the script tag. You can choose to include it (as per the HTML 4 spec) or omit it as all modern browsers already know that anything inside a script element will be JavaScript.

Listing 2.7 shows an HTML page that contains a sample function that looks for an element with an id of "year" and replaces what is in that element with the current year.

LISTING 2.7   The Full Text of javascriptdate.html

```
 1:  <!DOCTYPE html>
 2:  <html>
 3:    <head>
 4:      <title>JavaScript Date</title>
 5:      <meta charset="utf-8">
 6:      <style type="text/css">
 7:        p {text-align: center;}
 8:        #year {font-weight: bold;font-size:200%;}
 9:      </style>
10:    </head>
```

```
11:    <body>
12:       <p>When this page loads, the year below will switch to the current year
    that the client device is set to.</p>
13:       <p id="year">2000</p>
14:       <script type="text/javascript">
15:         window.onload = setYear;
16:         function setYear() {
17:           var currentYear = new Date();
18:           document.getElementById('year').innerHTML = currentYear.getFullYear();
19:         }
20:       </script>
21:    </body>
22: </html>
```

Starting on line 14 we see the start of our `script` element. Line 15 is where we use the `window` object in conjunction with the `onload` method and set it to `setYear`. This is the name of the function we want to run when the page loads. Line 16 shows the declaration of the `setYear()` function. On line 17 we create a variable named `currentYear` and set the value to be a `Date` object. Line 18 ties the function together as we use `document.getElementbyId('year')` to parse through the Document Object Model (DOM) and find an element with an `id` of "year". Then by using `.innerHTML = currentYear.getFullYear();` we are able to change the value of the found element to equal the current year.

Something worth noting about this code example is that the `Date` object is taken from the client machine. This means that if someone doesn't have their time set properly, the year that shows up on the site reflects whatever year the computer thinks it is. Because of that, using JavaScript to set the date is not a foolproof or terribly terrific idea. Whenever possible, try to use the time from the server instead of the client.

Figure 2.4 shows the code of javascriptdate.html being rendered on a browser that has the year set to 2011. Notice that it has changed the date from 2000 to 2011.

We can do more than simple data manipulation with JavaScript, we can actually make elements do things when clicked.

Event Binding

One thing that JavaScript is used for is to bind events. Binding events is useful when you want to make a mouse click trigger a function or submit a form.

FIGURE 2.4
A rendered HTML file with JavaScript manipulating the displayed content

Listing 2.8 shows an example of binding an event in JavaScript.

LISTING 2.8   A Code Snippet from javascriptalert.html

```
1: <script type="text/javascript">
2:    document.getElementById("btnAlert").addEventListener('click', clickAlert,
 false);
3:    function clickAlert() {
4:      alert("You clicked the button!");
5:    }
6: </script>
```

Line 1 shows the beginning of the `script` element. In line 2 we use `document.`
`getElementById("btnAlert")` to get the element with the `id` of `"btnAlert"` and then bind
the click event to it by attaching `.addEventListener('click', clickAlert, false)` to
it. Line 3 is where we start to create the `clickAlert` function. Line 4 shows an `alert` function being called. The value being passed inside the `alert` function is what will be displayed
in a dialog window by the browser that is rendering the site. Line 5 is the closing brace for the
`clickAlert` function and ends the code that will be executed when the function runs. Line 6
simply ends the `script` element.

In Figure 2.5 you see an alert window displaying the message "You clicked the button!" This window has a slightly different appearance depending on the browser and operating system you are using whenever the `alert()` function is called.

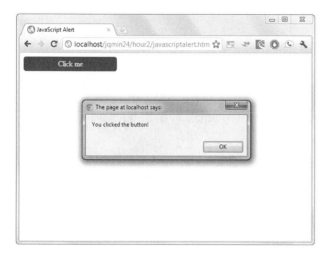

FIGURE 2.5
An alert window being displayed

CAUTION

Be Careful with the Alert

Using the `alert()` function shows a dialog window on your page. This is an application controlled message and stops users from being able to use your site until the message has been acknowledged. Some browsers detect multiple calls to this function and give the user an opportunity to ignore all alerts. For this reason you should think about nonintrusive messages through the use of light boxes or modal windows.

Summary

You just learned about the current use of HTML and CSS. You also learned that the separation of content and presentation is desirable for easy maintenance and site reconstruction with the use of CSS files.

You learned the different ways to apply CSS styles to your site by using the `style` element, including styles through the use of external .css files and by using inline styles.

You then learned the role of JavaScript in web development and how to include JavaScript by using external files or by placing code inside `<script>` tags inside the `head` or `body` elements of your HTML file.

Q&A

Q. **Does the single-line hierarchy style of formatting ever pose any rendering problems?**

A. Yes, using a single-line hierarchy style of formatting can occasionally be a problem with some browsers. When you are setting the property and value in your CSS, if you forget to add a space before the value the value may be skipped causing your styles to break. This is another reason why many developers prefer to use the paragraph style and then minify the code before using it on production.

Q. **Can I still use tables even though developers are using CSS now for styling?**

A. Of course you can. Just remember that tables should be used for displaying tabular data. You really should avoid using a table as a layout device and use it only for displaying lists and forms.

Q. **If the HTML 4 spec deprecates some HTML tags, why would I want to use the `Transitional DOCTYPE`?**

A. If you ever get the chance to work on a project where the code is inherited you may find yourself replacing portions of it at a time. When this is the case, using the `Transitional DOCTYPE` allows you to improve the site while maintaining the previous version.

Workshop

The workshop contains a quiz and some exercises to help you check your comprehension and understanding.

Quiz

1. Can the use of deprecated HTML tags can still be used in the HTML 4 `strict DOCTYPE`?

2. Why is inline styling discouraged?

3. Is JavaScript currently used for mouse trails and animated eyes or is it used for other things?

4. What version of HTML included support for CSS?

5. True or False: Using JavaScript to manipulate objects that have not been parsed and loaded into the DOM causes errors to be thrown and your JavaScript to fail.

Answers

1. No, but it can be used in the HTML 4.01 `Transitional DOCTYPE`.

2. Inline styles can be used, but they blur the line between content and presentation. This makes future upgrades to your site styles more involved and time intensive.

3. While that is possible, the current use of JavaScript is focused more on events and animation. While HTML5 and CSS3 are still growing, JavaScript is currently bridging the gap for interactivity and Flash replacement.

4. The HTML 4 specification was the first version of HTML to fully include support for CSS styles.

5. True. When you attempt to manipulate data that has not been parsed into the DOM you are grabbing at something that doesn't exist. Even if you know that it will exist you need to wait until it has been created to manipulate it.

Exercises

1. Write a simple web page that contains a click event similar to the one in Listing 2.8 and change what happens when the event is triggered.

2. Create a web page using the `HTML5 DOCTYPE` and add some elements and basic styles. View the page in the oldest and the newest version of Internet Explorer that you have. Note how the `HTML5 DOCTYPE` does not throw IE into standard "quirks" mode and still displays your page correctly (and in case you wondered, no, the `HTML5 DOCTYPE` will not save you from the ie6 double-margin issue). If you do not have Internet Explorer or run on OSX or Linux, try grabbing an old version of Firefox and see how the page renders.

3. Perform a search on your favorite search engine for HTML5 websites and get familiar with the new tags and proposed standards. Do another search on the current boilerplate code that is available when starting an HTML5 page and notice the fallbacks and compatibility that is built in for both modern and legacy browsers.

HOUR 3
Using the jQuery Framework

What You'll Learn in This Hour:

▶ How to include jQuery in your site
▶ How to use jQuery selectors
▶ How to include and use the jQuery framework

This hour covers the basics of the jQuery framework. This is important as it gives a developmental base and understanding to the framework that jQuery Mobile uses to function. Learning about jQuery also gives you an idea of how you can write scripts that can be used with jQuery Mobile. This hour is purely about the jQuery framework.

Unless you are running a static site or application, you are going to run into a few wishes and wants. You are probably going to want to load remote data. Maybe you want to create an area that rotates or changes displayed information. Perhaps you want to display a gallery of images. Another feature you may want is to add some friendly client-side validation to reduce server-side validation requests. Or of course maybe you want some special effects to use on your site and do not want to use a plug-in-based playback device.

By using JavaScript, everything on the previous list is not only possible but is already being used on millions of websites. There are pages built on the use of "vanilla" JavaScript, and there are plenty of sites built with various JavaScript libraries that help developers create everything on their wish list.

While we won't cover the other libraries here, I will tell you the reason why I absolutely adore jQuery. jQuery is simple, seriously simple. It may sound a little odd, but with jQuery you can learn and use JavaScript with little knowledge of the JavaScript language.

Using a framework is all about saving you time, reducing bandwidth, and making things easier. jQuery does all these things by taking the small bits of JavaScript that you may already know and blending that together with your expertise in CSS.

You save time in development by being able to ramp up new developers quickly by leveraging skills they already have. In larger projects that require hundreds or even thousands of lines of code, time is saved in the simplicity of creating and using objects.

The jQuery framework saves you bandwidth by reducing the amount of code needed to accomplish what you want and in turn reduces your overall file size. Even though including a framework takes up some bandwidth itself, if server-side compression is enabled on your server, the file-size of the jQuery framework is only 31kb.

During this hour, we learn how jQuery makes things easier through the use of selectors, filters, and chaining.

Including jQuery in Your Site

Implementing the jQuery framework into your site is as straightforward as adding any external JavaScript file. To add jQuery to your site, do the following:

▶ Include the jQuery library either from a local location or by using a Content Delivery Network.

▶ Include or inline your JavaScript after the jQuery library inclusion.

▶ Make sure that your code is initialized by calling the $(document).ready() function.

Use the following snippet to include the jQuery library just before the closing body tag in your HTML file. The following code snippet uses a Content Delivery Network (CDN) to host the library rather than loading a local copy of the jQuery library. Note that when using jQuery Mobile 1.0 the following snippet loads the version of jQuery you will use:

```
<script type="text/javascript" src="http://code.jquery.com/jquery-1.6.4.min.js">
</script>
```

When using jQuery Mobile 1.1 you use the following snippet to load jQuery:

```
<script type="text/javascript" src="http://code.jquery.com/jquery-1.7.1.min.js">
</script>
```

Loading the script file remotely provides a couple of nice benefits. First, most CDN locations will use compression on the file. Some web hosts do not allow server-side compression because of the extra cost in processing power on the server, so loading the file from a provider that does it automatically is nice. The second benefit is that by loading the script from a different domain you save yourself from possible HTTP request blocking. That in turn allows the browser to request an extra file and load your site faster. Another benefit of using the public CDN link is that the odds are good that a user has already visited a site using the same script, and therefore will already have a cached copy saved to their browser cache further speeding up the loading of your site.

Getting It Out of Your Head

Adding your JavaScript imports at the bottom of your HTML file increases the perceived loading speed of your page as the browser will not pause to request and parse the files until the rest of the DOM has been loaded.

Now that we have the jQuery framework is included in our page we add some inline JavaScript and use the `document.ready()` function to complete jQuery initialization.

Listing 3.1 shows the jQuery framework being included and an example of how to initialize it.

LISTING 3.1   The Scripts Required to Use jQuery

```
1:   <script type="text/javascript"
src="http://code.jquery.com/jquery-1.7.1.min.js"></script>
2:   <script type="text/javascript">
3:     $(document).ready(function() {
4:       // add your jQuery functions and code here
5:     });
6:   </script>
```

Line 1 is the jQuery framework being loaded from the remote CDN. On line 2 we start a `script` element. Line 3 may look a little odd, but this is the `$(document).ready()` function that I was talking about earlier. This is a jQuery selector that is getting the `document` object and running the `ready` function on it. You probably noticed that inside the `ready` function we are passing an anonymous or unnamed function. This anonymous function contains all the jQuery code we want to execute. This is why line 4 shows a JavaScript comment telling you where you may begin to add your jQuery code. Line 5 is the closing brace of the anonymous function, and the closing parentheses of the `ready` function. Line 6 then finishes out our `script` element.

jQuery and Other JavaScript Frameworks

Although the jQuery team would be thrilled if you only used their framework, that may not always be possible. When using other JavaScript frameworks the $ selector may already be in use, and will cause errors in your website or application. To get around this problem, jQuery provides the `jQuery.noConflict()` function that allows it to play nice with other frameworks. Learn more about using this function by visiting http://api.jquery.com/jQuery.noConflict/.

I mentioned last hour that when JavaScript functions attempt to manipulate objects that have not already been loaded into the DOM errors would occur. Some developers have overcome this problem by using the `window.onload` function and passing all their JavaScript functions to it. While doing this does force the code to delay executing, it must wait until all elements have been loaded (including external images, banners, scripts, pixels, and so on). jQuery handles both of these problems by using the `document.ready()` function.

The `document.ready()` function checks the DOM for the time when it can start executing your code. This way, you get your JavaScript code to execute safely at the first possible moment.

The caveat to this is that all your jQuery code needs to reside inside that particular function to execute. Doing this adds protection to your scripts from failing on objects that may not exist when your script is called. Your script holds on execution until the document is truly ready for it.

As a point of clarification, you must include the jQuery library before you include any code that uses the `$(document).ready()` method. Failure to do so results in JavaScript errors on your page and none of your jQuery code executing.

Making Your Selection

One of the greatest reasons to use the jQuery framework is that it makes getting the object or element you want simple. By using jQuery selectors you can get just about any element in your HTML code.

Let's say that in your document you have a particular element that you want like to get so that you can manipulate it. The element you want could be just about anything—an image, a link, or even a `div` element. Using traditional JavaScript you would have to invoke the `document` object and use the `getElementById()` function. The following is an example of using standard JavaScript to get an element.

Listing 3.2 shows the traditional JavaScript way of creating a variable and setting the value of it to an object with an id of `infoSlider`.

LISTING 3.2 Setting a Variable to an Object from the DOM

```
1: <script type="text/javascript">
2:    function init() {
3:      var infoSlider = document.getElementById("infoSlider");
4:    }
5:    window.onload = init;
6: </script>
```

On line 1 we begin our `script` element. Line 2 shows a function named `init` being started. Line 3 shows a variable named `infoSlider` being created and then set to a value of the object on the page that contains an id of `infoSlider`.

This is done by calling the getElementById function on the document object. That function parses the DOM and finds whatever element we passed into the function.

Line 4 simply closes out the init function. Line 5 calls the onload method on the window object and sets the value to the function above. By setting this value we are protecting our function from running too early and failing on an object that may not exist yet. Line 6 closes the script element.

Now that we've used some plain JavaScript, let's try doing the same thing using jQuery.

Listing 3.3 shows the jQuery version of Listing 3.2.

LISTING 3.3   A Simple jQuery Script

```
1: <script type="text/javascript">
2:   $(document).ready(function() {
3:     var infoSlider = $("#infoSlider");
4:   });
5: </script>
```

Line 1 starts out our script element. Line 2 initializes jQuery by calling the $(document).ready function and then passes an anonymous function into it. Line 3 shows the creation of a variable named infoSlider and sets the value to $("#infoSlider"). That odd-looking value is actually a jQuery selector. While it may look strange, it is calling the jQuery object and parsing through it for the id called infoSlider. This should sound familiar, as it is a shortcut of what the document.getElementById function was doing. Line 4 is the closing brace for the anonymous function and the closing parentheses for the document.ready() function. This leaves line 5 to close out the script element completing our jQuery script.

TIP

jQuery Called with an Alias

The method that jQuery actually uses to select objects is jQuery(). There is an alias set up that you can use to call the jQuery() method. The alias is $(), and it is generally used by developers instead of typing jQuery() to invoke the method.

What makes jQuery selectors so powerful and easy to use is that if you know the notation for CSS you already know how to write a jQuery selector.

To demonstrate, Listing 3.4 shows an example of creating some CSS properties for an element with an id with the value of infoSlider and also for a class with the value of widget.

LISTING 3.4 Standard CSS Notation for an Id and a Class

```
1: #infoSlider {
2:    /* CSS styles here */
3: }
4: .widget {
5:    /* CSS styles here */
6: }
```

Line 1 shows #infoSlider and an opening brace. If you are new to CSS you may not realize that the # symbol actually stands for an id. This means that #infoSlider is a reference to an element in the DOM that has an id of infoSlider. Line 2 is a comment telling you that you would normally put your properties and values on that line. Line 3 is the closing brace for any styles that would be applied to #infoSlider.

Line 4 holds some slightly different notation. It contains .widget and an opening brace. Just like the # symbol, the . has a special meaning as well; it is a reference to a class. This means that by using .widget you are actually referencing all elements in the DOM that contain a class with a value of widget. Line 5 is exactly the same as line 2, just a comment telling you that styles may be placed there. That leaves line 6 to close out the example with a closing brace for the .widget style properties.

Now that we've reviewed CSS notation, let's take a look at Listing 3.5 and see whether we can figure out what the script is doing.

LISTING 3.5 Another jQuery Script Using Selectors

```
1: <script type="text/javascript">
2:    $(document).ready(function() {
3:       var infoSlider = $("#infoSlider");
4:       var widget = $(".widget");
5:    });
6: </script>
```

Line 1 starts the script element, and line 2 initializes jQuery. Line 3 shows a variable named infoSlider being created and then being set to a value of $("#infoSlider"). With that value in mind, think of CSS notation. Can you tell what we are selecting to be used as the value? That's right, we are parsing the DOM for an element with an id of infoSlider and setting that object as the value for our variable.

Line 4 looks fairly similar to line 3. The differences here are that the variable is named widget, and the value that it is being set to is $(".widget"). Thinking of CSS notation again, this means that we are going to parse the DOM for any elements that contain the class with the value of widget and load them as the value for our variable.

Line 5 closes our anonymous function and the `document.ready()` function. Line 6 then completes our `script` element.

You can take using jQuery selectors even further by using more CSS notation. You can even cascade them just like you can in CSS.

The following are all valid jQuery selectors:

- `$("li")`

- `$("p")`

- `$("#id")`

- `$(".class")`

- `$("#nav li")`

- `$("img.class")`

You can make even more complex selections by looking inside selected elements for specific attributes, and by using a few helper methods.

By using [] after a specific element, you can look for a specific value or attribute, including custom attributes.

Listing 3.6 shows an example of how to use a jQuery selector to get a paragraph element that contains a custom attribute inside it.

LISTING 3.6   Selecting a Custom Attribute Inside a `p` Element Using jQuery

```
1: <script type="text/javascript">
2:    $(document).ready(function() {
3:      var productDesc = $("p[productdesc]");
4:    });
5: </script>
```

Walking through the code we see the usual `script` element set up on line 1. Line 2 is the `$(document).ready()` function to initialize jQuery. Line 3 is where we switch things up a little. You can see that a variable named `productDesc` is being created. You can also see that the value is a jQuery selector that contains some brackets. The brackets are attached to the element in front of it and searches that element for an attribute of whatever you typed into the brackets. In this example, our selector is going to perform a search through the entire DOM for all the p elements that contain an attribute of `productdesc`. Lines 4 and 5 close out the `$(document).ready()` function and the `script` element.

To see this snippet in action, view custom_attribute.html in your browser. It contains three p elements, with one having `productdesc` as a custom element. Figure 3.1 shows custom_attribute.html being viewed in a browser. The p element with the custom attribute has been given a border, and the text has been changed to bold.

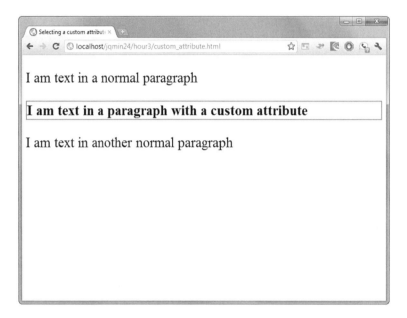

FIGURE 3.1
The selected element has been outlined and bolded.

There are other ways to select just the specific elements that you want. Listing 3.7 shows that by using a filter method you can select only the first `"li"` element in the list.

LISTING 3.7   Using the `.first()` Filter Method to Select an Element

```
1: <script type="text/javascript">
2:   $(document).ready(function() {
3:     var firstListItem = $("li").first();
4:   });
5: </script>
```

You should be familiar with lines 1 and 2 by now, so we'll move on to line 3. We can see that a variable named `firstListItem` is being created and being set to a selector of `$("li")`. It doesn't stop there though; there is a method being called on the selector. This is called a filter method, and this particular filter method finds the first child node in the DOM of whatever selector it is called on. By using `$("li").first()` we are selecting the value of the first li that is found in the DOM structure. Lines 4 and 5 should also look familiar as they are required to close the $(document).ready() function and the script element.

To see this code snippet in action, load child_filter.html in your browser. It contains an unordered list with three list items. Figure 3.2 shows child_filter.html being viewed in a browser. The first li element has been given a border and had the text changed to italicized.

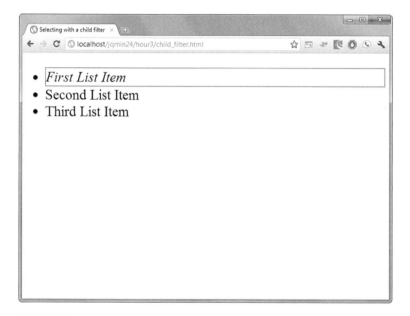

FIGURE 3.2
The selected element has been outlined and italicized.

jQuery comes with many filter methods that help you select the element or object you want. For a full list of filter methods and how you can use them to move around the DOM, view the official jQuery documentation found at http://api.jquery.com/category/traversing/.

A list of some of the filter methods you can use are

- ▶ .eq()
- ▶ .filter()
- ▶ .first()
- ▶ .has()
- ▶ .is()
- ▶ .last()
- ▶ .map()
- ▶ .not()
- ▶ .slice()

Another way you can use selectors to get what you want is through the use of child filters. These are applied in similarly to the way pseudo-classes are applied in CSS. Listing 3.8 shows the use of a child filter to get the first list item in an unordered list.

LISTING 3.8   Using a Child Filter to Select the First Child Node Using jQuery

```
1: <script type="text/javascript">
2:    $(document).ready(function() {
3:       var firstListItem = $("li:first-child");
4:    });
5: </script>
```

Lines 1 and 2 set up of our `script` element and the `$(document).ready()` function to initialize jQuery. On line 3 we create a variable named `firstListItem` and set the value to a selector. Inside the selector we use `:first-child` immediately after `li`. This is a child filter, and it works similarly to the `.first()` filter method. One of the main differences is that a child filter is done inside the selector while a filter method is attached at the end of the selector. Lines 4 and 5 close our `$(document).ready()` function and our `script` element.

Just as with filter methods, there are other child filters that you can use. The following is a short list of some of the child filters available within the jQuery framework:

- ▶ `:first-child`
- ▶ `:last-child`
- ▶ `:nth-child()`
- ▶ `:only-child`

Binding an Event

Now that you have had a brief introduction on how to get what you want, it is time to show you what you can do with it.

In the last hour we saw how you can bind events in JavaScript by using `addEventListener`. In fact we used it to bind a function that would display an alert when a certain element was clicked. Listing 3.9 shows how to bind a `click` event using the jQuery framework.

LISTING 3.9   Using jQuery to Bind a Click Event

```
1: <script type="text/javascript">
2:    $(document).ready(function() {
3:       $("#btnAlert").click(function() {
```

```
4:        alert("You clicked the button!");
5:      });
6:    });
7: </script>
```

Once again, lines 1 and 2 start things out with the opening `script` element and the `$(docu-ment).ready` function. Line 3 shows a selector getting an element with an id of `btnAlert`. Attached to the selector is a `.click()` function that has an anonymous function being called inside it. Line 4 shows that the anonymous function is going to run an `alert()` function and display "You clicked the button!" as the message. Line 5 is the closing brace of the anonymous function and the closing parentheses of the `.click()` function. Line 6 is the closing brace for the anonymous function being passed inside the `$(document).ready()` function, and the closing parentheses for the `$(document).ready()` function. Line 7 closes the `script` element.

How simple was that? We were able to bind the `click` event to the selected element just by using the `.click()` function on the selector.

There are many events that jQuery lets you bind in this manner. To view the full list of events that you can use with jQuery, visit the official documentation that can be found at http://api.jquery.com/category/events/. Here is a list of some of the events that can be used to bind events when used with selectors:

- `.blur()`
- `.change()`
- `.click()`
- `.dblclick()`
- `.focus()`
- `.focusin()`
- `.focusout()`
- `.hover()`
- `.keydown()`
- `.keypress()`
- `.keyup()`
- `.load()`

- `.mousedown()`
- `.mouseenter()`
- `.mouseleave()`
- `.mousemove()`
- `.mouseout()`
- `.mouseover()`
- `.mouseup()`
- `.resize()`
- `.scroll()`
- `.submit()`
- `.toggle()`

For the most part these event functions work just like they do when written in standard JavaScript notation. With jQuery you can also easily use callbacks to run other functions at the end of an event.

Using jQuery's Chaining

Sometimes you may run into a situation where you really want to run multiple jQuery functions on the same selector without having to write the same selector multiple times. In other instances, you may want to run multiple jQuery functions one after another inside another function during callback. In jQuery, this is referred to as chaining. Take a look at the following code snippet:

```
$('a[href^="http://"]').addClass('external').attr('target', '_blank');
```

For the preceding code snippet, we start off using a somewhat complex selector that will find every a element in the DOM that contains an attribute of href that starts with http://. We then use the .addClass() function to add a class with the value of external to all elements returned in the selection. We then chain the .attr() function on to add an attribute of target with a value set to _blank.

For the plain and simple description of what we just did, we added a class and an attribute to all `<a href="http://example.com">` elements that were in the DOM.

Chaining can be used on just about anything, including objects, events, and functions. Chaining can even be used inside callback functions. Callback functions allow you to execute code at a specific time. This is especially useful when you want to do some visual effects or animations that need to run in sequence instead of running in parallel.

Listing 3.10 shows an example of code running in parallel that when called will trip over itself creating a visual mess.

LISTING 3.10   An Example with Effects Running in Parallel

```
 1: <script type="text/javascript">
 2:   $(document).ready(function() {
 3:     $("#gallery").click(function() {
 4:       // everything below runs in parallel
 5:       $(".active").fadeOut();
 6:       $(".active").removeClass("active");
 7:       $(".gallery").addClass("active");
 8:       $(".active").fadeIn();
 9:     });
10:   });
11: </script>
```

Starting on line 3, we can see that a selector is being called for an element with an id of `gal-lery`. A `.click()` function is then called on the selector binding a `click` event to that element. Inside the `.click()` function, an anonymous function is set up. This moves us to line 4, which contains a comment telling us that everything below will be running in parallel. This means that the selectors and functions on lines 5 through 8 will all run as close to the same time as possible without waiting for the other functions to finish. Line 5 uses a selector to find an element with a class with the value of `active` and then uses the `.fadeOut()` function to make it disappear from the rendered page. Line 6 uses the same selector as line 5, but uses the `.removeClass()` function to take away the `active` class from itself. Line 7 uses a selector to find an element with a class with the value of `gallery` and uses the `.addClass()` function to add a class with the value of `active` to it. Line 8 uses the same selector as lines 5 and 6 but uses the `.fadeIn()` function to make the selected element appear in the rendered page. Line 9 closes out the anonymous and `.click()` functions; line 10 closes out the anonymous and `$(document).ready()` functions. Line 11 closes the `script` element.

The problem with running this code in parallel is that the `.fadeOut()` and the `.fadeIn()` functions will run at the same time, and it makes the animation jump when the `click` event is triggered.

To see this for yourself, view the file named parallel_effect.html in a browser. This file can be found in the code samples for this hour.

We can fix the effects by putting some of the functions inside a callback that allows them to run in sequence. Listing 3.11 shows the previous example rewritten to run in serial.

LISTING 3.11   An Example with Effects Running in Sequence

```
1: <script type="text/javascript">
2:    $(document).ready(function() {
3:       $("#gallery").click(function() {
4:          $(".active").fadeOut(function(
5:             // The following will run after .fadeOut finishes
6:             $(this).removeClass("active");
7:             $(".gallery").addClass("active");
8:             $(".active").fadeIn();
9:          });
10:      });
11:   });
12: </script>
```

Starting at line 3, we have used the exact same selector and `.click()` function as we did in Listing 3.10. On line 4 we are selecting an element with a class attribute having a value of `active` and removing it from the rendered page with the `.fadeOut()` function. Inside the

.fadeOut() function we are passing an anonymous function. Anything set up in this anonymous function will run after the .fadeOut() function is finished.

This is why line 5 shows a comment telling you that the following lines will be run later. Lines 6 uses a selector of this that points back to the parent selector. That means that $(this) is actually referring to the $(".active") selector on line 4. Knowing that you can see that it will remove the active class from itself as soon as the .fadeOut() function finishes running. Line 7 uses a selector to get the element with a class with the value of gallery and assigns it a class named active by use of the .addClass() function. Line 8 then uses a selector to look for the element with a class with value of active and makes it appear by using the .fadeIn() function.

Although the change in the jQuery script has been minor, it makes a major impact on the way the page is rendered to the end user. If you are ever having problems with the execution order of your code, it is a good idea to look at what code should be shifted so as not to run in parallel.

To see this for yourself, view the file named sequence_effect.html in a browser. This file can be found in the code samples for this hour.

Hopefully with the examples you've seen this hour, you can see why jQuery makes JavaScript easier to not only code with but also to read and understand.

Adding Custom Animation

We have played with making an element fade in and out of the rendered page, but what if we had an element that we wanted to change size of or even move to a different location on the screen when it was clicked?

jQuery has an animate function that is powerful and easy to use to help you make custom animations happen.

Let's say that we have a box that we want to grow taller when a button is clicked. Listing 3.12 shows how to make an element grow taller when clicked using a click event and the .animate() function.

LISTING 3.12   Animating the Height of an Element with the .animate() Function

```
1: <script type="text/javascript">
2:    $(document).ready(function() {
3:        $("#grow").click(function() {
4:            $("#box").animate({height: '200px'});
5:        });
6:    });
7: </script>
```

Lines 1 and 2 show the initial setup for our `script` element and jQuery initialization. Line 3 then shows a selector getting the element with the id of `grow`. Then we bind a `click` event to it by using the `.click()` function. On line 4 we then have a selector for the element with the id of `box` and set the `.animate()` function to run on it. The `.animate()` function works by passing values in pairs with name and value settings. Inside the `.animate()` function we passed the name of `height` and a value of `'200px'`. This means that every time `$("#grow")` is clicked, it will increase in height by 200px. The animate function also accepts a duration setting (for speeding up or slowing down your animation), an easing style, and a complete flag. Line 5 closes out the `.click()` function, and line 6 closes the `$(document).ready()` function. Line 7 closes our `script` element.

To see the snippet of code in action, view resizing_element.html in your browser and click on the button to watch the box grow. Figures 3.3 and 3.4 show the before and after results of running this snippet of code.

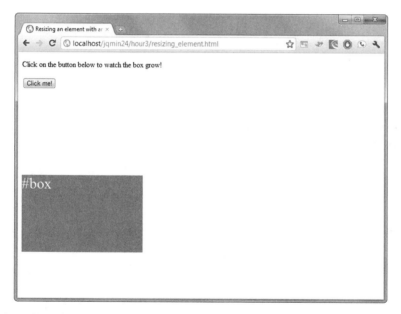

FIGURE 3.3
The box grows when the button is clicked.

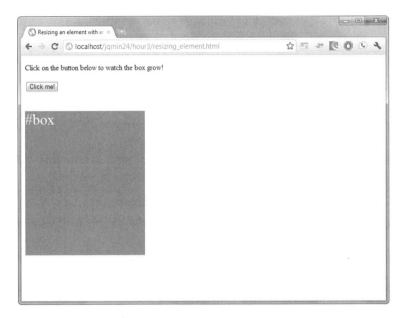

FIGURE 3.4
The button was clicked and the box has grown.

While it is good to know that we can make elements grow, how do we move an element across the screen or even to a specific location when it is clicked? This is also easily done using the .animate() function. Listing 3.13 shows us how to move an element around the page.

LISTING 3.13 Moving an Element Around the Page with the .animate() Function

```
1: <script type="text/javascript">
2:    $(document).ready(function() {
3:       $("#move").click(function() {
4:          $("#sprite").animate({left: '30px', top: '20px'});
5:       });
6:    });
7: </script>
```

Lines 1 and 2 set up our script element and jQuery initialization. Line 3 uses a selector to get the element with an id of move and uses the .click() function to add a click event to it. Inside the .click() function we have passed an anonymous function. Line 4 shows a selector getting the element with the id of sprite and then using the .animate() function on it to move from wherever it currently is on the page to 30px from the left and 20px from the top of the containing element that has a style value of position: relative. Line 5 closes the .click() function, and line 6 closes the $(document).ready() function. Line 7 closes our script element.

To view the code snippet in action, load moving_element.html in your browser. When the button is clicked, the `div` element with the id of `sprite` will move across the page. Figures 3.5 and 3.6 show the before and after the button has been clicked.

FIGURE 3.5
The sprite moves across the page when the button is clicked.

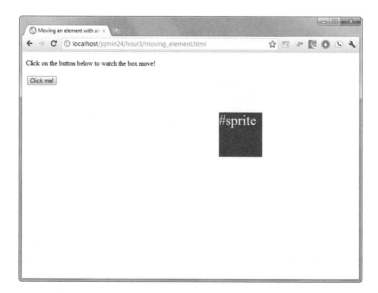

FIGURE 3.6
The button was clicked and the sprite moved to a new location.

Positioning Your Animation

Note that animation changes are called and run just like live CSS changes. This means that to adjust the `left`, `top`, `right`, and `bottom` properties of an element, that element must be positioned using `position: absolute` or `position: relative`. Failure to have the element positioned causes the animation to fail without throwing any JavaScript errors.

Animations are a great way to add interactivity and user enticement to your website. You can even use the animation function to build rudimentary games and effects.

Summary

You just learned about the jQuery framework and a few of its uses. You also learned how to add it to a website by either calling the file from a local location or by using a CDN.

You learned about jQuery selectors and how you can select various elements in the DOM so that you can manipulate them.

You learned about chaining functions together and about the possible errors that can occur when running all code parallel instead of running it in sequence.

You also learned that jQuery offers an `.animate()` function that can be used to make an object change size and even location on the page.

Q&A

Q. Why should you use a CDN?

A. A Content Delivery Network is a network of servers in various geographical locations that serve files from a location that is closer to your location. This helps you to load required files faster for everyone. Another reason why using a CDN is a good idea is that most of them will serve gzipped and minified versions of the file you requested. Serving gzipped and minified files is important as file size is greatly reduced. They are also useful as they do not count against the total number of URL connections that your browser is allowed to make in the same way as local files and resources do.

Q. I've included jQuery on the page but nothing is working, how do I fix it?

A. Including the jQuery library on your page is not enough. Remember that if you do not wrap your code in the `$(document).ready()` function it will not run. If on the other hand you are getting a `"$() is not defined"` error in your JavaScript console, make sure that you have included the jQuery library before your custom scripts.

Q. Why do you suggest that I include my JavaScript files at the bottom of my HTML file above the closing `body` element?

A. When a browser is rendering the Document Object Model, it starts at the top and works its way down to the bottom of your HTML file. HTTP requests are limited to two requests per domain, so if you have multiple JavaScript includes, you are stopping the page from loading while those resources are fetched. Even if the delay is for a split second, this delay can cause users to believe your site is unresponsive and slow. Including your JavaScript files before the closing `body` element ensures that the rest of the page loads quickly. Even if the site is not fully functional, users believe that the site is responsive and fast because they see things being rendered on the page.

Workshop

The workshop contains a quiz and some exercises to help you check your comprehension and understanding.

Quiz

1. True or False: jQuery only supports attaching a `click` event to an element.

2. True or False: jQuery selector notation is similar to CSS notation.

3. True or False: jQuery is for data manipulation only.

4. True or False: jQuery is incompatible with any other JavaScript frameworks.

5. True or False: Using jQuery selectors I am able to select only basic HTML elements such as `spans`, `ul`, `div`, and `table` elements.

Answers

1. False. jQuery offers many more events than just the `click` event to attach to events. You can use all the events that you are used to using in standard JavaScript notation with jQuery, and you can even use the jQuery `.bind` function for greater flexibility and customization.

2. True. jQuery notation is based on CSS notation so that developers who are not terribly familiar with JavaScript can immediately start using JavaScript using the skills they already have from working with CSS.

3. False. While jQuery excels at data and object manipulation, it is a fantastic effects package. By using the `.animate()` function, you can actually create your own effects.

4. False. jQuery is one of the friendliest frameworks available and includes a `jQuery.noCon-`
    `flict()` method in which the alias for "$" is unassigned from the global scope so as not
    conflict with other popular frameworks including prototype and mooTools.

5. Selectors are extremely powerful and allow you to get any element (including custom ele-
    ments) inside the DOM. The difficulty with getting the element you want may stem from not
    understanding where the element is that you are trying to select. Tools like Web Inspector
    and Firebug help you transverse the DOM and find what you want.

Exercises

1. Create some elements and bind various events to them. Add a `click` event to a button.
    Use the `mouseenter()` and `mouseleave()` functions to create hover effects over an
    element.

2. Check with your web host or your own local server and see whether gzip and minification
    services are available. Load your page with compression turned on and loading jQuery from
    a CDN. Look at the total download size of your site using various developer tools. Compare
    your results with compression turned off and jQuery loaded from a local location.

3. Either create your own animation or borrow from the examples earlier in the hour and
    change the animation properties and speed settings. Try speeding up the animation and
    slowing it down. Try making an element move across the screen. Find an animated gif and
    make it fly or run across the screen.

HOUR 4

Introduction to the jQuery Mobile Framework

What You'll Learn in This Hour:

▶ What files make up the jQuery Mobile framework
▶ How jQuery Mobile works with data attributes
▶ How to use jQuery Mobile to create a simple page
▶ How to use the mobile initialization event

The jQuery Mobile framework is the perfect place to get started with mobile development. Just like the standard jQuery framework, it is built to deliver speed, stability, and an excellent cross-browser experience to your visitors.

During this hour we start with adding jQuery Mobile to a web page and then discuss a little of how jQuery Mobile runs with the use of data roles. We then create a basic page with HTML and make it a mobile page using jQuery Mobile. Finally in this hour we cover the `pageinit` function and the difference between it and the standard jQuery `$(document).ready()` function.

Adding jQuery Mobile to Your Site

Adding the jQuery Mobile framework to your site is almost as easy as adding the standard jQuery framework to your site. In fact, jQuery Mobile requires the standard jQuery framework to function. In this respect, it could be considered part of the jQuery Mobile framework since it will not run without it.

Three files make up the complete jQuery Mobile framework:

▶ jQuery library JavaScript file

▶ jQuery Mobile library JavaScript file

▶ jQuery Mobile CSS style sheet

The two jQuery libraries are included as they contain all the logic that makes the frameworks work. The jQuery Mobile library extends on the base features of the jQuery library. Each of these libraries is available in a production version and a development version. The main difference between the two is that in the production version each file has been minified to remove excess whitespace and leaves out all comments. If you want to dive into what makes each framework tick, grab the development versions as they contain extra lines to help with legibility and comments to help explain some sections of code.

The jQuery Mobile CSS style sheet is included as it contains all the styles, themes, and swatches that are used with jQuery Mobile. These styles include various settings for backgrounds, colors, margin, padding, and sprites. jQuery Mobile does leverage CSS3 styles as this allows a smaller file size, and most modern mobile browsers have fairly good support for them.

When the files listed previously are included together in your HTML file, you are ready to get started using jQuery Mobile.

CAUTION

Including JavaScript in the head Element

Last hour we discussed putting all JavaScript includes just before the closing body tag and how this helps reduce HTTP request blocking and perceived loading speed. While that is a good practice on a standard HTML page, this will *not* work with all scripts when using jQuery Mobile. Because jQuery Mobile uses AJAX, scripts in the head element are considered to be "run once" scripts. If you have scripts that you want to execute only on a single or certain page you should either use the pageinit event, or you may include your scripts within the div element you are using as a page with the data-role="page" attribute.

Listing 4.1 shows the contents of basic_layout.html, which we use to start the layout of a simple mobile page including jQuery Mobile.

LISTING 4.1   Basic Page Layout Including jQuery Mobile

```
 1: <!DOCTYPE html>
 2: <html>
 3:    <head>
 4:       <title>Developing with jQuery Mobile</title>
 5:       <meta name="viewport" content="width=device-width, initial-scale=1">
 6:       <link rel="stylesheet"
href="http://code.jquery.com/mobile/1.1.0/jquery.mobile-1.1.0.min.css" />
 7:       <script src="http://code.jquery.com/jquery-1.7.1.min.js"></script>
 8:       <script
src="http://code.jquery.com/mobile/1.1.0/jquery.mobile-1.1.0.min.js"> </script>
 9:    </head>
10:    <body>
```

```
11:     <p>content will go here shortly</p>
12:   </body>
13: </html>
```

Let's take a walk through the basic structure. Beginning with line 1 we set up our HTML5 DOCTYPE. This allows most mobile browsers and even most modern desktop browsers to use all the features that jQuery Mobile offers. The HTML5 DOCTYPE also allows some backwards compatibility with older browsers.

The next few lines are all standard HTML, but line 5 contains a meta element with some attributes that you may not recognize. The name attribute tells the browser what type of data this meta element contains. In this case it tells the browser that it contains information for the viewport or the display size of the page. The content attribute is set to width=device-width, initial-scale=1. This means that when the page is viewed, it should not be zoomed in to a particular portion of the page or zoomed out and shrink everything down. Instead the page should be rendered with the same dimensions as the device it is being viewed on, averting the strange zoomed views that plague some websites that are viewed on mobile devices.

Line 6 is where we include the jQuery Mobile CSS file. This file contains all the default styles that will be applied when using jQuery Mobile, and it also contains some theme styles that can be overwritten.

Line 7 contains the include for the standard jQuery JavaScript library. Note that this include must be called before you call the jQuery Mobile JavaScript library or you will receive JavaScript errors on the page.

Line 8 is the include for the jQuery Mobile JavaScript library.

Lines 9 through 13 show basic HTML markup for the rest of the page.

You can try running the code from Listing 4.1 by running basic_layout.html in your browser. Don't be surprised or worried that the site doesn't look very mobile and that it only contains one line of text. This is normal and rendering exactly as expected. In fact it brings us to using data roles.

Using Data Roles

Before we dive into data roles, you need to first learn what they are. We know that HTML elements are limited in the attributes they can contain to be considered valid. For example an img element requires an src and an alt attribute to be valid. While there are some optional attributes that you can also put in the img element that would still allow it to be valid, if you were to throw in an attribute of imgtitle it would not validate. Listing 4.2 demonstrates this with two img elements; one is valid and the other is not.

LISTING 4.2   An Example of Valid and Invalid HTML Markup

```
1: <!-- The following img element is valid and will pass HTML validation -->
2: <img src="images/logo.png" alt="Site Logo" />
3: <!-- The following img element has been customized and will fail HTML
validation -->
4: <img src="images/logo.png" alt="Site Logo"
imgtitle="Tremble before our mighty logo of fury!" />
```

Let's walk through the code snippet in Listing 4.2. Line 1 is an HTML comment that I included to help you understand what is going on. Line 2 is a perfectly valid img element that contains both src and alt attributes. Line 3 is another HTML comment, and line 4 is an invalid img element because it contains a custom attribute with a custom value.

We know that the code in line 4 is invalid, but what happens when we need that extra text in that img element? For example, what if we had a tooltip function that was built in JavaScript that we wanted to use that would take the text from the custom imgtitle attribute and display it? This is why data attributes exist.

Data attributes are part of the HTML5 specification. They were created so that developers who need to use custom tags can use them without fear of breaking validation of the element they are customizing. To create a data attribute you must start the attribute with data- you may then use any letters you want as long as they are lowercase.

NOTE

In Reference to a data attribute

Due to the way data attributes are created some people refer to them as data-*. The asterisk is used to denote that after typing data- almost anything can be used. Creating data attributes named data-mine, data-billingaddress, data-phone, data-userid, data-a, and data-z are all perfectly acceptable. However, actually using a data attribute named data-* in your code, is not.

Experienced jQuery users may already be familiar with data attributes and the use of the jQuery .data() function when working with them. If you decide to reference data attributes with this function, be aware that after the first dash any extra text will be formatted in CamelCase. For example, data-my-attribute will become data-myAttribute. To get around this you can use the jQuery .attr() method instead to specify your custom attribute. For more information on the .attr() method, visit http://api.jquery.com/attr/.

Using a data-attribute and an HTML5 DOCTYPE informs the browser to ignore the attribute and any data contained in it, thereby allowing it to validate.

jQuery Mobile uses these data attributes to create data roles for data storage. This allows the jQuery Mobile library to find the data contained in custom attributes and manipulate them without making any of the code invalid.

Creating a Simple Page

We have already covered the code it takes to build the basic structure for a mobile site, but we have not actually made it look like a mobile site. Let's expand that into a one-page and one-button site so that we can get a better feel for how jQuery Mobile works.

In Listing 4.3 we add several elements to the page and use data attributes to apply functionality and style.

LISTING 4.3   Expanding the Mobile Site to Include a Header and a Button

```
 1: <!DOCTYPE html>
 2: <html>
 3:   <head>
 4:     <title>Developing with jQuery Mobile</title>
 5:     <meta name="viewport" content="width=device-width, initial-scale=1">
 6:     <link rel="stylesheet"
href="http://code.jquery.com/mobile/1.1.0/jquery.mobile-1.1.0.min.css" />
 7:     <script src="http://code.jquery.com/jquery-1.7.1.min.js"></script>
 8:     <script
src="http://code.jquery.com/mobile/1.1.0/jquery.mobile-1.1.0.min.js"> </script>
 9:   </head>
10:   <body>
11:     <div data-role="page">
12:       <div data-role="header"><h1>Single Page Site</h1></div>
13:       <div data-role="content">
14:         <p>Look at the button!</p>
15:         <a href="#" data-role="button">I am a button</a>
16:       </div>
17:     </div>
18:   </body>
19: </html>
```

The preceding code was based on the code from Listing 4.1 and can be viewed by opening the file expanded_layout.html. Let's go over the changes that were made from the original code.

Inside the `body` element we have added a new `div` element on line 11. This `div` has an attribute of `data-role="page"`, which allows jQuery Mobile to treat this `div` as a single page. This functionality also allows you to have a multipage site contained in one HTML file. Continuing on to line 12 you can see that it contains a div with an attribute of data-role="header". This tells jQuery Mobile to treat this as a container for the header section of the page. Inside this div element is an h1 element. It is important that we have this element in the header, not only for Search Engine Optimization (SEO) purposes, but because it gets a specific style applied to it that helps complete the look of the header section.

Line 13 contains another div with an attribute of data-role="content". This applies some padding and other styles and designates this div as the container for the content section of the page. Line 14 shows a p element with some text inside it. This is included as an example of what text looks like inside the content section. Also inside the content section line 15 shows a link that we have set up. While this link currently does not go anywhere (the href attribute is set to #), it is important to notice that the a element contains the data-role="button" attribute. jQuery Mobile uses this attribute to transform the standard link into a fully styled button.

If you were to render the page in a browser, the whole page should now look more like a mobile site. The default theme is applied including a clearly defined header section and content section. The button that we added is in the content section and automatically expands to fit the size of the screen it is being viewed on.

I mentioned previously that the button that was added does not actually do anything when clicked. This is fine for personal amusement and practical jokes, but we can make it do something if we set the href attribute to link somewhere. In Listing 4.4, which shows the contents of button_click.html, you can see that the button has been set to point to another page, and a second page section has been set up within our HTML file.

LISTING 4.4   The Mobile Site with a Working Button and Second Page Section

```
 1:  <!DOCTYPE html>
 2:  <html>
 3:    <head>
 4:       <title>Developing with jQuery Mobile</title>
 5:       <meta name="viewport" content="width=device-width, initial-scale=1">
 6:       <link rel="stylesheet"
href="http://code.jquery.com/mobile/1.1.0/jquery.mobile-1.1.0.min.css" />
 7:       <script src="http://code.jquery.com/jquery-1.7.1.min.js"></script>
 8:       <script
src="http://code.jquery.com/mobile/1.1.0/jquery.mobile-1.1.0.min.js"> </script>
 9:    </head>
10:    <body>
11:       <div data-role="page">
12:          <div data-role="header"><h1>Single Page Site</h1></div>
13:          <div data-role="content">
```

```
14:            <p>Look at the button!</p>
15:            <a href="#dpop" data-role="button" data-rel="dialog">I am a button</a>
16:         </div>
17:       </div>
18:       <div data-role="page" id="dpop" data-theme="d">
19:         <div data-role="header"><h1>Clicked!</h1></div>
20:         <div data-role="content">
21:           <p>clicked content!</p>
22:           <a href="#" data-rel="back" data-role="button">Go back</a>
23:         </div>
24:       </div>
25:       </body>
26: </html>
```

The first change is on line 15. We changed the link to now point at a populated anchor instead of an empty one. We also added another attribute to the a element. Using `data-rel="dialog"` allows jQuery Mobile to display the linked element as a `dialog` page instead of a standard page. Using a `dialog` gives a different style and feel than a standard page and also shows the page with a special `pop` transition by default.

If you look farther down in the code for the referenced anchor you will find it on line 18. This is where we set up a second `page`. We gave the second `page` an `id` of dpop, and just like the `page` on line 11, it is a `div` element. Something else we have done is added `data-theme="d"`, which styles the dialog window a little differently than the current color scheme.

There are currently five basic swatches in the jQuery Mobile default theme. The swatches are selected by passing either a, b, c, d, or e into the `data-theme` attribute.

Line 19 shows that we set up another `header` section and added another h1. Line 20 is the same as line 13, which is a `div` with an attribute of `data-role="content"`, and just like line 13 it tells jQuery Mobile that this `div` element will be used as a `content` section. Within this section we created a back button on line 22. The back button works through the use of the `data-rel="back"`. This attribute sends the browser back one step in history. This is why the `href` has an empty anchor value.

Figure 4.1 shows the first page, and Figure 4.2 shows the dialog page.

As you can see from the preceding coding exercise, jQuery Mobile allows you to easily make mobile sites with very little code. You can also create your own events, or even tweak the default ones. To get started adding your own customization we need cover some subtle differences between the standard jQuery framework and the jQuery Mobile framework.

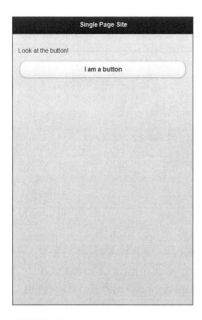

FIGURE 4.1
A simple page with one button linking to the dialog page

FIGURE 4.2
The dialog page that appears when linked from the first page

Understanding the Mobile Initialization Event

You already learned that one of the problems with using standard JavaScript happens when including scripts and attaching events or even when trying to manipulate data that may not exist at the time the function is called. The jQuery framework uses the $(document).ready() function to circumvent manipulation and loading problems by giving you access to your functions as soon as possible. While this is fantastic for single page sites, it becomes a small problem for the jQuery Mobile framework.

jQuery Mobile uses AJAX to load the contents of each page rather than reload the entire DOM structure. The $(document).ready() function only runs once per page load, not per AJAX call. In jQuery Mobile, the $(document).ready() function doesn't run once per page, but rather once per site unless a page refresh is requested or performed by the user. This means that some of the default settings that need to be set by jQuery Mobile cannot be set in the $(document).ready() function because they would not be applied to pages included through AJAX.

The answer to setting and changing these defaults is to use the mobileinit event because it runs before the $(document).ready() function ever does. To use the mobileinit event you must first include the jQuery framework and then either inline or include an external JavaScript file that contains an event binding for the mobileinit event and finally the include for jQuery Mobile. That may sound a little confusing, so let's look at Listing 4.5 for an example of this process.

LISTING 4.5   Including jQuery, an Inline mobileinit Script, and jQuery Mobile

```
1: <script src="http://code.jquery.com/jquery-1.7.1.min.js"></script>
2: <script type="text/javascript">
3:    $(document).on("mobileinit", function() {
4:       $.extend( $.mobile , {
5:          pageLoadErrorMessage:
'Either the page cannot be found or it cannot be loaded.'
6:       });
7:    });
8: </script>
9: <script
src="http://code.jquery.com/mobile/1.1.0/jquery.mobile-1.1.0.min.js"></script>
```

Line 1 starts out with the include for the jQuery framework. Line 2 is the beginning of our inline JavaScript for setting the mobileinit event. Line 3 is where we actually set up the mobileinit event by using the .on() function (which is part of the version 1.7 of the jQuery framework and is why we needed to include the jQuery framework before our inline script). If we had been using a version of jQuery Mobile prior to 1.1 we would be using the .bind() function instead of the .on() function. The .on() function can take quite a few arguments, but in our case we pass two. The first argument passed is the event you want to bind, and the second is usually an anonymous function that contains the code you want to run when the event runs. You can learn more about the `.on()` function by visiting http://api.jquery.com/on/. On line 4 we used the `$.extend()` function, which allows us to merge two objects together, and passed `$.mobile` to be used as the target object that we want to add or merge to. We then used an opening brace to begin the array of settings that we want to merge or change into the `$.mobile` object. Continuing to line 5 you can see that we are going to overwrite the default for `pageLoadErrorMessage` by setting the value to `"Either the page cannot be found or it cannot be loaded"`. The notation used here may look a familiar. It is a name-value pair and is commonly known as JavaScript Object Notation (JSON). It is commonly used in jQuery plug-ins, configurations, and functions (including the jQuery `.css()` function). Line 6 shows the closing brace and closing parentheses of the `$.extend()` function. Line 7 is the closing brace and closing parentheses of the `.on()` function. Line 8 is the closing tag for our inline script. Line 9 then includes the jQuery Mobile framework that now has the default value for `pageLoadErrorMessage` changed.

Now that we know that we can change some of the default settings of jQuery Mobile with the `mobileinit` event what do we do when we want an event or function to be triggered when a new page is loaded? I'm fairly sure that you are thinking, "That's easy! Just use the `$(document).ready()` function on the page you are loading and you'll be all set!" While that is normally the correct answer, we have to remember that all pages are inserted into the DOM through AJAX. This means that the DOM is only loaded once, making the `$(document).ready()` function load on the first page only. Luckily jQuery Mobile has a solution for this problem: You just need to use the `pageinit` event.

Using the `pageinit` Event Instead of `$(document).ready()`

To use the `pageinit` event on your page, you have to take a slightly less dynamic and more planned approach to your code. There are a few different ways you can attach the `pageinit` event in your code. When using a version of jQuery Mobile prior to 1.1, you will be using jQuery 1.6.4, which means you use the `.bind()` function instead of the `.on()` function. When using jQuery Mobile 1.1+ you use the `.on()` function to bind the event.

The `.on()` function introduced in jQuery 1.7 is a unification of previous functions used to bind events. Instead of having to worry about using `.bind()`, `.live()`, or `.delegate()`, you can now use the `.on()` function to find events. More about this function can be found by visiting http://api.jquery.com/on/. If you are using a version of jQuery Mobile prior to 1.1, you should not use the `.on()` method, but should instead use the `.delegate()` or `.live()` function.

In Listing 4.6 the contents of multipage_one.html, which is the first page of a multipage site are shown. It includes a button that then loads a second page through AJAX.

LISTING 4.6 A Page Containing the Setup for the `pageinit` Event

```
1:  <!DOCTYPE html>
2:  <html>
3:    <head>
4:      <title>Developing with jQuery Mobile</title>
5:      <meta name="viewport" content="width=device-width, initial-scale=1">
6:      <link rel="stylesheet"
href="http://code.jquery.com/mobile/1.1.0/jquery.mobile-1.1.0.min.css" />
7:      <script src="http://code.jquery.com/jquery-1.7.1.min.js"></script>
8:      <script type="text/javascript">
9:        $(document).on("mobileinit", function() {
10:         $.extend( $.mobile , {
11:           pageLoadErrorMessage: 'Either the page cannot be found or it
cannot be loaded.'
12:         });
13:       });
14:       $(document).on("pageinit","#pageinit2", function() {
15:         alert("pageinit is bound!");
16:       });
17:     </script>
18:     <script
src="http://code.jquery.com/mobile/1.1.0/jquery.mobile-1.1.0.min.js"></script>
19:   </head>
20:   <body>
21:     <div data-role="page">
22:       <div data-role="header"><h1>pageinit event example</h1></div>
23:       <div data-role="content">
24:         <p>The button below will use AJAX to load another page and trigger
a bound event</p>
25:         <a href="multipage_two.html" data-role="button">Click to open a new
page</a>
26:       </div>
27:     </div>
28:   </body>
29: </html>
```

Looking at the preceding code, do you see the `.on()` function and the `pageinit` event? Let's walk through the code and I will explain what we have done and how it makes things work.

The beginning lines should seem familiar by now, so we'll start at line 9. Line 9 uses `$(document)` as the selector, and then uses the `.on()` function to bind the `mobileinit` event to the current page. In comparison line 14 also uses the `.on()` function to bind the `pageinit` event. The binding takes place through the second parameter passed in the `.on()` function. The `.on()` function allows events to be delegated to elements that do not currently exist in the DOM, but that will exist in the future. This is why the `pageinit` event will be bound to the object that will have an `id` of `pageinit2` once it is added to the DOM.

Continuing onto line 15 we can see that an `alert()` function is going to be called as soon as the page is initialized into the DOM. Line 16 then closes the `.on()` function.

Continuing onto line 18 we see the include for jQuery Mobile. Line 19 closes the `head` element. Line 20 starts the `body` element. Lines 21 through 27 make up the actual code that will be presented as a page to the user. Line 25 shows the setup for a button, and if you look closely you see that our button is set to link to another file instead of an anchor tag farther down the page. We cover multipage sites in Hour 7, "Learning About Page Layout."

To finish out the file, lines 28 and 29 are closing tags for the `body` and `html` elements that complete our page.

We set up a function inside the `pageinit` event that triggers anytime a page with an `id` of `pageinit2` is loaded. Even though we are binding the `pageinit` event on the first page, it will not run on there because it does not have an `id` of `pageinit2`.

Now let's look at Listing 4.7, which shows the contents of multipage_two.html and is the second page that Listing 4.6 links to.

LISTING 4.7 This Page Has an Event Tied to It That Will Trigger on Page Load

```
 1: <!DOCTYPE html>
 2: <html>
 3:   <head>
 4:     <title>Developing with jQuery Mobile</title>
 5:     <meta name="viewport" content="width=device-width, initial-scale=1">
 6:     <link rel="stylesheet"
href="http://code.jquery.com/mobile/1.1.0-rc.1/jquery.mobile-1.1.0-rc.1.min.css"
/>
 7:     <script src="http://code.jquery.com/jquery-1.7.1.min.js"></script>
 8:     <script
src="http://code.jquery.com/mobile/1.1.0-rc.1/jquery.mobile-1.1.0-rc.1.min.js">
</script>
 9:   </head>
10:   <body>
11:     <div data-role="page" id="pageinit2">
12:       <div data-role="header"><h1>pageinit event example </h1></div>
13:       <div data-role="content">
14:         <p>Fantastic! I am a new page and was loaded through AJAX.</p>
15:         <a href="pageinit.html" data-role="button" data-rel="back">
Amazing, now take me back</a>
16:       </div>
17:     </div>
18:   </body>
19: </html>
```

Look closely at the code for a minute and see if you can spot anything that would make it trigger an event when it loads.

A quick glance over lines 1 through 9 shows the typical setup of a mobile site. We can see the HTML5 DOCTYPE being used on line 1. The head element starts on line 3 and includes a title element set on line 4, the meta element set for mobile devices on line 5, the include for the jQuery Mobile style sheet on line 6, the include for the jQuery library on line 7, the include jQuery Mobile library on line 8, and the closing tag for the head element on line 9.

The only thing that appears different on this page from the page in Listing 4.6 is the lack of binding for both the mobileinit event and the pageinit event. Let's keep looking down the code and see if we can see anything else.

Skipping over line 10, line 11 shows us setting up a div element with a data-role="page" attribute and an id="pageinit2". That is the line that contains the attribute that ties this whole thing together. The attribute is id="pageinit2". That is the id that we used for the .on() function to bind the pageinit event to. Since this page contains that particular id, as soon as it is loaded into the DOM it triggers the pageinit event and calls the alert function that we placed inside the event.

Continuing down the rest of the page, you can see the content section being created on line 13. We also added a button that allows us to link back to the first page being created on line 15. This button contains both a link back to the first page through the attribute href="pageinit. html" and an attribute of data-rel="back" that defaults to a sliding-back page transition to the first page. Lines 16 through 19 are closing tags for various HTML elements that complete our page.

Perceived `pageinit` **Processing Speed**

When using the pageinit event, the transition between pages does not actually take place until whatever code has been placed into the pageinit event has finished processing. This can cause some delay between page transitions and may make users who are unprepared for the wait think the site has some lag or is slow. Plan ahead and keep the functions that you need to have on page-load short and direct.

The following figures show the use of the pageinit event. These figures were taken on an Android device running version 4.0.1. Depending on what browser and device you use, the alert message will appear styled differently. Figure 4.3 shows the page we built in Listing 4.6. Figure 4.4 shows the alert that is triggered by the function called in the pageinit event. Figure 4.5 shows the page that triggered the pageinit event and is the code from Listing 4.7.

You can set up more pageinit events for other pages by using a unique id for each page you want like to attach the event to. By doing this you can trigger functions that you only want happening when certain pages load.

FIGURE 4.3
When the button is pressed, the `pageinit` event will be called.

FIGURE 4.4
This alert message was triggered by the `pageinit` event.

FIGURE 4.5
This is the second page. It appears only after the code in the `pageinit` event has completed.

Summary

This hour discussed the jQuery Mobile framework. You learned that it is dependent on the standard jQuery framework to function. You learned what files are included and required to use the jQuery Mobile framework, and also learned about HTML5 data attribute and how jQuery Mobile leverages them to apply style and functionality to the page.

The basic requirements needed for a mobile page were discussed as well as how to add some extra HTML elements into the page to complete the look and feel of a mobile site.

Finally you learned how to overwrite some of the default jQuery Mobile settings and that you can use the `pageinit` event to run a function when a page is called to get around the problems associated with the `$(document).ready` function only running on the first page load.

Q&A

Q. Can I use my own data attributes within jQuery Mobile or will that break the site?

A. Generally you are free to use whatever data attribute you want, but quite a few data attributes are reserved by jQuery Mobile. For a short list stay away from the following: `data-theme`, `data-ajax`, `data-filter`, `data-icon`, `data-grid`, `data-rel`, `data-icon`, `data-url`, `data-role`, and `data-type`. A good practice is to add a prefix that is unique to you or your site so you would end up with a custom attribute that looked similar to `data-mcn-username`, where the prefix "mcn" stands for "my custom name." Just as a reminder, if you use a dash in your data-attribute, you should avoid using the jQuery `.data()` function and instead use the `.attr()` function.

Q. Regarding the `pageinit` event, can I bind the event on the page I want it to run on instead of on the first page using the `.on()` function?

A. You can, but keep a few things in mind. When running jQuery Mobile 1.1+, if you use the `.on()` function on the page you want to have the `pageinit` event work on, then the first time that page is loaded, your `pageinit` function will run once. The second time that page is loaded, the function will run twice instead of once. This is because the event is being bound over and over again instead of just once. You can get around this with the `.off()` function. If you forget to unbind the `pageinit` event you run the risk of crashing the browser on the mobile device that is viewing your site due to the amount of memory that will be taken up in binding and running your function over and over again. See http://api.jquery.com/off/ for information about unbinding events set with the `.on()` function.

Q. You warned me to watch out when adding scripts outside the `head` element. Can you explain why the scripts are "run once"?

A. When you are browsing a mobile site that uses jQuery Mobile, any scripts included in the `head` element will be read only on the page that you start from. So you start on the home page and then the scripts that are in the `head` element of that page will be run. If you use a button or a navigation bar to move to another page, the scripts in the `head` element on those pages will be ignored because only the `title` element and the `div` element that contains the `data-role="page"` attribute will be parsed and brought into the DOM.

Workshop

The workshop contains a quiz and some exercises to help you check your comprehension and understanding.

Quiz

1. What files make up the jQuery Mobile framework?

2. True or False: The $(document).ready() function cannot be used on pages that are added to the DOM through AJAX.

3. How is the .on() function different from the .bind() function?

4. True or False: You can use the .on() function with jQuery 1.6.4.

5. True or False: The use of data attributes in HTML has been around since HTML 3.2.

Answers

1. The jQuery Mobile framework is made up of a JavaScript file and a CSS style sheet. However, to function, the jQuery framework must be included.

2. True. The document is only loaded once per page and will not run on subsequent pages that are inserted into the DOM through AJAX.

3. The main difference is that you can use the .on() function to bind events to objects that do not exist on initial page load. This is extremely helpful with binding events to elements that appear through AJAX.

4. False. The .on() function was not added to the jQuery framework until version 1.7. Prior to that you could use .delegate() or the .bind() functions for event binding.

5. False. The use of data attributes is new to HTML5 and has been added to the specification specifically for easier data manipulation and storage.

Exercises

1. Create your own data-attribute and add it to a page. Try using some jQuery scripts to get data from it or as a way to help create a selector for the element.

2. Take some of the code from the chapter and add more links and more pages. Experiment with setting up multiple pageinit events for your new pages.

3. Try using the .on() function with another event and with an object that is on a separate page. Try binding different events with it. Something as simple as a click event that triggers an alert() function is a good way to get started with understanding how the .on() function works with events.

HOUR 5
Building Your First Mobile Site

What You'll Learn in This Hour:

▶ The basic structure of a page
▶ How to add a header and a footer bar to your page
▶ How to add some simple formatting to your layout
▶ How to attach an image and make it scale
▶ How to use a button to link to another page

You've been introduced to most of the basic building blocks that make up jQuery Mobile. In this hour we put them together to make a rudimentary but usable website.

We start with the basics of site structure and move on to adding content. When we are finished you'll have a small two-page site that features an auto-scaling image and a link to a second page. The link is triggered by a button and gives you a look at page transitions.

Structuring the Page

The structure of your site is important, both for the ease of maintaining your site and for the user experience. The layout you choose is going to determine the entire user experience. Your layout should let users know where they are and make them want to continue to scroll down or click on a button and dive deeper into your site. While many pieces and elements make up a mobile site, we are going to focus on three major areas as shown in Figure 5.1.

Not every site follows this exact formula, but most use a similar layout. Let's take a look at each of the three sections a little more in depth.

The Header

This section is the first thing a user sees, and may be the most prominent feature of your mobile site. This informs users where they are, and may include a search bar, a call-to-action button, and/or a logo.

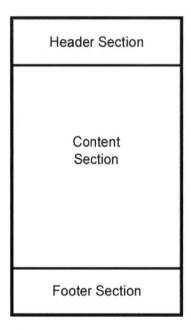

FIGURE 5.1
This shows a basic wireframe of the site with a header, content, and footer section.

The Content Area

Content areas are exactly what they sound like: buttons, text, call-outs, and everything else that is not already included in the other sections. The content area houses the core of your site and displays everything you want the user to see, absorb, or spend time on.

The Footer

The footer is an often overlooked but important area of your site. It can contain everything from extra links to a simple credit line for ownership of the site. In mobile development the footer is often omitted and replaced with a navigation bar or other static element.

Now that we have that covered, let's start on your first mobile site. Listing 5.1 shows the beginning of a mobile site.

LISTING 5.1 A Basic Mobile Site Layout

```
 1: <!DOCTYPE html>
 2: <html>
 3:   <head>
 4:     <title>My first mobile site</title>
 5:     <meta name="viewport" content="width=device-width, initial-scale=1">
 6:     <link rel="stylesheet"
href="http://code.jquery.com/mobile/1.1.0/jquery.mobile-1.1.0.min.css"/>
 7:     <script src="http://code.jquery.com/jquery-1.7.1.min.js"></script>
 8:     <script
src="http://code.jquery.com/mobile/1.1.0/jquery.mobile-1.1.0.min.js"></script>
 9:   </head>
10:   <body>
11:     <div data-role="page">
12:       <div data-role="content">
13:         Welcome to my first mobile site.
14:       </div>
15:     </div>
16:   </body>
17: </html>
```

I'll step through the code so you know exactly what is going on in this setup.

On line 1 you can see that we start our HTML file by using the HTML5 DOCTYPE that jQuery Mobile requires.

In lines 3 through 9 we set up the head element and include the styles for jQuery Mobile, the jQuery library, and the jQuery Mobile library. Note that you can use a local location for your required files, or you can use a Content Delivery Network (CDN) hosted location.

On line 11 we set up a containing div and gave it an attribute of data-role="page". This allows jQuery Mobile to know what belongs onscreen as a page and how to handle the elements within the page.

Within the page we then added another div with an attribute of data-role="content". This sets up the area that will hold all your content pieces. For now we have a simple sentence that we are using as a sort of informational placeholder.

Figure 5.2 shows the site we just created rendered in a mobile browser.

Welcome to my first mobile site.

FIGURE 5.2
While it may look like a line of text on a gradient, this figure shows the beginning of our mobile site.

Adding a Header and Footer

I know what you are thinking: "That's not a site, that's a sentence!" Let's add a header and a footer to make it feel a bit more like a real site.

In Listing 5.2 we add a header section to the site.

LISTING 5.2   The Mobile Site with a Header Section Added

```
1:  <!DOCTYPE html>
2:  <html>
3:    <head>
4:      <title>My first mobile site</title>
5:      <meta name="viewport" content="width=device-width, initial-scale=1">
6:      <link rel="stylesheet"
href="http://code.jquery.com/mobile/1.1.0/jquery.mobile-1.1.0.min.css"/>
7:      <script src="http://code.jquery.com/jquery-1.7.1.min.js"></script>
8:      <script
src="http://code.jquery.com/mobile/1.1.0/jquery.mobile-1.1.0.min.js"></script>
9:    </head>
10:   <body>
11:     <div data-role="page">
12:       <div data-role="header">
```

```
13:          My First Mobile Site
14:        </div>
15:        <div data-role="content">
16:          Welcome to my first mobile site.
17:        </div>
18:      </div>
19:    </body>
20: </html>
```

On line 12 we added a `div` with an attribute of `data-role="header"`. This tells jQuery Mobile to apply the necessary header styles to that section including any custom themes that have been defined.

Let's complete the basic layout by adding a footer section. The code for adding a footer is similar to the header. Go ahead and give it a try, and then check Listing 5.3 see whether you've gotten the hang of it.

LISTING 5.3   **The Mobile Site with a Header and Footer Section Defined**

```
1: <!DOCTYPE html>
2: <html>
3:   <head>
4:     <title>My first mobile site</title>
5:     <meta name="viewport" content="width=device-width, initial-scale=1">
6:     <link rel="stylesheet"
href="http://code.jquery.com/mobile/1.1.0/jquery.mobile-1.1.0.min.css"/>
7:     <script src="http://code.jquery.com/jquery-1.7.1.min.js"></script>
8:     <script
src="http://code.jquery.com/mobile/1.1.0/jquery.mobile-1.1.0.min.js"></script> 9:
</head>
10:    <body>
11:      <div data-role="page">
12:        <div data-role="header">
13:          My First Mobile Site
14:        </div>
15:        <div data-role="content">
16:          Welcome to my first mobile site.
17:        </div>
18:        <div data-role="footer">
19:          Viva la footer!
20:        </div>
21:      </div>
22:    </body>
23: </html>
```

On line 17, the footer is set by adding a `div` and adding an attribute of `data-role="footer"`. This works in the same way as the code for the header section, meaning that a series of styles will automatically be applied. Note that some styles are dependent on child elements and if not found will not fully render the styles defined for that section.

In Figure 5.3 you can see how each section has started to take shape. While each section is defined and clearly separated, it is apparent that we are missing some necessary elements that will complete the expected definition of each section.

FIGURE 5.3
This shows the rendered site with a header, content, and footer section. While the page is being rendered as coded, some styles are definitely missing.

Formatting Text Content

Now that the basic page layout is finished we should add some polish to the page. Let's do the following:

- ▶ Add an `h1` tag around the text in the header.
- ▶ Add some `paragraph` tags around the text in the content area.
- ▶ Add a `strong` tag around some of the text.
- ▶ Add some centered text.
- ▶ Add an `h3` tag around the text in the footer.

TIP

Search Engine Optimization

Search Engine Optimization is important! The higher your h1 tag is on the page the more "weight" the content inside it will have. Make sure you are using your site name or relative keywords for your site in your h1 tag.

Listing 5.4 shows the mobile site with the addition of various formatting elements.

LISTING 5.4   The Mobile Site with Included Formatting Tags

```
 1: <!DOCTYPE html>
 2: <html>
 3:   <head>
 4:     <title>My first mobile site</title>
 5:     <meta name="viewport" content="width=device-width, initial-scale=1">
 6:     <link rel="stylesheet"
href="http://code.jquery.com/mobile/1.1.0/jquery.mobile-1.1.0.min.css"/>
 7:     <script src="http://code.jquery.com/jquery-1.7.1.min.js"></script>
 8:     <script
src="http://code.jquery.com/mobile/1.1.0/jquery.mobile-1.1.0.min.js"></script> 9:
</head>
10:   <body>
11:     <div data-role="page">
12:       <div data-role="header">
13:         <h1>My First Mobile Site</h1>
14:       </div>
15:       <div data-role="content">
16:         <p>Welcome to my first mobile site.</p>
17:         <p>Try me on all of your mobile devices! You can use any
<strong>valid HTML</strong> on this page</p>
18:         <p style="text-align:center;">Powered by jQuery Mobile</p>
19:       </div>
20:       <div data-role="footer">
21:         <h3>Viva la footer!</h3>
22:       </div>
23:     </div>
24:   </body>
25: </html>
```

Figure 5.4 demonstrates some of the styles that jQuery Mobile applies automatically with the built-in theme system on our basic code additions.

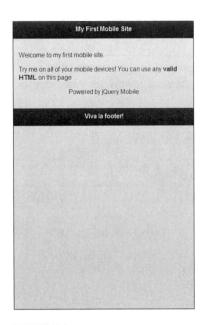

FIGURE 5.4
This shows the changes we have made. Note the newly applied styles that make the header and footer stand out.

Let's review what we just changed. By adding the `h1` tag on line 13 and the `h3` tag on line 21 in the respective header and footer sections we automatically added some extra styling (a gradient background along with centered text). Adding the `p` tags as well as the extra text on lines 16, 17, and 18 helped to extend and shape the content area. On line 17 we added a `strong` tag to make some of the text bold. On line 18 we applied some inline styling to center the text inside the `p` tag.

I used the `strong` tag on line 17 to show you that within the content area of a page you can use any valid HTML tag and it will render just as it would on any standard web page. Keep in mind that some tags will be rendered in a different style or theme (we cover this more in Hour 13, "Changing the Default Theme," when we look at the theme system).

Attaching an Image

Images are usually thought about during the design process and generally thought of as staying at a constant size. In mobile design you need to think about the size of the image, the size of the screen, and the best way to serve the image. We go into detail about these issues in Hour 15, "Responsive Site Layout." For now we'll put up an image and add a `style` element within the `head` element in our HTML file to allow the image to shrink as needed.

Listing 5.5 shows the addition of a `style` element within the `head` element, and the addition of an image inside the content area of our page.

LISTING 5.5　The Mobile Site with the Addition of an Image That Will Scale

```
 1: <!DOCTYPE html>
 2: <html>
 3:   <head>
 4:     <title>My first mobile site</title>
 5:     <meta name="viewport" content="width=device-width, initial-scale=1">
 6:     <link rel="stylesheet"
href="http://code.jquery.com/mobile/1.1.0/jquery.mobile-1.1.0.min.css"/>
 7:     <script src="http://code.jquery.com/jquery-1.7.1.min.js"></script>
 8:     <script
src="http://code.jquery.com/mobile/1.1.0/jquery.mobile-1.1.0.min.js"></script> 9:
<style>
10:       img {max-width:100%;}
11:     </style>
12:   </head>
13:   <body>
14:     <div data-role="page">
15:       <div data-role="header">
16:         <h1>My First Mobile Site</h1>
17:       </div>
18:       <div data-role="content">
19:         <p>Welcome to my first mobile site.</p>
20:         <p>Try me on all of your mobile devices! You can use any
<strong>valid HTML</strong> on this page</p>
21:         <img src="sf_600.jpg" alt="Golden Gate Bridge" />
22:         <p style="text-align:center;">Powered by jQuery Mobile</p>
23:       </div>
24:       <div data-role="footer">
25:         <h3>Viva la footer!</h3>
26:       </div>
27:     </div>
28:   </body>
29: </html>
```

On line 9 we started a `style` element. Inside the `style` element we set up a style that changes the `max-width` of all `img` elements on the page to 100%. By doing this we force the image to become somewhat "stretchy." We then closed the `style` element on line 11. On line 21 we added an `img` element and set the `src` to point at a local file and added some appropriately descriptive `alt` text.

Figure 5.5 and Figure 5.6 give a visual representation of the `img` element scaling to fit the different sizes of the devices viewing the page.

FIGURE 5.5
Notice the image has scaled itself down to accommodate the taller screen.

FIGURE 5.6
Also notice the same image has expanded to fill the wider one.

Linking to a Second Page

The last thing we are going to add is a link to a second page. There are a few different ways you can link to another page, but for simplicity we are going to use a second page container in the same HTML file that we have been working in.

Listing 5.6 shows the content of multipage.html and details the current mobile site with the addition of a second page section along with links to navigate between the pages.

LISTING 5.6   A Multiple Page Site

```
 1:  <!DOCTYPE html>
 2:  <html>
 3:    <head>
 4:      <title>My first mobile site</title>
 5:      <meta name="viewport" content="width=device-width, initial-scale=1">
 6:      <link rel="stylesheet"
href="http://code.jquery.com/mobile/1.1.0/jquery.mobile-1.1.0.min.css"/>
 7:      <script src="http://code.jquery.com/jquery-1.7.1.min.js"></script>
 8:      <script
src="http://code.jquery.com/mobile/1.1.0/jquery.mobile-1.1.0.min.js"></script>
 9:      <style>
10:        img {max-width:100%;}
11:      </style>
12:    </head>
13:    <body>
14:      <div id="pageone" data-role="page">
15:        <div data-role="header">
16:          <h1>My First Mobile Site</h1>
17:        </div>
18:        <div data-role="content">
19:          <p>Welcome to my first mobile site.</p>
20:          <p>Try me on all of your mobile devices! You can use any
<strong>valid HTML</strong> on this page</p>
21:          <img src="sf_600.jpg" alt="Golden Gate Bridge" />
22:          <a href="#pagetwo" data-role="button">Go to Page 2</a>
23:          <p style="text-align:center;">Powered by jQuery Mobile</p>
24:        </div>
25:        <div data-role="footer">
26:          <h3>Viva la footer!</h3>
27:        </div>
28:      </div>
29:      <div id="pagetwo" data-role="page">
30:        <div data-role="header">
31:          <h1>My First Mobile Site</h1>
32:        </div>
33:        <div data-role="content">
```

```
34:          <p>You've made it to page 2!</p>
35:          <p>Isn't that awesome?</p>
36:          <a href="#pageone" data-role="button">Go Back to Page 1</a>
37:          <p style="text-align:center;">Powered by jQuery Mobile</p>
38:        </div>
39:        <div data-role="footer">
40:          <h3>Viva la footer!</h3>
41:        </div>
42:      </div>
43:  </body>
44: </html>
```

The first thing we changed was on line 14 where we added an id of "pageone" to our first page. Continuing onto line 22 we added a link to the second page by using an a tag with the href value set to #pagetwo. We made the link appear as a button by adding an element of data-role="button" to the a tag.

On line 29 we added another page to the site by simply adding a second container div with an attribute of data-role="page". On line 30 in that we added the data-role="header" attribute to the div element. For the content area on line 33 we added the data-role="content" attribute to the div element. We need a way to link back to the first page, so on line 36 we added an a tag with an href value of #pageone. We also added a data-role="button" so that it would render in the browser as a button. Line 39 shows the data-role="footer" attribute being added to the div element that will be the footer section.

The following figures show the rendered output of the site. Figure 5.7 shows the first page, and Figure 5.8 shows the second page.

CAUTION

Multiple Page Elements

Using multiple "page" sections in one HTML file can be disastrous to SEO as the search bot sees all "pages" but records the inactive pages as intentionally "hidden" in CSS. This can cause false black-hat reports that can negatively impact your search ranking.

As you test your site, a feature you may have noticed is that when you resize your browser or change the orientation of your screen, each section stays in its relative place and stretches out to fill in the entire area. While this feature is somewhat dependent on the device and browser you are using, each section always tries to stay where it should while using jQuery Mobile.

FIGURE 5.7
The left side shows the first page.

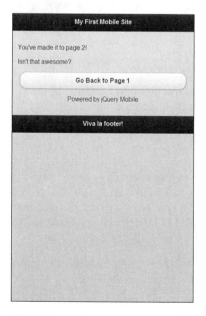

FIGURE 5.8
The right side shows the second page of your first mobile site.

Summary

In this hour you learned that the three basic sections of a mobile site are the header, the content area, and the footer. You put those elements together on a page and had them render with the jQuery Mobile library in a browser as a mobile site.

You also learned that you can use valid HTML inside each section and saw that you can control the styling of the content within each section using inline styles. Styles can also be controlled through an external CSS file.

You learned how to add an image to the site and to make it scale. Finally you learned about using multiple "page" elements in one HTML file and how to use a button to navigate between pages.

Q&A

Q. I see mobile sites with a navigation section, a hero or splash, and several call-to-action buttons. How does this fit into the "three major sections" of a mobile site?

A. A navigation section can be placed in multiple areas. Some navigation sections are included in the header section while others replace the entire footer section. As for callouts, many sites keep one in the header section, or have a static location inside the content area that stays the same as you navigate through the site. Many elements make up a mobile site. The "three major sections" are a way to help you carve up your site and think about your layout.

Q. Can I use any HTML tags inside any section or just ones like you used?

A. Any tag, as long as it is a valid HTML tag, can be used. Some tags may be styled by the internal theme system, but you can always override the style or use a different tag. Tags that may fail are ones that are not valid or created tags.

Q. Why did we set the image to `"max-width:100%"`?

A. This allows the image to scale itself. By setting the style to `"max-width: 100%"` on all the image tags, we are telling the browser that the image cannot exceed the parent container, but that it should be as close to it as possible. This way, when the parent container is less the 100% of the image size the image scales down to fit. Note that if you are viewing the mobile site on an older browser, the image may still break out of the container.

Workshop

The workshop contains a quiz and some exercises to help you check your comprehension and understanding.

Quiz

1. Is jQuery Mobile only available when invoked through a CDN?

2. Does jQuery Mobile use a custom `DOCTYPE` that works only with jQuery Mobile?

3. How can you link to multiple pages if you only have one HTML file?

4. Is a header absolutely required for the site to work when using jQuery Mobile?

5. When changing the browser size or rotating the screen, what happens to the layout of your site?

Answers

1. Of course not; jQuery Mobile can be used locally or from a CDN.

2. No, jQuery Mobile uses the standard `HTML5 DOCTYPE` ensuring compatibility with future browsers and the HTML5 specification.

3. When you set up your `div` elements that will be used for each page in your single HTML file you should give each one a unique `id`. Then whenever you want to link to another page you can simply use the `id` of the desired page with a hash or pound symbol in front of it. For example you could set up an `a` tag and set the `href` to a value of `#pagethree` and that would transition you from your current page to the one with the `id` of `"pagethree"`.

4. While we did cover three major sections of a site, there is no rule that states that you must have all three sections. Some sites get rid of the header or footer section altogether and use a navigation section or put an image there instead.

5. jQuery Mobile detects the change and changes the size of your elements to match the new resolution or orientation.

Exercises

1. Continue working with the mobile site and add another image to one of the pages. Try removing the style for the image and see what happens on your mobile when you use a larger image than the screen has space for.

2. Modify the site some more. Remove the header or footer and replace it with a button, an image, or leave it blank. Add an external style sheet and see what styles you can add to the header or footer replacement.

3. View a few of your favorite websites on your mobile and see whether they redirect or offer you a mobile version of their site. Look to see whether they are using jQuery Mobile or some other framework to serve mobile content.

PART II

Creating the User Interface

HOUR 6
Knowing the Capabilities of Mobile Devices

What You'll Learn in This Hour:

▶ The current screen resolutions of mobile devices
▶ The various extras mobile devices have
▶ The current selection of mobile operating systems
▶ jQuery Mobile support for various mobile devices

Since we have been through the basics of creating a mobile site, in this hour we focus on some of the aspects of a mobile device.

We start with the various screen sizes and resolutions of different mobile devices and move on to understand the screen depth. We then take a quick look at some current mobile operating systems and finally finish out the hour discussing the jQuery Mobile graded support matrix.

Understanding Screen Resolutions and PPI

Not all mobile devices are created equal, and not just in memory or processing power. The screen sizes of most mobile devices are different and may vary significantly even when compared to a previous version.

Let's look at the iPhone as an example. Apple originally created the iPhone with a screen size of 3.5 inches and a resolution of 320×480. Apple continued using that screen size and resolution until the iPhone 4, which has the same 3.5-inch display but a substantially increased resolution of 640×960.

While that is great to designers and geeks who obsess over product specifications, you may be asking yourself why the resolution matters and whether it has an effect on anything.

Clearing Up Resolution

Resolution is the amount of pixels displayed on a screen and is generally shown in a width-by-height format. You may already be familiar with resolution and not realize it. For years the most common resolution on a computer was 640×480. If we take that measurement as width-by-height that would mean the screen is 640 pixels wide by 480 pixels tall. As time moved on 800×600 became the next most common resolution, and then 1024×768. Web development has been pushing a maximum width anywhere between 920 and 980 pixels over the last few years as using this width fits the website inside a viewing resolution of 1024×768 and only requires visitors to scroll vertically.

Knowing what the average website visitor screen size is, or what the minimum and maximum resolutions are can drastically alter your website design and style. Visitors who attempt to view or use your site who have a lower resolution than your design will only able to see a small portion of it on initial page load. They can see your content, but they will be forced to scroll horizontally and vertically, and they may miss out on the message or any call to action you are trying to send. This is especially important to mobile devices and can be a design headache as you shift your design to handle the differences in various mobile devices.

Let me bring up one more resolution example that is commonly viewed but not commonly thought too much about. Take a moment and consider the television. I won't spend time going into the specifics of how a picture is displayed on a television, but try to think about the last time you watched a program in Standard Definition (SD). Now think about the first time you watched a program in High Definition (HD). Did you notice the difference? After viewing a program in HD, watching something SD will have softer edges and may seem to have a touch blur applied to everything. This is because of the resolution differences between SD and HD. The default resolution of SD is generally 640×480, while HD tends to be either 1280×720 or 1920×1080. The difference in resolution is also typically the reason why SD content on some HD televisions has a tendency to look blocky, distorted, or show artifacts since the lower resolution image is forced to be "blown up" to fit the much larger resolution.

Another factor to take into account is not only the resolution of the device, but the physical size of the screen as well. The physical display size and resolution go together to form pixel density.

Pixel Density

Pixel density or Pixels Per Inch (PPI) is the amount of pixels that can be placed in a given area. Going back to the iPhone example, the early generation iPhone contained a resolution of 320×480 with a physical display size of 3.5 inches. After some number crunching, that gives that screen a PPI of 163. The iPhone4 has a resolution of 640×960 and the same physical display size of 3.5 inches. This doubles the PPI to 326. The difference in density is due to the physical screen size and the amount of pixels that can be placed in that area, thereby increasing the resolution that can be displayed.

TIP
Calculating the PPI of a Screen

To figure out the PPI of a display you need to know the physical size of the screen and the resolution that it displays. Starting with the resolution of the device, you take the square root of both the width-squared and height-squared added together and divide it by the physical diagonal display size of the display. For example, a display with a 4-inch screen and a resolution of 480x800 would be calculated by the following:

$$\sqrt{480^2 x 800^2} = 932.95$$

$$932.95/4 = 233.24 \text{ PPI}$$

While there are many heated debates over whether PPI matters with digital images when being viewed on a display, you can live by this guideline: It is not the PPI of the image that matters, but the overall resolution of the image and the device that is viewing it.

Let me explain that a little more. Devices with a higher PPI will have a higher resolution, meaning that images appear smaller when displayed on devices with a higher PPI. A great example of this is when you look at an image on a monitor with a display resolution of 640×480 and then switch to a monitor with a resolution of 1280×1024. The image will be displayed twice as big on the 640×480 screen as it will be on the 1280×1024 even though the PPI of the image itself didn't change. Figure 6.1 and Figure 6.2 illustrate this.

FIGURE 6.1
640×480 viewing an image that is 400px × 300px

FIGURE 6.2
1280×1024 viewing an image that is 400px × 300px

When dealing with mobile devices you need to be aware of the differences in screen resolutions so that images and buttons on your site are still big enough for users to access.

Just in case you have started to wonder about common screen resolutions of mobile devices, the following is a list of current sizes. Note that in the list the width and height are generally reversed in most phones.

▶ Quarter Video Graphics Array (QVGA): 240×320

▶ Wide Quarter Video Graphics Array (WQVGA400): 240×400

▶ Wide Quarter Video Graphics Array (WQVGA432): 240×432

▶ Half Video Graphics Array (HVGA): 320×480

▶ Wide Video Graphics Array (WVGA800): 480×800

▶ Wide Video Graphics Array (WVGA854): 480×854

▶ iPhone 4 (Retina™): 640×960

▶ Wide eXtended Graphics Array (WXGA): 1280×800

Figure 6.3 shows an overlay of these different sizes so that you can get an idea of just how different the viewing area and aspect are.

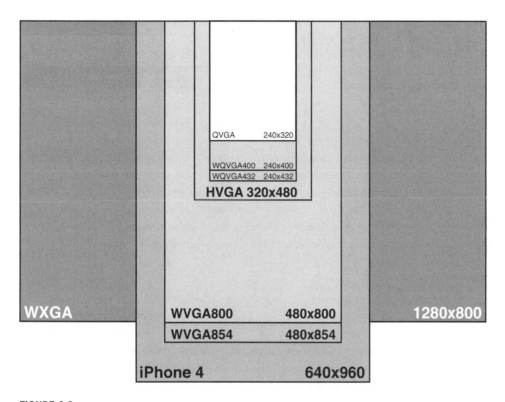

FIGURE 6.3
The many screen resolutions of mobile devices

The preceding list covers most mobile devices but not all of them. Some phones, tablets, and netbooks may contain sizes similar to 1024×600 or 1366×768.

As you look over the list you can see that with the wide variety of resolutions available it can be a daunting task to think of a design and usability that will work for all devices. Luckily this is one of the benefits of using jQuery Mobile. jQuery Mobile allows you to create lists, buttons, and more that remain usable across these devices allowing you to focus on your content and message instead of worrying about users who may not be able to view or use your site.

Additional Mobile Features

Along with a display, mobile devices come with a wide array of additional hardware components that allow them to behave differently than other devices.

Touchscreens

Most modern mobile devices feature a touchscreen for data display and functionality. There are actually many types of touchscreen technologies, but the two most popular for mobile devices are usually resistive and capacitive.

Resistive

Touchscreens that use resistive technology function by using a multilayered screen with two conductive layers in them separated by a gap. When the screen is touched or tapped, the layers touch together to create a point. Those who remember older Personal Digital Assistant devices and even some current gaming devices should be familiar with this type of screen. Devices that use this type of touchscreen generally include a stylus to increase the accuracy of the touch or tap. A downside to this screen type is that it can have a delay when tracking movement making applications and websites feel a bit sluggish compared to capacitive screen devices.

Capacitive

Touchscreens that are capacitive function through the use of sensors placed in various areas of the screen that detect the tiny frequency changes between an insulator and a transparent conductor that occur when the screen is touched or pressed. Frequency changes are dependent on a conductive material touching the screen. This is why when a nonconducting stylus, glove, or similar material touches the screen the frequency will not change and the touch will not be detected. Many mobile devices opt for this type of touchscreen technology because of increased precision when touching the screen.

Orientation

Many portable devices can detect how they are being held and will change how data is displayed to the screen, or use this information as an input device. While it may not seem terribly helpful at first, device orientation can make a large impact on some activities such as reading. This displays the inherent benefit of supporting two viewing resolutions.

Accelerometer

Some devices include a gyroscope or three-way sensor that can return feedback by analyzing movement along the x, y, and z axis. This information is then processed and can be used to adjust the screen orientation, or can be used by some programs or games as a way to move objects along the surface.

Proximity Sensor

This is one sensor that few people think about or even know exists. This may not be included in your mobile device but is found in many current mobile handsets. The main function of this sensor is to perform operations when the device is close to something. An example of this is automated screen operation when the device is placed in a pocket or up to your head. A quick way to tell whether your phone has this feature is to take a call and check to see whether the screen turns off instantly when you place the phone up to your ear. When you pull it away, look to see whether the screen turns back on by itself.

Physical Keyboard

This is another feature that you might not think about when you look at a mobile device. Some devices rely on software keyboards that display keys onscreen that are then touched or typed to use. Other mobile devices have a full set of hardware keys that slide out or are placed below the screen of the device. It is important to be aware that not all devices have a keyboard, especially when designing form input or application controls that use hardware keys as a shortcut.

GPS

If your device contains a Global Positioning System (GPS), it has the ability to look for a network of satellites that are then used to "fix" your location by using a series of coded radio waves and timestamps. This data is then used by various applications for everything from plotting your position on a map, tracking where you've been, or even displaying your current speed and direction.

Acquiring your position can take a few minutes so some devices include Assisted GPS. This works by using known positions of cell towers and other known access points to assist the GPS in determining your location.

Barometer

Yes, some mobile devices come with a barometer sensor inside them. While this can help weather applications display air pressure and help predict future weather at your location, the actual intent for this sensor is quite different. The barometer is actually included to assist the GPS unit. The barometer can get a better fix on your altitude and speed up the GPS acquisition of your location.

Camera

Some devices have one camera on the back of the device. Other devices have two cameras, one on the back and one on the front. Generally the front-facing camera has a smaller megapixel count and is used for video chatting or for quick self-portraits.

The camera included on most mobile devices can be used in a variety of ways. Some applications use the camera for simple picture sharing, while others use the image taken to reference against a library of similar pictures to identify it. Other uses of the camera include Alternate

Reality, which allows you to view the world through your mobile device while pictures, menus, routes, and guides are superimposed into the environment. A current trend with the camera in your device is to use it so scan Quick Response (QR) codes to view special promotions or to receive coupons for the item you are looking at. Figure 6.4 shows a QR code that you can scan with a mobile device.

FIGURE 6.4
QR codes are popular for displaying text, address information, and links.

Not all mobile devices include a camera, and some official application marketplaces will not be available if a camera is not included with the device.

Wireless

Many mobile devices come with WiFi for network and Internet usage at home or at various business establishments. The 802.11 version of a wireless card inside varies per device. Some mobile devices opt for a cheaper 802.11g wireless card that may use less power to save battery, while other devices may include a 802.11n wireless card for possible increased speed and distance.

Other mobile devices may include a 3G connection for cellular service. Other devices may also include 4G, LTE, WiMAX, or similar cellular technology for increased bandwidth, connection sharing, and speed. Generally devices that include cellular access capability cost more than their WiFi only counterparts. Also worth noting is that while a data plan is required to use the cellular access, it can still be used with the cellular access turned off.

Looking at Mobile Operating Systems

Just as there are a wide variety of mobile devices there are also a wide variety of operating systems that run them.

iOS

Many are familiar with iOS as it powers many of the "iDevices." It has been around since 2007 and was originally named iPhone OS. It features tight integration with the Apple OS (known as OSX), iTunes, and the App Store.

When it was originally introduced few apps were available in the App Store, so many developers built web apps that would run in the dimensions of the iPhone. Web apps are still supported by the platform and run inside Mobile Safari (the web browser packaged inside iOS).

Other web browsers are available for iOS and can be purchased in the App Store.

Developers can download the Software Development Kit (SDK) for free but are required to pay a registration fee per year to publish applications in the App Store. Applications must go through a submission process where they are either accepted and placed in the App Store, or rejected and sent back to the developer to fix. While native code is written and compiled from Objective-C, there are frameworks that take HTML, CSS, and JavaScript and compile it to be run as a native app.

Android

Mobile devices that run the Android OS have been on the rise during the last few years. Android was started in 2008 by Google and the Open Handset Alliance and is currently used in tablets, mobile phones, and personal media players. It features the Play Store, Play Music, Play Books, widgets, and extra customization through the use of "rooting" the device to install modified versions of the OS (please be aware that rooting a device will usually void your warranty).

Android originally branched out into versions for small screen devices (phones) and large screen (tablet) devices but is coming into a unity with future versions.

Android ships with a built-in browser based on WebKit (the same WebKit that Chrome is based on). Similar in support to Mobile Safari (which is also based on WebKit) many CSS3 and HTML5 features are supported.

Native application development is done with the Android SDK, which can be downloaded for free. Code is written in Java, extended with API calls, and then compiled for device usage. There is a one-time developer fee to release your app in the Android Market. While applications are somewhat reviewed, the Android Market is much less strict than other marketplaces. When installing an application on Android the app must disclose what features of the phone it is going to access. This puts the onus of responsibility on the individual user instead of the developer. This has also caused some backlash in marketplaces if users believe an app is accessing personal data without reason.

Several external "markets" exist that may be used to download applications. Some of these marketplaces exist due to the restriction that Google has placed on hardware running the Android OS. Devices that do not pass Google certification do not receive access to the Android Market and must either provide their own or make users sideload applications onto their device. This does not mean that all external marketplaces are necessarily less legitimate than the official Play market. For example, the Amazon Market drives the applications available for the Kindle Fire, which is a third-party device that runs a customized version of Android. Other Android-based devices also run customized markets that make sure applications run on their devices before allowing users to download them.

Windows Phone

This is the current name of the mobile OS developed by Microsoft. It was announced in 2010 as a replacement for the Windows Mobile OS. It features a completely redesigned interface dubbed "metro."

While the initial release of the OS was met with only 10 devices supporting it, Microsoft made a partnership with Nokia in 2011 to help bolster hardware support. The agreement with Nokia also brought support for the Ovi store and Nokia maps to the OS. In addition to these Windows Phone has integration with Bing services and has a Marketplace where applications can be downloaded and installed.

The current release of Windows Phone sports a new version of Internet Explorer Mobile that is based on the desktop version of Internet Explorer 9.

Applications are built using the Windows Phone SDK, which is used in conjunction with Visual Studio and can be downloaded for free. To release an app in the Marketplace you must be either a licensed Xbox Live or Windows Phone developer. All applications are subject to approval and must pass to appear in the Marketplace.

The future of Windows Phone is currently geared toward a more complete integration with Windows 8, including tighter integration for desktops, tablets, and mobile phones.

Bada

This OS is created by Samsung and is still trying to gain traction in the mobile device market. It was introduced in 2010 with a limited number of hardware devices. If you have ever used an Android device from Samsung that runs the touchwiz launcher, then Bada will feel somewhat familiar. Also if you have ever had a Samsung phone before, then you may recognize some of the features as Bada is the current evolution of Samsung's existing proprietary OS.

Applications are distributed and downloaded through Samsung Apps, the native store for the OS.

Bada currently features a web browser that is based on WebKit. It features many similar functions that you would expect in today's smartphones, meaning multitouch, pinch-to-zoom, OpenGL support for 3D applications and games, as well as copy and paste features.

Currently the SDK is available for free download as long as you are either a registered developer or have a Samsung user account.

Applications are coded in C++ but share many similarities with Android development. To publish an app you must create a seller account and go through an approval process.

BlackBerry

This OS was created by Research In Motion and was one of the first of the mobile devices to include and support a trackball. The BlackBerry OS was also one of the first devices to offer integration with corporate email systems, making it an ideal choice for businesses worldwide.

BlackBerry Messenger has been one of the most successful features of the OS. It allows users to interact with each other in a chat-like environment, including building chat rooms and groups. Unlike traditional texting, BlackBerry Messenger instead relies on sending messages over the Internet allowing messages to be sent when out of cell phone coverage but within a wireless access point.

BlackBerry currently runs a proprietary browser that varies on each version of the OS. This means that older BlackBerry devices lack support for newer web technologies such as HTML5 and CSS3.

Applications can be downloaded to the device through BlackBerry App World, the official store for BlackBerry apps.

To develop an app for BlackBerry you need to download the SDK and then create your application using either HTML5 or Java. Once your application is completed you must submit the app to App World for approval. If approved it will be placed in App World and become available for download or purchase.

The BlackBerry OS 7 will be the last release not based on QNX, which is what the BlackBerry PlayBook OS was based on. The new BlackBerry OS, named BlackBerry 10 is slated for launch during 2012 and will run on phones and tablet devices. The PlayBook OS supports BlackBerry WebWorks applications as well as Adobe AIR applications. Recent developments allow the tablet to also run Android applications that have gone through a repackaging process. A new development kit is also in the works to allow native application building in C and C++.

Many more mobile operating systems are available, and more are currently in active development. Some mobile devices feature an OS that has taken the core of another mobile OS and applied heavy modifications to both the look and functionality of the system to create a unique user experience.

Learning About Mobile Graded Browser Support

With so many mobile devices in existence, the team at jQuery Mobile has decided to keep a matrix of supported devices.

Before you get too excited, it does not cover every mobile device in existence, but it does cover the popular ones. The list is carved into four major sections or grades.

The A-grade section is a list of browsers that support all the features that jQuery Mobile adds to your site. This means all the special effects including page transitions appear, and all theme and styles will be applied. This also means that pages will be loaded through AJAX and will be dynamically inserted into the DOM giving the user a smoother experience.

The B-grade section still offers an excellent viewing experience with most styles being enabled. Navigation may feel a touch on the slow side because AJAX page loading is not supported. This means that rather than receive loading messages while pages are fetched and inserted into the DOM, pages will have to be navigated to and displayed.

The C-grade section gets you a basic albeit usable site. The pages will still load, and your content will still be there, but everything is reduced to fallbacks. The fancy styles will not be applied. Page transitions will not work.

The last section is more of a message from the development team letting users know that they have not tested every mobile OS and device. What is nice is that there is usually a note why a device is on the list. The reasons may vary from OS not supported to unable to test due to lack of emulation software or hardware available. To view the list of currently supported devices for yourself browse to http://jquerymobile.com/gbs/.

Summary

In this hour you learned about some of the aspects of mobile devices, including screen size and resolution and that each mobile device may display an image at a different size due to resolution.

You learned about the different feature sets that can be found in mobile devices. You also learned about some of the functionality of these features and have an idea about they can be used by developers.

Mobile devices do not all run the same mobile OS, and now you know that mobile devices are generally tied to a store where apps can be purchased or downloaded. Different mobile browsers are used to surf the Internet and view web applications and mobile websites, and you learned that you could develop for these mobile devices with an SDK and knowledge of the native programming language.

Finally you learned that the jQuery Mobile team keeps a support matrix of devices with the expected level of style and functionality for those devices.

Q&A

Q. What is the difference between a native application and a web application?

A. A native application means that the code was written and compiled either using the same language as the OS or into a file that can be understood by the device at an OS level. Native applications give deeper control and access to the hardware components of the device and usually grant access to the local file system. Native applications generally must be coded for each mobile OS individually.

Web applications on the other hand are built to be displayed in the browser or through a special viewer on the mobile device. Web applications are usually built to look and function like a native app but have the advantage of only being written once. There are a few frameworks such as PhoneGap, Sencha Touch, Appcelerator, and Rhodes that you can use to write a web application that will allow you to tie into some of the functionality that native apps can use.

Q. Why isn't there a mobile standard for devices that everyone can follow so that developing is easier?

A. Some companies have put together agreements to try to standardize some of the feature sets of mobile devices. The problem, however, isn't really the devices, it is the demand. If a manufacturer has customers demanding a device with a specific size, they will cater to the customer needs. This is also what continues to drive mobile evolution and progress. It may be easier for developers to have cookie-cutter devices, but without new features and changes in device technology development wouldn't evolve much either.

Q. How does jQuery Mobile help me deal with all these device differences?

A. jQuery Mobile bridges the gap in many places for you. It helps you with a uniform layout that looks nearly the same on every mobile device that views it. It gives you the tools to make a response layout that has the ability to work with browsers on your standard computer as well as on your mobile device. It is geared toward speed and functionality, both of which are important to mobile users. Finally it helps you reduce the bandwidth spent on your mobile site and lets users get to your content faster than loading a full site.

Workshop

The workshop contains a quiz and some exercises to help you check your comprehension and understanding.

Quiz

1. True or False: All mobile devices have the exact same pixel density.

2. True or False: Mobile devices can come with a GPS included that allows users to see where they are on a map, or even how fast they are travelling.

3. True or False: Some mobile devices cannot use cellular technologies for Internet access.

4. True or False: Resistive screens respond quicker than conductive screens, allowing a smoother experience.

5. True or False: All devices will work with all the features of jQuery Mobile.

Answers

1. False. All mobile devices do not even have the same screen size or resolution; it would be impossible for them to all have the exact same pixel density.

2. True. Some mobile devices have a GPS included that can show you where you are, how long it took you to get there, and give a live update of how fast you are currently moving.

3. True. Not every device that is considered mobile is connected through cellular networks. Many devices such as personal media players, tablets, or eReaders use WiFi to connect to the Internet.

4. False. Resistive screens have a harder time tracking movement and may give the feeling of added lag when used.

5. False. Unfortunately not all devices support all the styles or even the JavaScript required for jQuery Mobile to function fully. On the bright side, the jQuery Mobile team has gone to great lengths to include fallback support for legacy devices making sites built with jQuery Mobile still function on older or nonsupported devices.

Exercises

1. Either using your mobile device or a borrowed one, experiment with the various features of the device and see what apps have been developed that use these features. This may include weather applications that use the barometer, image apps that use the cameras, or even apps that track your walking, jogging, or biking.

2. Determine what type of mobile OS and version your mobile device is currently running. Look at the version history online and see what features have been added up to the point of your device. Check to see whether you are even using the new features or whether there are ones that you should be using.

3. Open the browser on your mobile device and browse a few sites. Check to see whether your browser can support multiple tabs or windows. Go to your app marketplace and search for other browsers. Read about them and see what extra functionality they give when compared to the stock or included browser on your mobile device.

HOUR 7
Learning About Page Layout

What You'll Learn in This Hour:

- ▶ How to create a single page layout
- ▶ How to create a multiple page layout
- ▶ How to align content with a grid
- ▶ How to make content collapsible

This hour we dive deeper into the use of single and multiple page layouts. We also learn about using a grid to help align content, and then finish the hour by learning how to add collapsible content on a mobile site.

Using a Single Page Layout

As you start to think about your mobile projects, you may find that a single page site is a viable option. Single page sites are great for profile sites or simple applications. But of course there is much more than just using a single page layout. A single page layout is the starting point for any jQuery Mobile project. Every page in your site will share the attributes of a single page template.

We previously discussed the three main sections of a mobile page; the head, content, and footer sections. Regardless of your overall site structure, every page you include will use portions of a single page layout.

Listing 7.1 shows the contents of singlepage.html. This is a simple single page layout that can be used as a base for any page you are going to build.

LISTING 7.1   A Single Page Template

```
1: <!DOCTYPE html>
2: <html>
3:   <head>
4:     <title>Sample template</title>
```

```
5:        <meta name="viewport" content="width=device-width, initial-scale=1">
6:        <link rel="stylesheet"
href="http://code.jquery.com/mobile/1.1.0/jquery.mobile-1.1.0.min.css" />
7:        <script src="http://code.jquery.com/jquery-1.7.1.min.js"></script>
8:        <script src="http://code.jquery.com/mobile/1.1.0/jquery.mobile-1.1.0.min.
js"></script>
9:    </head>
10:    <body>
11:      <div data-role="page">
12:        <div data-role="header">
13:          <h1>header section</h1>
14:        </div>
15:        <div data-role="content">
16:          <p>Page content goes in this content section</p>
17:        </div>
18:        <div data-role="footer">
19:          <h4>footer section</h4>
20:        </div>
21:      </div>
22:    </body>
23: </html>
```

You should recognize this code from the pages we put together previously. Since you should have a pretty good grasp on what is going on with this code, I'll briefly touch on some of the lines that you should pay particular attention to.

Line 1 shows the `!DOCTYPE html` declaration. We previously covered why this is important, so make sure that you always start your HTML files with this declaration.

Line 4 is the `title` element, which is important for Search Engine Optimization (SEO) and descriptive purposes. Line 5 is the `meta` element that allows the page to fit mobile devices. If you leave it out, your end user will have to pinch and zoom, and your site may suffer from some unexpected layout issues.

Lines 6, 7, and 8 all show the required files for using jQuery Mobile. In this example we load them from a Content Delivery Network (CDN). You need to keep these links up to date to use all the newest features.

Line 11 is the container for our `page`. Due to the Ajax nature of jQuery Mobile, all pages are kept separate and loaded when called. Note that in single page documents, this container is not necessarily required and will be inserted automatically when not included. With that being said, it is still good practice to always include a container for your page.

Line 12 begins our `header` section. Note that you do not have to use an `h1` here if you do not want to. I strongly recommend you do for SEO purposes, but if you have a different strategy you may change this value to an h2, h3, h4, h5, or h6 and still retain the same styling.

Line 15 starts our `content` section. This area contains everything you want displayed that doesn't belong in the header or the footer. This may include lists, forms, images, and more.

Line 18 is the beginning of the `footer` section. We mentioned before that this section might not exist on all of your mobile sites or projects. You may want a nice footer with some links or legal text, or you may want to switch the entire section out for a group of buttons to make your mobile site feel more like an application.

Figure 7.1 shows a screenshot of what the page looks like in a mobile browser.

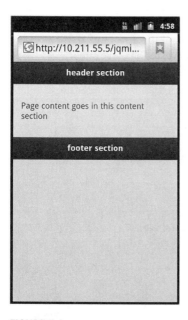

FIGURE 7.1
A single page layout showing the head, content, and footer sections

While you may be just fine creating a single page site with jQuery Mobile to host a mobile version of your contact information, there are times when you need to share more, show more, or just do more. This is when you should use multiple pages.

Using a Multiple Page Layout

A multiple page layout is simply a collection of single page layouts. This can be achieved in a couple of different ways. You can create one HTML file and include multiple pages inside it, or you can create multiple HTML files that each contain a page and then link them together.

To illustrate this, let's create a single file named single_multipage.html that contains multiple pages and buttons to change between them. Listing 7.2 shows a single HTML file that contains multiple pages.

LISTING 7.2   The single_multipage.html File

```
1: <!DOCTYPE html>
2: <html>
3:   <head>
4:     <title>Multiple Pages in a Single File</title>
5:     <meta name="viewport" content="width=device-width, initial-scale=1">
6:     <link rel="stylesheet"
href="http://code.jquery.com/mobile/1.1.0/jquery.mobile-1.1.0.min.css" />
7:     <script src="http://code.jquery.com/jquery-1.7.1.min.js"></script>
8:     <script src="http://code.jquery.com/mobile/1.1.0/jquery.mobile-1.1.0.min.
js"></script>
9:   </head>
10:   <body>
11:     <!-- Start: Page 1 -->
12:     <div id="page1" data-role="page">
13:       <div data-role="header">
14:         <h1>Page 1 Header</h1>
15:       </div>
16:       <div data-role="content">
17:         <p>The content for page one is here</p>
18:         <a href="#page2" data-role="button">Go to page 2</a>
19:       </div>
20:       <div data-role="footer">
21:         <h4>Page 1 Footer</h4>
22:       </div>
23:     </div>
24:     <!-- End: Page 1 -->
25:     <!--Start: Page 2 -->
26:     <div id="page2" data-role="page">
27:       <div data-role="header">
28:         <h1>Page 2 Header</h1>
29:       </div>
30:       <div data-role="content">
31:         <p>The content for page two is here</p>
32:         <a href="#page3" data-role="button">Go to page 3</a>
33:       </div>
34:       <div data-role="footer">
35:         <h4>Page 2 Footer</h4>
36:       </div>
```

```
37:      </div>
38:      <!-- End: Page 2 -->
39:      <!-- Start Page 3 -->
40:      <div id="page3" data-role="page">
41:        <div data-role="header">
42:          <h1>Page 3 Header</h1>
43:        </div>
44:        <div data-role="content">
45:          <p>The content for page three is here</p>
46:          <a href="#page1" data-role="button">Go to page 1</a>
47:        </div>
48:        <div data-role="footer">
49:          <h4>Page 3 Footer</h4>
50:        </div>
51:      </div>
52:      <!-- End: Page 3 -->
53:    </body>
54: </html>
```

The beginning of our file looks about the same as our single page example, so we'll start with line 11.

Line 11 is an HTML comment added to help with readability in the file. It simply lets you know that the code following it will be the first page.

Line 12 is the container for the first page. It is a div element with an id of page1 and contains the data-role="page" attribute. The id on this container is important, as it is what will be used as the reference for this page.

Line 13 contains a div element with a data-role="header" attribute to set up our header section for page1. Line 14 shows an h1 element with some text that informs us what page we are on. This text will be displayed as the text in our header section.

Line 15 is the closing div element for our header section. Line 16 uses a div element with data-role="content" to start the content section for page1. Line 17 is a p element with some text informing us that content for page1 should be in this section.

Line 18 shows an a element with the attributes href="#page2" and data-role="button". This makes a link to our second page and styles the link as a button.

Line 19 is the closing div element for the content section. Line 20 shows the opening of the footer section for page1 by using a div element with data-role="footer". Line 21 is an h4 element that contains the text that will appear in the footer section.

Line 22 is the closing `div` element for the `footer` section. Line 23 is the closing `div` element for `page1`. Line 24 shows a comment telling us that the lines above it contain the code for the first page. Line 25 starts the process over, only this time it is a comment telling us that we are starting the second page.

Lines 26-37 are almost identical to lines 12-23, with a few changes that I'd like to point out. Line 26 has a `div` element with an `id` of `page2` and is designated as a page by including the `data-role="page"` attribute. This allows us to reference everything within this container as a separate page from the first page container. By default jQuery Mobile displays only the first `div` element with a `data-role="page"` attribute when the page is loaded. While there are minor text changes in these lines, another difference to point out is on Line 32; the line still contains an a element with the `data-role="button"` attribute, but now it contains `href="#page3"`. This of course changes the button to link to `page3`, which is the `id` of another `div` element farther down in the file.

Line 38 is an HTML comment letting us know that we have reached the end of the code that makes up `page2`. Line 39 is another HTML comment telling us that the code following it is for the third page.

Lines 40-51 are also almost identical to lines 12-23, with the similar changes we saw made on `page2`. Line 40 shows the page container being created by using a `div` element with an `id` of `page3` and the `data-role="page"` attribute. Just like on `page2` we changed what page the button links to. Line 46 shows the a element containing an attribute of `href="#page1"` setting the link to point back to the first page.

Line 52 contains an HTML comment telling us that the code above it was for `page3`. Line 53 is the closing `body` element. Line 54 is the closing `html` element, and it completes the single_multipage.html file.

Figures 7.2, 7.3, and 7.4 show each one of the pages that we just created in our single file.

While creating a multipage site in one HTML file is definitely an option, and I have built sites that way before, I strongly recommend that you opt to create your mobile site using multiple files.

Using multiple HTML files, let's re-create the previous example. Listing 7.3 shows multi_page1.html, the first page. Listing 7.4 shows multi_page2.html, the second page. Listing 7.5 shows multi_page3.html, the third page.

FIGURE 7.2
The rendered content from page1

FIGURE 7.3
The rendered content from page2

FIGURE 7.4
The rendered content from page3

LISTING 7.3 The multi_page1.html File

```
1: <!DOCTYPE html>
2: <html>
3:   <head>
4:     <title>Multi-page - Page 1</title>
5:     <meta name="viewport" content="width=device-width, initial-scale=1">
6:     <link rel="stylesheet"
href="http://code.jquery.com/mobile/1.1.0/jquery.mobile-1.1.0.min.css" />
7:     <script src="http://code.jquery.com/jquery-1.7.1.min.js"></script>
8:     <script src="http://code.jquery.com/mobile/1.1.0/jquery.mobile-1.1.0.min.
js"></script>
9:   </head>
10:   <body>
11:     <div id="page1" data-role="page">
12:       <div data-role="header">
13:         <h1>Page 1 Header</h1>
14:       </div>
15:       <div data-role="content">
16:         <p>The content for page one is here</p>
17:         <a href="multi_page2.html" data-role="button">Go to page 2</a>
18:       </div>
19:       <div data-role="footer">
20:         <h4>Page 1 Footer</h4>
21:       </div>
22:     </div>
23:   </body>
24: </html>
```

LISTING 7.4 The multi_page2.html File Linked from multi_page1.html

```
1: <!DOCTYPE html>
2: <html>
3:   <head>
4:     <title>Multi-page - Page 2</title>
5:     <meta name="viewport" content="width=device-width, initial-scale=1">
6:     <link rel="stylesheet"
href="http://code.jquery.com/mobile/1.1.0/jquery.mobile-1.1.0.min.css" />
7:     <script src="http://code.jquery.com/jquery-1.7.1.min.js"></script>
8:     <script src="http://code.jquery.com/mobile/1.1.0/jquery.mobile-1.1.0.min.
js"></script>
9:   </head>
10:   <body>
11:     <div id="page2" data-role="page">
12:       <div data-role="header">
13:         <h1>Page 2 Header</h1>
14:       </div>
15:       <div data-role="content">
```

```
16:            <p>The content for page two is here</p>
17:            <a href="multi_page3.html" data-role="button">Go to page 3</a>
18:        </div>
19:        <div data-role="footer">
20:            <h4>Page 2 Footer</h4>
21:        </div>
22:    </div>
23:  </body>
24: </html>
```

LISTING 7.5 The multi_page3.html File Linked from multi_page2.html

```
1: <!DOCTYPE html>
2: <html>
3:   <head>
4:     <title>Multi-page - Page 3</title>
5:     <meta name="viewport" content="width=device-width, initial-scale=1">
6:     <link rel="stylesheet"
href="http://code.jquery.com/mobile/1.1.0/jquery.mobile-1.1.0.min.css" />
7:     <script src="http://code.jquery.com/jquery-1.7.1.min.js"></script>
8:     <script src="http://code.jquery.com/mobile/1.1.0/jquery.mobile-1.1.0.min.
js"></script>
9:   </head>
10:   <body>
11:     <div id="page3" data-role="page">
12:       <div data-role="header">
13:         <h1>Page 3 Header</h1>
14:       </div>
15:       <div data-role="content">
16:         <p>The content for page three is here</p>
17:         <a href="multi_page1.html" data-role="button">Go to page 1</a>
18:       </div>
19:       <div data-role="footer">
20:         <h4>Page 3 Footer</h4>
21:       </div>
22:     </div>
23:   </body>
24: </html>
```

Looking at each of the pages you can see how similar they are to each other. In fact only six lines are different in each file. Let's cover the lines that are different from each other.

Line 4 in each file contains a `title` element. When a new page is requested, the text that is currently in the `title` element is automatically replaced with the text in the `title` element on the page that has been requested.

Line 11 contains the next difference between all three files. The only difference on this line is the value of the id in the div element.

Line 13 also contains a small difference between each file. Each file contains an h1 element that contains different text on the inside. This will be the text that appears in the header bar on each page.

Line 16 has a text change in the p element just to let us know what page we are on.

Line 17 contains the change with the most impact. We can see that we have set up an a element and set it to point to another page. The a element is styled as a button automatically due to the included data-role="button". The file multi_page1.html uses this line to link to multi_page2. html, which in turn uses this line to link to multi_page3.html. Finally, multi_page3.html uses this line to link back to the multi_page1.html to complete the loop through all three files.

The difference between all three files is on line 20. The text inside the h4 elements has been changed to match the page number and will be displayed on the footer bar of each page when loaded.

While using multiple files to create your site does create more initial work and setup, it pays off when it comes to individual page maintenance and separate event triggers.

Now that we've seen how to create pages and link them together using a button, let's take a look at adding multiple buttons and aligning them.

Aligning Content with a Grid

A grid is just what it sounds like. It is a tool for placing objects to make them align. jQuery Mobile uses a grid system to help with content alignment. This system is useful as it helps to create a cross-device experience that takes the guesswork out of dealing with devices that have different dimensions than you originally planned for.

The grid system in jQuery Mobile allows you to create columns of equal width. To apply the grid system to your content you need to add a class to the container you want to use the grid, and a secondary class to the items inside the container.

Grid container classes are as follows:

▶ ui-grid-a creates a two-column grid.

▶ ui-grid-b creates a three-column grid.

▶ ui-grid-c creates a four-column grid.

▶ ui-grid-d creates a five-column grid.

Content classes are as follows:

- ui-block-a is used on the first block.
- ui-block-b is used on the second block.
- ui-block-c is used on the third block.
- ui-block-d is used on the fourth block.
- ui-block-e is used on the fifth block.

When using a grid on a container that has elements with content that is wider than the available screen resolution, the content will be moved into a new row in the grid. This helps keep content organized and viewable.

Figure 7.5 shows a page created without using the grid system.

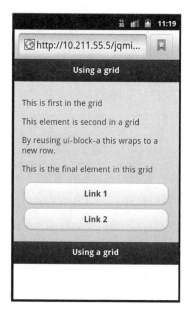

FIGURE 7.5
A page that has not been aligned using the grid system

Listing 7.6 shows grid.html, a file we create to implement the grid system on the page seen in Figure 7.5, which contains the code from the first page of our multiple page site using buttons and content aligned with a grid.

LISTING 7.6   Aligning Buttons on a Page Using a Grid

```
1: <!DOCTYPE html>
2: <html>
3:   <head>
4:     <title>Using a grid</title>
5:     <meta name="viewport" content="width=device-width, initial-scale=1">
6:     <link rel="stylesheet"
href="http://code.jquery.com/mobile/1.1.0/jquery.mobile-1.1.0.min.css" />
7:     <script src="http://code.jquery.com/jquery-1.7.1.min.js"></script>
8:     <script src="http://code.jquery.com/mobile/1.1.0/jquery.mobile-1.1.0.min.
js"></script>
9:   </head>
10:   <body>
11:     <div id="page1" data-role="page">
12:       <div data-role="header">
13:         <h1>Using a grid</h1>
14:       </div>
15:       <div data-role="content">
16:         <div class="ui-grid-a">
17:           <div class="ui-block-a">
18:             <p class="ui-bar ui-bar-b" style="height: 80px;">
19:               This is first in the grid
20:             </p>
21:           </div>
22:           <div class="ui-block-b">
23:             <p class="ui-bar ui-bar-b" style="height: 80px;">
24:               This element is second in a grid
25:             </p>
26:           </div>
27:           <div class="ui-block-a">
28:             <p class="ui-bar ui-bar-b" style="height: 80px;">
29:               By reusing ui-block-a this wraps to a new row.
30:             </p>
31:           </div>
32:           <div class="ui-block-b">
33:             <p class="ui-bar ui-bar-b" style="height: 80px;">
34:               This is the final element in this grid
35:             </p>
36:           </div>
37:         </div>
38:         <div class="ui-grid-a">
39:           <div class="ui-block-a">
40:             <a href="#" data-role="button">Link 1</a>
41:           </div>
42:           <div class="ui-block-b">
43:             <a href="#" data-role="button">Link 2</a>
44:           </div>
```

```
45:            </div>
46:          </div>
47:          <div data-role="footer">
48:            <h4>Using a grid</h4>
49:          </div>
50:        </div>
51:    </body>
52: </html>
```

In the preceding code you can see we start our grid on line 16. We add `class="ui-grid-a"` to a `div` element. This `class` sets the `div` element up as a container for a two-column grid. If we wanted to use a three-column grid we would have used `class="ui-grid-b"`.

Line 17 shows another `div` element with `class="ui-block-a"`. This puts all the content within this `div` in the first column of the grid that was set up on line 16.

Line 18 contains a p element with two `class`es and an inline style applied. The first `class` is `ui-bar`. This `class` is not required for using the grid system but adds some extra styles that help to illustrate the grid. The second `class` is `ui-bar-b`, and yes, this is another `class` that is not required for use with the grid system. The `ui-bar-b` is actually part of the theming system in jQuery Mobile, and one that we cover in Hour 13, "Changing the Default Theme." The `style="height: 80px;"` that has been applied was also done to help illustrate the grid.

In lines 19-21 you can see the content we want shown and the closing tags for the p element and the `div` element.

Line 22 begins the `div` element that contains the content for the second column in the grid. This element contains `class="ui-block-b"`, which is how we get the content into the second column of the grid.

We can see that line 23 contains the same code as line 18, so we know that the classes and inline style are applied to help us see the grid when the page is viewed in a browser.

There is a possible surprise on line 27, however. We can see that the `div` element there is still a child of the containing `div` element that has `class="ui-grid-a"`, but what may be a little odd is that it repeats the same class that we saw on line 17, `class="ui-block-a"`. This is actually how you create a new row in a grid. By repeating `class="ui-block-a"` on the `div` element we are using a clear to move the content down one row. This is also why line 32 uses `class="ui-block-b"` to move the `div` element to the second column in the grid on the second row.

Just in case you wanted a second example, without any extra classes that are not required getting in the way, take a look at line 38.

Line 38 begins another grid by using a container `div` element with `class="ui-grid-a"`. Line 39 then creates a block for the first column by using a containing `div` with `class="ui-block-a"`.

Line 40 shows an a element that has been styled as a button using `data-role="button"`. Line 41 closes the `div` element that is the block in the first column of the grid. Line 42 creates the block that goes in the second column of the grid by using `class="ui-block-b"` on a container `div` element.

Line 43 shows another a element that has been styled as a button by using `data-role="button"`. Line 44 is the closing `div` element for the block that is in the second column of the current grid. Line 45 is the closing `div` element for the current grid.

Figure 7.6 shows what the page looks like now that we have applied the grid to it.

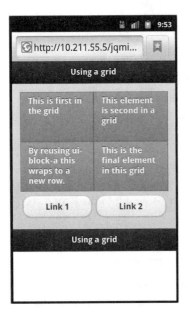

FIGURE 7.6
The page from Figure 7.5 now aligned using the grid system

The grid is designed to scale and will make use of whatever space it is told to fit in. This means that on high-resolution devices the grid columns will be wider than on small-resolution devices. Figure 7.7 shows the grid.html file being viewed on a tablet-sized device.

Content can be more than just aligned. We can also add content to a page and make it collapse or expand when clicked or touched.

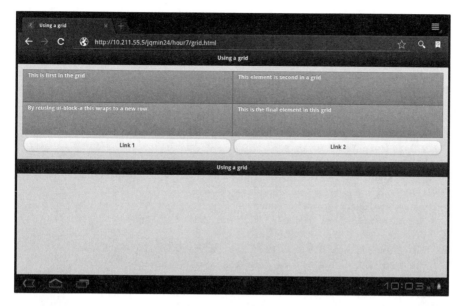

FIGURE 7.7
Large devices still show content aligned in a grid; the content will just be stretched out to take advantage of the screen space.

Conquering Collapsible Content

Collapsible content can be hidden or shown with a click or a touch. You probably have already seen this type of behavior on websites before. You may have seen it in the Frequently Asked Questions sections on multiple sites. Usually on those sites it is a question or an answer with the title viewable and then a little "+" or "-" next to it to show that it can be opened or closed. This same functionality is built into jQuery Mobile.

To create collapsible content, you just need to add `data-role="collapsible"` to the containing element that you want to make collapsible. Listing 7.7 gives an example of using collapsible content on a page. You can view this example by loading collapsible.html in your browser.

LISTING 7.7   The Contents of collapsible.html

```
 1: <!DOCTYPE html>
 2: <html>
 3:   <head>
 4:     <title>Collapsible Content</title>
 5:     <meta name="viewport" content="width=device-width, initial-scale=1">
 6:     <link rel="stylesheet"
href="http://code.jquery.com/mobile/1.1.0/jquery.mobile-1.1.0.min.css" />
 7:     <script src="http://code.jquery.com/jquery-1.7.1.min.js"></script>
```

```
 8:     <script src="http://code.jquery.com/mobile/1.1.0/jquery.mobile-1.1.0.min.
js"></script>
 9:    </head>
10:    <body>
11:      <div id="page1" data-role="page">
12:        <div data-role="header">
13:          <h1>Collapsible Content</h1>
14:        </div>
15:        <div data-role="content">
16:          <div data-role="collapsible">
17:            <h3>I'm a single collapsible element</h3>
18:            <p>I'm the content inside of the single collapsible element.</p>
19:          </div>
20:          <div data-role="collapsible-set">
21:            <div data-role="collapsible" data-collapsed="false">
22:              <h3>I'm expanded on page load</h3>
23:              <p>I am collapsible content that is visible on page load.</p>
24:              <p>That's because of the data-collapsed="false" attribute</p>
25:            </div>
26:            <div data-role="collapsible">
27:              <h3>Expand me I have something to say</h3>
28:              <p>I am closed on page load, but still part of an accordion.</p>
29:              <div data-role="collapsible">
30:                <h3>Wait, are you nested?</h3>
31:                <p>Yes! You can even nest your collapsible content!</p>
32:              </div>
33:            </div>
34:          </div>
35:        </div>
36:        <div data-role="footer">
37:          <h4>Collapsible Content</h4>
38:        </div>
39:      </div>
40:    </body>
41: </html>
```

To see where the collapsible content starts, take a look at line 16. There is a `div` element that contains `data-role="collapsible"`; this is the container that will be collapsed on page load.

Line 17 shows an h3 element with some text inside it. Collapsible content displays a "+" or "-" on a title bar, to show the collapsed state. You must include an h1, h2, h3, h4, h5, or h6 element inside your collapsible container for them to appear and function.

Line 18 contains a p element that contains some text. This is an example of content that remains hidden inside the collapsed container until it is expanded. Also, you are not limited to using only p elements. You can put any HTML element that you want inside the `div` container.

Line 19 is the closing `div` element for our collapsible container.

The collapsible container we just looked at would be great for holding some information, a secondary navigation section, or even an options bar. However, you may be wondering about a collapsible set that expands and closes containers semiautomatically. This is commonly referred to as an accordion, and if you look at line 20 you can see how to begin one.

Line 20 is the beginning of a `div` element that contains a `data-role="collapsible-set"` attribute. This is the wrapper or the container for multiple collapsible content containers.

Line 21 shows another `div` element containing two attributes, `data-role="collapsible"` and `data-collapsed="false"`. We already know what `data-role="collapsible"` will do, but the `data-collapsed="false"` attribute is new. When it is present, it informs jQuery Mobile that it needs to be expanded by default on page load instead of collapsed.

Lines 22-24 show the content that will be shown on page load, and line 25 shows the closing `div` element for the collapsible section.

Line 26 shows another collapsible section being set up through the use of another `div` element containing the `data-role="collapsible"` attribute.

Lines 27 and 28 should look pretty much the same as the content in our previous collapsible containers.

Line 29 shows something you may not have expected. It is another `div` element with the `data-role="collapsible"` attribute. In case you were wondering, it's not a fluke. This was done completely on purpose to show you that you can nest collapsible content sections inside each other. Inside this nested collapsible section you can see that we have thrown in some content following the exact same rules as any other collapsible section. The nested collapsible content section is closed on line 32, and the section that was holding it is closed on line 33.

Line 34 is the closing `div` element for the `collapsible-set` container.

Remember that when using collapsible sets only one collapsible section remains open at a time; the rest are automatically collapsed.

Figure 7.8 shows collapsible.html being rendered on a mobile device.

Using collapsible content is a great way to increase the user-friendliness of your mobile site. It is also a great way to pack in extra content without forcing the end user to scroll through the parts that are not relevant to them. You can benefit from the use of collapsible content on everything from product pages to blog posts.

FIGURE 7.8
Collapsible content being viewed on a mobile device, with a section of an accordion expanded

Summary

In this hour you just learned about single and multiple page layouts. You learned that you are able to create a multiple page layout within the same file, or by using links to external files.

Aligning content with a grid, and what grid options are available within the jQuery Mobile framework also were discussed.

Finally, you then learned about collapsible content and that it can be used to make accordions and can also contain nested collapsible content.

Q&A

Q. When using the grid system, are there any dangers with low resolution?

A. I wouldn't call it a danger, but there are some difficulties you may run into. For example, if you have a three-column grid and you have buttons with more than one word on them, there is a good chance that your text will not be seen on low-resolution devices. A user may see only the first letter or two of your link text.

Q. How would using collapsible content be beneficial on a blog?

A. While you may have run into blogs with short intro sections, on a mobile device you still have to scroll through all that text. By using a collapsible content section for your post or intro section, you can still show the title of a blog post and allow the visitor to decide whether it is worth expanding the section and reading through.

Q. What do I do if I want to use more than five columns in my grid?

A. The short answer is to re-evaluate what you are trying to accomplish. The long answer is that you need to remember that you are using a mobile framework. When screen widths are as small as 240px, you are left with columns that are only 48px wide. That is wide enough to get between two and four characters per column, any smaller and the column would be completely illegible. Note that when using the grid system with jQuery Mobile, your columns will be equal width. If you really want to use more than five columns or even two columns with one at 75% width and the other at 25% width, I would suggest adding some custom CSS to your page and not using the built-in grid system.

Workshop

The workshop contains a quiz and some exercises to help you check your comprehension and understanding.

Quiz

1. What type of site is it a good idea to use a single page layout contained in a single file?

2. How does using a grid system help with displaying content?

3. True or False: It is impossible to nest collapsible content.

4. How do you add a title and a "+" or "-" to a collapsible content section?

5. True or False: You can also create multiple rows when using a grid for columns

Answers

1. A profile or contact site is a great candidate for a single page.

2. Using a grid brings visual balance to your site; however, when combined with navigation or with buttons a grid system excels. Most native mobile applications use a grid when aligning buttons or icons.

3. False. You can nest collapsible content by simply creating a collapsible container within another one.

4. Within the collapsible container you need to add an h1, h2, h3, h4, h5, or h6 element. jQuery Mobile then applies the required styles to create a title bar and applies the "+" and "-" icon.

5. True. After you have defined a column size by applying the correct class, you may then create rows by repeating the ui-block-a, ui-block-b, ui-block-c, ui-block-d, and ui-block-e classes on container elements you want included per row.

Exercises

1. Create a multipage site either using a single HTML file or by using multiple HTML files. Create button links to each page on every page so that each page is reachable from each page.

2. Using the page you created in the first activity, align your buttons in a grid. Experiment with using two, three, or even four buttons per row. Note how much the buttons change size depending on screen resolution and orientation of your device.

3. Using the sample collapsible.html file as a base, either create a new file or a copy and modify it to be a Frequently Asked Questions page with at least five questions and answers in an accordion.

HOUR 8
Tuning the Toolbars

What You'll Learn In This Hour:

▶ How to add a header toolbar
▶ How to add buttons to the header toolbar
▶ How to add a navigation toolbar
▶ How to add a footer toolbar
▶ How to use positioning with toolbars
▶ How to use a persistent navigation toolbar

Whether you are building a mobile site or a mobile app, you are probably going to want to use a toolbar. Toolbars allow you to present content in a familiar and useful way. Toolbars are generally used for the header and footer sections of your pages.

You may not always opt for, or even use a toolbar on every page of your mobile site. However, there are several occasions where they are useful. I have frequently used footer toolbars to house my navigation sections, allowing my site to give a more mobile-application feel. By including a persistent header or footer toolbar, you allow the user instant access to important options or links within your site without making them scroll around to find the links they are looking for.

Now that we know a little about what we can do with toolbars, let's learn how to add them to a mobile site.

Adding a Header Toolbar

This may seem a little like déjà vu, but I'm going to show you how to add a header toolbar to a page. Listing 8.1 shows the code from a standard page section with a header toolbar added.

LISTING 8.1 Setting Up a Header Toolbar

```
1: <div data-role="page">
2:    <div data-role="header">
3:       <h1>I am a header toolbar</h1>
4:    </div>
5: </div>
```

Just in case you were wondering, you have done the code in Listing 8.1 before. Whenever you use `data-role="header"` on a `div` element, you are actually setting up a header toolbar. Figure 8.1 shows the output from the code snippet in Listing 8.1.

FIGURE 8.1
An empty page with a header toolbar

You can do more than just use the header toolbar as a title for your page; you can also add up to two buttons. This makes the header toolbar useful for displaying options on data-entry or similar pages.

To add a button into the header toolbar you simply need to add a link and style it as a button. Listing 8.2 shows an excerpt of page code where one button has been applied.

LISTING 8.2 Adding a Button to a Header Toolbar

```
1: <div data-role="page">
2:   <div data-role="header" data-position="inline">
3:     <a href="#">Contacts</a>
4:     <h1>I am a header toolbar</h1>
5:   </div>
6: </div>
```

By adding an a element on line 3, we set up a button that will be displayed on the left side of the header toolbar. Note that we did not have to apply a `data-role` to style the link as a button. The link will be styled as a button automatically when it is inside the header toolbar.

The first link in the header toolbar always defaults to display on the left side of the header toolbar. This happens even if you include the link after the `h1` element. That means that if you swap lines 3 and 4, the button still appears on the left.

Figure 8.2 shows what the toolbar looks like now that we have added a button to it.

FIGURE 8.2
A link has been added to the left side of the header toolbar and automatically styled as a button.

Now that you know that the first link that is added automatically goes on the left side of the header toolbar, where do you think a second button goes? Let's find out by looking at Listing 8.3 and the resulting output shown in Figure 8.3.

LISTING 8.3   Adding a Second Link to the Header Toolbar

```
1: <div data-role="page">
2:    <div data-role="header" data-position="inline">
3:       <a href="#">Contacts</a>
4:       <h1>I am a header toolbar</h1>
5:       <a href="#">Config</a>
6:    </div>
7: </div>
```

FIGURE 8.3
Two links have been added to the header toolbar. The first is aligned to the left, while the second is aligned to the right.

The second link defaults to display on the right side of the header toolbar. It doesn't matter whether both links are before the `h1` element or after, they still get the same treatment. I do recommend that you code your header toolbar with an a-h1-a approach as we did in Listing 8.3 as it makes it much easier to keep track of where your code will end up on the page.

You can add more links to the header if you want, but they will not be styled correctly. They will receive the button styles, but will be displayed inline, smashing right up next to each other. Figure 8.4 shows an example of this bad behavior.

If you absolutely need to use more links in your header, consider adding a `navbar` to the header, instead of stacking links in this way.

FIGURE 8.4
Using excessive links in the header toolbar proves that just because you can doesn't mean you should.

Attaching a Navigation Toolbar

A navigation toolbar, or `navbar`, is a widget built into jQuery Mobile that allows you to add navigation links to your page. Similar to the built-in grid system, the `navbar` is capable of containing five columns. To add a `navbar` to your page, you must use a container element with an attribute of `data-role="navbar"`. Inside the container you must have an unordered list with each column inside an `li` element. Listing 8.4 shows the markup for using a `navbar`.

LISTING 8.4   Setting Up a `navbar`

```
1: <div data-role="navbar">
2:    <ul>
3:       <li><a href="#">Link 1</a></li>
4:       <li><a href="#">Link 2</a></li>
5:    </ul>
6: </div>
```

It really is pretty simple markup. We use a `div` element to create the container and then put the `ul` element with two `li` elements inside it to create a `navbar` that contains two columns. The only thing you need to do when dropping this snippet into your code is to remember to change out the empty anchors with actual links.

Let's take the snippet in Listing 8.4 and build a page that contains a header toolbar and a navbar with three extra links in it. Listing 8.5 shows the code for a header toolbar with a navbar placed inside it. You can find this example code by opening header_navbar.html.

LISTING 8.5   A Page with a `navbar` Inside the Header Toolbar

```
 1: <!DOCTYPE html>
 2: <html>
 3:   <head>
 4:     <title>Toolbars with jQuery Mobile</title>
 5:     <meta name="viewport" content="width=device-width, initial-scale=1">
 6:     <link rel="stylesheet"
href="http://code.jquery.com/mobile/1.1.0/jquery.mobile-1.1.0.min.css" />
 7:     <script src="http://code.jquery.com/jquery-1.7.1.min.js"></script>
 8:     <script
src="http://code.jquery.com/mobile/1.1.0/jquery.mobile-1.1.0.min.js"></script>
 9:   </head>
10:   <body>
11:     <div data-role="page">
12:       <div data-role="header" data-position="inline">
13:         <a href="#">Contacts</a>
14:         <h1>I am a header toolbar</h1>
15:         <a href="#">Config</a>
16:         <div data-role="navbar">
17:           <ul>
18:             <li><a href="#">Rock</a></li>
29:             <li><a href="#">Paper</a></li>
20:             <li><a href="#">Scissors</a></li>
21:           </ul>
22:         </div>
23:       </div>
24:     </div>
25:   </body>
26: </html>
```

On line 12 you can see the header toolbar being created. Lines 13, 14, and 15 show the standard links and heading that make up the standard header toolbar.

Line 16 shows the container for the navbar being created as a div element with an attribute of data-role="navbar". Notice how the navbar is attached to the header toolbar by being created inside it.

Line 17 begins the `ul` element that contains all the links we want inside of the `navbar`. Lines 18, 19, and 20 show `li` elements that each contain a link. Lines 21 closes the `ul` element, and line 22 closes the `div` container for the `navbar`.

That is all it takes to create a `navbar` in the header. Figure 8.5 shows the output of the page with the `navbar` in place.

FIGURE 8.5
A `navbar` contained inside a header toolbar

The other place on your page that you can use a `navbar` is in the footer toolbar. Let's learn about the footer toolbar and what we can do with it.

Adding a Footer Toolbar

Just like the header toolbar, the footer toolbar is added by adding an attribute of `data-role="footer"` to a container element. There are a few differences between the header and footer toolbars. The footer toolbar does not automatically format the placement of links; this must be done manually through the use of custom styles, a layout grid, a `navbar`, or by using a `controlgroup`.

Let's start with a basic footer toolbar and then look at adding content through some of the other methods. Listing 8.6 shows the code needed to set up a footer toolbar.

LISTING 8.6 A Code Snippet for Setting Up a Footer Toolbar

```
1: <div data-role="footer">
2:    <h4>I am a footer toolbar</h4>
3: </div>
```

This snippet of code should be as familiar as the header toolbar was, as we have covered it before. Let's do something new and switch up the footer toolbar by removing the h4 element and replacing it with a few buttons. Listing 8.7 shows the modified footer toolbar.

LISTING 8.7 Buttons Added to the Footer Toolbar

```
1: <div data-role="footer" class="ui-bar">
2:    <a href="#" data-role="button">Link 1</a>
3:    <a href="#" data-role="button">Link 2</a>
4:    <a href="#" data-role="button">Link 3</a>
5: </div>
```

This should look straightforward. On line 1 we added class="ui-bar" to add some padding to the toolbar. The ui-bar class alone sets a default font size and sets the margins to 0. It is more commonly combined with other classes to create padding, clear floats, and change the display property and the positioning of an element. We also removed the h4 element and replaced it with three a elements that each contain attributes of data-role="button" to style the links as buttons. Take a look at Figure 8.6 to see results of our changes.

As shown in Figure 8.6, we now have three buttons that are styled inline with each other. They look pretty good, but we can make them look a little better by applying a controlgroup to them. A control group is a container that surrounds the buttons and applies either a vertical or horizontal style to them so that they appear to be one long button that has been sliced into portions. Listing 8.8 shows the code for adding a controlgroup with the buttons aligned horizontally.

LISTING 8.8 Using a Control Group to Align and Style Buttons

```
1: <div data-role="footer" class="ui-bar">
2:   <div data-role="controlgroup" data-type="horizontal">
3:     <a href="#" data-role="button">Link 1</a>
4:     <a href="#" data-role="button">Link 2</a>
5:     <a href="#" data-role="button">Link 3</a>
6:   </div>
7: </div>
```

As shown in Figure 8.7 you see the styles applied from wrapping the buttons in a controlgroup container.

FIGURE 8.6
Adding buttons into the footer toolbar

FIGURE 8.7
The buttons have been styled to be displayed inline, and the corners on the buttons on the ends have been rounded.

NOTE

Button Clipping

If you are developing with jQuery Mobile 1.0 you may notice that buttons sometimes have borders or shadows that appear clipped. This does not affect all browsers but is visible in both desktop and mobile WebKit- and Opera-based browsers. The solution to this issue is to upgrade to using jQuery Mobile 1.1+.

Another option for content formatting in our footer is to use a grid system. Let's keep our buttons but use a grid system to separate them from each other. Listing 8.9 shows the footer toolbar with a three-column grid layout applied.

LISTING 8.9   A Footer Toolbar with a Grid Layout Applied

```
1: <div data-role="footer" class="ui-bar">
2:    <div class="ui-grid-b">
3:       <div class="ui-block-a"><a href="#" data-role="button">Link 1</a></div>
4:       <div class="ui-block-b"><a href="#" data-role="button">Link 2</a></div>
5:       <div class="ui-block-c"><a href="#" data-role="button">Link 3</a></div>
6:    </div>
7: </div>
```

Line 2 shows us starting our grid by using class="ui-grid-b" on the div element. This class sets up a three-column grid.

Line 3 shows a div element with an attribute of class="ui-block-a", which means it will be shown in the first column. Lines 4 and 5 use a similar class to put their content into the second and third column. Line 6 closes our grid by closing the div element.

Each of the buttons will now be displayed inside a separate column in the footer toolbar. We can see what this looks like in Figure 8.8.

Using the grid looks good for spacing, but you can see that each button is aligned to the left side of the column. This may be problematic to your design, however, as it throws off the symmetry of the page.

We can solve this problem by using a navbar to display the links. In Listing 8.10 the buttons have been changed to standard links and have been placed in a navbar.

LISTING 8.10   Using a navbar in the Footer Toolbar

```
1: <div data-role="footer">
2:    <div data-role="navbar">
3:       <ul>
4:          <li><a href="#">Link 1</a></li>
5:          <li><a href="#">Link 2</a></li>
```

```
6:          <li><a href="#">Link 3</a></li>
7:      </ul>
8:    </div>
9: </div>
```

FIGURE 8.8
Using a three-column grid in the footer toolbar

Using a `navbar` in the footer toolbar is identical to the way it is applied to the header toolbar. A container element with an attribute of `data-role="navbar"` is created and then a `ul` element containing `li` elements is placed inside. As shown in Figure 8.9 the `navbar` centers the links and gives them a matching style to the `navbar` in the header toolbar.

NOTE

Toolbar Styles When Using a `navbar`

When using a `navbar` make sure that you do not have a `class="ui-bar"` applied to the header or footer toolbar. If you do, the extra padding on the header or footer toolbar will force the `navbar` to cling to the right side of the screen and will force parts of the site offscreen and to appear broken.

FIGURE 8.9
Using a `navbar` in both the header and footer toolbars

Now that we've seen some different options for placing content into the header and footer toolbars, there is one last thing we need to cover—the default behavior for how toolbars are displayed onscreen.

Positioning the Toolbars

Toolbars are generally placed before and after the content section, as is standard in web development. Sometimes though you may find yourself wanting the header and footer to stay visible all the time, especially when you are using a `navbar`. There are two different ways of doing this. You can either use fixed or full screen positioning on the toolbar.

Using a Fixed Position

When using a fixed position, jQuery Mobile checks the page to see whether the positioned toolbar is already in view. If the toolbar is out of the view, it will be inserted into the document at the top or bottom of the viewable area (depending on whether it is a header or footer toolbar). To make a toolbar use the fixed position, you need to add `data-position="fixed"` to the toolbar. Listing 8.11 shows the code for a page that contains a header and footer toolbar using fixed positioning.

LISTING 8.11 The Source Code of toolbar_fixed.html

```
 1: <!DOCTYPE html>
 2: <html>
 3:   <head>
 4:     <title>Toolbars with jQuery Mobile</title>
 5:     <meta name="viewport" content="width=device-width, initial-scale=1">
 6:     <link rel="stylesheet"
href="http://code.jquery.com/mobile/1.1.0/jquery.mobile-1.1.0.min.css" />
 7:     <script src="http://code.jquery.com/jquery-1.7.1.min.js"></script>
 8:     <script
src="http://code.jquery.com/mobile/1.1.0/jquery.mobile-1.1.0.min.js"></script>
 9:   </head>
10:   <body>
11:     <div data-role="page">
12:       <div data-role="header" data-position="fixed">
13:         <h1>Fixed example</h1>
14:       </div>
15:       <div data-role="content">
16:         <a href="#" data-role="button">A button!</a>
17:         <p style="height: 400px;">This has been styled to take up more space</p>
18:         <p>This way you can see what happens when you scroll down the page</p>
19:         <p>The toolbars will reappear when you stop scrolling</p>
20:         <p>You can hide them by clicking or tapping the screen</p>
21:       </div>
22:       <div data-role="footer" data-position="fixed">
23:         <div data-role="navbar">
24:           <ul>
25:             <li><a href="#">Link 1</a></li>
26:             <li><a href="#">Link 2</a></li>
27:             <li><a href="#">Link 3</a></li>
28:           </ul>
29:         </div>
30:       </div>
31:     </div>
32:   </body>
33: </html>
```

On lines 12 and 22 you can see that we added data-position="fixed" to make both the header and footer toolbars use the fixed position.

To get a feel for how they work we added a button and some p elements to the content section so it would be large enough to scroll. The button was added to show you that as you scroll down the page, the header toolbar might cover it up. If this happens you can either scroll back up the page, or you can click or tap the screen to make the fixed toolbars disappear. A second click or tap on the screen brings them back. When you hide the toolbars this way, they will still be at the top and bottom of your page.

Figures 8.10 and 8.11 show the toolbars using a fixed position at different points of the page.

FIGURE 8.10
The footer toolbar has been moved to the bottom of the viewable area.

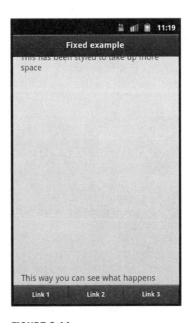

FIGURE 8.11
The header toolbar has been moved to the top of the viewable area. It now covers up a button and some text.

That is really all there is to setting your toolbars up to use a fixed position. Let's take a look at using the full screen position.

Using a Full Screen Position

The full screen position is closely related to the fixed position. The main difference is that the toolbars are placed above the page rather than be a part of it. This can create some navigation problems as links that would normally be available farther down or farther up the page from the toolbars are now sitting directly underneath them.

Full screen positions are good to use when you are displaying an image gallery or for showing videos. In these instances the controls can be put in the navbar, letting the user open and close the controls when they need them.

To use the full screen position you need to add data-fullscreen="true" to the div element that also has the attribute of data-role="page". You then need to make sure that both the header and footer toolbars contain data-position="fixed". For example, in Listing 8.11 there is only one line we need to modify.

The code on line 11 that originally reads

```
<div data-role="page">
```

should be changed to now read

```
<div data-role="page" data-fullscreen="true">
```

That's it. That's the only change we need. This is because we already had both the header and footer toolbars using data-position="fixed", so no other changes are necessary.

Figure 8.12 shows what our page looks like with our one line change.

FIGURE 8.12
The header toolbar now blocks access to the button when the page is loaded.

Remember that items covered by toolbars using the full screen position are still accessible by clicking or tapping somewhere on the screen to hide the toolbars.

Adding Persistent Navigation

By mixing together the things we have just learned we can create a `navbar` in the footer toolbar that will persist on screen between pages. We can even add a few extra styles to give the user a visual cue to the page they are currently on.

Listing 8.12 shows code required to create a persistent `navbar` in the footer toolbar. Refer to persistent_rock.html, persistent_paper.html, and persistent_scissors.html for the full source code.

LISTING 8.12   Setting Up a Persistent `navbar` in the Footer Toolbar

```
1: <div data-role="footer" data-position="fixed" data-id="rps">
2:    <div data-role="navbar">
3:       <ul>
4:          <li><a href="persistent_rock.html" class="ui-btn-active ui-state-
persist">Rock</a></li>
5:          <li><a href="persistent_paper.html">Paper</a></li>
6:          <li><a href="persistent_scissors.html">Scissors</a></li>
7:       </ul>
8:    </div>
9: </div>
```

Line 1 shows a `div` element with the attributes of `data-role="footer"`, `data-position="fixed"`, and `data-id="rps"`. The first two attributes are the required setup for creating a footer toolbar and using fixed positioning. The `data-id="rps"` keeps `navbar` visible while the page is transitioning. This works only when the value inside the `data-id` attribute is the same on the current page and the one being transitioned to.

Line 2 is a `div` element with an attribute of `data-role="navbar"`, which is the required attribute for adding a `navbar`. Line 3 begins the `ul` element that is required when using a `navbar`. Line 4 is an `li` element that contains an `a` element that has a few new classes that we haven't seen before inside it. The first class is `ui-btn-active`. This makes the button appear to be active on page load. The second class is `ui-state-persist`. This allows the button to retain the active status when transitioning back to this page from another one. Lines 5 and 6 are the other `li` elements and links to other pages that complete our `navbar`. Lines 7-9 contain the closing tags of our `ul` element, the `div` element for the `navbar`, and the `div` element for the footer toolbar.

Figures 8.13, 8.14, and 8.15 show the files being viewed on a mobile browser.

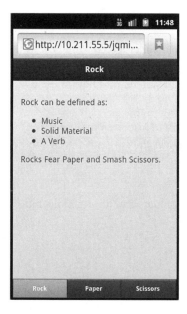

FIGURE 8.13
Viewing persistent_rock.html on a mobile browser

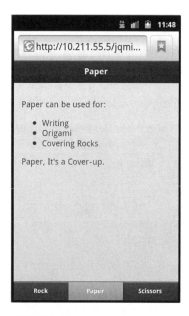

FIGURE 8.14
Viewing persistent_paper.html on a mobile browser

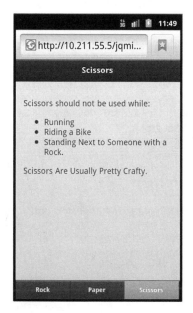

FIGURE 8.15
Viewing persistent_scissors.html on a mobile browser

Summary

In this hour you learned about the built-in support for links in the header toolbar and how to add a `navbar` to include more links. You learned about the footer toolbar and how to add buttons, how to use a control group to style them, how to apply a grid system, and how to use a `navbar` to contain your links.

You also learned about positioning toolbars using the `fixed` and `fullscreen` positions. You learned that using fixed positioning will insert the toolbars whenever they are not detected in the current view, while using full screen will attach the toolbars above the rest of the elements on the page.

You then learned about using a persistent `navbar` in the footer toolbar, and how to make buttons appear active when the page is loaded.

Q&A

Q. What happens when I add more than five links inside a navbar? Does it break like the header does when adding extra links?

A. No, it doesn't break. The `navbar` changes the formatting of the columns to display two columns and stacks the links below as rows.

Q. Can I apply my own custom styles to the header instead of using the built-in ones?

A. Yes, you may always write your own CSS to style the header the way you want. This is actually something you may want to do to display custom pages or message pages.

Q. Can I use a navbar outside the toolbars?

A. Yes, you can use a `navbar` anywhere on your page, but depending on your design you may be better off styling with a grid system and/or a button control group.

Workshop

The workshop contains a quiz and some exercises to help you check your comprehension and understanding.

Quiz

1. What do you add to create a header toolbar?

2. How many buttons are automatically styled in the header?

3. How do you create a `controlgroup`?

4. True or False: Using `fullscreen` position requires the header and footer toolbars to have an attribute of `data-position="fixed"`.

5. True or False: When styled with `fixed` or `fullscreen` positioning, you can make the header and footer toolbars disappear and reappear by tapping or clicking on the screen.

Answers

1. The same way you define a header section will create a header toolbar. You need to create a `div` element and add an attribute of `data-role="header"`.

2. The header toolbar supports two buttons and automatically puts the first button on the left side and the second button on the right side of the toolbar. You can override the default behavior and styles with custom styles if wanted.

3. To apply a `controlgroup` to your buttons, you need to wrap the buttons in a container element that contains an attribute of `data-role="controlgroup"`. By adding a second attribute you can adjust the alignment of the `controlgroup`. By default the `controlgroup` aligns the buttons vertically, but by using `data-type="horizontal"` the buttons will be lined up next to each other.

4. True. Using the `fullscreen` position applies some additional styling to the toolbars and requires the header and footer toolbars to be using a `fixed` position.

5. True. This is built-in functionality that allows users to see more of the screen or access otherwise hidden content when the toolbars are present.

Exercises

1. Either using the included sample files or on your own create your own pages that use a `navbar` to switch between.

2. Create a few pages that each contain a large image and use the full screen position to add toolbars that contain links that let you move to the next picture.

3. Use a grid in the footer to set up some buttons or text that you want displayed in the footer.

Designing Buttons

What You'll Learn In This Hour:

▶ When button are used

▶ Button default settings and how to override them

▶ How to add icons to buttons

▶ How to add custom icons to buttons

This hour we learn about the button system in jQuery Mobile. We've lightly covered buttons before, and we've used them to switch pages and to trigger dialog windows, but you can do much more with them.

Beginning with Buttons

Buttons are tightly integrated into jQuery Mobile. Buttons are useful in mobile sites and applications because they improve the user experience. Few things are more frustrating than being able to see a link on your screen but being unable to activate or use it. jQuery Mobile solves this problem by allowing you to style your links as buttons that scale to the device they are being viewed on. This in turn creates elements that are easy to read and access.

Creating a Link-Based Button

Let's take a quick review on how to create a button. First we need to create a link and then give it an attribute of `data-role="button"`. This does not create an actual button element or object, but instead uses the underlying styling and markup to make the link appear to be button.

Here is a one-line snippet of code that shows an a element being styled as a button:

```
<a href="#" data-role="button">Button</a>
```

This creates what is referred to as a link-based button. Because link-based buttons only use the styles and markup of the button plug-in, they cannot natively tap into the button functions and methods. You can create and use link-based buttons wherever you want, but I've found that it is best to use them in navigation, or for triggering custom functions.

While link-based buttons do not use the actual button plug-in of jQuery Mobile, it turns out that input and button elements do.

Inputs and Buttons

In HTML many types of input elements create buttons. Anytime that you use an input element with an attribute type having a value of submit, reset, button, or image it automatically is styled as a button.

With these input types being automatically styled as buttons, you do not need to add the data-role="button" attribute like you did when using a link-based button. Just in case you were wondering, the button element is also automatically styled as a button and does not require any extra markup. Listing 9.1 shows the contents of the file button_examples.html. This file contains example code for creating all the buttons supported by jQuery Mobile.

LISTING 9.1   A Series of Input Elements Being Styled as Buttons

```
 1: <!DOCTYPE html>
 2: <html>
 3:   <head>
 4:       <title>Buttons jQuery Mobile</title>
 5:       <meta name="viewport" content="width=device-width, initial-scale=1">
 6:       <link rel="stylesheet"
href="http://code.jquery.com/mobile/1.1.0/jquery.mobile-1.1.0.min.css" />
 7:       <script src="http://code.jquery.com/jquery-1.7.1.min.js"></script>
 8:       <script
src="http://code.jquery.com/mobile/1.1.0/jquery.mobile-1.1.0.min.js"></script>
 9:   </head>
10:   <body>
11:     <div data-role="page">
12:       <div data-role="header"><h1>Buttons</h1></div>
13:       <div data-role="content">
14:         <p>Link-based button</p>
15:         <a href="#" data-role="button">Link-based</a>
16:         <p>&lt;button&gt; Element</p>
17:         <button type="button">Button</button>
18:         <p>&lt;input type="submit"&gt;</p>
19:         <input type="submit" value="Submit" />
20:         <p>&lt;input type="button"&gt;</p>
21:         <input type="button" value="Button" />
22:         <p>&lt;input type="reset"&gt;</p>
23:         <input type="reset" value="Reset" />
24:         <p>&lt;input type="image"&gt;</p>
25:         <input type="image" value="Image" />
```

```
26:        </div>
27:      </div>
28:    </body>
29: </html>
```

Line 15 shows the creation of a link-based button. This was done by adding the attribute `data-role="button"` to the a element. Line 17 shows that the button element can also be used to create a button. Lines 19, 21, 23, and 25 show the various input types that can be used to create buttons.

The lines with p elements are there for descriptive purposes. These lines contain HTML entities that render as symbols that are normally rendered as parts of code by the browser.

If you haven't already rendered the code in a browser, you probably have a vague idea of what the page would look like. By looking at Figure 9.1 you can see the way jQuery Mobile styles the input elements. Figure 9.2 shows how they appear when not using the jQuery Mobile framework.

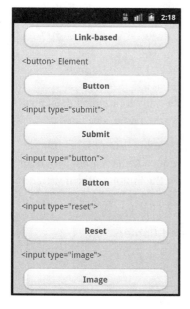
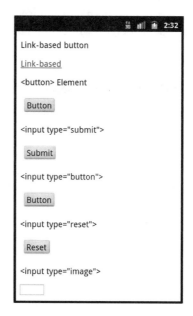

FIGURE 9.1
jQuery Mobile applying style to input elements automatically

FIGURE 9.2
When not using jQuery Mobile, the input elements do not get optimal styles for mobile devices.

A nice feature of using buttons with jQuery mobile is that any events bound to the original elements will still be accessible. In fact, the original input element is still on the page but has been made transparent and is hovering over the button area. If you view the source code of the rendered page you will see that your input element has been wrapped in a div element that has been given a style of position: relative. A span element is also created, and while it appears before the input element, it contains another span element with a style of z-index: 1. The input element appears next and has been styled with position: absolute and z-index: 2. This is how the input elements maintain the original events that are bound to them as you are clicking on it instead of on the stylized button.

Sometimes you may not want jQuery Mobile to restyle your input or button elements automatically. You can easily turn off the automatic styles by adding data-role="none" to the element.

Buttons also have some options or defaults that can be set or overwritten. Let's take a few minutes and learn about what they are and what we can do with them.

Overriding Button Defaults

By default, buttons are given a certain appearance. While this appearance looks good on most mobile devices, it may not look good when combined with your design. Lucky for us, we can change a good portion of button aesthetics.

Putting the Edges Back On

Sometimes you don't want to have your corners shaved off. Occasionally a nice brick-looking button is the best choice for your design. To achieve this, you may use a data attribute.

By adding the attribute data-corners="false" to the element you are using as a button, it will be styled without rounded corners. Listing 9.2 shows a section of code that contains buttons with the data-corners="false" attribute. Figure 9.3 shows how the buttons appear with and without the rounded corners.

LISTING 9.2 Creating Buttons with Rounded and Squared Corners

```
1: <div data-role="content">
2:    <a href="#" data-role="button" data-corners="false">Squared</a>
3:    <a href="#" data-role="button">Rounded</a>
4:    <a href="#" data-role="button" data-corners="false">Squared</a>
5: </div>
```

Just by looking at the attributes inside the a elements, you can tell that the elements on lines 2 and 4 will create square buttons. Line 3 lacks the data-corners="false" attribute, so it will appear with the standard rounded corners.

FIGURE 9.3
A mixture of rounded corner and squared corner buttons

Removing the Shadow

Another option you may want to change is the appearance of a drop shadow under your button. This can be changed by using the `data-shadow="false"` attribute. You are not limited to using only one data attribute per element. You can combine them to get different styles. Listing 9.3 shows the use of the `data-shadow="false"` attribute as well as a button with mixed `data-` attributes.

LISTING 9.3   Changing Button Appearance with Data Attributes

```
1: <div data-role="content">
2:    <a href="#" data-role="button" data-shadow="false">No Shadow</a>
3:    <a href="#" data-role="button">Shadow</a>
4:    <a href="#" data-role="button" data-corners="false" data-shadow="false">
5:       Squared no Shadow
6:    </a>
7: </div>
```

Line 2 shows that we are removing the shadow from the button by using `data-shadow=` `"false"`. Line 3 is our default button as no extra data attributes have been attached to change the appearance. Line 4 shows a button that contains both `data-corners="false"` and `data-shadow="false"`. The button created on this page will not have a drop shadow, and it will have squared corners.

Figure 9.4 shows the code from Listing 9.3 being rendered in a mobile browser.

FIGURE 9.4
A button without a drop shadow, a standard button, and a button without a drop shadow and with squared corners

Not only can we change the corners and drop shadow of buttons, but we can also change the button size.

Changing the Button Size

Whenever we previously created a button, we didn't worry about the size of the button. While you may not ever need to change the default size of a button, you may run into a few problems or some unexpected results with the default size.

By default, buttons take as much width as they have available to them. If you design your site and test only with a low-resolution device you may never notice what happens to your buttons when they are viewed on a tablet. Figure 9.5 shows a page with a couple of buttons being viewed on a tablet in landscape orientation.

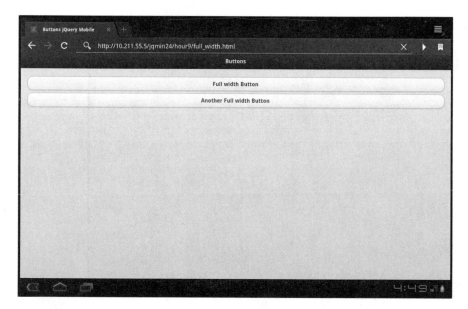

FIGURE 9.5
When buttons are viewed on high-resolution devices, they appear rather wide.

This default behavior is good, as it allows screens with similar widths to see the buttons at about the same size. However, as we saw in Figure 9.5, this is not always the desired behavior. We can use an attribute to force the buttons to take up only as much width as the content within them. Listing 9.4 shows two buttons; one has not been modified and takes up the entire width of the page. The second button takes up only as much room as the content within it uses.

LISTING 9.4   Changing the Default Button Width with a Data Attribute

```
1: <div data-role="content">
2:   <a href="#" data-role="button">Full Width Button</a>
3:   <a href="#" data-role="button" data-inline="true">Inline Button</a>
4: </div>
```

Did you see what attribute made the second button change width? Look at line 3, and you can see that we added `data-inline="true"` as an attribute to the a element. Adding this attribute causes the button to use only as much space as the content inside it.

Figure 9.6 shows the code from Listing 9.4 rendered on a mobile browser. You can see that each button is now on a separate line, and that the button without the `data-inline="true"` attribute has taken up the entire screen width.

FIGURE 9.6
Buttons with different onscreen widths

Using the `data-inline="true"` attribute does a little more than just change the width of the button. It also allows you to place multiple buttons next to each other when the attribute is applied to all buttons. Listing 9.5 shows what happens when we have two buttons using the `data-inline="true"` attribute.

LISTING 9.5 Placing Buttons Inline

```
1: <div data-role="content">
2:    <a href="#" data-role="button" data-inline="true">An Inline Button</a>
3:    <a href="#" data-role="button" data-inline="true">Also an Inline Button</a>
4: </div>
```

The a elements on lines 2 and 3 both have the attribute `data-inline="true"`. This means that both buttons will appear next to each other. Adding more buttons with the same attribute will continue to line them up next to each other. Buttons will continue to line up next to each other until the maximum width has been reached. When that happens, the buttons will wrap down to a new line and repeat the process. Figure 9.7 shows some buttons aligned inline.

While this is nice to make buttons appear on the same line and not take up the full width of the screen, what do we do when we want to get the buttons to take up the full screen but still align up next to each other? We use a grid.

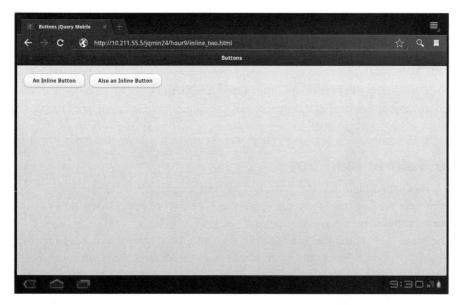

FIGURE 9.7
Buttons using `data-inline="true"` appear on the same line.

Setting up a grid container and putting our buttons inside allows each to fill up the maximum space available in the column. Listing 9.6 shows a grid container being set up and two buttons placed inside.

LISTING 9.6 Adjusting Button Width and Placement by Using a Grid

```
1: <div data-role="content">
2:   <div class="ui-grid-a">
3:     <div class="ui-block-a"><a href="#" data-role="button">Left</a></div>
4:     <div class="ui-block-b"><a href="#" data-role="button">Right</a></div>
5:   </div>
6: </div>
```

In this example, we see a simple two-column grid being set up on line 2. Lines 3 and 4 show that each button has been placed inside a containing `div` element. The only difference between the containers is the class that has been applied to them. A class of `ui-block-a` aligns content in the first column of the grid, while a class of `ui-block-b` aligns content in the second column.

Now that we know how to place buttons and change the options for them, we should give them a little something extra.

Adding Icons to Buttons

When you think of a native mobile application, are all the buttons text only? Of course not; they tend to have images in them.

These images, or icons, allow us to know what the button is without having to read it. They also make some buttons appear less awkward if there is not enough room to spell out what they are supposed to do.

Using the Built-in Icon Set

jQuery Mobile comes with a built-in set of icons that you can use on your buttons to help with styling for mobile devices. These icons are applied to your buttons by including a `data-icon=""` attribute in the element you are using as a button. The icon you want to display on the button is the value for the attribute. For example, if I wanted to display a search icon in my button I would use `data-icon="search"` as an attribute on the element that I am using as a button.

The included icons are

- Left Arrow - `data-icon="arrow-l"`
- Right Arrow - `data-icon="arrow-r"`
- Up Arrow - `data-icon="arrow-u"`
- Down Arrow - `data-icon="arrow-d"`
- Delete - `data-icon="delete"`
- Plus - `data-icon="plus"`
- Minus - `data-icon="minus"`
- Check - `data-icon="check"`
- Gear - `data-icon="gear"`
- Refresh - `data-icon="refresh"`
- Forward - `data-icon="forward"`
- Back - `data-icon="back"`
- Grid - `data-icon="grid"`
- Star - `data-icon="star"`

- ▶ Alert - `data-icon="alert"`

- ▶ Info - `data-icon="info"`

- ▶ Home - `data-icon="home"`

- ▶ Search - `data-icon="search"`

Listing 9.7 shows a few buttons using some of the built-in icons from the preceding list.

LISTING 9.7   Adding Icons to Buttons

```
1: <div data-role="content">
2:    <a href="#" data-role="button" data-icon="back">Back</a>
3:    <a href="#" data-role="button" data-icon="home">Home</a>
4:    <a href="#" data-role="button" data-icon="forward">Forward</a>
5: </div>
```

Lines 2-4 show link-based buttons being created with the use of `data-role="button"`. Each button has had a different icon applied to it by using `data-icon="back"`, `data-icon="home"`, and `data-icon="forward"`.

In Figure 9.8 you can see what the buttons look like with the icons applied to them.

FIGURE 9.8
Buttons with icons applied to them

The icons have all been placed on the buttons, and we can see that the icons have all been placed to the left of the text on the button. This is the default behavior of icon placement on buttons. We can change the icon placement using the `data-iconpos=""` attribute and a value of `top`, `right`, or `bottom`. It should not come as a surprise that the placement of the icon will be exactly where the value says to place it. We can also use a value of `notext` to leave only the icon on the button and remove the text. This resizes the button to be to be barely larger than the icon itself and can come in handy when you need to place many buttons on a single line for a small screen. Listing 9.8 gives an example of buttons using different values to change the default icon placement.

LISTING 9.8   **Examples of the Values Used in the** `data-iconpos` **Attribute**

```
1: <div data-role="content">
2:    <a href="#" data-role="button" data-icon="back">Back</a>
3:    <a href="#" data-role="button" data-icon="home" data-iconpos="top">Home</a>
4:    <a href="#" data-role="button" data-icon="forward"
data-iconpos="right">Forward</a>
5:    <a href="#" data-role="button" data-icon="gear"
data-iconpos="bottom">Config</a>
6:    <a href="#" data-role="button" data-icon="info"
data-iconpos="notext">information</a>
7: </div>
```

Line 2 lacks the `data-iconpos` attribute as the icon will already be positioned on the left side of the button. Line 3, however, does include the `data-iconpos` attribute with the value of `top`. This will make the button taller than it would normally be. Line 4 shows that our icon will be positioned on the right side of the button. We know this because of the `data-iconpos="right"` attribute. Line 5 causes an icon to be placed under the text on the button. Buttons that position icons under the text have the same height as buttons that have icons positioned above the text. Line 6 is probably the most interesting button because it uses `data-iconpos="notext"`. This really does make the button minimal and easy to place on even the smallest mobile screens.

Figure 9.9 shows how our buttons look now with the icons located in different positions.

The built-in icons are an appreciated feature of jQuery Mobile, but when you have a particular style or brand, these built-in icons might not work. Let's take a look at customization.

Using Custom Icons

The custom icons that you use need to be 18×18 pixels. The icon itself needs to be white, and the file should be saved as a PNG-8 with alpha transparency. If you want you may also use a high-resolution icon file for use on Retina and similar displays. The high-resolution icon should be 36×36 instead of 18×18 and also needs to be saved as a PNG-8 with alpha transparency.

FIGURE 9.9
The various ways button icons can be positioned

CAUTION

The Icon Disc

You may have noticed that all the built-in icons are sitting on top of a round circle or disc. This is to help the icon stand out and work on any color of background. This disc must fit within the 18×18 pixel space. This means that when you are designing a custom button, you want to add a few pixels of space so that your custom icon does not appear broken or out of place when the disc is applied.

To use your own icons you need to pass a custom value to the `data-icon=""` attribute. The value that you pass is then used by jQuery Mobile to apply a custom class to the button that you can then use to apply your custom icon through the use of CSS. Listing 9.9 shows an example of the markup required to use a custom icon, and Listing 9.10 shows the CSS that applies the custom icon.

LISTING 9.9   Required HTML Markup for a Custom Icon

```
1: <div data-role="content">
2:    <a href="#" data-role="button" data-icon="custom-sams">Custom icon</a>
3: </div>
```

Nothing too fancy here—we still use the `data-icon` attribute and pass in a custom value. The value `custom-sams` is used to generate a class named `ui-icon-custom-sams`.

LISTING 9.10   Required CSS Markup for a Custom Icon

```
1:  .ui-icon-custom-sams {
2:    background-image: url("custom-icon-sams.png");
3:  }
4:  @media only screen and (-webkit-min-device-pixel-ratio: 2) {
5:    .ui-icon-custom-sams {
6:      background-image: url("custom-icon-sams-hd.png");
7:      background-size: 18px 18px;
8:    }
9:  }
```

Lines 1-3 show the style definition for our custom `ui-icon-custom-sams` class. On line 2 we set the `background-image` property to use our standard-resolution icon file.

Lines 4-9 show the setup required for using a high-resolution icon. Line 4 uses a media query to check the mobile browser for support of high-resolution icons. If the browser supports them, then the CSS code inside the `media-query` will run. Line 6 sets up the `background-image` property again, only this time it points to a high-resolution file. Line 7 sets the image to fit within a space of 18×18 pixels. Without this property being set, the larger image will try to scale up and will end up being mostly hidden, leaving only a small portion of your custom icon visible. Figure 9.10 shows our custom icon being applied to a button.

FIGURE 9.10
A custom icon has been applied to the button.

We used a single image file set as the background image for the custom icon. If you want, you may use an image sprite instead of a single file. Using image sprites is usually a good idea as they reduce the amount of HTTP requests that the mobile device needs to make to get all the assets of the page. If you plan on using more than a few custom icons, you should give serious consideration to combining them into an image sprite.

Summary

This hour you learned all about buttons. You learned that link-based buttons are created by adding `data-role="button"` to any a element. You also learned that form input elements with an attribute type of `submit`, `reset`, `button`, or `image` are automatically styled into buttons and can access all the button functions.

You learned how to override button defaults. You can take off a button's rounded corners and remove the drop shadow. Buttons will use as much width as possible to display themselves. To change this behavior you use the attribute `display-inline="true"` and a grid to make them align on the same row but still use the maximum width available to them.

This hour also discussed using the built-in icon set for your buttons. By default the icons are placed to the left of the text included in the button, but this can be changed to have the icon above, below, or to the right of the text, or the icon can appear by itself with the text of the button removed.

Finally you learned about adding your own custom icons to buttons and what image size and file type are needed for the buttons to display properly.

Q&A

Q. Can I use a `controlgroup` on buttons like we did in the `navbar`?

A. Yes, the `controlgroup` will work outside of toolbars and will work on any buttons you have on your page.

Q. After talking about using image sprites, would there ever be a time when I wouldn't want to use them?

A. The only time you may not want to use image sprites is when they are exceptionally large. When the image sprite is delivered to the mobile browser, it is placed into memory. If your mobile device has a small or limited amount of memory, storing the sprite along with all the other assets of the website may crash the browser. That being said, the goal of a mobile site is to make the entire site as light as possible, so I would use image sprites and then test them on as many devices as possible.

Q. When using custom icons, your example showed the value being "custom-sams". Do I need to use a dash in the value I use?

A. No, I used that value because when the class is applied it comes out as "ui-icon-custom-sams". When I am working on my CSS files I know that this class will be for part of the "ui" as an "icon" that is "custom" that will have a file attached to it named "sams". I use this as a personal system to keep my files organized. You can name it whatever you want as long as you remember to apply your custom styles to the class that is generated.

Workshop

The workshop contains a quiz and some exercises to help you check your comprehension and understanding.

Quiz

1. What is a link-based button, and how do you create one?

2. What data attribute do you use to remove the rounded corners from buttons?

3. What do the dimensions of a custom icon need to be to use them with your buttons?

4. True or False: You cannot use icon-only buttons; all buttons must include text.

5. True or False: When using input elements that are automatically turned into buttons with jQuery Mobile, any event handlers for the elements that had been previously bound are removed.

Answers

1. Link-based buttons are buttons that have only the styles of a button applied. They cannot use any of the button functions. To create one you need an `a` element that contains an attribute of `data-role="button"`.

2. To make corners square, you need to include the `data-corners="false"` attribute.

3. For standard resolution devices you need to use 18x18 pixel dimensions. For HD or Retina supported icons you need to use 36x36 pixel dimensions.

4. False. You may use `data-iconpos="notext"` to remove the text from the button and show only the icon. Although all buttons do not require text inside them, when using icon-only buttons usability is a key factor in keeping text in your code. Browsers that do not support the features of jQuery Mobile still benefit from being able to see what the button is supposed to do.

5. False. When jQuery Mobile changes the input element into a button it keeps the original element and places it above the button. The input element is changed to be transparent so it is not visible, but any clicks on the button really are clicks on the original input element.

Exercises

1. Try creating a multiline section of buttons that use grids to separate them. Try using an odd and even number; for example, try using two buttons on the top row and three buttons on the bottom row.

2. Create or find a set of custom icons and apply one or even a few to your buttons. Change the positioning of the icon on the button and note the change it has on your button.

3. Try using a `controlgroup` to align a few buttons together in the content section of a page. Add icons to the buttons and see how the buttons change in appearance. Remove the text from the buttons, leaving only the icons and note the difference in width and accessibility.

HOUR 10
Formulating Your Forms

What You'll Learn in This Hour:

▶ The basic elements of a `form` element
▶ What jQuery Mobile does with `form` elements
▶ How to use the `slider`, `flip toggle switch`, and `search input`
▶ How to submit forms using jQuery Mobile

Depending on the site you are building, you may need to use a form. Forms are a terrific way to get information from a user. This information may be then used with backend processing logic to determine what to do with the data. This hour you learn about `form` elements and how they work with jQuery Mobile.

Getting Started with Forms

Don't sweat it if you have never used a form before. I've met plenty of developers that have never actually used a form, and even some that have built a form, but just sent it off to who-knows-where without understanding exactly what they just did.

Personally, I like to think of forms as Mad Libs, those humorous word games we all loved as kids. A Mad Lib generally is a short story template printed on a piece of paper that has blank fields asking for different things, such as a part of the body or a part of speech. When you are finished filling it out, you give it to your friend to read and process. This is just about the same way the `form` element works. The `form` element is the paper, and various elements such as `input`, `select`, and `label` make up the fields that either contain data or tell you what to write in them. When you are finished filling out the form you then submit it for processing.

A Basic Form

Let's dive right in and make a form. Listing 10.1 shows the contents of simple_form.html.

LISTING 10.1 An HTML Page That Contains a Form with Some Input Elements

```
 1: <!DOCTYPE html>
 2: <html>
 3:   <head>
 4:     <title>Simple Form</title>
 5:   </head>
 6:   <body>
 7:     <div id="content">
 8:       <form id="login" name="login" action="login.php" method="POST">
 9:         <label for="username">Username: </label>
10:         <input type="text" name="username" id="username" value="" /><br />
11:         <label for="password">Password:</label>
12:         <input type="password" name="password" id="password" value="" /><br />
13:         <input type="hidden" name="hiddenInput" id="hiddenInput"
value="secret message" />
14:         <input type="submit" name="loginSubmit" id="loginSubmit"
value="Login" />
15:       </form>
16:     </div>
17:   </body>
18: </html>
```

On line 8 you see the start of the form element. Inside this element are several attributes. The id and name attributes match and are put there mostly for referencing purposes. The action attribute is similar to the href attribute in an a element, in that it tells the form where to go when submitted. Finally the method element has been included with a value of POST. The method element has two values; the default, GET, takes all form values and puts them in the URL that is visible in the browser. While this is good for pages that need to be bookmarked or shared, it is bad on a page that is asking for personal information. Could you imagine seeing your password in plain sight in your browser's location bar? This is why the method attribute was set to POST. Using POST sends the values without displaying them in the URL.

Lines 9 and 11 each contain label elements. The label element is nice way to attach an accessible area to another input. When you click on a label, the associated element is automatically selected and will have the cursor placed inside it. In the case of line 9, the element with the id of username will be selected when the label is clicked because the label element has a value of username inside the for attribute.

A text field has been created on line 10 through the use of an input element with an attribute of type="text". Any text typed into this field will be visible to the user. While the text field that is created on line 12 is also an `input` element, the attribute `type="password"` masks anything typed into the field. This is useful for letting users know how many characters they have entered, but not displaying what they typed.

Line 13 is another `input` element with a different `type` attribute. The attribute `type="hidden"` hides the element from being viewed directly on the page but still passes values when the form is processed. This is especially useful when dealing with identification values. Some values may not make sense to the user viewing your site, but might be important for your backend logic.

Line 14 is an `input` element containing the attribute `type="submit"`; this element creates a button that sends all the data within the `form` element to the processor when clicked.

Figure 10.1 shows the form rendered on a browser.

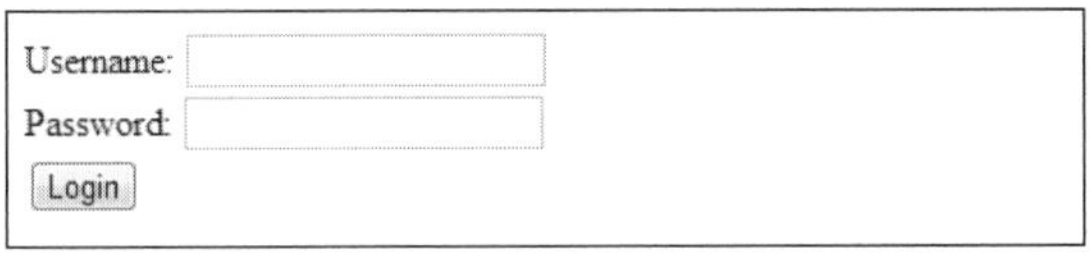

FIGURE 10.1
A simple login form

Now that we've seen an example of a few of the different elements that can be placed inside a form, let's take a look at how jQuery Mobile handles `form` elements.

Enhancing Forms with jQuery Mobile

jQuery Mobile has exceptional support for forms on mobile devices. Each element has been restyled to be accessible and easily usable on a mobile device. Keep in mind that some of the `form` styles vary slightly depending on the platform and mobile browser that you are using.

Standard Input Elements

To give you an idea of just how jQuery Mobile handles the look and layout of forms let's update the code we used in Listing 10.1 to include jQuery Mobile. Listing 10.2 shows the content of jqm_simple_form.html.

LISTING 10.2   The Simple Form Updated to Use jQuery Mobile

```
1: <!DOCTYPE html>
2: <html>
3:   <head>
4:     <title>Forms with jQM</title>
5:     <meta name="viewport" content="width=device-width, initial-scale=1">
```

```
 6:        <link rel="stylesheet"
href="http://code.jquery.com/mobile/1.1.0/jquery.mobile-1.1.0.min.css" />
 7:        <script src="http://code.jquery.com/jquery-1.7.1.min.js"></script>
 8:        <script
src="http://code.jquery.com/mobile/1.1.0/jquery.mobile-1.1.0.min.js"></script>
 9:      </head>
10:      <body>
11:        <div data-role="page">
12:          <div data-role="header"><h1>Forms with jQM</h1></div>
13:          <div data-role="content">
14:            <form id="login" name="login" action="login.php" method="POST">
15:              <label for="username">Username: </label>
16:              <input type="text" name="username" id="username" value="" /><br />
17:              <label for="password">Password:</label>
18:              <input type="password" name="password" id="password" value="" />
<br />
19:              <input type="hidden" name="hiddenInput" id="hiddenInput"
value="secret message" />
20:              <input type="submit" name="loginSubmit" id="loginSubmit"
value="Login" />
21:            </form>
22:          </div>
23:        </div>
24:      </body>
25: </html>
```

Strange as it may seem, the only thing that we really changed was the addition of the jQuery Mobile files and section containers. The entire form was left intact and just copied into the content area of the page. Take a look at Figure 10.2 to see the change that jQuery Mobile made on the original form.

When jQuery Mobile applies styles to the form it takes the text and password elements and automatically makes them display to the full width of the screen. Because this is done automatically the line breaks on lines 16 and 18 are not needed and can be removed if you want to take back a few pixels of space.

If you are worried about the input elements being too wide when displayed on a tablet or other large screen device, you can wrap the label and input elements inside a div with an attribute of data-role="fieldcontain". This puts the label and the input on the same line when there is room for both. If the screen is too narrow to display both on the same line, then they will still be on different lines. Listing 10.3 shows a code snippet from a page using jQuery Mobile with a form modified for this behavior.

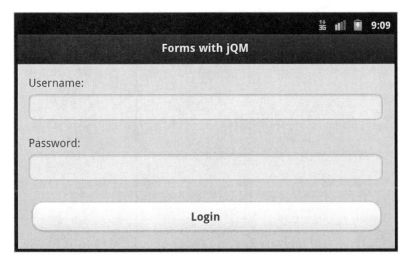

FIGURE 10.2
The mobile version of a simple login form, viewed in landscape

LISTING 10.3 Using `data-role="fieldcontain"` to Align Elements

```
 1: <form id="login" name="login" action="login.php" method="POST">
 2:    <div data-role="fieldcontain">
 3:       <label for="username">Username: </label>
 4:       <input type="text" name="username" id="username" value="" /><br />
 5:    </div>
 6:    <div data-role="fieldcontain">
 7:       <label for="password">Password:</label>
 8:       <input type="password" name="password" id="password" value="" /><br />
 9:    </div>
10:    <input type="hidden" name="hiddenInput" id="hiddenInput"
value="secret message" />
11:    <input type="submit" name="loginSubmit" id="loginSubmit" value="Login" />
12: </form>
```

Figure 10.3 shows the code from Listing 10.3 rendered in a mobile browser viewed in landscape orientation.

Now that we've seen the use of text elements, let's take a look at some other `input` elements styled with jQuery Mobile.

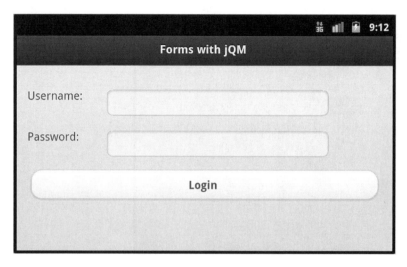

FIGURE 10.3
The label and input elements are displayed on the same line.

Radio Buttons and Check Boxes

Radio buttons are useful when you want to present more than one option to the user but have the user select only one of them. They remind me of multiple-choice tests, or those "fill in the bubble" forms. jQuery Mobile takes radio buttons a bit further than your standard radio button by using the label element to display the radio button on a touch-friendly bar.

To create a radio button you start with an input element and then use an attribute of type="radio". You also want to give your radio button the value and id attributes. To make multiple radio buttons work together, you must give them all the same name. Your radio button should look similar to the following snippet:

```
<input type="radio" name="radio-1" id="radio-1" value="Option 1" />
```

You can group radio buttons together inside a div or a fieldset using a controlgroup, and they will display without any breaks between them. If you use the fieldset element, you can also use the legend element to give a description for the group.

If you want your radio buttons to appear horizontally you can use an attribute of data-role="controlgroup" and the attribute data-type="horizontal". This, however, makes your radio buttons appear as a row of standard buttons instead of a row of radio buttons.

Check boxes are similar to radio buttons, but they allow the user to select as many of the options as they want instead of just one. Just like radio buttons, you must include a label element for each checkbox element as jQuery Mobile uses it to create the touch-friendly bar. To create a check box you start with an `input` element and add an attribute of `type="checkbox"`. Your check box should look similar to the following snippet:

```
<input type="checkbox" name="checkbox-1" id="checkbox-1" />
```

You can group check boxes together by using a container element with an attribute of `data-role="controlgroup"`.

Listing 10.4 shows a form snippet from a page using jQuery Mobile that contains radio buttons and check boxes that are grouped with and without using a `controlgroup`.

LISTING 10.4 Using Radio Buttons and Check Boxes in a Form

```
 1: <form id="login" name="login" action="login.php" method="POST">
 2:    <div class="ui-grid-a">
 3:       <div class="ui-block-a">
 4:         <fieldset>
 5:         <legend>Radio Buttons:</legend>
 6:           <input type="radio" name="radio-group-1" id="radio1" value="Fruit"
checked="checked" />
 7:           <label for="radio1">Fruit</label>
 8:           <input type="radio" name="radio-group-1" id="radio2" value="Robot" />
 9:           <label for="radio2">Robot</label>
10:         </fieldset>
11:       <fieldset data-role="controlgroup">
12:         <legend>Using a controlgroup:</legend>
13:           <input type="radio" name="radio-group-2" id="radio3" value="Sing"
checked="checked" />
14:           <label for="radio3">Sing</label>
15:           <input type="radio" name="radio-group-2" id="radio4" value="Yell" />
16:           <label for="radio4">Yell</label>
17:       </fieldset>
18:    </div>
19:    <div class="ui-block-b">
20:       <fieldset>
21:       <legend>Checkboxes:</legend>
22:         <input type="checkbox" name="checkbox-1" id="checkbox-1" />
23:         <label for="checkbox-1">Rain</label>
24:         <input type="checkbox" name="checkbox-2" id="checkbox-2" />
25:         <label for="checkbox-2">Snow</label>
26:       </fieldset>
27:       <fieldset data-role="controlgroup">
28:         <legend>Grouping checkboxes:</legend>
29:         <input type="checkbox" name="checkbox-3" id="checkbox-3" />
30:         <label for="checkbox-3">Sunny</label>
31:         <input type="checkbox" name="checkbox-4" id="checkbox-4" />
32:         <label for="checkbox-4">Cloudy</label>
```

```
33:        </fieldset>
34:      </div>
35:    </div>
36: </form>
```

In the example I used a `grid` to separate the radio buttons from the check boxes. The grid container starts on line 2 with the columns being created on line 3 and line 19. Starting with the first column, lines 4-10 show a set of radio buttons contained in a `fieldset` element that have been added to the page. They will appear with space between them and not be visibly grouped together. Lines 11-17 show another group of radio buttons being contained in a `fieldset` element along with a property of `data-role="controlgroup"`. This removes the extra spacing and makes the radio buttons appear to be grouped tightly together. An interesting side note about radio buttons is that the `label` elements for each radio button can be placed before or after the `input` element that creates the radio button. In the preceding code we placed the labels after the `input` elements because the page always renders `label` after the `radio` button. The other difference between the two radio button groups is the use of the `legend` element. The `legend` element can only be used inside a `fieldset` element and uses different spacing than the p element.

Looking at the second column of our grid, lines 20-33 show the use of check boxes. Just like the radio buttons there are two groups. Lines 20-26 show the check boxes being created inside a `fieldset` element. Due to check boxes only having a "checked" value, they do not contain a `value` attribute. Lines 27-33 show the check boxes being grouped together by using a `fieldset` element with a property of `data-role="controlgroup"`.

Figure 10.4 shows the code from Listing 10.4 being run on a mobile browser.

The `select` Element

The `select` element is a little different from the previous elements because it doesn't extend the `input` element. Instead it acts like a container for `option` elements. Each `option` element has a `value` and contains some text. The text for each `option` element appears when the `select` element is clicked or tapped. When the user is shown the list of `option` elements and selects one of them, the value within the selected `option` element becomes the value of the `select` element.

With jQuery Mobile the `select` element is styled as a button with an arrow pointing down. It also takes up as much space as is available and can be used with a container that has an attribute of `data-role="fieldcontain"` to place the `label` and `select` elements on the same line (if there is enough room onscreen).

FIGURE 10.4
Radio buttons and check boxes displayed with and without a control group

Just as we did with the radio buttons and check boxes we can also group `select` boxes with a `controlgroup`. If you add the `data-type="horizontal"` to the `controlgroup`, then the `select` boxes line up next to each other on the same line.

Listing 10.5 shows a snippet of code from a page using jQuery Mobile using `select` boxes with various formatting options.

LISTING 10.5   Using the `select` Element with jQuery Mobile

```
 1: <form id="login" name="login" action="login.php" method="POST">
 2:     <label for="size-select">Select your Size:</label>
 3:     <select name="size-select" id="size-select">
 4:        <option value="small">small</option>
 5:        <option value="medium">medium</option>
 6:        <option value="large">large</option>
 7:     </select>
 8:     <div data-role="fieldcontain">
 9:        <label for="radius-select">Choose a Radius</label>
10:        <select name="radius-select" id="radius-select">
11:          <option value="radius-5">5</option>
12:          <option value="radius-15">15</option>
13:          <option value="radius-25">25</option>
14:        </select>
```

```
15:    </div>
16:    <div data-role="fieldcontain">
17:      <fieldset data-role="controlgroup" data-type="horizontal">
18:        <legend>Set Time:</legend>
19:        <label for="hour-select">Hour</label>
20:        <select name="hour-select" id="hour-select">
21:          <option>Hour</option>
22:          <option value="hour-08">08</option>
23:          <option value="hour-09">09</option>
24:          <option value="hour-10">10</option>
25:        </select>
26:        <label for="minute-select">Minute</label>
27:        <select name="minute-select" id="minute-select">
28:          <option>Minute</option>
29:          <option value="minute-10">10</option>
30:          <option value="minute-20">20</option>
31:          <option value="minute-30">30</option>
32:        </select>
33:      </fieldset>
34:    </div>
35: </form>
```

Lines 2-7 show a label and select box being set up. Remember to always include labels as they help with the accessibility of your site. Lines 8-15 show a select box being contained inside a div element with an attribute of data-role="fieldcontain". This tries to keep the label and select box on the same line.

Lines 16-34 show a more complex select box setup. Line 17 shows the use of a fieldset element with the attributes data-role="controlgroup" and data-type="horizontal". This groups the select boxes next to each other on the same line. Line 18 is important because the legend element will be the overall label for the group of select boxes. If you omit the legend element and still use your labels, the formatting of your select boxes will appear somewhat broken. If you are going to use a fieldset with select boxes, make sure you use the legend element as well.

Figure 10.5 shows the code from Listing 10.5 running in a mobile browser.

jQuery mobile tries to style the select element to appear with a similar skin across all devices; however this does not always work. There are noticeable differences between the native Android browser and the Opera Mobile browser. The size of the select box is about the same between browsers, but on Opera Mobile it still appears as a standard select box.

While you may already be familiar with these elements, there are a few more that you probably haven't used before. Let's take a look at some of the extra or extended input elements that jQuery Mobile provides.

FIGURE 10.5
Various ways that `select` boxes can be displayed with jQuery Mobile

Extended Input Elements

Mobile devices have a few new ways of collecting user input. Some of these ways have existed with desktop browsers for quite some time, but they are not used enough to be considered common. When thinking about the various control or input features of a mobile device, often included is a slider to change settings, a flip toggle switch to change from one setting to another, and a search feature. All three of these are supported in jQuery Mobile.

Slider

The slider is typically used on pages where a user would click and drag or tap and drag to select a value rather than type it. This makes the slider great for use as a volume control, a brightness or opacity control, and even for use on pages that perform calculations. Take a look at the following code and see whether you can tell what each attribute does.

```
<input type="range" name="slider" id="slider" value="10" min="0" max="100" />
```

The attribute `type="range"` is what jQuery Mobile looks for to create the slider, and yes even though it is a `type="range"`, it is still called a slider. There isn't anything special about the `name` and `id` attributes; they work just like they do with other input elements. The `value` attribute, however, is important because it sets where the slider button or handle starts. The min attribute sets how low the slider can go, while the max attribute sets how high the slider is allowed to go.

You should use a label with each slider you include on your page. This should be done not only for display and accessibility reasons, but also because it is required when using jQuery Mobile. Listing 10.6 shows a form with three sliders taken from a page using jQuery Mobile.

LISTING 10.6 Using Sliders Inside a Form

```
 1: <form id="volume" name="volume" action="volume.php">
 2:    <div data-role="fieldcontain">
 3:       <label>Bass:</label>
 4:       <input type="range" name="" id="" min="10" max="110" value="80" />
 5:    </div>
 6:    <div data-role="fieldcontain">
 7:       <label>Mid:</label>
 8:       <input type="range" name="" id="" min="0" max="90" value="80" />
 9:    </div>
10:    <div data-role="fieldcontain">
11:       <label>Treble:</label>
12:       <input type="range" name="" id="" min="5" max="105" value="80" />
13:    </div>
14: </form>
```

You can see that we used div containers on lines 2, 6, and 10 to separate each slider from one another. I also included labels for each slider, and because the container has the data-role="fieldcontain" attribute, it attempts to put both label and slider on the same line.

There is only one curve in this example. You may not notice it immediately, but when you look at Figure 10.6 you can see that even though each slider has the same value, it shows up in a different place on each slider. This is because I changed the min and max settings of each slider. Keep this in mind as you build sliders on your page.

Flip Toggle Switch

The flip toggle switch is pretty much a binary toggle. Either it is turned on, or it is turned off. This is common in settings where you turn various parts of your mobile device on or off.

To create a flip toggle switch you need to start with a select element that has two option elements. You then need to add an attribute of data-role="slider" to the select element. Just like the other input elements, you can also wrap the flip toggle switch inside a container with the data-role="fieldcontain" to keep the label and the flip toggle switch on the same line (if room is available). Listing 10.7 shows two flip toggle switches being set up on a page using jQuery Mobile. One is placed inside a div element with the data-role="fieldcontain" attribute.

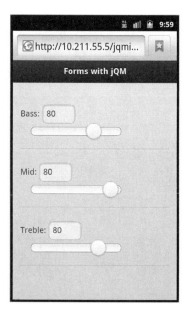

FIGURE 10.6
Sliders are adjustable relative to their min and max settings.

LISTING 10.7 Adding the Flip Toggle Switch to a Form

```
 1: <form id="flip" name="flip" action="flipswitch.php">
 2:    <label for="flip-1">Brightness:</label>
 3:    <select name="flip-1" id="flip-1" data-role="slider">
 4:      <option value="Bright">Bright</option>
 5:      <option value="Dark">Dark</option>
 6:    </select>
 7:    <div data-role="fieldcontain">
 8:      <label for="flip-2">Flip switch:</label>
 9:        <select name="flip-2" id="flip-2" data-role="slider">
10:          <option value="Loud">Loud</option>
11:          <option value="Silent">Silent</option>
12:        </select>
13:    </div>
14: </form>
```

Lines 2-6 show the first label and flip toggle switch being created and set up. Since it is not in a container, the flip toggle switch will take as much screen space as is available. Lines 7-13 show a div container wrapping another label and flip toggle switch.

Figure 10.7 shows the code from Listing 10.7 rendered in a mobile browser with one of the switches toggled.

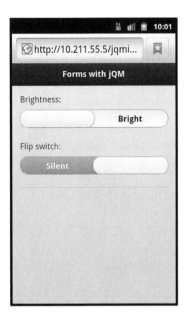

FIGURE 10.7
A pair of flip toggle switches with one toggled

Search Input

The search input is a new type of input that is part of the HTML5 specifications. This input is an enhanced text field that has an icon to help users know what it is for. When the user starts typing an "x" icon appears that when tapped or clicked erases all the user text entry in the field.

To create a search input, use the following one-line snippet:

```
<input type="search" name="search-input" id="search-input" value="" />
```

As with the other elements we've covered this hour, be sure to include a label to increase your form accessibility. You can also use a container with `data-role="fieldcontain"` to keep the label and search input on the same line when enough room is available onscreen. Listing 10.8 shows two search inputs being created.

LISTING 10.8 Creating Search Inputs

```
1: <form id="search-form" name="search-form" action="search.php" method="get">
2:    <label for="search-1">Search the site:</label>
3:    <input type="search" name="search-1" id="search-1" value="" />
4:    <div data-role="fieldcontain">
5:      <label for="search-2">Find:</label>
```

```
6:    <input type="search" name="search-2" id="search-2" value=""/>
7:    </div>
8: </form>
```

The code should look pretty familiar. On line 2 we set the `label` for the search input created on line 3. Line 4 is a `div` element with the `data-role="fieldcontain"` attribute that keeps the `label` on line 5 and the search input on line 6 displayed on the same line when screen space is available.

Figure 10.8 shows what the code from Listing 10.8 looks like when rendered on a mobile browser when included on a page using jQuery Mobile.

FIGURE 10.8
Search inputs add extra visuals to the text field.

Remember that the search input is an enhanced text input. This means that it will not submit a form by itself. You must either wire it up with some extra JavaScript or include a submit input in the form. While we are talking about form submission, let's take a look at how it works with jQuery Mobile.

Submitting Forms

Form submission is a little different when using jQuery Mobile. On most websites when a form is submitted, the user is redirected to a page based on whatever backend code has run and determined what to do with the user. While that is still possible, the default way forms are handled with jQuery Mobile is to handle all form submissions through AJAX. Also, the default method for sending form data is through the use of GET.

Submitting Forms with AJAX

As I mentioned before, all form submissions are handled with AJAX by default. This means that the results of the form are injected into the DOM and a page transition is triggered to move the current view of the page to it. This is the same way new pages are loaded by default with jQuery Mobile.

While you can use any backend processing language you are familiar with for handling forms, we are going to use some PHP mixed with jQuery Mobile to demonstrate how form submission works. Listing 10.9 shows a PHP file that contains some rudimentary logic to display data from a form submit.

LISTING 10.9   The Contents of login.php

```
 1: <!DOCTYPE html>
 2: <html>
 3:   <head>
 4:     <title>Forms with jQM</title>
 5:     <meta name="viewport" content="width=device-width, initial-scale=1">
 6:     <link rel="stylesheet"
href="http://code.jquery.com/mobile/1.1.0/jquery.mobile-1.1.0.min.css" />
 7:     <script src="http://code.jquery.com/jquery-1.7.1.min.js"></script>
 8:     <script
src="http://code.jquery.com/mobile/1.1.0/jquery.mobile-1.1.0.min.js"></script>
 9:   </head>
10:   <body>
11:     <div data-role="page">
12:       <div data-role="header"><h1>login.php</h1></div>
13:       <div data-role="content">
14:         <p>You tried to login as "<strong><?php echo $_POST['username']; ?>
</strong>"</p>
15:         <p>You used "<strong><?php echo $_POST['password']; ?>
</strong>" as your password</p>
16:         <p>The input element with type="hidden" contained "<strong>
<?php echo $_POST['hiddenInput']; ?></strong>"</p>
17:         <a href="jqm_simple_form.html" data-rel="back"
data-role="button">Go Back</a>
```

```
18:        </div>
19:        </div>
20:    </body>
21: </html>
```

While that does appear to be an awful lot of HTML to be a PHP file, you can see that on line 14 we used some PHP to output what was passed through as the `'username'` on our form. Line 15 shows more use of PHP as we get what was passed out of the `'password'` field on our form. The last bit of PHP appears on line 16 of our form where we display what was passed through the form in a `hidden` input element.

In Listing 10.2 we referenced the file jqm_simple_form.html that used a login.php as the action for the `form`. Since we just created the login.php file, you can now place both of these files in the same folder on a web server and run them together to see the form working for yourself.

As for the page using AJAX, if you open Web Inspector, Firebug, or a similar debugging program, you can actually watch the DOM being manipulated as the form is submitted and the contents of login.php are injected into the DOM. Because of this the page is never reloaded, and the user never actually leaves the page they are on.

NOTE

Duplicate Form id with AJAX

If you are using multiple forms on your mobile site make sure that you are using a unique id on every one of them. Because pages and forms are injected into the DOM, they are moved into memory and stay there. Having a unique id on every form will save you hours of headache as you try to fix seemingly phantom problems.

Submitting a Form Without AJAX

Occasionally you may need to submit a form that reloads the entire page instead of making an AJAX request and inserting it into the DOM. When this is the case you only need to add the attribute `data-ajax="false"` to the `form` element. This forces jQuery Mobile to load the result page as a new page. The following is a one-line snippet that shows the modification required to your opening `form` element.

```
<form id="login" name="login" action="login.php" method="POST" data-ajax="false">
```

If you take the previous snippet and replace line 14 of jqm_simple_form.html with it, you will find that even though the form appears to handle the same, a page load is actually happening instead of a DOM injection. You can verify this by using Web Inspector, Firebug, or similar tools.

Summary

In this hour you learned about forms and how jQuery Mobile uses them. You learned about the modifications to standard form inputs that jQuery Mobile makes, as well as some of the new form inputs that jQuery Mobile offers. You learned how to add a slider, a flip toggle switch, and a search input to a form.

This hour also discussed form submission. The default method for submitting a form is with a GET request, although this can be changed to a POST request if you want. You also learned that the default handling method of form submission is through an AJAX call where the results are then injected into the DOM. Finally you learned that you can override the AJAX setting and require the page to be reloaded through the use of the `data-ajax="false"` attribute on the form element.

Q&A

Q. You mentioned that some mobile browsers ignore styles or replace them. Why does this happen?

A. The jQuery Mobile team does its absolute best at trying to accommodate as many browser types as they can. While most modern mobile browsers are based on WebKit and use a similar preset CSS and browser chrome, some use completely different rendering methods. Opera Mobile for example is focused on speed and handles element rendering a little differently than the rest to deliver pages quickly and efficiently.

Q. What if I don't want to use any jQuery Mobile styles on my form elements?

A. While I'm not sure exactly why you would want to do that, I'm sure you have your reasons. In this case you can simply add `data-role="none"` to any form element that you want to have rendered natively by the browser.

Q. When submitting forms through AJAX, the URL in my location bar changes; is it really using AJAX?

A. Yes, jQuery Mobile will update the displayed URL in your location bar, but if you watch with debug tools you will see that the original page is just marked as `display:none` and the page that was AJAX'd in will appear.

Workshop

The workshop contains a quiz and some exercises to help you check your comprehension and understanding.

Quiz

1. How do you change a form to use a `POST` request instead of a `GET`?

2. What do you need to do to disable AJAX form submission?

3. True or False: By default, jQuery Mobile only adds new input types. It does not change the style of any existing input types.

4. How do you create a flip toggle switch?

5. True or False: Search inputs are actually just restyled Submit buttons.

Answers

1. In your `form` element, add the attribute `method="POST"`.

2. In your `form` element, add the attribute `data-ajax="false"`.

3. False. jQuery Mobile changes all `form` elements by default, but can be told to let the browser handle them natively by using the `data-role="none"` attribute.

4. You need to create a `select` element with an attribute of `data-role="slider"` and then place two `option` elements inside it.

5. False. A search input is part of the HTML5 specification that is more closely related to a text field.

Exercises

1. Create a contact form using jQuery Mobile. Think of all the fields that you want to capture and use the various `input` elements to make your form.

2. Create a preferences page using the slider and flip toggle switch.

3. Using whatever backend programming knowledge you have, create a page that handles a form submit using jQuery Mobile. If you do not have any backend experience, try changing the login.php file that we used in this hour to get data from more fields, or to display the data in different `input` elements.

Learning About Lists

What You'll Learn in This Hour:

▶ How unordered lists work with jQuery Mobile

▶ How to number items in a list

▶ How to add icons and thumbnails to `list items`

▶ How to search through `list items`

▶ How to use a form with a list

List elements are used often in web development. Their versatility helps developers display content, navigation, and links with minimal effort. jQuery Mobile uses both ordered and unordered lists to display content and links in a mobile friendly way, while continuing the original ease of use.

Creating Standard and Inset Lists

While you may already be familiar with standard list behavior in HTML, jQuery Mobile brings some new options to list behavior and display. Whether you want to create a list that takes up the entire screen or create a list that appears to jump off the page, you can do it with jQuery Mobile.

Standard lists behave similar to buttons; they take up the full amount of space available to them. Inset lists still take up the full amount of space, but add rounded corners and a shadow to make the list appear to jump off the page.

Creating a Standard List

Using HTML, you can make a standard list by creating a `ul` element and placing `li` elements inside it. To make a standard list in jQuery Mobile you follow the same setup only you need to add an attribute of `data-role="listview"` to the `ul` element. Listing 11.1 shows the creation of a standard list.

LISTING 11.1   Creating a Standard List

```
1: <ul data-role="listview">
2:    <li data-role="list-divider">List Items</li>
3:    <li>I am a list item!</li>
4:    <li>I am another list item!</li>
5:    <li data-role="list-divider">List Items with Links</li>
6:    <li><a href="#">I am a link in a list item!</a></li>
7:    <li><a href="#">I am another link in a list item!</a></li>
8: </ul>
```

On line 1 a standard list is created with the `ul` element and styled by jQuery Mobile because of the `data-role="listview"` attribute. If you do not include the `data-role="listview"` attribute, the standard list styles will be applied instead of the jQuery Mobile styles. This can be useful if you want to use a standard list without the styles that jQuery Mobile adds.

Lines 2 and 5 are both `li` elements, but they contain an extra attribute of `data-role="list-divider"`. When used, this attribute changes the display styles of the `li` element to help create grouped content. The text within the element is displayed like a title to help users understand the grouping.

Lines 3 and 4 show some `li` elements that have been created. These two elements will be styled with a darker gray background and will not be clickable. Lines 6 and 7, however, will be styled with a lighter gray background and will be given an icon on the right to indicate that they are clickable. When links within a standard list are clicked, jQuery Mobile makes an AJAX request to the target and injects the results into the DOM and then triggers a page transition to bring it into view.

Figure 11.1 shows the standard list we made rendered in a mobile browser. Just like buttons and toolbars, the styling may be a little different based on the mobile browser you are using.

Now that we have a standard list created, let's take a look at creating an inset list.

Creating an Inset List

To create an inset list, you start by creating a standard list and then add an attribute of `data-inset="true"` to the `ul` element. This means that we could use the code from Listing 11.1 and only change the first line to make our list inset:

```
<ul data-role="listview" data-inset="true">
```

Figure 11.2 shows what our one-line change has done to our list.

Now that we know how jQuery Mobile styles standard lists and how to create inset lists, let's learn about the extras we can do with lists.

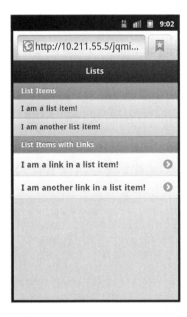

FIGURE 11.1
A standard list rendered in a mobile browser

FIGURE 11.2
An inset list rendered in a mobile browser

Adding Extras to Lists

You may be wondering what extras can be added to a list. There are quite a few things we can do. We can add numbers, insert a counter, include thumbnail images, include an icon, and even create split lists. Let's start with using numbered lists.

Using Numbered Lists

To create a numbered list you need to start with an `ol` lement and include `li` elements inside it. Each `li` element is automatically numbered based on the position it is placed in the `ol` element. Listing 11.2 shows the creation of a numbered list.

LISTING 11.2 Creating a Numbered List

```
1: <ol data-role="listview">
2:    <li data-role="list-divider">Numbered List Items with Links</li>
3:    <li><a href="#">Polar</a></li>
4:    <li><a href="#">Grizzly</a></li>
5:    <li><a href="#">Brown</a></li>
6:    <li><a href="#">Black</a></li>
7: </ol>
```

On line 1 we begin with an `ol` element that has an attribute of `data-role="listview"` to apply the jQuery Mobile styles to make this a numbered list. Just like the standard list if you omit the `data-role="listview"` attribute the styles will not be applied and it will remain an ordered list instead of being rendered as a numbered list.

Line 2 contains an `li` element that contains an attribute of `data-role="list-divider"`. This works the same as it does in the standard list allowing this particular element to act as a separator. Even though it is an `li` element inside an `ol` element, it will not be numbered.

Lines 3-6 show four `li` elements with a elements with some text inside them. Just like the standard list, these elements will be styled with arrows on the right indicating that they can be clicked and tapped. Line 7 closes the `ol` element and completes our numbered list.

Figure 11.3 shows what a numbered list looks like on a mobile browser.

While this numbered list was not set up as an inset numbered list, it can be created as one by using the `data-inset="true"` attribute on the `ol` element.

Another thing we can do with numbers is add count bubbles.

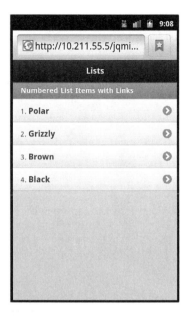

FIGURE 11.3
A numbered list rendered in a mobile browser

Adding a Count

A style that is popular with some messaging or email apps is to display the number of items, or count of items, contained within a subsection or link. You can replicate this style using an element with `class="ui-li-count"` inside your `li` elements. Listing 11.3 shows a standard list with a count.

LISTING 11.3   Implementing a Count in a Standard List

```
1: <ul data-role="listview">
2:    <li data-role="list-divider">List Items with Links and a Count</li>
3:    <li><a href="#">Bugs<span class="ui-li-count">5</span></a></li>
4:    <li><a href="#">Comments<span class="ui-li-count">12</span></a></li>
5:    <li><a href="#">Suggestions<span class="ui-li-count">8</span></a></li>
6:    <li><a href="#">Tickets<span class="ui-li-count">27</span></a></li>
7: </ul>
```

Since we've already covered the basic setup of a standard list you should know what lines 1 and 2 are doing. Lines 3-6 should also look familiar as they contain `li` elements that each have an `a` element inside them. However, inside the `a` element is some text followed by a `span` element with an attribute of `class="ui-li-count"`. You can see that each line has a different number inside the span element. This is the number that will appear in a "bubble" on the right side of the rendered list item bar. Figure 11.4 shows what this standard list looks like when rendered.

FIGURE 11.4
A standard list with a count applied rendered in a mobile browser

We are not limited to only adding a count or using a numbered list, we can also add icons and thumbnail images.

Using Icons and Thumbnails

When you are styling a list you may want to include an icon or thumbnail image with each item in the list. This is not only possible but is easy to do.

Adding a Thumbnail

A thumbnail image is a preview or smaller version of a full-sized image. Thumbnail images can be added to list items by including them inside an a element in your li element. Listing 11.4 shows a snippet of code taken from thumbnail_list.html that gives an example of how to add thumbnail images inside li elements.

LISTING 11.4 Adding Thumbnails to List Items

```
1: <ul data-role="listview">
2:    <li data-role="list-divider">List Items with Links and Thumbnails</li>
3:    <li><a href="#"><img src="thumb_bridge.jpg" alt="Bay Bridge" />Bridges</a></li>
4:    <li><a href="#"><img src="thumb_food.jpg" alt="Food" />Food</a></li>
5:    <li><img src="thumb_sleepy.jpg" alt="People" />People</li>
6:    <li><img src="thumb_grass.jpg" alt="Grass" />Nature</li>
7: </ul>
```

Lines 3 and 4 show `li` elements that contain an `a` element within them. When using links inside lists, the visual style will be changed for list items containing them. A hover and click-state style will be applied to the list item giving a visual clue to the user that it is a link. Within the `a` element is an `img` element that will be used at the thumbnail. After the `img` element is some text that will be displayed to the right of the thumbnail.

Lines 5 and 6 show that thumbnails can also be applied to `li` elements that do not contain an `a` element within them. These lines are also set up with the image first and then the text that should be displayed with the image. Figure 11.5 shows what the list items look like when they have thumbnail images applied to them.

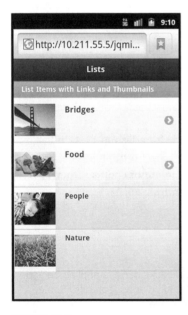

FIGURE 11.5
Using thumbnails with and without links

jQuery Mobile automatically reduces the size of whatever image is specified down to 80×80 pixels. If you elect to use an image smaller than 80 pixels wide or tall, the image is not resized but is used as is. Even though image resizing is handled somewhat automatically, it is still a good idea to presize your images to keep the file size of your image down and to format them how you want them.

Adding an Icon

Icon images are similar to thumbnails only much smaller. Where the thumbnail was an 80×80 pixel image, an icon is a 16×16 pixel image. While some automatic resizing is applied, I highly recommend you use resized images to save you from some possible image overlap issues with the text you include in your list item.

To use an icon, you start the same way you do when applying a thumbnail, only on the `img` element you need to add a `class="ui-li-icon"` attribute. Listing 11.5 shows a snippet of code from icon_list.html that shows an example of adding icons to list items.

LISTING 11.5   Adding Icons to List Items

```
1: <ul data-role="listview">
2:    <li data-role="list-divider">List Items with Links and Thumbnails</li>
3:    <li><a href="#">
<img class="ui-li-icon" src="icon_bridge.jpg" alt="Bay Bridge" />Bridges</a></li>
4:    <li><a href="#"><img class="ui-li-icon" src="icon_food.jpg" alt="Food" />
Food</a></li>
5:    <li><img class="ui-li-icon" src="icon_sleepy.jpg" alt="People" />People</li>
6:    <li><img class="ui-li-icon" src="icon_grass.jpg" alt="Grass" />Nature</li>
7: </ul>
```

The code should look familiar, since it is a modification to the code from Listing 11.4. In fact, the only change we really made was adding the `class="ui-li-icon"` attribute to the `img` elements, and changing the images that are used. While these were minor changes, they have quite an impact on the visible space used as Figure 11.6 demonstrates.

NOTE

Rounded Border Clipping

When using links inside lists, an arrow is automatically added and a background is applied behind the arrow that is actually square with all corners rounded to give it a circular appearance. Some devices and browsers clip the rounded background slightly and may make the image appear somewhat jagged.

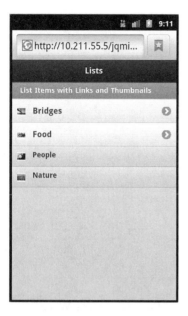

FIGURE 11.6
Icons used with list items

Now that we have made our lists look more exciting and visually descriptive, let's make them even more useful by using a split list.

Creating a Split List

A split list is a list that contains list items that have more than one link in them. When you place two a elements inside an li element, jQuery Mobile automatically creates a split list.

The first a element takes the majority of space of the list item leaving the second a element a small section with space for an icon on the right side of the list item. Because split lists are automatically created by adding a second link, you can mix other list extras together. Listing 11.6 shows a snippet of code used to make a split list.

LISTING 11.6   Creating a Split List

```
1:   <ul data-role="listview" data-split-theme="e">
2:     <li data-role="list-divider">Split List</li>
3:     <li>
4:       <a href="#">
5:         <h3>First link in a split list</h3>
6:         <p>The icon on the right is the default icon</p>
7:       </a>
8:       <a href="#" title="Second Link">Second link in a split list</a>
```

```
 9:    </li>
10:    <li>
11:      <a href="#">
12:        <img class="ui-li-icon" src="icon_bridge.jpg" alt="Bay Bridge" />
13:        <h3>Use with an icon</h3>
14:        <p>Yep, you can use icons with split lists</p>
15:      </a>
16:      <a href="#" title="Another link">Another split list link</a>
17:    </li>
18:    <li>
19:      <a href="#">
20:        <img src="thumb_grass.jpg" alt="Grass" />
21:        <h3>Use with a thumbnail</h3>
22:        <p>Wow, you can also use thumbnails in split lists.</p>
23:      </a>
24:      <a href="#" title="Titles are accessible">Another split list link</a>
25:    </li>
26: </ul>
```

There is a lot going on here so we're going to walk through most of the lines of code. When looking at line 1, in the previous examples we had only added the `data-role="listview"` attribute; this time we added `data-split-theme="e"`. This changes the colors that will be applied to the icon used on the second link in the split list. Each theme swatch is assigned a different letter and is accessed by passing this letter into the attribute.

Line 2 does not have any surprises; it is an `li` element with the `data-role="list-divider"` attribute making it a differently styled list item.

Lines 3-9 show the first list item in our split list. Line 3 is the opening `li` element, and line 4 is the opening a element for the first link. To change the formatting up a little, Line 5 contains an `h3` element that will style the text inside as a large bold title, while the text in the p element on line 6 will be displayed as a subtitle. Line 7 closes the first link, and line 8 contains the second link. The `title` attribute inside the a element on this line is important for accessibility. This is important because any text placed between the opening a element and closing a element will be removed. I placed the text "Second link in a split list" in-between the opening and closing a element, but when the page is rendered this text will not be shown, so having the `title` attribute set with a value is strongly recommended.

Lines 10-17 show another list item in our split list. Line 10 starts us out with an opening `li` element, and line 11 contains an opening a element to set up our first link. Line 12 shows that we are including an `img` element with an attribute of `class="ui-li-icon"`, which is the required class for using an icon inside our list item. On line 13 we are using an `h3` element again to add some title text to our list item, making line 14 a p element displaying some subtitle text. Line 15 closes the a element, and line 16 shows the second link being created.

Lines 18-25 show the last list item in our split list. This list item starts out like the other with an opening `li` element on line 18 and the opening a element on line 19. Line 20 then uses an `img` element that will be styled as a thumbnail for the list item. Line 21 is an h3 element that is used for title text, and line 22 is our p element that is used for subtitle text. Line 23 is the closing a element for our first link, and line 24 contains the a element for the second link. Line 25 is the closing `li` element for this list item, leaving line 26 to close out the entire split list.

In Figure 11.7 we can see what our split list that contains a plain list item, a list item with an icon, and a list item with a thumbnail looks like when rendered on a mobile browser.

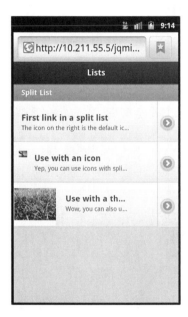

FIGURE 11.7
Split lists can be combined with other list item extras.

The default icon that is shown for the second link in the split list is an arrow. If you would prefer to use a different icon you can add another by adding another attribute to the `ul` element specifying one of the standard icon names. For example, if I wanted to change the default icon to a star, I would add `data-split-icon="star"` to the `ul` element for the list. Using the default settings of jQuery Mobile, you cannot specify more than one icon per list. That means that you have to overwrite styles inside your CSS if you want to use different icons.

Now that we've seen the extras that we can add to a list, let's take a look at adding a search feature to it.

Searching List Content

If you are using a list to display a large number of items you may want to include a search filter to help users navigate through your selection to find what they need.

Creating a search filter is easier than you might think. All you need to do is add an attribute of data-filter="true" to the ul element of your list. Listing 11.7 shows a list with a search filter applied.

LISTING 11.7   Adding a Search Filter to a List

```
 1:   <ul data-role="listview" data-filter="true">
 2:     <li data-role="list-divider">Signed Bands</li>
 3:     <li>Planned obscolencense</li>
 4:     <li>S.E.P. (Scortched Earth Policy)</li>
 5:     <li>Ground Pounder</li>
 6:     <li>Decibel Hertz</li>
 7:     <li>Ultra Violent Lights</li>
 8:     <li>Southern Tempo</li>
 9:     <li>Candy Lab</li>
10:     <li>Brother Tobias</li>
11:     <li>Silent Squall</li>
12:     <li>Red Air Day</li>
13:     <li>Fourty Floor</li>
14:     <li>Marvelous Makeover</li>
15:     <li>Anthem</li>
16:     <li>Groupraiser</li>
17:     <li>Nine Knights</li>
18:     <li>Modulation</li>
19:     <li>Saw the Sine</li>
20:   </ul>
```

On line 1 the data-filter="true" attribute was applied on the opening ul element. Line 2 is an li element that contains a data-role="list-divider". We already know that this creates a list divider, but when using the search filter, the list divider is visible only as long as at least one thing comes back as a result. Lines 3-19 show li elements being created with different names in them for the purpose of demonstrating the search filter. Figure 11.8 shows what the list looks like with the search filter.

As you type into the search filter box, the displayed list automatically hides list items based on matches between the entered text and the list item text content. Text entered into the search filter is not case sensitive and filters even on partial matches. For example, if you were to put the code from Listing 11.7 into a page and type "rou" into the search filter, it would remove all entries except for "Ground Pounder" and "Groupraiser".

FIGURE 11.8
A populated list with a search filter to help find content

Just in case you were wondering, the initial text inside the search filter can be changed from the default "Filter items...". To change the text, you need to include the `data-filter-placeholder=""` attribute on your `ul` element with the value set to what you want displayed. You can also use search filters on inset lists. Listing 11.8 is an example of using an inset list with customized text in the search filter.

LISTING 11.8   Customizing the Search Filter Text on an Inset List

```
1: <ul data-role="listview" data-filter="true"
data-filter-placeholder="Find Album..." data-inset="true">
2:    <li data-role="list-divider">Discography</li>
3:    <li>Inverted Distortion</li>
4:    <li>Tekknowlegy</li>
5:    <li>Spectralillium</li>
6:    <li>Bar Foo</li>
7:    <li>Vigilante Hyperbole</li>
8:    <li>4 Chords and 88 Keys</li>
9: </ul>
```

While the list data has changed, the only major code change to note is on line 1. Included in the `ul` element is `data-filter-placeholder="Find Album..."` and `data-inset="true"`. While those changes are easy and small, they change things up nicely. Figure 11.9 shows what our customized text and inset list looks like now.

FIGURE 11.9
An inset list with customized search filter text

The last thing we are going to look at this hour is using a list within a form.

Using a List Within a Form

While you can always use a div element to help contain and style your form elements, another option is to use a list.

Using a list with a form is straightforward; you begin with a form element and then use list elements inside it to contain your form data. Listing 11.9 shows a form using a list.

LISTING 11.9   Using List and Form Elements

```
 1: <form name="login" id="login" action="process.php" method="POST">
 2:    <ul data-role="listview">
 3:      <li>
 4:       <label for="username">Username:</label>
 5:        <input type="text" name="username" id="username" value="" />
 6:      </li>
 7:      <li>
 8:        <label for="password">Password:</label>
 9:        <input type="password" name="password" id="password" value="" />
10:      </li>
11:      <li>
```

```
12:        <input type="hidden" name="hiddenInput" id="hiddenInput"
value="secret message" />
13:        <input type="submit" name="loginSubmit" id="loginSubmit"
value="Login" />
14:    </li>
15:   </ul>
16: </form>
```

Line 1 shows a `form` element with relevant attributes being set up. Line 2 is where we start our list by using a `ul` element with the `data-role="listview"` attribute. Line 3 is a starting `li` element that wraps both the `label` and `input` elements found on lines 4 and 5. Line 6 is the closing tag of the `li` element. Lines 7-10 are similar, showing another `li` element that contains a `label` and `input` element inside it. Line 11 begins another `li` element this time containing a hidden form input on line 12 and a submit button on line 13. Lines 14 and 15 are the closing elements for `li` and `ul` elements, respectively. Line 16 shows the closing tag of our `form` element.

This form was previously built using `div` elements with `data-role="fieldcontain"` attributes to help with the appearance of the form elements. By replacing the `div` elements with a list we changed the appearance of the form with gradient backgrounds and borders. Figure 11.10 shows what the form styled with a list looks like on a mobile browser.

FIGURE 11.10
The appearance of your form changes when used with a list

Summary

In this hour you learned how lists work when used with jQuery Mobile. Lists can be displayed either in full screen or inset, and both `ul` and `ol` elements can be used and styled with jQuery Mobile.

You learned about adding extras such as thumbnails, icons, and a count to list items. You also learned about split lists and how to use them with the other extras that can be added to list items.

You saw how to add a search filter to your list, how it works with list dividers, and how to customize the initial search filter text. You also learned that you can combine a list with a form to include a different visual style and that it can be used in place of `div` elements with the `data-role="fieldcontain"` attribute.

Q&A

Q. Is there a reason why I would or would not want to use inset lists?

A. I believe this comes down to personal preference and style. An example of when inset lists come in handy is when creating complex layouts that use media queries to hide or show content based on screen size. If your screen layout splits into multiple columns, a standard list will fill up the entire column but not include any side borders. This can give your list an incomplete feel.

Q. Do I always have to enter the number to display in the count manually?

A. No. But to make the number dynamic you need to include either a backend language to write the value out, or use some JavaScript to change the values on an event such as `pageInit()` or `pageCreate()`.

Q. I included a thumbnail that was shorter than 80px. It looks wrong. Isn't it supposed to center my image?

A. Unfortunately jQuery Mobile will not figure out the vertical center of your image. Instead it places it at the top and leaves empty space at the bottom. To fix this I suggest trimming your image manually in some photo-manipulation software and then placing it on either a transparent background or other color so that the image is 80×80 px with your image centered. If you look at Figure 11.5 you can see that is what I had to do with my thumbnail images because they came out at 80×60 px.

Workshop

The workshop contains a quiz and some exercises to help you check your comprehension and understanding.

Quiz

1. True or False: It is impossible to stop jQuery Mobile from styling your lists.

2. True or False: You can mix multiple list extras together to create uniquely styled list items.

3. How do you create a split list?

4. What is the default size for an icon when used with a list?

5. How do you add a count to a list item?

Answers

1. False. jQuery Mobile always checks for a `data-role="listview"` element on the `ul` element of your list before it styles it. If you do not include the attribute your list will use default styles instead of the jQuery Mobile ones.

2. True. You can mix almost any of the various extras together to make your lists stand out and perform the tasks you need. This includes mixing thumbnails with a count, or icons with a split list, and so on.

3. To create a split list you need to include two `a` elements inside a list item.

4. The default size of an icon is 16×16 pixels. This is different from the default icon size used with buttons, which is 18×18 pixels.

5. You create a count by adding an element with an attribute of `class=" ui-li-count"` that contains a number. This number is then displayed on the right side of the list item when rendered.

Exercises

1. Create either an inset or standard list and apply a thumbnail and a count.

2. Create a form and try adding various form elements to different list items. Experiment with how the list changes when displayed as an inset list.

3. Create an address book using list dividers and a search filter to quickly find a name that you are looking for.

HOUR 12
Handling Events

What You'll Learn in This Hour:

▶ How to use page initialization events

▶ How to use touch events

▶ How to use virtual mouse events

▶ How to trigger an event when device orientation changes

An event is basically a trigger that happens either by user interaction or by a process that is being run. As a developer, you can tie into an event to enable custom scripts to run, or to change the default behavior of an action or process. During this hour, we look at some of the different ways that you can use an event to extend your site when using jQuery Mobile.

Events for Page Initialization

When pages are initialized they go through three stages:

▶ Before page creation

▶ Page creation

▶ Page initialization

These stages all have an event that can be used to help you dynamically insert or manipulate code.

Let's start at the first event you can use during the page initialization process.

Using the `pagebeforecreate` Event

The `pagebeforecreate` event is used when you have content that you want modified before jQuery Mobile has had a chance to lock in and write the `data-roles` and attributes of page elements to the DOM. Listing 12.1 shows the content of pagebeforecreate.html, which is a file that contains a list that will be modified during the `pagebeforecreate` event.

LISTING 12.1   Using `pagebeforecreate` to Dynamically Add an Attribute

```
 1: <!DOCTYPE html>
 2: <html>
 3:    <head>
 4:       <title>Developing with jQuery Mobile</title>
 5:       <meta name="viewport" content="width=device-width, initial-scale=1">
 6:       <link rel="stylesheet"
href="http://code.jquery.com/mobile/1.1.0/jquery.mobile-1.1.0.min.css" />
 7:       <script src="http://code.jquery.com/jquery-1.7.1.min.js"></script>
 8:       <script>
 9:         $(document).on('pagebeforecreate', function(event) {
10:            $(".modify").attr('data-inset','true');
11:         });
12:       </script>
13:       <script
src="http://code.jquery.com/mobile/1.1.0/jquery.mobile-1.1.0.min.js"></script>
14:    </head>
15:    <body>
16:       <div data-role="page" id="home">
17:         <div data-role="header"><h1>pagebeforecreate event</h1></div>
18:         <div data-role="content">
19:           <p>The following list will be inset during the pagebeforecreate
event</p>
20:           <ul class="modify" data-role="listview">
21:             <li>A</li>
22:             <li>B</li>
23:             <li>C</li>
24:           </ul>
25:         </div>
26:       </div>
27:    </body>
28: </html>
```

The file starts out as a standard HTML file that uses jQuery Mobile, but on line 8 we see the start of a `script` element. Line 9 contains some jQuery code that is used to bind the `pagebeforecreate` event to the document. This is done by using the `.on()` function that is available when using jQuery 1.7+. Line 10 shows that when the `pagebeforecreate` event runs it searches for any elements that have an attribute of `class="modify"` and applies an attribute of `data-inset="true"` to any that are found by using the `.attr()` function. Line 11 ends the `.on()` function, and line 12 closes the `script` element.

Because the `pagebeforecreate` event runs before the page code is added to the DOM, jQuery Mobile sees the `data-inset="true"` attribute and styles it as an inset list. Figure 12.1 shows what the page looks like when loaded on a mobile browser.

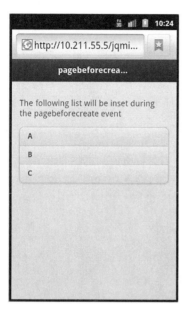

FIGURE 12.1
The list has been changed to an inset list during the `beforepageload` event.

If you want to see the list without the changes made on the `beforepageload` event, remove lines 8-12 and reload the page. The list will then be created as a standard list.

Let's move on to the next stage in the page initialization stage, page creation.

Using the `pagecreate` Event

The `pagecreate` event can be used either to apply your own widgets or to use the built-in widget or plug-in controls that jQuery Mobile provides. Listing 12.2 shows the contents of pagecreate.html. This file uses the `pagecreate` event to apply the `listview` plug-in to style a list on the page.

LISTING 12.2 Using the **`pagecreate`** Event in Conjunction with the `listview` Plug-In

```
1: <!DOCTYPE html>
2: <html>
3:   <head>
4:     <title>Developing with jQuery Mobile</title>
5:     <meta name="viewport" content="width=device-width, initial-scale=1">
6:     <link rel="stylesheet"
href="http://code.jquery.com/mobile/1.1.0/jquery.mobile-1.1.0.min.css" />
7:     <script src="http://code.jquery.com/jquery-1.7.1.min.js"></script>
```

```
8:      <script>
9:        $(document).on('pagecreate', function(event) {
10:          $(".modify").attr('data-inset','true').listview();
11:        });
12:      </script>
13:      <script
src="http://code.jquery.com/mobile/1.1.0/jquery.mobile-1.1.0.min.js"></script>
14:    </head>
15:    <body>
16:      <div data-role="page" id="home">
17:        <div data-role="header"><h1>pagecreate event</h1></div>
18:        <div data-role="content">
19:          <p>The following list will be styled during the pagecreate event</p>
20:          <ul class="modify">
21:            <li>A</li>
22:            <li>B</li>
23:            <li>C</li>
24:          </ul>
25:        </div>
26:      </div>
27:    </body>
28: </html>
```

The code starts out as a standard page using jQuery Mobile, and on line 9 you can see that the
.on() function is using the pagecreate event to run the code on line 10. The code on line 10
shows a selector that finds any element on the page that has a class="modify" attribute and
then adds an attribute of data-inset="true". After that has been done you can see that a
function called listview() is being run. This function is known as the listview plug-in and
is used to apply the styles and markup for a list. Line 11 then closes the .on() function, which
is the binding to the pagecreate event.

Looking down at line 20 we can see a ul element that contains only an attribute of
class="modify". The data-role="listview" attribute is not present, and neither is the
data-inset="true" attribute. Figure 12.2 shows that even with the missing attributes, the
script that runs during the pagecreate event will apply the necessary styles to make the ul
element an inset list.

It is important to note that the listview plug-in cannot be called during the pagebeforecreate event. It must be called after you have applied any data attributes or classes that you want
parsed. If you call a widget or plug-in before you call the .attr() function or similar functions,
the widget or plug-in will not parse the additional data and it will be skipped.

The next event during page initialization is pageinit.

FIGURE 12.2
You may use widgets or plug-ins, such as the `listview` plug-in, during the `pagecreate` event.

Using the `pageinit` Event

The `pageinit` event is best described and used as you would use the `$(document).ready()` function of jQuery. This event is triggered after the DOM has been loaded and all widgets and plug-ins have been run. This event also is triggered whenever a page is loaded either directly or through the AJAX call of another page. This event is triggered only once when included in the DOM. Listing 12.3 shows the contents of pageinit.html, which gives an example of the page-init event in action.

LISTING 12.3   Using `pageinit` When Loading the Second Page

```
1:  <!DOCTYPE html>
2:  <html>
3:    <head>
4:      <title>Developing with jQuery Mobile</title>
5:      <meta name="viewport" content="width=device-width, initial-scale=1">
6:      <link rel="stylesheet"
href="http://code.jquery.com/mobile/1.1.0/jquery.mobile-1.1.0.min.css" />
7:      <script src="http://code.jquery.com/jquery-1.7.1.min.js"></script>
8:      <script>
9:        $(document).on('pageinit','#away' function(event) {
10:          alert("The pageinit event has been run");
11:        });
```

```
12:      </script>
13:      <script
src="http://code.jquery.com/mobile/1.1.0/jquery.mobile-1.1.0.min.js"></script>
14:    </head>
15:    <body>
16:      <div data-role="page" id="home">
17:        <div data-role="header"><h1>pageinit event</h1></div>
18:        <div data-role="content">
19:          <p>I am the #home page</p>
20:          <a href="#away" data-role="button">Go Away</a>
21:        </div>
22:      </div>
23:      <div data-role="page" id="away">
24:        <div data-role="header"><h1>pageinit event</h1></div>
25:        <div data-role="content">
26:          <p>
27:            I am the #away page. The pageinit event runs on first page load.
28:          </p>
29:          <a href="#home" data-role="button">Go Back</a>
30:        </div>
31:      </div>
32:    </body>
33: </html>
```

The initial page setup should be familiar by now. Starting at line 8 you can see the same method is employed to bind the pageinit event as was used to bind the pagebeforecreate and pagecreate events. The difference of course is on lines 9 and 10 where a selector for an element with an id="away" is used in the .on() function to bind an alert() function that will only run on the page with that selector when it is first loaded into the DOM.

Continuing down the code you can see that a page has been set up with a div element using the data-role="page" attribute on line 16. The page continues down to line 22. Another page has been set up on line 23 and continues down to line 31. Each of these pages has been given an id, and a button that uses the id to link to and load the other page.

When the button is clicked on the first page for the first time, the pageinit event will fire and launch the alert() function from line 10. When you use the button to go back to the first page and then click to return to the second, the event will not be triggered a second time. This is because it is still part of the DOM and has already been run. However, if you manually reload the second page, the pageinit event will also be triggered as soon as the page is loaded. The event will then not be triggered again until another manual page refresh.

Figure 12.3 is a screenshot of the alert() function running in a mobile browser when triggered for the first time during the pageinit event. Remember that when using the alert function, the way the alert is displayed is determined by the browser. If your alert message doesn't look exactly like the one in Figure 12.3, it doesn't necessarily mean that anything is broken, just that you are using a different browser or device.

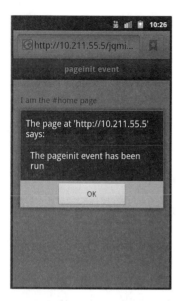

FIGURE 12.3
As seen on the stock browser of Android 2.3, the `alert()` function runs only once during the `pagecreate` event.

Brushing Up on Touch Events

Whenever users interact by touch with your site they are triggering touch events. You can tap (pardon the pun) into these events to run custom functions.

Using Tap Events

The main difference between a `click` and `touchstart` event is about 300ms. While that may not seem like a lot of time, an almost 1/3 of a second delay can make your mobile site or application feel slow and unresponsive. While the `tap` event is used by default on links, lists, and similar jQuery Mobile plug-ins and widgets, you can use the `tap` event to trigger custom functions on different elements on your page.

You can also use the `taphold` event on your pages. This event waits for almost an entire second before it is triggered. Listing 12.4 shows the contents of tap_events.html where both a `tap` and `taphold` event are being used on an image.

LISTING 12.4   Using the `tap` and `taphold` Events

```
1: <!DOCTYPE html>
2: <html>
3:   <head>
```

```
4:       <title>Developing with jQuery Mobile</title>
5:       <meta name="viewport" content="width=device-width, initial-scale=1">
6:       <link rel="stylesheet"
href="http://code.jquery.com/mobile/1.1.0/jquery.mobile-1.1.0.min.css" />
7:       <script src="http://code.jquery.com/jquery-1.7.1.min.js"></script>
8:       <script>
9:         $(document).on("pageinit", function(){
10:          $("#home").on('tap', '#image', function(event, ui) {
11:            var tapCaption = $(this).data("tap");
12:            $("#caption").addClass("comment").html(tapCaption);
13:          });
14:          $("#home").on('taphold','#caption', function(event, ui) {
15:            var $this = $(this);
16:            var tapholdCaption = $this.data("appTaphold");
17:            $this.html(tapholdCaption);
18:          });
19:        });
20:     </script>
21:     <script
src="http://code.jquery.com/mobile/1.1.0/jquery.mobile-1.1.0.min.js"></script>
22:     <style type="text/css">
23:        img {max-width: 100%}
24:        .comment {background: #FFF;border-radius: 5px;
border: 2px solid #000;padding: 5px}
25:     </style>
26:   </head>
27:   <body>
28:     <div data-role="page" id="home">
29:       <div data-role="header"><h1>Tap Events</h1></div>
30:       <div data-role="content">
31:         <p>Tap or tap-and-hold the image below.</p>
32:         <img id="image" src="river.jpg" alt="An image of a river"
data-tap="You tapped the picture, try tap-and-holding on this caption"  />
33:         <div id="caption"
data-app-taphold="This picture was taken during a flood.">Caption</div>
34:       </div>
35:     </div>
36:   </body>
37: </html>
```

The `tap` and `taphold` events must be bound in either the `document.ready()` function or inside the `pageinit` event. Since we already know that using the `document.ready()` function is not recommended for use with jQuery Mobile, line 9 shows that we are binding the `pageinit` event using the `.on()` function. Inside the function on line 10, you can see the `.on()` function attaching the `tap` event to an element with an attribute of `id="image"`. Lines 11 and 12 show the code that will run when the `tap` event is triggered. Line 11 shows a variable being created containing the value of what has been placed in the `data-tap` attribute of the element containing an attribute of `id="image"`. This is done by using the `$(this)` selector, which refers to the value of the original selector that is used on line 10. The function `.data("tap")` is used to check for an attribute of "data-tap". Line 12 shows a selector being used to find the element that contains an attribute of `id="caption"`. This element will then be given another attribute of `class="comment"`, and will also have the contents changed to the value of the `tapCaption` variable. Line 13 closes the `.on()` function.

Line 14 shows the use the `.on()` function to bind the `taphold` event to the element with a property of `id="caption"`. Those using jQuery Mobile 1.0 or lower should know that the `.live()` function is not compatible with the `taphold` event, and the `.bind()` function must be used instead.

If you haven't played with jQuery very much, line 15 may look a little odd. Every time a selector is used, it takes up extra space in memory, and jQuery is forced to parse the entire DOM to find the element. To save on both speed and memory, the selector we are currently using is set to a variable that can be reused.

Line 16 shows another variable being set up that contains the content of the `data-app-taphold` attribute. In general, it is a wise idea to stay away from using more than one dash in your code; however I've left an example of how to select data from a custom data attribute if there is absolutely no other way around it. Remember that when using the `.data()` function, anything after the first dash will be merged in CamelCase with the words before it. This means that the value of `data-app-taphold` is referenced by passing `appTaphold` to the `.data()` function. For more information on the `.data()` function visit http://api.jquery.com/data/.

On line 17 we set the contents of the element with an attribute of `id="caption"` (that is what is stored in the `$this` variable) to the value of the `tapholdCaption` variable. Line 18 then closes our `.on()` function to the `taphold` event, and line 19 closes the `.on()` function to the `pageinit` event.

Continuing down to lines 22-25 you can see that a `style` element has been set up and contains the styles for keeping the image scalable for mobile devices, as well as the styles that will be used with elements containing `class="comment"`.

Moving into the code that contains our mobile page you can see on line 32 that the `img` element has been given the `id="image"` attribute. This is what will have the `tap` event bound to it. Line 33 shows a `div` element containing an attribute of `id="caption"`. This element will have the `taphold` event bound to it, and will also have the contents changed during both `tap` and `taphold` events.

Figure 12.4 shows the page rendered in a browser after the `tap` event has been triggered.

FIGURE 12.4
The `tap` event has been called changing the text and visual style of the caption.

Another series of events similar to `tap` events are `swipe` events. Let's take a look at how to use them.

Using Swipe Events

Swiping at your mobile device is common when moving through image galleries, deleting email, bringing up contact information, and more. With jQuery Mobile you can tap into three swipe events: `swipe`, `swipeleft`, and `swiperight`. A `swipe` is similar to a click-and-drag action on a computer. For any of the swipe events to trigger, the touch must travel more than 30px horizontally and take less than 1 second to complete. It also may not move more than 20px vertically or the event trigger will be cancelled. Listing 12.5 shows the contents of the file swipe_events.html, which shows the use of the `swipe`, `swipeleft`, and the `swiperight` events.

LISTING 12.5 Using the **`swipe`, `swipeleft`, and `swiperight`** Events

```
1: <!DOCTYPE html>
2: <html>
3:   <head>
4:     <title>Developing with jQuery Mobile</title>
5:     <meta name="viewport" content="width=device-width, initial-scale=1">
6:     <link rel="stylesheet"
href="http://code.jquery.com/mobile/1.1.0/jquery.mobile-1.1.0.min.css" />
7:     <script src="http://code.jquery.com/jquery-1.7.1.min.js"></script>
```

```
 8:      <script>
 9:        $(document).on('pageinit', function() {
10:          $("#home").on('swipe','#swipe', function(event, ui) {
11:            $("#caption").html("Swipe detected!");
12:          });
13:          $("#home").on('swipeleft','#swipe-box', function(event, ui) {
14:            $("#caption").html("Swipe to the left detected!");
15:          });
16:          $("#home").on('swiperight','#swipe-box', function(event, ui) {
17:            $("#caption").html("Swipe to the right detected!");
18:          });
19:        });
20:      </script>
21:      <script
src="http://code.jquery.com/mobile/1.1.0/jquery.mobile-1.1.0.min.js"></script>
22:      <style type="text/css">
23:        #swipe-box {width: 200px;height: 200px;background: #FFF;
border: 2px solid #000}
24:        .comment {background: #FFF;border-radius: 5px;border: 2px solid #000;
padding: 5px}
25:      </style>
26:    </head>
27:    <body>
28:      <div data-role="page" id="home">
29:        <div data-role="header"><h1>Swipe Events</h1></div>
30:        <div data-role="content">
31:          <p id="swipe">Take a swipe this text or at the box below.</p>
32:          <div id="swipe-box"></div>
33:          <br />
34:          <div id="caption" class="comment">Waiting for swipe...</div>
35:        </div>
36:      </div>
37:    </body>
38: </html>
```

Starting at line 9 you can see that the pageinit event is being bound using the .on() function. On line 10 you can see the selector that finds the element on the page with id="swipe" as an attribute and then the binding of the swipe event to it. Line 11 shows what the swipe event will do when triggered. It finds the element with the id="caption" attribute and changes the text content of the element to "Swipe detected!".

Line 13 shows the swipeleft event being bound to an element with an attribute of id="swipe-box". Line 14 shows that when the swipeleft event is triggered, the element with an attribute of id="caption" will have its content changed to "Swipe to the left detected!"

Line 16 shows the `swiperight` event being bound to the same element that the `swipeleft` event was bound to. You can bind both of these events to the same element to trigger different functions based on user interaction. Line 17 shows that when the `swiperight` event is triggered, the content inside the element with the attribute of `id="caption"` will be changed to "Swipe to the right detected!".

NOTE

Using `swipe` **Versus** `swipeleft` **and** `swiperight`

The `swipe` event works for swipes made in either direction; however, if the `swipeleft` and/or `swiperight` events are bound to the same object that the `swipe` event is, the `swipe` event will be overwritten and not run. Double-check your event bindings to make sure you are not overwriting your `swipe` events.

Lines 28-36 show the markup used to create the page. Line 31 shows the element that will have the `swipe` event bound to it. Line 32 shows the element that the `swipeleft` and `swiperight` events are bound to. Even though the element looks empty, it will be styled with CSS into a rather sizeable square that can be used for swiping. Figure 12.5 shows the page rendered on a mobile browser.

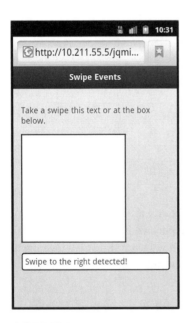

FIGURE 12.5
The `swiperight` event has been triggered changing the caption text.

Looking at Virtual Mouse Events

The virtual mouse events are an answer to compatibility problems between mobile and desktop browsers. For example, some mobile browsers support an event called touchstart, while other mobile browsers do not. Desktop browsers support the mousemove event and have support for hover through the use of the mouseover event while mobile devices have a hard time emulating or using the correct event. These problems are solved in jQuery Mobile by using virtual mouse events. When a page is loaded with jQuery Mobile, the browser is checked for event support. Events are then supported based on the virtual mouse events. While this happens in the background, you can bind virtual mouse events to run specific functions, or even to get data that can be used in other functions.

The virtual mouse events that are available are

- ▶ vmouseover
- ▶ vmousedown
- ▶ vmousemove

- ▶ vmouseup
- ▶ vclick
- ▶ vmousecancel

Listing 12.6 shows a snippet of code taken from vmouse_events.html. This snippet shows the vmousedown, vmousemove, and the vmouseover events being bound on a page.

LISTING 12.6   Using the **vmousedown, vmousemove, and vmouseover** Events

```
 1: <script>
 2:   $(document).on('pageinit', function() {
 3:     $(".sub-nav").hide();
 4:     $("#home").on('vmousedown','#hover-nav', function(e) {
 5:       $("#debug").prepend("vmousedown: x: "+e.pageX+" y: "+e.pageY+"<br />");
 6:     });
 7:     $("#home").on('vmousemove','#hover-nav', function(e) {
 8:       $("#debug").prepend("vmousemove: x: "+e.pageX+" y: "+e.pageY+"<br />");
 9:     });
10:     $("#home").on('vmouseover','#hover-nav', function(e) {
11:       $("#debug").prepend("vmouseover: x: "+e.pageX+" y: "+e.pageY+"<br />");
12:       $(".sub-nav").show();
13:     });
14:   });
15: </script>
```

Just like swipe events, virtual mouse events need to run inside the pageinit event. Line 2 binds the pageinit event by using the .on() function. Line 3 is a line of jQuery script that searches the DOM for any element with an attribute of class="sub-nav" and removes it from view. Line 4 shows the vmousedown being bound to the element with an attribute of id="hover-nav", as well as passing the event object (shown as the variable e) through the anonymous function that is used as a callback. Line 5 shows the .prepend() function besing used on a selector for the element with an attribute of id="debug". Inside the .prepend() function is some text that details what is happening during the vmousedown event. Virtual mouse events carry data about where they are triggered; we are displaying that data by using .pageX and .pageY on the event object (variable e) that was passed through the anonymous function. Line 6 closes the .on() function that we are using to bind the vmousedown event.

Line 7-9 are similar to lines 4-6. On line 7, vmousemove is bound to the same element that vmousedown was bound to. Also just like the code for the vmousedown event found on line 4, the event object (shown as the variable e) being passed through the anonymous function which will allow the code on line 8 to run as a callback. Line 8 shows the same element with the attribute of id="debug" getting some text added to it by use of the .prepend() function. Line 9 closes out the .on() function that we are using to bind vmousemove.

Lines 10-13 are also similar to the previous lines. Line 10 shows that the same selector that was used for binding vmousedown and vmousemove is used again with the .on() function to bind vmouseover. Line 11 shows that once again the element with an attribute of id="debug" is going to get some text added to it by use of the .prepend() function. Line 12 shows a selector that will select any elements with an attribute of class="sub-nav" and make them visible by using the .show() function on them. Line 13 closes the .on() function that is being used to bind vmouseover, and line 14 closes out the .on() function that is used to bind pageinit to the page.

The code shown behaves a little differently on desktops than it does on a mobile device. On a mobile device, vmouseover is triggered when the area that has been bound to it is tapped. The vmousemove event is triggered when the screen is swiped (but before the swipe event is triggered). The mousedown event also is triggered whenever the screen is tapped.

Figure 12.6 shows the file vmouse_events.html being run in a mobile browser. A few events have been triggered so that you see the output from the code.

When using virtual mouse events, the jQuery Mobile team gives a warning about using the vclick event. While it does work, there are instances where the element or object clicked may shift, move, or be incorrectly calculated. This can cause frustration during development and especially for end users when they are interacting with it. It is suggested that you use a plain click event instead.

The vmouseup and vmousecancel events work in as close to the same manner as the mouseup and mousecancel events in JavaScript work. The differences are tied to the user tapping instead of clicking.

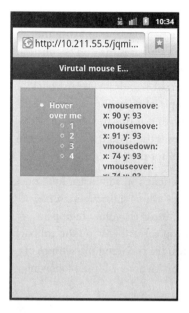

FIGURE 12.6
The area on the left has been bound to a few virtual mouse events. The area on the right displays the output of the events being triggered.

Adapting to the Orientation Event

When viewing a mobile device, there are two options or modes for screen orientation. When a page is viewed in portrait, it means that the height of the screen is greater than the width of the screen. When a page is viewed in landscape, the width of the screen is greater than the height of the screen.

Unless the device is locked into one viewing mode, the screen can be rotated and content shifted dynamically to make use of the extra space. While jQuery Mobile handles the resize of many of your elements, you may want to trigger a custom function whenever a screen change is detected.

Listing 12.7 shows a snippet of code used to bind the `orientationchange` event to a page and run code when it is triggered.

LISTING 12.7 Using the `orientationchange` Event

```
1: $(document).on('pageinit', function() {
2:   $(window).on('orientationchange', function(e) {
3:     $("#mode").html('orientation is currently '+e.orientation);
4:   });
5: });
```

The `orientationchange` event needs to run inside either the `$(document).ready()` function or the `pageinit` event. Line 1 shows that we are binding the `pageinit` event with the `.on()` function. Line 2 starts with a selector for the `window` object and uses the `.on()` function to attach the `orientationchange` event to the window. The event object (variable e) is passed to the anonymous function and contains a property called `orientation` that will pass back a value of either "landscape" or "portrait". Line 3 gives an example of using the event object (variable e)and the `orientation` property by showing the value of it inside the element with an attribute of `id="mode"` when the event is triggered. Line 4 closes the `.on()` function for the `orientationchange` event, and line 5 closes the `.on()` function for the `pageinit` event.

As a failsafe, devices that do not support the use of `window.orientation` will instead fall back to the `resize` event. Some developers have reported a timing issue where the `orientationchange` event fires before the screen has actually rotated, causing incorrect values to appear or causing the event to not function as desired. To get around this you can either wrap the callback function you are using in the `setTimeout()` function, or you can try changing the settings of jQuery Mobile to not use the `orientationchange` event. This can be done with the following snippet:

```
$.mobile.orientationChangeEnabled = false;
```

Figures 12.7 and 12.8 show a page with the snippet of code from Listing 12.7 running in landscape and portrait modes.

FIGURE 12.7
A mobile page using the `orienationchange` event in portrait

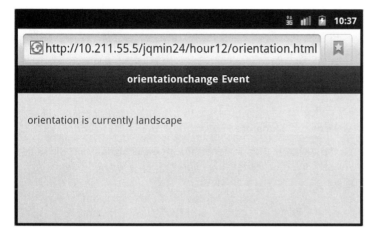

FIGURE 12.8
A mobile page using the `orientationchange` event in landscape

If you are using the `orientationchange` event to trigger a change in your styles, I suggest that you consider the use of CSS3 media queries instead.

Summary

This hour covered several of the events available when using jQuery Mobile. You should now have a good idea of how to tie into an event and when it will run. You saw that many events rely on the use of the `pageinit` event.

You learned about the use of touch events including `tap`, `taphold`, `swipe`, `swipeleft`, and `swiperight`. You also learned about the virtual mouse events and how they can be used to normalize event handling between desktop and mobile browsers.

Q&A

Q. Is it possible to use a hover on a mobile device?

A. Not exactly. Because a hover is similar to a `mouseover` event, it can be triggered. However, when your finger is removed from the screen the virtual mouse will also be removed making the code running in the `mouseover` event no longer function. You can create a pseudo-hover by attaching a `vmouseover` event to an element and then assigning another `vmouseover` event to every other element in the DOM that will close, cancel, or complete the code from the first `vmouseover`. This is an expensive and somewhat clumsy solution, but it is possible.

Q. So I can't use the `$(document).ready()` or `$(function() {})` on my mobile pages?

A. You can, but it's not recommended. Remember that because jQuery Mobile runs your site through AJAX, the only page that will execute your `$(document).ready()` function will be the first page. If that is the behavior you are expecting, then go for it. Although you will be miles better off by planning ahead and using the `pageinit` event, especially if you plan on growing your application or site.

Q. Will the screen orientation work on a desktop browser?

A. Yes, it does actually work on the desktop. This is done through a calculation that runs during the `resize` event. When the screen is resized the current width and height are compared, and the event will trigger based on the window size.

Workshop

The workshop contains a quiz and some exercises to help you check your comprehension and understanding.

Quiz

1. During page initialization, what three stages does a page go through?

2. What is the time difference in processing between a touch and click event?

3. How do you bind the `pageinit` event to a specific page?

4. What virtual mouse events are available with jQuery Mobile?

5. True or False: The `swipe` event will be triggered for screen swipes to both the left and the right.

Answers

1. Before page creation, page creation, and page initialization.

2. There is roughly a 300ms difference between a click event and a touch event.

3. When you create your page container using `data-role="page"`, you also need to make sure that it has an `id` attribute set. The `.live()` function is then used on the `id` through a selector to bind the `pageinit` event to it.

4. The virtual mouse events that are accessible are `vmouseover`, `vmousedown`, `vmouse-move`, `vmouseup`, `vclick`, and `vmousecancel`.

5. True. You can use the `swipeleft` and `swiperight` events when you want to tie specific functions to a swipe in a specific direction.

Exercises

1. Using the example code for page events, try adding some new elements to your page. Explore adding them during different stages of the page load and see whether they were styled as expected.

2. Build a page that uses swipe events. Make two functions and trigger them with the `swipeleft` and `swiperight` events.

3. Build a function that runs during the `orientationchange` event. Try adding a function that changes the classes applied to elements on your page depending on what orientation the device is currently. Test it out on a desktop browser and a mobile browser.

HOUR 13

Changing the Default Theme

What You'll Learn in This Hour:

▶ How the theme framework is used

▶ How to load your own theme

▶ How to apply different swatches to elements

▶ How to customize and create swatches

While the default styles of jQuery Mobile already look fantastic, you may want to change them to match your brand. The theme system in jQuery Mobile is modular and flexible enough to allow you to present your site with the unique colors and styles that give users your branded experience instead of a generic one size fits all.

Learning About the Theme Framework

As you have noticed when using jQuery Mobile, a set of styles is applied to elements by default. The styles applied are part of the theme framework. The theme framework uses a combination of CSS2 and CSS3 styles to apply all the formatting as well as rounded corners, shadows, and gradients for backgrounds without loading extra images. This helps save on file size allowing the client browser to add most of the special effects used instead of forcing the browser to download multiple static images.

The theme framework is a powerful part of the jQuery Mobile system and allows you to easily create multiple color schemes and even new icon sets with minimal effort. Let's take a look at how you can leverage the theme framework.

Using Icons and Classes

Even though CSS3 is in use and helps reduce file size, some static assets are still used. They have been put together into a minimum amount of files that are downloaded only when needed. Currently the default theme uses five static image files:

► ajax-loader.png—This is the animated loader or spinner.

► icons-18-white.png—This sprite contains 22 white icons.

► icons-18-black.png—This sprite contains 22 black icons.

► icons-36-white.png—This sprite contains 22 high-res white icons.

► icons-36-black.png—This sprite contains 22 high-res black icons.

The file ajax-loader.png is the spinner or loader image that appears when pages are being loaded through AJAX. The image dimension is 35×35 pixels and is downloaded by the browser on page load.

The files icons-18-white.png and icons-18-black.png are sprite files. They are horizontal sprites that measure 776×18 pixels each. They contain 22 icons or images that are 18×18 pixels separated by an 18-pixel space. Most of the icons found in this file do not take up the full 18×18 pixel space. This is because a circular disc is applied through CSS as a background to help the icons maintain visibility on whatever object they are placed. Each image has between 2 and 4 pixels of empty space around the edges to make room for the disc.

The files icons-36-white.png and icons-36-black.png are also sprite images, and they contain the same images as the other two sprite files. The difference here is that the icons contained in these sprites are 36×36 pixel images with a 36-pixel space between them that is used for high-resolution displays, like those with Retina™ displays. These high-resolution icons are loaded only on devices that support them, so you do not need to worry about wasting mobile bandwidth on devices that cannot use them. This is done through the following snippet that checks for device compliance:

```
@media only screen and (-webkit-min-device-pixel-ratio: 1.5),
  only screen and (min--moz-device-pixel-ratio: 1.5),
  only screen and (min-resolution: 240dpi) {}
```

If the device viewing the page does not meet the requirements of the media query, then any code inside it is skipped and not loaded.

Figure 13.1 shows the images included with jQuery Mobile so you can see what each file looks like.

Now that we've discussed the default images used in the theme framework, let's discuss the classes that can be applied to invoke different swatches from the theme.

Swatches are a set of defined styles that can be applied when using a theme. By default five swatches are included with jQuery Mobile. You can change the default swatch used for an entire page by including an attribute of data-theme with the value set to the swatch you want loaded. When the page loads, every component except the header and footer will have that swatch color scheme applied to it. Listing 13.1 shows a snippet of code from the file single_swatch.html that demonstrates using a single swatch for an entire page.

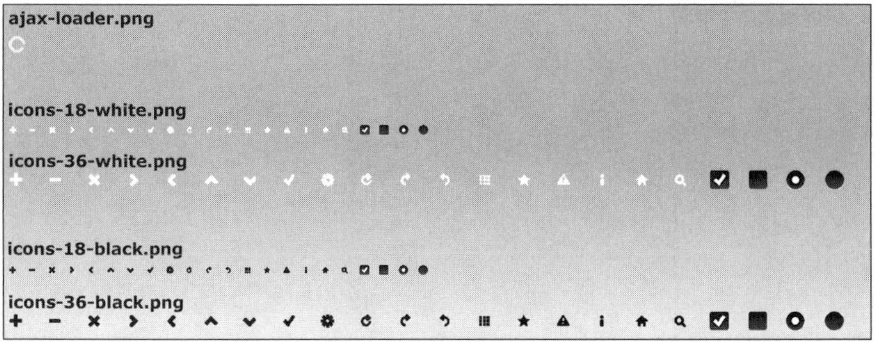

FIGURE 13.1
These files are included with jQuery Mobile by default. They have been placed on a colored background for visibility.

LISTING 13.1   Using a Single Swatch on a Page

```
 1: <div data-role="page" data-theme="b">
 2:   <div data-role="header"><h1>Single Swatch</h1></div>
 3:   <div data-role="content">
 4:     <p>Look at the button!</p>
 5:     <a href="#" data-role="button">I am a button</a>
 6:     <ul data-role="listview" data-inset="true">
 7:       <li>List Item 1</li>
 8:       <li>List Item 2</li>
 9:       <li>List Item 3</li>
10:     </ul>
11:   </div>
12: </div>
```

Line 1 shows the standard markup for setting up a page; however, an attribute of data-theme="b" has been added. This attribute will change the applied swatch for the entire page. It will not, however, change the swatch for the header and footer. To change those you must include the data-theme attribute separately. We discuss the swatches in greater detail later in this hour, but for now you should know that swatches are referenced by a single letter designation. The value of b that is passed into the data-theme attribute designates the second swatch of the theme. By taking the code from Listing 13.1 and changing the value in the data-theme attribute, you can see how the theme affects the different components on the page when rendered in a browser. Figure 13.2 shows this page rendered in a mobile browser.

FIGURE 13.2
A page using the b swatch

While the page looks good using a different swatch, there may be times where you have a special page or a dialog page that you need to use only a certain part of a swatch. For this you can
use classes to style individual elements. Listing 13.2 shows a snippet of code from class_swatch.
html where a few elements use different swatches by including different class values on some
elements.

LISTING 13.2   Specifying the Swatch Used on Elements by Class Attribute Value

```
 1: <div data-role="page">
 2:   <div data-role="header"><h1>Class Swatch</h1></div>
 3:   <div data-role="content" class="ui-body-a">
 4:     <p>The body or content area is using class="ui-body-a"</p>
 5:     <a href="#" data-role="button" class="ui-btn-up-e">class="ui-btn-up-e"</a>
 6:     <ul data-role="listview" data-inset="true" class="ui-bar-d">
 7:       <li>This list</li>
 8:       <li>is using</li>
 9:       <li>class="ui-bar-d"</li>
10:     </ul>
11:   </div>
12: </div>
```

Starting at the top you can see that both the page and the header sections do not have a data-
theme attribute used, so theme defaults will be used on these sections. Line 3 shows the content

section with an attribute of `class="ui-body-a"`. This will style the content section with the a swatch. Line 4 is content that will inherit the same swatch style from the content section. Line 5 shows a link with an attribute of `data-role="button"` that will turn it into a button. It also contains an attribute of `class="ui-btn-up-e"`. This will change the default style of the button to use the styles from the e swatch. Line 6 shows a `ul` element that contains an attribute of `data-role="listview"` that will change the list to appear as a jQuery Mobile list. It also contains the attribute `data-inset="true"` that will give the list rounded corners and add some margin and padding to the list. The list also has `class="ui-bar-d"` applied to it that will change the default swatch applied to the d swatch.

Take a look at Figure 13.3 to see what the page looks like when displayed using classes to change the swatch used on various components.

FIGURE 13.3
Using classes to change the swatches used on a page

While only a few classes were used, you can customize just about every facet of the base jQuery Mobile styles by overwriting classes like the following:

▶ `ui-bar-(a-z)`

▶ `ui-body-(a-z)`

▶ `ui-btn-up-(a-z)`

▶ `ui-btn-down-(a-z)`

▶ ui-btn-active

▶ ui-corner-all

▶ ui-br

▶ ui-icon

▶ ui-icon-alt

▶ ui-overlay

▶ ui-shadow

To see all the classes that you can use, open the noncompressed or minified CSS file that is part of the jQuery Mobile framework. This file has been commented and is really helpful when trying to create your own customized styles. Let's take a look at how to create our own styles and include them.

Applying a Custom Theme

Now that you know you are able to customize the styles of jQuery Mobile by using CSS classes, it is time to learn how to modify the default styles and even include your own. To do this you need to either edit the existing CSS file, or create your own and add it to the mobile page. Because I believe in using nondestructive methods when learning something new, we create a new CSS style sheet and add it to our page. Listing 13.3 shows the contents of custom_styles.css.

LISTING 13.3   A Custom Style Sheet That Overrides the Default Styles

```
 1: /* Straighten out the Top Right button corner */
 2: .ui-btn-corner-tr {
 3:    -moz-border-radius-topright: 0em;
 4:    -webkit-border-top-right-radius: 0em;
 5:    border-top-right-radius: 0em;
 6: }
 7: /* Straighten out the Bottom Left button corner */
 8: .ui-btn-corner-bl {
 9:    -moz-border-radius-bottomleft: 0em;
10:    -webkit-border-bottom-left-radius: 0em;
11:    border-bottom-left-radius: 0em;
12: }
13: /* Change the default shadow */
14: .ui-shadow {
15:    -moz-box-shadow: 2px 4px 3px rgba(0,0,0,.3);
16:    -webkit-box-shadow: 2px 4px 3px rgba(0,0,0,.3);
```

```
17:    box-shadow: 2px 4px 3px rgba(0,0,0,.3);
18:  }
19:  /* Change the default nav-bar */
20:  .ui-navbar {
21:     -moz-box-shadow: 0px 4px 7px rgba(0,0,0,.7);
22:     -webkit-box-shadow: 0px 4px 7px rgba(0,0,0,.7);
23:     box-shadow: 0px 4px 7px rgba(0,0,0,.7);
24:  }
25:  /* Change the default icon set */
26:  .ui-icon,
27:  .ui-icon-searchfield:after {
28:     background-image: url(icons-18-white-custom.png);
29:  }
```

Starting with line 1, you can see a comment that tells you what lines 2-6 are going to do. Those lines are going to remove the rounded corner from the top-right corner of any buttons that use this class. Note that it will not remove all the rounded corners from buttons, only ones that use this specific class. A look at lines 3 and 4 show styles being set up using browser-specific styles. Even though recent versions of both Firefox- and Webkit-based browsers support CSS3, these styles help with legacy browsers that have been embedded on mobile devices or with users who are unable to update to current versions. Line 5 shows the CSS3 style that will be used by any browser that supports it.

This same pattern is used throughout the file. A comment is placed to let you know what the class will do, and then each class is set up using browser-specific styles for Firefox and Webkit browsers as well as the CSS3 style for all other modern browsers.

One thing you should notice is that on line 28, a custom icon set is used. This file has been modified from the original that comes with jQuery Mobile. If you opt to use custom icons this way you can apply them to buttons using the same classes and data attributes that would apply the images normally. For example, if you wanted to use a custom home icon, you would use `data-icon="home"` and it would pull the custom icon from the spot where the home icon would normally be.

Figure 13.4 shows custom.html, which uses the custom style sheet including the custom icon set.

Let's take a look at how themes can be applied to different types of elements using jQuery Mobile.

FIGURE 13.4
Using custom styles and a custom icon set

Theming Site Components

You just learned that you can use classes to change various aspects of the theme of your site, but there are a few extra options that you can use when theming individual components. Some components also have a default setting that you should be aware of.

Buttons

Buttons automatically use the swatch that is assigned to the parent container. If you place a button in a content block that uses swatch b, then the button will use swatch b.

You can change this by using the data-theme attribute on the button directly to change what swatch it uses. The following one-line snippet shows the markup for changing a button theme using this method:

```
<a href="#" data-role="button" data-theme="e"></a>
```

Should be simple enough. Figure 13.5 shows two buttons on a page, one inheriting the swatch, and the other being set by the data-theme attribute.

FIGURE 13.5
Buttons either inherit the swatch, or can use one that is manually set.

Bars

Component bars include the header and footer sections of your page. By default they use the a swatch, but they can be changed to use any swatch you prefer by adding the `data-theme` attribute. The following one-line snippet shows a `div` element being used to create a header section that uses the `data-theme` attribute to change the swatch applied to it.

```
<div data-role="header" data-theme="e"><h1>Using the e swatch</h1></div>
```

Figure 13.6 shows a page with this snippet of code in it.

Content Blocks

Content block theming can be a little tricky. The jQuery Mobile team suggests that you do not apply a `data-theme` attribute directly to the content section of your page. This is because of the potential that the content section will not take up the entire viewable space of the page. When this happens the background applied cuts off abruptly leaving you with a page that appears broken. Instead you should apply the swatch you want used by using a data attribute on the element that contains the `data-role="page"` attribute.

FIGURE 13.6
A header using a specified swatch instead of the default swatch

Content blocks can also accept a second theme attribute, `data-content-theme`. This second theme attribute applies to content that is inside collapsible containers. It can also be applied to the element with the `data-role="page"` attribute and will be inherited by child elements. Listing 13.4 shows a snippet of code with a collapsible content area that is styled using the `data-theme` and `data-content-theme` attributes.

LISTING 13.4 Theming Content Blocks

```
 1: <div data-role="page" data-theme="b">
 2:   <div data-role="header"><h1>Custom Styles</h1></div>
 3:   <div data-role="content">
 4:     <div data-role="collapsible" data-collapsed="false" data-content-theme="e">
 5:       <h3>Different Swatch</h3>
 6:       <p>
 7:         This collapsed content area uses a different style for the collapsed
 8:         content than the rest of the page.
 9:       </p>
10:     </div>
11:   </div>
12: </div>
```

Line 1 shows the attribute of `data-theme="b"` added to the containing `div` element for the page. This will apply the b swatch to all the components on the page. Line 4 shows the use of `data-content-theme="e"` on a collapsible content area. By including this here, the collapsed content will use a different style.

Figure 13.7 shows what the page and collapsible content areas look like with the specified swatches being used.

FIGURE 13.7
The content area and collapsible area have specified swatches applied to them.

Switching the Swatches

We briefly talked about swatches and that jQuery Mobile includes five of them by default. We also used swatches to create mix-and-match styles on a page. Let's take a closer look at what swatches are and how to create our own.

Learning About Swatches

A swatch is a set of CSS rules that are applied whenever the swatch is used. The swatches are labeled using letters of the alphabet; the included five swatches are labeled a, b, c, d, and e. Each swatch has a different meaning when used. The first swatch, a, is considered the most important and contains the highest level of visual priority. The second swatch, b, is considered a secondary color, and the third swatch, c, is a neutral gray. The fourth swatch, d, is considered a secondary level color palette. The fifth swatch, e, is considered an accent swatch.

When modifying or creating your own themes you do not have to follow this same convention, but it does make for an easy-to-follow guide. Each theme can have up to 26 swatches, with each swatch using one letter of the alphabet. This allows you to create an extremely large amount of colors and options for your theme.

If you were to open up the default jQuery Mobile style sheet, you would see a few sections related to swatches. Each swatch section is labeled so that it is easy to find. Each section is also commented for readability and is roughly 135 lines long. To get you familiar with the swatch section, Listing 13.5 shows a 40-line snippet of the a swatch.

LISTING 13.5   The First 40 Lines of the a Swatch of jQuery Mobile

```
1: .ui-bar-a {
2:    border: 1px solid #2A2A2A /*{a-bar-border}*/;
3:    background: #111111 /*{a-bar-background-color}*/;
4:    color: #ffffff /*{a-bar-color}*/;
5:    font-weight: bold;
6:    text-shadow: 0 -1px 1px #000000;
7:    background-image: -webkit-gradient(linear, left top, left bottom,
from( #3c3c3c ), to( #111 )); /* Saf4+, Chrome */
8:    background-image: -webkit-linear-gradient(#3c3c3c, #111);
/* Chrome 10+, Saf5.1+ */
9:    background-image: -moz-linear-gradient(#3c3c3c, #111); /* FF3.6 */
10:    background-image: -ms-linear-gradient(#3c3c3c, #111); /* IE10 */
11:    background-image: -o-linear-gradient(#3c3c3c, #111); /* Opera 11.10+ */
12:    background-image: linear-gradient(#3c3c3c, #111);
13: }
14: .ui-bar-a,
15: .ui-bar-a input,
16: .ui-bar-a select,
17: .ui-bar-a textarea,
18: .ui-bar-a button {
19:    font-family: Helvetica, Arial, sans-serif;
20: }
21: .ui-bar-a .ui-link-inherit {
22:    color: #fff;
23: }
24:
```

```
25: .ui-bar-a .ui-link {
26:   color: #7cc4e7;
27:   font-weight: bold;
28: }
29:
30: .ui-bar-a .ui-link:hover {
31:   color: #2489CE;
32: }
33:
34: .ui-bar-a .ui-link:active {
35:   color: #2489CE;
36: }
37:
38: .ui-bar-a .ui-link:visited {
39:   color: #2489CE;
40: }
```

Since style sheets are not terribly new, you should be able to understand a good portion of what is going on. If you look at the class that is declared on line 1, you should recognize it as one of the classes that you can apply directly to an element to change the theme swatch. Lines 2-5 are standard CSS2 markup that set up the border, background, and text color that will be used when the class is applied. Line 6 shows the use of CSS3 to apply a `text-shadow` that will be centered on the x-axis, up 1 pixel on the y-axis (web browsers run the y-axis positive down and negative up), have a spread or radius of 1px, and have a shadow color of #000000. Lines 7-12 are also important to look over as they show the fallback support for browsers that do not support the CSS3 `linear-gradient`. Each of these lines has been commented so that you know which browser that line supports. The order that the styles are placed in makes the fallback support work, so if you are creating your own or modifying this swatch, make sure to keep the order there if you want the support for the listed browser.

Lines 14-18 give a good example of setting up multiple classes with the same settings. These particular lines are resetting all the classes to use the same `font-family`. Lines 21-40 show various nested classes being created and styled. If you were to open the full swatch style sheet you would see even more of these being created and used. All these styles help define and shape a swatch. Now that we've taken a peek at a swatch file, let's create our own.

Creating a Swatch

You have a few different options when it comes to creating a swatch. You can either modify an existing swatch, code one from scratch, or copy one and change the swatch letter and change the settings to something you'd prefer. One other option is also available that we cover in detail in Hour 16, "Rolling Your Own Theme with ThemeRoller."

To create our own swatch, we are going to copy one of the exisiting swatches and then modify the styles to be what we want. Listing 13.6 shows an entire swatch that was copied and then changed to be a custom swatch.

LISTING 13.6 Creating Custom Swatch

```
 1:  .ui-bar-f {
 2:     border: 1px solid #4a4a4a;
 3:     background: #333333;
 4:     color: #ffffff;
 5:     font-weight: bold;
 6:     text-shadow: 0 -1px 1px #000000;
 7:     background-image: -webkit-gradient(linear, left top, left bottom,
    from( #014D88), to( #111 )); /* Saf4+, Chrome */
 8:     background-image: -webkit-linear-gradient(#014D88, #111);
    /* Chrome 10+, Saf5.1+ */
 9:     background-image: -moz-linear-gradient(#014D88, #111); /* FF3.6 */
10:     background-image: -ms-linear-gradient(#014D88, #111); /* IE10 */
11:     background-image: -o-linear-gradient(#014D88, #111); /* Opera 11.10+ */
12:     background-image: linear-gradient(#014D88, #111);
13:  }
14:  .ui-bar-f,
15:  .ui-bar-f input,
16:  .ui-bar-f select,
17:  .ui-bar-f textarea,
18:  .ui-bar-f button {
19:     font-family: Helvetica, Arial, sans-serif;
20:  }
21:  .ui-bar-f .ui-link-inherit {
22:     color: #fff;
23:  }
24:  .ui-bar-f .ui-link {
25:     color: #F7E065;
26:     font-weight: bold;
27:  }
28:  .ui-bar-f .ui-link:hover {
29:     color: #FFFF7F;
30:  }
31:  .ui-bar-f .ui-link:active {
32:     color: #FFFF7F;
33:  }
34:  .ui-bar-f .ui-link:visited {
35:       color: #FFFF7F;
36:  }
37:  .ui-body-f,
38:  .ui-dialog.ui-overlay-f {
39:     border: 1px solid #3f3f3f;
```

```
40:     background: #444444;
41:     color: #fff;
42:      text-shadow: 0 1px 0 #000;
43:     font-weight: normal;
44:     background-image: -webkit-gradient(linear, left top, left bottom,
from( #0C8DD2 ), to( #014D88 )); /* Saf4+, Chrome */
45:     background-image: -webkit-linear-gradient(#0C8DD2, #014D88 );
/* Chrome 10+, Saf5.1+ */
46:     background-image: -moz-linear-gradient(#0C8DD2, #014D88); /* FF3.6 */
47:     background-image: -ms-linear-gradient(#0C8DD2, #014D88/); /* IE10 */
48:     background-image: -o-linear-gradient(#0C8DD2, #014D88); /* Opera 11.10+ */
49:     background-image: linear-gradient(#0C8DD2, #014D88);
50:   }
51:   .ui-body-f,
52:   .ui-body-f input,
53:   .ui-body-f select,
54:   .ui-body-f textarea,
55:   .ui-body-f button {
56:     font-family: Helvetica, Arial, sans-serif;
57:   }
58:   .ui-body-f .ui-link-inherit {
59:     color:   #fff;
60:   }
61:   .ui-body-f .ui-link {
62:     color: #FFFF7F;
63:     font-weight: bold;
64:   }
65:   .ui-body-f .ui-link:hover {
66:     color: #FFFF7F;
67:   }
68:   .ui-body-f .ui-link:active {
69:     color: #FFFF7F;
70:   }
71:   .ui-body-f .ui-link:visited {
72:       color: #FFFF7F;
73:   }
74:   .ui-btn-up-f {
75:     border: 1px solid #222;
76:     background: #065BDB;
77:     font-weight: bold;
78:     color: #fff;
79:     text-shadow: 0 -1px 1px #000;
80:     background-image: -webkit-gradient(linear, left top, left bottom,
from( #1065E4 ), to( #065BDB )); /* Saf4+, Chrome */
81:     background-image: -webkit-linear-gradient(#1065E4, #065BDB);
/* Chrome 10+, Saf5.1+ */
82:     background-image: -moz-linear-gradient(#1065E4, #065BDB); /* FF3.6 */
83:     background-image: -ms-linear-gradient(#1065E4, #065BDB); /* IE10 */
```

```
84:     background-image: -o-linear-gradient(#1065E4, #065BDB); /* Opera 11.10+ */
85:     background-image: linear-gradient(#1065E4, #065BDB);
86:   }
87:   .ui-btn-up-f a.ui-link-inherit {
88:     color: #fff/;
89:   }
90:   .ui-btn-hover-f {
91:     border: 1px solid 000;
92:     background: #444444;
93:     font-weight: bold;
94:     color: #fff;
95:     text-shadow: 0 -1px 1px #000;
96:     background-image: -webkit-gradient(linear, left top, left bottom,
from( #1A6FEF ), to( #1065E4 )); /* Saf4+, Chrome */
97:     background-image: -webkit-linear-gradient(#1A6FEF, #1065E4);
/* Chrome 10+, Saf5.1+ */
98:     background-image: -moz-linear-gradient(#1A6FEF, #1065E4); /* FF3.6 */
99:     background-image: -ms-linear-gradient(#1A6FEF, #1065E4); /* IE10 */
100:    background-image: -o-linear-gradient(#1A6FEF, #1065E4); /* Opera 11.10+ */
101:    background-image: linear-gradient(#1A6FEF, #1065E4);
102:  }
103:  .ui-btn-hover-f a.ui-link-inherit {
104:    color: #fff;
105:  }
106:  .ui-btn-down-f {
107:    border: 1px solid #014D88;
108:    background: #012E50;
109:    font-weight: bold;
110:    color: #fff;
111:    text-shadow: 0 -1px 1px #000;
112:    background-image: -webkit-gradient(linear, left top, left bottom,
from( #013B66), to( #0261A9 )); /* Saf4+, Chrome */
113:    background-image: -webkit-linear-gradient(#013B66, #0261A9/);
/* Chrome 10+, Saf5.1+ */
114:    background-image: -moz-linear-gradient(#013B66, #0261A9); /* FF3.6 */
115:    background-image: -ms-linear-gradient(#013B66, #0261A9); /* IE10 */
116:    background-image: -o-linear-gradient(#013B66, #0261A); /* Opera 11.10+ */
117:    background-image: linear-gradient(#013B66, #0261A9);
118:  }
119:  .ui-btn-down-f a.ui-link-inherit {
120:    color: #fff;
121:  }
122:  .ui-btn-up-f,
123:  .ui-btn-hover-f,
124:  .ui-btn-down-f {
125:    font-family: Helvetica, Arial, sans-serif;
126:    text-decoration: none;
127:  }
```

To create this new f swatch, the a swatch was copied and then modified. The fastest way to start the modification is to do a search-and-replace of the entire file for "-a" and replace it with a dash and the letter of the swatch you are creating. When performing a search and replace, make sure you do not replace -o, -m, -w, -g, -s, or -i, or you will either break your styles altogether or break the fallback support for other browsers.

Even though this listing is large, it is not actually that much work to customize the entire file. Each section contains several lines of fallback code meaning that once you have picked a color you can just copy and paste into the fallback sections. For example, lines 7-12 are the styles that will be applied to the ui-bar for several different browsers with each containing roughly the same values but with a different declaration. Lines 24-36 are the styles that will be applied to links that appear in any ui-bar sections on your mobile page. Since most links will want to retain the same link color, you can pick one color and use it on each section. Lines 44-49 are the background gradient colors for the ui-body section, again with fallback support. Lines 61-73 show the color setup for links that appear inside the ui-body section. Lines 74-127 all contain the setup for button states. Lines 74-89 contain the styles that will be applied to a button when it is normally displayed. Lines 90-105 show the styles that will be applied when a mouse is hovered over the button. Lines 106-121 show the styles that will be applied when the button is clicked or tapped. Lines 122-127 show the reset styles that will be applied to all button states.

Now that we have our swatch made, let's take a look at including it on a page.

Using Custom Swatches

You can continue to make swatches and import them into the jQuery Mobile style sheet, or your own custom style sheet. Then you can use the data-theme attribute or the various other theme classes to apply your custom styles to your page. Listing 13.7 shows the contents of custom_swatches.html, which has included the file custom_swatches.css that contains a couple of custom swatches that will be used on the page.

LISTING 13.7 Using Custom Swatches

```
 1: <!DOCTYPE html>
 2: <html>
 3:   <head>
 4:     <title>Developing with jQuery Mobile</title>
 5:     <meta name="viewport" content="width=device-width, initial-scale=1">
 6:     <link rel="stylesheet"
href="http://code.jquery.com/mobile/1.1.0/jquery.mobile-1.1.0.min.css" />
 7:     <link rel="stylesheet" href="custom_swatches.css" />
 8:     <script src="http://code.jquery.com/jquery-1.7.1.min.js"></script>
 9:     <script
src="http://code.jquery.com/mobile/1.1.0/jquery.mobile-1.1.0.min.js"></script>
10:   </head>
```

```
11:   <body>
12:     <div data-role="page" data-theme="f" id="page1">
13:       <div data-role="header"><h1>Custom swatch f</h1></div>
14:       <div data-role="content">
15:         <p>Use the button to change pages</p>
16:         <a href="#page2" data-role="button">Second Swatch</a>
17:         <ul data-role="listview" data-inset="true">
18:           <li>List Item 1</li>
19:           <li>List Item 2</li>
20:           <li>List Item 3</li>
21:         </ul>
22:       </div>
23:     </div>
24:     <div data-role="page" data-theme="g" id="page2">
25:       <div data-role="header"><h1>Custom swatch g</h1></div>
26:       <div data-role="content">
27:         <p>Use the button to go back</p>
28:         <a href="#page1" data-role="button">First Swatch</a>
29:         <ul data-role="listview" data-inset="true">
30:           <li>List Item 1</li>
31:           <li>List Item 2</li>
32:           <li>List Item 3</li>
33:         </ul>
34:       </div>
35:     </div>
36:   </body>
37: </html>
```

Two pages are included in this example with each using a different custom swatch. The custom style sheet that contains our custom swatches is included on line 7. Note that when including custom styles, you should always include them after the jQuery Mobile styles have been included.

The button on line 16 will change from the first page to the second one. The button on line 28 will change back. Both pages are setting the data-theme on the element that contains the data-role="page" attribute so that the swatch is applied to all components on the page. Figures 13.8 and 13.9 show the first and second pages rendered in a mobile browser.

You can continue to add swatches to your custom CSS file all the way to the z swatch. Just in case you wondered, you do not have to go in alphabetical order if you do not want to; you can start at any letter.

FIGURE 13.8
The first page is using the custom f swatch.

FIGURE 13.9
The second page is using the custom g swatch.

Summary

In this hour you learned about the theme framework included with jQuery Mobile. The theme can be controlled by using classes or by using the `data-theme` and `data-content-theme` attributes on page sections.

You learned that you can apply a custom icon set using CSS, and that if you replace the included sprite files you can still use the built-in classes to call your sprite images. You learned about the swatch system and that swatches are designated by any letter from a to z. Of these letters, the first five are already included by default with jQuery Mobile and may be modified or extended.

Finally, you learned how to create a swatch based on one of the included swatches, and how to include it in an external file to your page.

Q&A

Q. Do I have to keep the default styles that are included with jQuery Mobile?

A. No, the jQuery Mobile team included the first five swatches as an example of what can be done but expects you to modify, break, extend, and play with any and every style they include.

Q. How many themes can I use on my site?

A. Many sources on the Internet reference "theme" and "swatch" interchangeably creating some serious confusion. That being said, you are allowed one theme that can contain up to 26 swatches. You can then mix and match various parts of the swatches to create a unique blend of swatches.

Q. Can I use a custom icon set that doesn't match up with the included one—for example, a sprite that uses images that are separated by a single pixel instead of 18?

A. Yes, you just need to make sure that you create the classes to back up your custom sprite set. As long as you reference the sprite file and your custom classes the icon set works with jQuery Mobile just like it would with any other site.

Workshop

The workshop contains a quiz and some exercises to help you check your comprehension and understanding.

Quiz

1. What data attribute is used to apply a swatch to an element?

2. What is the default icon size in the included sprites?

3. True or False: All mobile browsers load both the standard icon set and the high-resolution icon set.

4. How does jQuery Mobile include fallback support for legacy browsers in regards to swatches?

5. True or False: You can overwrite any of the included swatches with your own styles.

Answers

1. You can use `data-theme` or `data-content-theme` to apply swatches.

2. The default icon size is 18px for regular screen resolution and 36px for high-resolution or Retina displays.

3. False. The files are referenced in CSS and downloading them is determined by a media query. If the mobile device is unable to use the icon file, it will not download it.

4. Each swatch includes several lines of browser-specific styles to add support for most mobile browser types. This helps to make sure that your swatch appears as close to the same as possible in cross-browser situations.

5. True. You can alter, edit, change, modify, remove, and add as much as you want to any swatch style. In fact each swatch is commented to help you know what you are modifying and why a particular line was included.

Exercises

1. Either find a different sprite set online or open an image editor and change the sprite files that come with jQuery Mobile and load them on a page.

2. If you have access to a few mobile devices try loading a page on all of them and compare the styles. If you do not have access to multiple devices then download different browsers or emulators and use them to view a page using jQuery Mobile. Note the differences between the browsers and then open the CSS file and tweak the settings to see what browsers are affected.

3. Create your own swatch by copying an existing swatch or from scratch. Change the button colors, the body colors, and other styles. Notice what happens when you change the text color but forget to change the color of the text shadow. Look for other changes that affect the way the page is displayed.

PART III

Customizing Your Content

Sprucing Up Your Design

What You'll Learn in This Hour:

▶ Popular copyrights and licenses used with software
▶ Where to find custom icons and icon sets
▶ Where to find stock images
▶ How to use custom fonts in your site
▶ Using plug-ins with jQuery Mobile

You are probably at the point where you would like to expand on some elements of your design to help make it personal and unique. This is where custom icon sets, images, and custom fonts come into play. Also not to be ignored is the addition of plug-ins that can help manage the look, flow, and feel of your site. But before we get into that, we need to square away a few technical details that keep you out of trouble and operating your site smoothly.

Understanding Copyrights and Licensing

Oddly enough those who know the most about copyrights and licensing are the ones who are either enforcing them or breaking them. While you already may have your opinions on copyrights and licenses, you should know about them. Ignorance may work a bit when dealing with a cease and desist letter, but it will not save you when you try to publish your application or try to pass someone's work off as your own.

There are several types of copyrights and licenses that you should be aware of when you are creating a site or mobile application. No matter what license is in use, the best thing to do when in doubt is to contact the artist, owner, or company of any copyrighted work. Let's go over some of the common licenses that you will find when looking to extend your mobile site.

General Public License (GPL)

This license has gone through a few different versions and currently resides at version 3. It was first created in February 1989 to help developers publish code that could not be taken by others and redistributed as another's work. It required developers to release human-readable source code with any binary or compiled code.

Version 2 of the GPL (GPLv2) was released in 1991 and is still used in a considerable amount of projects and programs today. It added clauses to fix some loopholes that hardware manufacturers had exposed through the use of software detection that would not let hardware function when a software modification was made. It also included a clause making it illegal to distribute any software using the GPLv2 if the software had been legally required or court-ordered to be distributed without source code.

Version 3 of the GPL was released in 2007 and was geared to address some of the areas concerning the license with patents, compatibility with other licenses such as the MIT and Apache licenses, and to define source code. This version also added some room for developers to release source code over peer-to-peer connections as long as it is clear to the user where they may obtain the code. The most current Linux kernel has been released using this version of the GPL.

When any version of this license is applied to software, it can be distributed but must remain under the specified license. Software released under this license may be sold to other parties, but they may not build proprietary software from it.

This means that if you are running a website you are generally free to run with software (including plug-ins) that are licensed through the GPL because it is not being distributed. The tricky part becomes when you attempt to bundle your site and sell it in an application store or market as it now becomes somewhat of a proprietary software package or program. Projects that use jQuery and jQuery Mobile may use the GPL license.

You can learn more about the GPL and the version used by jQuery (GPLv2) by visiting the following links:

- http://www.gnu.org/licenses/gpl.html
- http://en.wikipedia.org/wiki/GNU_General_Public_License
- http://en.wikipedia.org/wiki/Tivoization
- https://github.com/jquery/jquery/blob/master/GPL-LICENSE.txt

The Massachusetts Institute of Technology (MIT)

The Massachusetts Institute of Technology (MIT) license is a popular license used with software. The MIT license was originally created for use with the X Windows System and is popular with open source projects. Part of the reason for the popularity is that it allows code and programs to be released as open source, but also to be incorporated into proprietary projects and applications. The jQuery Mobile framework is dual licensed to use either the GPL and/or the MIT license.

This is the license that enables you to include the jQuery Mobile framework in any applications that you publish to any application store or marketplace.

The MIT license is occasionally referred to as the Expat and X11 license although there are slight differences between them.

You can read more about the MIT license and the version jQuery uses by visiting the following links:

- http://www.opensource.org/licenses/MIT
- http://en.wikipedia.org/wiki/MIT_License
- https://github.com/jquery/jquery/blob/master/MIT-LICENSE.txt

The Berkeley Software Distribution (BSD)

This license was originally created for Berkeley Software Distribution, which was a UNIX variant created at Berkeley. It is similar to the MIT license in the respect that any software using the license is freely available for modification, redistribution, and inclusion provided that the text of the license is included.

Today a couple of versions of the BSD license are available to use. These are sometimes referred to as modified BSD licenses.

The Modified BSD license was created in 1999 and contains three clauses that state that the software must be released with a copy of the license, the binary form of the software must also include a copy of the license, and the original developer(s) or institution does not endorse work or can be used as an endorsement on derivatives of the original code.

There is also a simplified version that contains two of the three clauses choosing to omit the clause about endorsement. While it does remove that clause, it adds a paragraph about the views and opinions of the software author(s).

The jQuery framework includes the Sizzle selector engine created by the Dojo Foundation and released for development under the GPL, MIT, and BSD license. To learn more about the BSD license visit the following links:

- http://www.opensource.org/licenses/BSD-3-Clause
- http://www.opensource.org/licenses/bsd-license.php
- http://en.wikipedia.org/wiki/BSD_licenses
- http://en.wikipedia.org/wiki/Berkeley_Software_Distribution
- http://www.linfo.org/bsdlicense.html
- https://github.com/jquery/sizzle/blob/master/LICENSE

Creative Commons

Creative Commons created the Creative Commons license in 2002. It originally aimed to help content creators easily distribute works with clearly defined rules for what could be done with the work. Four major rights were attached to the license. These were Attribution (must give credit to original author), Noncommercial (may not be used for any commercial work), No Derivative Works (may not create new works based on, or using any part of the original work), and Share-alike (may be used, but must be verbatim with no modifications). These rights could then be mixed and matched to create a license that was suitable by the content creator.

Currently six variations are in common use today. These are

▶ Attribution alone (BY)

▶ Attribution + NoDerivatives (BY ND)

▶ Attribution + ShareAlike (BY SA)

▶ Attribution + Noncommercial (BY NC)

▶ Attribution + Noncommercial + NoDerivatives (BY NC ND)

▶ Attribution + Noncommercial + ShareAlike (BY NC SA)

Currently using any version of the license requires that the original author be given credit or attribution rights for the work.

This license is not recommended for software and instead is used on copyrighted works such as books, music, pictures, blogs, and so on. Any work released under this license cannot be reverted or restricted to another license provided that it was originally received under the license.

To learn more about the Creative Commons license, you can visit the following links:

▶ http://en.wikipedia.org/wiki/Creative_Commons_licenses

▶ http://en.wikipedia.org/wiki/Creative_Commons

▶ http://creativecommons.org/licenses/

▶ http://www.flickr.com/creativecommons/

▶ http://soundcloud.com/101/creative-commons

Mobile Application Licensing

Using licenses with mobile applications can be tricky. Most application stores or markets have a policy in place that gives you a legal outline of what licenses are allowed for distribution in their store. Some stores allow distribution of apps that contain GPL code; others do not.

While you may create a web app that uses GPL code and allows users to browse, view, and interact with your site through a web browser, packaging that site up in a webview or repacked native application may violate the terms of the store agreement. This is true even when you offer the application for free inside the marketplace.

Always remember to read the licensing agreements before you distribute the application as some licenses require you to provide the source code if someone asks for it. For store Terms of Service visit the following links:

- iTunes Store

  http://www.apple.com/legal/itunes/us/terms.html

- Android Market/Play

  http://www.android.com/us/developer-distribution-agreement.html

- App Hub (Windows Phone and Xbox LIVE)

  http://create.msdn.com/en-US/home/legal/terms_of_use

- BlackBerry

  http://us.blackberry.com/legal/terms.jsp

Now that we've learned a bit about licensing, let's learn where we can find images and plug-ins that we can use in jQuery Mobile projects.

Finding Images

Whether you are looking for a custom set of icons or some stock imaging to use as a background you need images. If you are a designer then you are probably already in good shape where images are concerned; however, every now and then it's good to know where to go to get images when you are in a pinch or need some inspiration.

Getting Icons and Icon Sets

You already know that some icons are included with jQuery Mobile by default, but when you are trying to make a unique app or just want to see what other developers and designers are doing, looking up icons can be beneficial.

Icons can be located from several difference sources. They can be downloaded or acquired from commercial websites that specialize in maintaining large libraries of icon files, or from several free or social sites. Let's go over a few sites and learn about what is offered and what you can expect to find.

Using Commercial Sources

Commercial sites generally offer the best-looking resources and have a wide selection. Not all commercial sites are equal, and not all offer you the same type of product. For example, some sites happily sell you an icon set delivered in multiple .png files with different dimensions. This may not bother you too much because you might be able to rescale the images without too much pixelation, but it might have been nicer if they had given you a vector image set that you could use to create your own size without any loss in original quality.

Whenever you go to make a purchase, try to get a sample first. This way you will know for sure whether the files you are purchasing work with your setup. Another thing to keep in mind when buying icons and icon sets is the license they are using to sell them to you with. Many commercial sites sell icons under a royalty-free model. This doesn't mean that you are buying the work and it becomes yours; it means that you are buying the work to use on your site or application and you pay once. It does not give you the right to bundle or redistribute the icons for resale.

The following is a list of sites that sell commercial icons and icon sets:

- ▶ http://icondock.com/
- ▶ http://stockicons.com/
- ▶ http://www.iconshock.com/
- ▶ http://icondrawer.com/
- ▶ http://graphicriver.net/category/icons
- ▶ http://www.shutterstock.com/
- ▶ http://www.icojoy.com/allicons/
- ▶ http://somerandomdude.com/work/iconic/
- ▶ http://tipogram.com/

Getting Free Icons

Not every project is going to require you to use a commercial set of icons, and even if they do you may not have a budget that is big enough to support getting a set to get it done. You don't have to worry, though; plenty of places still offer free icons and icon sets.

If you've done some searching or read a few design blogs, you know that there are tons of "free icons!" and "free for download!" resources. What you may have missed is that those same links usually contain a link to a commercial set of icons that comes dual licensed—one for personal projects under a CC license, and one that usually includes a royalty-free license. An example of this is the "gentleface" icon set (http://www.gentleface.com/free_icon_set.html). This is an icon set that has been released for public works under the CC (a, nc) license. You can use it on your own site as long as you give credit back to where you acquired the icons and as long as you are not using it for commercial purposes.

Not all icon sets will be free, and some of them will pale in comparison with the detail and time spent on making them look polished and good; however, that doesn't mean that you won't be able to find anything.

The following sites all contain free icons or icon sets:

▶ http://www.famfamfam.com/lab/icons/

▶ http://www.defaulticon.com/

▶ http://www.greepit.com/open-source-icons-gcons/

▶ http://www.iconza.com/

▶ http://www.iconeden.com/icon/category/free

Using the Web to Find Icons and Icon Sets

One of the best things about the Web right now is that there are so many different ways to find the resources you need. You can use search engines, blogs, and social sites to find links to icons and icon sets.

Some of my favorite resources of images and designs are blogs. The following list is a great place to get started with finding icons:

▶ http://www.smashingmagazine.com/

▶ http://www.noupe.com/

▶ http://speckyboy.com/

▶ http://www.webresourcesdepot.com/

▶ http://www.hongkiat.com/blog/

While you can visit each of these sites and dig through all the posts to find icons and icon sets, the easiest way I've found is to use Google to do it for you. All you need to do is open http://www.google.com and then type the following into the search box:

```
site:smashingmagazine.com icons
```

When you press the Enter key on your keyboard or click the Google Search button on the page, the results returned will all be from smashingmagazine.com and will contain the word "icons." You can refine the search further by adding "sets" or "free" to the search. To search other sites, just replace the "smashingmagazine.com" portion with the site you want to check.

You can also sort through Twitter the same way. Just put twitter.com in and watch the links come pouring in. Of course you can also visit http://twitter.com and use the search box on the site to find icons and icon sets. Another way to find icons through Twitter is to check the tweets from the sites mentioned previously. I've found that many sites and blogs share links through Twitter that they leave off their sites. Many of them are also very friendly and helpful, so if you have a question, feel free to contact them and see if they can give you some direction.

Now that you know how to find icons, let's go over stock images.

Sorting through Stock Images

Before I jumped into dealing with ecommerce and marketing, I really had no idea how big the stock image market was. For some reason I had it stuck in my head that whenever someone needed a picture they'd either hire a photographer or grab a camera and run out to take pictures. While that does happen, there are occasional problems such as weather, season, time, and location that really tend to mess things up. When this is the case, using stock images is a good way to get the images you need. Another use for stock images that you may not have thought about is using them for textures. You can use textures to add noise or depth to an otherwise visually bland background or logo. Let's take a few minutes to go over how to get stock images.

Commercial Stock Images

Just like icons and icon sets, stock images are available through many commercial sites. Most images are offered through a royalty-free system allowing you to use the images anyway you want as long as you do not distribute or sell them. Be sure to read the licensing terms when you make your purchase though so that you know exactly what you can do with the image.

Many commercial sites allow you to purchase individual images, or sign up for a monthly plan where you pay a set amount and in return are allowed a set number of credits or downloads.

Popular commercial sites for acquiring stock images are

- http://www.istockphoto.com/
- http://www.shutterstock.com/
- http://us.fotolia.com/
- http://www.veer.com/

Just like with icons, you can find several sites that allow you to use some images for free. Let's take a look at free stock images.

Free Stock Images

Some stock images can be acquired for free and used without cost, even on commercial projects. Others allow you to use them, but only for nonprofit projects. You can mix some of them to create new images or derivative works without worrying about violating any licenses.

The free side of stock images seems to be from artists who are trying out new styles, new equipment, or are just trying to make a name for themselves without too much worry about having a perfect high-end product. While that is not always the case, it is much more difficult to find exactly what you are looking for when dealing with free. The saying "You get what you pay for" definitely holds true in this instance. Still, I've found many free stock images that I've used as textures, or even masks to make some interesting images and backgrounds. As I've said before, always check the license and give credit where credit is due.

The following is a list of sites that offer free stock images:

- ▶ http://www.sxc.hu/
- ▶ http://www.everystockphoto.com/
- ▶ http://flickr.com/
- ▶ http://www.stockvault.net/
- ▶ http://www.deviantart.com/
- ▶ http://search.creativecommons.org/

Another element that you may want to add to your mobile site is extra functionality. Some of that can be added through the use of plug-ins.

Functionality Enhancement with Plug-ins

When developing with frameworks like jQuery Mobile, plug-ins can help you easily enhance your functionality. Plug-ins are functions or methods that come packed together that can be added to help with special effects, change default behavior, or help with some of your logic.

Finding Plug-ins

jQuery Mobile is new, so the amount of plug-ins is not as large as say the original jQuery framework. However, as it continues to gain popularity, more developers will use it and release plug-ins to help others do what they have already done. This is beneficial for developers who know what they want, but are unsure of how exactly to do it. The part that I love most about plug-ins is digging through the source code so I can tell what they are doing, and so I can modify it to fit my exact needs.

Locating jQuery Mobile plug-ins can be difficult at first, but as soon as you know where to look, it becomes much easier. The first place to start is with a fantastic page that the jQuery Mobile team has put together at http://jquerymobile.com/resources/#Plugins.

This resource page contains sites that currently run jQuery Mobile, applications and frameworks that you can use to build jQuery Mobile sites, plug-ins and extensions, and even some templates for use with stencil or wireframe building software.

The second place I suggest looking is Twitter. The official jQuery Mobile team @jquerymobile does a terrific job of posting new plug-ins and resources when they are available.

Using Plug-ins

Because plug-ins cover anything that is added to the base library, they can be included through different means. Some plug-ins are JavaScript files that you include along with jQuery Mobile, and others are additional CSS files. We're going to take a quick look at using the `960 grid` plug-in with a page that is using jQuery Mobile.

The `960 grid` is a popular grid system that is in use on desktop websites. It allows pages to be flexible and allows content to grow and shrink based on the viewable space of the browser. The jQuery Mobile port of the 960 grid plug-in for this system can be found at http://jeromeetienne. github.com/jquery-mobile-960/.

Listing 14.1 shows the contents of plugin_960gs.html, where the plug-in is being used on a page with jQuery Mobile.

LISTING 14.1   Using a Plug-in Along with jQuery Mobile

```
 1:  <!DOCTYPE html>
 2:  <html>
 3:    <head>
 4:      <title>Developing with jQuery Mobile</title>
 5:      <meta name="viewport" content="width=device-width, initial-scale=1">
 6:      <link rel="stylesheet"
href="http://code.jquery.com/mobile/1.1.0/jquery.mobile-1.1.0.min.css" />
 7:      <link rel="stylesheet"
href="http://jeromeetienne.github.com/jquery-mobile-960/css/
jquery-mobile-fluid960.min.css" />
 8:      <script src="http://code.jquery.com/jquery-1.7.1.min.js"></script>
 9:      <script
src="http://code.jquery.com/mobile/1.1.0/jquery.mobile-1.1.0.min.js"></script>
10:    </head>
11:    <body>
12:      <div data-role="page">
13:        <div data-role="header"><h1>960gs plugin example</h1></div>
14:        <div data-role="content">
```

```
15:         <div class="container_12">
16:           <div class="grid_2"><a href="#" data-role="button">2 column</a>
</div>
17:           <div class="grid_6">
18:             <a href="#" data-role="button">6 column</a>
19:             <p>The fluid grid allows this layout to adapt to screen size</p>
20:             <p>You can see how it adjusts by changing device orientation</p>
21:             <p>When orientation changes, the size of the columns changes</p>
22:           </div>
23:           <div class="grid_4">
24:             <a href="#" data-role="button">4 column</a>
25:           </div>
26:         </div>
27:       </div>
28:     </div>
29:   </body>
30: </html>
```

The 960 grid is a style framework that allows a grid of 12 columns to be divided up into a custom size. Because this is done through a CSS file, adding the plug-in to a page is as simple as adding the code on line 7. Looking at that line you can see that this program is loading off a github link. The plug-in is loaded after the jQuery Mobile styles are loaded so that it will not be overwritten by jQuery Mobile when it loads. Continuing down the code you can see the standard markup for a jQuery Mobile page. Line 15 shows a div element that contains an attribute of class="container_12". This class works with the 960 grid plug-in that uses the div as a container with 12 columns. Line 16 shows another div element with an attribute of class="grid_2". This is another attribute that works with the 960 grid. This time it creates a two-column section inside the 12-column container. Line 17 follows a similar patter but uses the attribute class="grid_6" to create a six-column section inside the 12-column container. Line 23 shows another div element that contains a familiar attribute. You can probably guess that the attribute class="grid_4" is going to create a four-column section inside the 12-column container. What you also may have noticed is that these three sections all add up to 12 (2 + 6 + 4). When using the 960 grid plug-in, anything you set up must equal the size you set in the container. You can learn how to use the 960 grid by visiting http://960.gs/.

Using the plug-in adds some extra functionality that some developers may already be familiar with. This is the point of plug-ins, to add speed to the development and functionality to your site. Even though plug-ins can greatly increase the speed or functionality of a site, you need to be aware of some side effects. Figure 14.1 shows the results of the plug-in shown on a smaller phone screen. Figure 14.2 shows the same page being rendered on a tablet. As you can see from both images, this particular plug-in has a much better look on tablets than it does on small-screen devices.

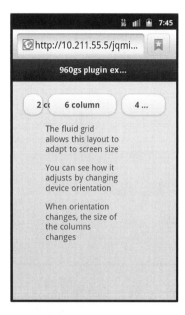

FIGURE 14.1
Viewing the `960 grid` plug-in on a mobile device

FIGURE 14.2
Viewing the `960 grid` plug-in on a tablet

This particular plug-in has been released under the MIT license giving anyone the right to use it in mobile site and application development. Most plug-ins are released under a license, so make sure that you read what license the plug-in is released under and that you are in compliance.

Something else you may want to do is add a custom font to your mobile site. Let's look over a few ways that this can be accomplished.

Adding Custom Fonts

As soon as fonts were created, everyone wanted to use one of their own. I remember one of the first sites I built used the `font` element, and I spent hours looking for exactly the right font to use. I didn't know back then that anyone who didn't have the font I wanted to use installed on their system saw a much different site than I had created. Luckily the Web has moved forward, and several solutions have been developed to help overcome custom font issues.

For a while any custom font work was done with images. There's nothing wrong with that; in fact, it is still a great way to make sure that your font looks exactly the way you want it to look. The downside of using images is that you lose accessibility, and SEO. This leads us to what common fonts are available to use.

Keeping It Generic

Just about all computers and mobile devices have a set of common or generic fonts installed on them that are accessible by a browser. These fonts are called as web safe fonts. These fonts are generally put together into a font family, and are applied using CSS. The idea is that when a font family is used, if the first font listed is unavailable, the second font listed will be used instead. Each font in the font family should be similar to the one before it, with the first being the font preferred overall. A few web safe fonts listed in font family form are

- ▶ Arial, Helvetica, sans-serif
- ▶ Times New Roman, Times, serif
- ▶ Impact, Charcoal, sans-serif
- ▶ Tahoma, Geneva, sans-serif
- ▶ Lucida Console, Monaco, monospace

While serif, sans-serif, and monospace may be used as base generic fonts, you can also use cursive and fantasy. These fonts can be combined to create a custom font family that can be used on your site. A browser will do the best it can to match listed fonts; however, if it is unable to match the exact font it usually just defaults to a built-in system font. A good place to test web safe fonts is at typetester (http://www.typetester.org/). This site allows you to see how the text will render in different styles and sizes.

The benefits of using web safe fonts are all in speed. Applying web safe fonts is only a line or two of CSS, and the browser does not have to download any external files or use extra processing power to render the fonts. The drawback is that your font choices are limited to the same fonts that everyone else has. This can put a serious cramp in your creative style. To remedy that, let's take a look at font embedding through @font-face.

Using Custom Fonts with @font-face

While it looks like a Twitter user who is just crazy about fonts, @font-face is actually a technique available in CSS that allows the use of downloaded fonts that work on just about every system. Using some intelligent CSS selectors, you can actually choose which file should be downloaded and applied.

Browsers occasionally lack support for certain file types and the functionality of one another. You have already seen this when dealing with CSS3, as some browser-specific styles need to be applied to make sure that all browsers display your styles the way you want them to. This same level of planning is used with @font-face. You can download @font-face kits that contain the following font files:

▶ TTF—For all browsers except IE, iPhone, and iPad

▶ EOT—For IE browsers

▶ WOFF—A new web font standard that supports compression

▶ SVG—A graphics format supported by the iPhone and iPad

These files are placed inside a directory and then referenced in a CSS file. When a browser parses the CSS file, it grabs the file that it supports and downloads it. Although this has been known to cause occasional page flashes when the text on a page has rendered before the font has been downloaded and is removed and replaced, it is still a well-received solution and is in use on many websites today.

Listing 14.2 shows the contents of fontface.html where an @font-face font is being used on a jQuery Mobile page.

LISTING 14.2   Using @font-face on a jQuery Mobile Page

```
1: <!DOCTYPE html>
2: <html>
3:   <head>
4:     <title>Developing with jQuery Mobile</title>
5:     <meta name="viewport" content="width=device-width, initial-scale=1">
```

```
6:        <link rel="stylesheet"
href="http://code.jquery.com/mobile/1.1.0/jquery.mobile-1.1.0.min.css" />
7:        <style type="text/css" media="screen">
8:         @font-face {
9:         font-family: 'BitstreamVeraSansBoldOblique';
10:          src: url('ff/Vera-Bold-Italic-webfont.eot');
11:          src:
url('ff/Vera-Bold-Italic-webfont.eot?#iefix') format('embedded-opentype'),
12:              url('ff/Vera-Bold-Italic-webfont.woff') format('woff'),
13:              url('ff/Vera-Bold-Italic-webfont.ttf') format('truetype'),
14:              url('ff/Vera-Bold-Italic-webfont.svg#BitstreamVeraSansBoldOblique')
format('svg');
15:          font-weight: normal;
16:          font-style: normal;
17:        }
18:        p.fft {font: 20px/27px 'BitstreamVeraSansBoldOblique', Arial,
sans-serif;}
19:        </style>
20:        <script src="http://code.jquery.com/jquery-1.7.1.min.js"></script>
21:        <script
src="http://code.jquery.com/mobile/1.1.0/jquery.mobile-1.1.0.min.js"></script>
22:      </head>
23:      <body>
24:        <div data-role="page">
25:          <div data-role="header"><h1>Using @fontface</h1></div>
26:          <div data-role="content">
27:            <p class="fft">This text is using a custom font</p>
28:            <p>This text is using the default font</p>
29:          </div>
30:        </div>
31:      </body>
32: </html>
```

Starting at line 7, a `style` element is set up after the styles for jQuery Mobile have been loaded. Line 8 shows the declaration for the `@font-face` style. This works similarly to declaring a class or an id in CSS. Line 9 shows the setup for a `font-family` with the value of `'BitstreamVeraSansBoldOblique'`. This is important because it defines the name that is used later to call this custom font. Lines 10-14 should look similar to each other. Each line is pointing to a different font file. This is how the font works cross-browser. Lines 15 and 16 are reset lines that normalize the font so that browsers do not add any extra custom styles to them. Lines 17 closes the `@font-face` declaration for the `'BitstreamVeraSansBoldOblique'` font. If you are using more than one custom font, you need to create another `@font-face` declaration. You need to use one per font that you want to include. Line 18 is the setup for applying the font to any p elements that contain an attribute of `class="fft"`. The values set on this line are shorthand CSS for setting the font size and line height, and what fonts to use. While this works, the full CSS font shorthand order is font: font-style, font-variant, font-weight, font-size/line-height font-family;. You can see that we left out the font-style, font-variant, and font-weight. Since we already declared the BitstreamVeraSansBoldOblique font, it works. If you remove the @font-face declaration the custom font will not work. If you are having problems loading a custom font, make sure that it has been declared in the CSS file above where you are trying to use it. You also do not have to include the style element if you do not want to. You can instead choose to copy all the styles out and place them in an external CSS file. The rest of the file shows some basic markup for a mobile page, with line 27 containing a p element with an attribute of class="fft". The text inside this p element will have the custom font applied to it.

Figure 14.3 shows the page being rendered on a mobile browser.

FIGURE 14.3
Using a custom font on a mobile browser with @font-face

You can create your own @font-face kits by visiting FontSquirrel (www.fontsquirrel.com/) and using the @font-face generator to make your own. There are stipulations on @font-face generation and a blacklist. This is because there are many fonts that are licensed and using @font-face is effectively giving away the font to the end user.

If you decide that you do not want to use @font-face but would still like a custom font, you can look at using the Google Web Fonts.

Using Google Web Fonts

Google maintains a set of open source fonts that are licensed for use in both personal and commercial projects. There are currently a few hundred different fonts that you can choose from, and loading the font is as simple as loading a CSS file from Google and using some styles to call the font on the page.

Listing 14.3 shows the contents of google_web_font.html where a page is using a font from Google Web Fonts.

LISTING 14.3 Using Google Web Fonts for a Custom Font

```
 1: <!DOCTYPE html>
 2: <html>
 3:   <head>
 4:     <title>Developing with jQuery Mobile</title>
 5:     <meta name="viewport" content="width=device-width, initial-scale=1">
 6:     <link rel="stylesheet"
href="http://code.jquery.com/mobile/1.1.0/jquery.mobile-1.1.0.min.css" />
 7:     <link rel='stylesheet'
href='http://fonts.googleapis.com/css?family=Terminal+Dosis' type='text/css'>
 8:     <script src="http://code.jquery.com/jquery-1.7.1.min.js"></script>
 9:     <script src="http://code.jquery.com/mobile/1.1.0/
jquery.mobile-1.1.0.min.js"></script>
10:     <style type="text/css" media="screen">
11:       p.gwf {
12:         font-family: 'Terminal Dosis', sans-serif;
13:         font-size: 20px;
14:         text-shadow: 3px 3px 3px #999;
15:       }
16:     </style>
17:   </head>
18:   <body>
19:     <div data-role="page">
20:       <div data-role="header"><h1>Google Web Font</h1></div>
21:       <div data-role="content">
22:         <p class="gwf">This text uses a Google Web Font</p>
23:         <p>This is plain text</p>
24:       </div>
25:     </div>
26:   </body>
27: </html>
```

Line 7 shows a call to an external style sheet that is hosted on a server at Google. Inside the href attribute you can see a variable containing Terminal+Dosis being passed as the font that we want to use. This acts similarly to the @font-face method in that the returned style sheet contains all the necessary styles needed to use the custom font. Line 10 shows a style element being created that holds the styles needed to use the custom font. Line 11 begins the styles that will be applied to any p elements with an attribute of class="gwf". Line 12 contains the font-family style with the value set to our custom font and a fallback font of sans-serif. Line 13 contains the setting for how big we want the font to be. Line 14 uses some CSS3 to throw a drop shadow on the text. You can add text effects with CSS to your custom fonts. This can help make your text look more polished and less like fancy plain text. Line 15 closes the styles that will be applied to the p element with the attribute of class="gwf", and line 16 closes the style element. Continuing down the page you can see the standard markup of a mobile page using jQuery Mobile. Line 22 shows the p element that will have our custom font as it has an attribute of class="gwf".

Figure 14.4 shows the custom font being rendered on a mobile device.

FIGURE 14.4
Using a custom font on a mobile browser with Google Web Fonts

You can choose fonts for yourself by visiting http://www.google.com/webfonts. Google cares about loading time, so you are given the option of only applying the parts of the font that you need. You can even take it a step further and use a beta technique where you pass the characters you need and you are passed back a font that contains only those characters. This is useful when you are only using a specific font for your header. The request should be URL encoded, so that the value in the `href` attribute for the font would appear as follows:

```
http://fonts.googleapis.com/css?family=Terminal+Dosis&text=The%20Site
```

Even with as much optimization for speed as you can get, you still may experience a little page jump as the text loads, so make sure you test thoroughly and that you are aware of how your page behaves.

Summary

In this hour you learned about licenses for software and images. Some licenses permit you to use the work for free as long as the work is noncommercial, while others require a fee. You learned how to find icons, icon sets, and stock images, and you learned how to include and use plug-ins with jQuery Mobile. Finally, you learned about using custom fonts inside your jQuery Mobile projects by using either the @font-face method or Google Web Fonts.

Q&A

Q. If I find something on the Internet and there isn't a license posted with it, is it free?

A. Unfortunately it is not free. Code that is posted on blogs is considered copyrighted by the original author. While the author may not choose to pursue and take action, it is much better to ask permission, even if it's just in a comment to the author for permission to use the work.

Q. Why do some software releases specifically use the GPLv2 instead of the newer GPLv3. Shouldn't they use the newer version?

A. Authors can decide for themselves which version of any license they want to attach to their software. The GPLv2 is still considered a good license for developers, and some developers do not feel the need to attach the newest version to their software.

Q. You mentioned earlier that using an image makes me lose SEO. How exactly does using a custom font help me gain the SEO back?

A. SEO is a funny thing because it changes often; however, machines still have some restrictions when it comes to reading images. Most search bots do not take the time to even process the images. They see an `img` element and they index the `alt` text for the image. When you use a custom font, your original text is still on the page and will be indexed by the bot when it makes a sweep through the site. This way you can put your text inside an `h1`, `h2`, or `h3` tag and get the full weight of the text instead of an `alt` tag reference.

Workshop

The workshop contains a quiz and some exercises to help you check your comprehension and understanding.

Quiz

1. True or False: The GPLv3 is currently compatible with the MIT license.

2. What license is not recommended for use with software?

3. What can be used to extend the functionality, accessibility, or appearance of a site?

4. What are web safe fonts?

5. True or False: You can take and use any image you want from public sources like flickr.com.

Answers

1. True. GPLv3 is fully compatible with the MIT license.

2. The Creative Commons license is not recommended for use with software. Instead developers should consider using a GPL, MIT, or BSD license.

3. Plug-ins, custom fonts, and icons can be used to extend the functionality, accessibility, and appearance of a site.

4. Fonts that are commonly installed on most computer systems and mobile devices are referred to as web safe fonts.

5. False. You may not use any image you find on flickr, or any other image-searching website. Just because an image is viewable on the Internet does not mean that you have the right to use the image. Always check for a license on the work. If a license cannot be found, contact the artist directly, or the entity hosting the image file.

Exercises

1. Spend some time searching for an icon set that you think would look good in your application. Try to find a free set that you can download and experiment with. If the icon set comes with multiple resolutions, experiment using a higher resolution version for retina displays.

2. Do some research on jQuery Mobile plug-ins and see whether some already are available that fit with a project you have in mind. If you do not have one in mind, grab an image slider or gallery plug-in and some stock images and combine them into an image gallery or slider.

3. Using either an @font-face kit or a Google Web Font create a page using jQuery Mobile and add your own custom font to it. Try using it for a list or navigation section. Watch the page load on your emulator or mobile device and see what effects the custom font has on your load time. If you have enough time, create a custom logo in an image manipulation program with the same or similar font and benchmark the mobile site using the image against using the custom font with load times.

Responsive Site Layout

What You'll Learn in This Hour:

▶ Understanding responsive design
▶ How to use media queries
▶ How to build a responsive page
▶ How to change styles based on device orientation

Creating a site layout that is responsive is not necessarily something that everyone needs, but when used can create a better layout and user interface. A responsive site layout gives you the ability to build your site for both large and small screen devices while allowing just the right amount of screen space to be used. There are a few different methods that you can use to attain a responsive layout including CSS3 media queries. Let's start by learning how to use them.

Appreciating Media Queries

A few years ago I was working on a project that required the width and height of the browser so that some calculations could be run to decide how the layout of the site should appear. While the project was finished to a satisfactory conclusion, the end result was more JavaScript intensive than I had originally hoped. What made it even worse was that it relied on extra scripts to add support for all major browsers. While at the time this was as good as I could get it, today I could have used media queries to shape my site layout.

You may recognize the `media` attribute from CSS2 where it was mostly used to inform the browser whether the style sheet was to be used for screen display or for printing. CSS3 has taken this original functionality and expanded it. For example, if I wanted to include a style sheet on a page when viewed on a browser with a screen that had a maximum width of 480px, I would use the following:

```
<link rel="stylesheet" type="text/css"
media="screen and (max-device-width: 480px)" href="mobile.css" />
```

The `media` attribute allows us to set up certain terms that must be met to include the referenced CSS file. We can also use them inside an existing style sheet. Listing 15.1 shows the setup for a couple of media queries that would be included either inside a CSS file or inside a style element.

LISTING 15.1   Media Queries for Use with Mobile Devices

```
 1: @media only screen
 2: and (min-device-width : 480px)
 3: and (max-device-width: 800px) {
 4:    /* styles go here */
 5: }
 6: @media only screen
 7: and (min-device-width: 768px)
 8: and (max-device-width: 1024px) {
 9:    /* styles go here */
10: }
```

The first media query starts on line 1 and continues to line 5. The first three lines could be moved onto a single line, but in this example I broke them up to make them easier to read. Line 1 declares that this is a media query by using `@media`. Using `only` allows older browsers to skip this media query, while using `screen` allows browsers running on devices with screens to use the media query. Line 2 shows a keyword of `and` being used with `min-device-width: 480px` inside parentheses. This means that not only does the browser have to support the arguments on line 1, but now must also have a screen width of at least 480px. By using `min-device-width` instead of `min-width`, the browser is checking the actual dimensions of the screen, not the viewable area. Line 3 adds another requirement to the mix; the device must have a maximum screen resolution of 800px. That means that all together the query runs only if the device is equipped with a browser that supports media queries, has a screen, and has an exact resolution of either 480×800 or 800×480. Any styles that you want applied to a device that meets that exact specification are entered on line 4 and beyond, just like you would do with normal CSS.

The second media query runs on lines 6-10 and follows the same pattern as the first media query. This query runs only on devices that are equipped with a browser that supports media queries, have a screen, and have an exact resolution of either 1024×768 or 768×1024.

Now that you have a taste of how media queries work, it's time to look at how they can be applied to site layout.

Adjusting Layouts Based on Screen Size

The method to building a traditional website has usually been centered on choosing a supported screen resolution, and then making a choice between a static or fluid layout. While my personal favorite size has been either 960px or 1140px, this becomes a problem for most mobile devices.

When thinking about responsive design, you can start from either end of the sizing spectrum. You can start from either the largest to smallest or from smallest to largest screen size. Both methods have pros and cons, and both should be considered for your target audience.

The pros of starting large and working small:

▶ You can retrofit an existing site by working down from the current size.

▶ Using "fallback" techniques may already be familiar for developers.

▶ The design may be compatible with older desktop browsers and systems.

The cons of starting large and working small:

▶ The site is generally bloated from the start with all of your features.

▶ Extra detection methods may be required to decide what to load after all assets have been downloaded to the client.

▶ CSS may get larger than necessary to scale down the existing site.

The pros of starting small and working large:

▶ Your CSS should be lighter as you will be adding options instead of checks for them.

▶ You do not have to worry about hiding features as they are added as the screen gets bigger.

▶ By starting small you are forced to focus on what really matters on your site.

The cons of starting small and working large:

▶ It is an entirely new mindset and may take an extended period of time to get a design working.

▶ By the time you get around to the full site, some features may be left out.

▶ It may feel like starting with the least common denominator and working up to what everyone else is using.

I personally prefer to start with the smallest size I am going to support and then build up and enhance the experience. Something else that you need to do when using a responsive design is to use either a grid system or a fluid system using percentages. Let's take a walk through setting up a site starting with the mobile layout.

Creating a Mobile Layout

To get started on the mobile design you first need to know what you are going to design. For this example we create a single-page portfolio. Knowing that, here is a list of things that to include in our page:

- Name
- Picture
- Contact Information
- My Work
- Interests
- Social

Using a block model layout for a page that is 480×800px, we can create a layout that has a header, then a picture and a name, contact information, a list of work, a list of interests, and a social links section. Figure 15.1 shows a block level layout of each area.

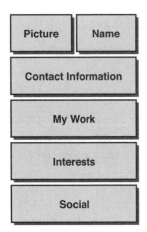

FIGURE 15.1
A block-level or wireframe of the mobile version of the portfolio site

Now that we have the layout, let's get it coded up. Listing 15.2 shows the contents of portfolio_mobile.html.

LISTING 15.2   A Mobile Portfolio Site

```
 1: <!DOCTYPE html>
 2: <html>
 3:   <head>
 4:     <title>Developing with jQuery Mobile</title>
 5:     <meta name="viewport" content="width=device-width, initial-scale=1">
 6:     <link rel="stylesheet"
href="http://code.jquery.com/mobile/1.1.0/jquery.mobile-1.1.0.min.css" />
 7:     <style type="text/css" media="screen">
 8:       img {max-width: 100%;}
 9:       #app-pic {width: 50%;float: left;}
10:       #app-name {width: 50%; margin-left:50%;min-height: 80px;}
11:     </style>
12:     <script src="http://code.jquery.com/jquery-1.7.1.min.js"></script>
13:     <script
src="http://code.jquery.com/mobile/1.1.0/jquery.mobile-1.1.0.min.js"></script>
14:   </head>
15:   <body>
16:     <div data-role="page" id="home">
17:       <div data-role="header"><h1>My Portfolio</h1></div>
18:       <div data-role="content">
19:         <div id="app-pic"><img src="pd_logo.gif" alt="My logo" /></div>
20:         <div id="app-name"><h2>Portfolio Developer</h2></div>
21:         <div id="app-contact">
22:           <ul data-role="listview" data-theme="d" data-divider-theme="e"
data-inset="true">
23:             <li data-role="list-divider">Contact Information</li>
24:             <li>
25:               <h3>Phone number</h3>
26:               <p>Office: 555-555-5555 ext. 512</p>
27:               <p>GVoice: 555-555-5551</p>
28:             </li>
29:             <li>
30:               <h3>Email</h3>
31:               <p>developer@emailaddress.com</p>
32:             </li>
33:             <li>
34:               <h3>Websites</h3>
35:               <p>http://www.mywebsite.com</p>
36:               <p>http://www.myotherwebsite.com</p>
37:             </li>
38:           </ul>
39:         </div>
40:         <div id="app-work">
41:           <ul data-role="listview" data-theme="d" data-divider-theme="a"
data-inset="true">
42:             <li data-role="list-divider">My Work</li>
43:             <li>
44:               <h3>Famous Company</h3>
```

```
45:                 <p>Developed an entirely new way to parse and process.</p>
46:             </li>
47:             <li>
48:                 <h3>Start-up</h3>
49:                 <p>Lead a small team to success through innovation.</p>
50:             </li>
51:             <li>
52:                 <h3>Meh Incorporated</h3>
53:                 <p>Engineered and designed a revolutionary new mobile app.</p>
54:             </li>
55:             </ul>
56:         </div>
57:         <div id="app-interests">
58:             <ul data-role="listview" data-theme="d" data-divider-theme="a"
data-inset="true">
59:             <li data-role="list-divider">Interests</li>
60:             <li>Mobile Development</li>
61:             <li>Technology</li>
62:             <li>Media</li>
63:             </ul>
64:         </div>
65:         <div id="app-social">
66:             <ul data-role="listview" data-theme="d" data-divider-theme="b"
data-inset="true">
67:             <li data-role="list-divider">Social</li>
68:             <li>
69:                 <h3>Twitter - <a href="#">Follow me!</a></h3>
70:                 <p>loading twitter feed...</p>
71:             </li>
72:             <li>
73:                 <h3>Find me on Google+</h3>
74:                 <p>
75:                     <a rel="author" href="https://profiles.google.com/">
76:                         <img
src="http://www.google.com/images/icons/ui/gprofile_button-32.png"
width="32" height="32">
77:                     </a>
78:                 </p>
79:             </li>
80:             <li>
81:                 <h3><a href="#">Friend me</a> on Facebook</h3>
82:                 <p>The world is a better place when we are all friends.</p>
83:             </li>
84:             </ul>
85:         </div>
86:         </div>
87:     </div>
88: </body>
89: </html>
```

This file shows the markup for a profile page that is using jQuery Mobile. The file starts out with all the requirements for a page using jQuery Mobile. With that in mind, we start with the `style` element that begins on line 7. This element contains all the extra styles that are going to be used on top of the ones included with jQuery Mobile. Line 8 shows the image style that is used to keep images within the bounds of the viewable page. Lines 9 and 10 contain styles that are used for layout. Line 11 closes our `style` element, and then we move into the rest of the code for the page setup. Lines 16-87 show the actual code and structure that make up our page. You can see that each section has been grouped into a `div` element and given an `id` that describes what the section contains. For example line 19 shows a `div` element with an attribute of `id="app-pic"` that contains an `img` element. Following the code down the page you can see the next `div` container is on line 20, with the next on line 21, and so on. This effectively matches up each section to the wireframe that was shown in Figure 15.1. Let's see how closely it appears when rendered by looking at Figure 15.2

FIGURE 15.2
The portfolio site viewed on a small-screen mobile device

You may be asking yourself where all the media queries went since there do not appear to be any in the markup. They have not been included yet because when you create a page with a mobile-first design you do not need any media queries for the mobile layout. Let's remedy the lack of media queries by moving onto a tablet layout and add our first media query.

Creating a Tablet Layout

Tablets have the advantage of higher resolutions than most smaller mobile devices. That generally means that you have more room to use in your design and allows you to change the layout to accommodate the extra space. This also means that some elements of your design may now appear stretched and out of place. To take that into account, Figure 15.3 shows a wireframe of what the design should change to when viewed on a tablet.

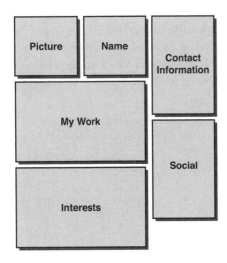

FIGURE 15.3
A wireframe of the tablet version of the portfolio site

With the new layout in mind, Listing 15.3 shows the `style` element portion of portfolio_tablet. html.

LISTING 15.3 Using a Media Query to Adjust the Page Layout for Tablets

```
 1: <style type="text/css" media="screen">
 2:    img {max-width: 100%;}
 3:    #app-pic {width: 50%;float: left;}
 4:    #app-name {width: 50%; margin-left:50%;min-height: 80px;}
 5:    @media all and (min-width: 800px){
 6:       /* Tablet styles go here */
 7:       #app-pic {width: 30%;}
 8:       #app-name {width: 30%;float: left;margin: 0;}
 9:       #app-contact {width: 30%;float: right;}
10:       #app-work {clear: left;width: 63%;padding-top: 1%;}
11:       #app-interests {width: 63%;float: left}
12:       #app-social {width:30%;clear: right;float: right;}
13:    }
14: </style>
```

Since this is an addition to the `style` element, lines 1-4 show the styles that we used to set up our mobile layout defaults. Line 5 shows our media query being set up. Something to note about this query is that we left out the keyword `only` and are using `min-width` instead of `min-device-width`. This is done to target a broader range of devices instead of a particular device or set of devices. This also means that this media query will be compatible with all devices with a modern browser instead of just mobile devices. By combining this with jQuery Mobile, we get a clean consistent site across all devices.

Continuing with line 6 you can see a comment that is left letting you know that anything inside this query is considered for tablets and devices with similar resolutions of a tablet. Line 7 then shows that we're adjusting the base style that was originally set on line 3 to be a width of `30%` instead of `50%`. Line 8 does a similar style change for the styles originally set on line 4. Note that when you are using media queries, you must be careful to overwrite or reset styles so that they display correctly. You can see that we are handling for that exact issue by resetting the margins with a `margin: 0` instead of leaving the base styles as `margin-left: 50%`.

Lines 9-12 are new styles set by using the jQuery Mobile default styles.

Now that you've seen the style changes to the page, take a look at Figure 15.4 and see what the site looks like on a tablet with the styles applied.

FIGURE 15.4
The portfolio site viewed on a tablet

We now have a site that looks great on a small-screen mobile device and a tablet. There may still be a problem, though. What happens when we view the site on a desktop with a high-resolution screen? The site still suffers from the stretching effect that happened when we viewed the mobile version on a tablet device. Let's look at using another media query to take care of views from desktop computers.

Creating a Desktop Layout

Unless you are specifically targeting mobile devices and routing them to special content or a special section of your site, you will have desktop users using your mobile site. This means that you really need to consider using a media query to at least put a size restriction on the amount of space you want the entire page to take up. Of course it is personal preference, and some designs work well with long buttons, lists, and content areas.

You may have already known or heard about some research that suggests that users follow an "F" pattern when viewing information on a site using a desktop. By choosing to follow that pattern, I am going to change the layout quite a bit in the hopes that it will increase the odds of what I want the user to read and remember.

NOTE

Analytical Awareness

You should do as much analytical research for your site as possible. Also keep in mind that just because a pattern or theory works today, that doesn't mean it won't change or become a rule. The "fold" for instance was a design law that is now becoming far less important than it once was.

Figure 15.5 shows the wireframe for the site when viewed on a desktop or high-resolution device.

Now that we have a wireframe to work with, let's look at Listing 15.4, which shows the `style` element portion from portfolio_desktop.html.

LISTING 15.4 Using Media Queries to Change Site Layout for Mobile, Tablet, and Desktop Devices

```
 1: <style type="text/css" media="screen">
 2:    img {max-width: 100%;}
 3:    #app-pic {width: 50%;float: left;}
 4:    #app-name {width: 50%; margin-left:50%;min-height: 80px;}
 5:    @media all and (min-width: 800px){
 6:       /* Tablet styles go here */
 7:       #app-pic {width: 30%;}
 8:       #app-name {width: 30%;float: left;margin: 0;}
 9:       #app-contact {width: 30%;float: right;}
10:       #app-work {clear: left;width: 63%;padding-top: 1%;}
```

```
11:     #app-interests {width: 63%;float: left}
12:     #app-social {width:30%;clear: right;float: right;}
13:   }
14:  @media all and (min-width: 1024px){
15:     /* Desktop styles go here */
16:     #home {position: relative;}
17:     #app-pic {position: absolute; top: 59px; left: 15px;width: 22%;
height: auto;text-align: center;}
18:     #app-name {position: absolute;top: 139px; left: 15px;width: 22%;
margin: 0;text-align: center;}
19:     #app-contact {position: absolute;top: 199px;left: 15px;width: 22%;}
20:     #app-work {margin-left: 25%;width: 50%;padding: 0;}
21:     #app-interests {margin-left: 25%;width: 50%;}
22:     #app-social {position: absolute;top: 59px;right: 15px;width: 22%;}
23:   }
24: </style>
```

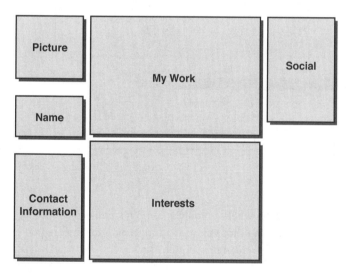

FIGURE 15.5
A wireframe of the desktop version of the site

This style element should be familiar as we are adding onto it. Lines 1-5 show the base styles that will be applied in addition to the jQuery Mobile styles that create the mobile layout of the site. Lines 6-13 show the styles applied to the tablet view. Previously this block contained the styles that applied to any device that had a minimum viewable screen area of 800px. Line 14 shows the media query that we are using for desktop or devices with a resolution of at least 1024px. Line 15 is an informational comment telling you that all desktop styles should be placed in this block. Line 16 shows an interesting change in our styles. The entire page container is set up to be used as a base for positional arrangement. Line 17 shows that positioning coming into use as you can see that it will be positioned an exact 59px from the top of the page, 15px away from the left edge, and will contain a width of 22%. The widths in this media query may not make sense as they do not add up to a full 100%, but this is to accommodate the margins and padding that are added to each element by the jQuery Mobile styles. Line 18 follows a similar padding and position setup. To make sure that the image will be in the center of the available space, `text-align: center` is also applied. Lines 19-22 continue to show the setup for each of the section containers.

Figure 15.6 shows what the site looks like when viewed on a desktop browser.

FIGURE 15.6
The portfolio site viewed on a desktop browser

We've now seen the portfolio site change based on whether you are using a small-screen mobile device, a tablet, or a desktop. There is one last thing that you may need to plan for in case you have not already thought about it: how to handle screen orientation.

Rotating Site Layout

In the example portfolio site we used a responsive design and then used media queries with a `min-width` setting to allow the change in site layout. This worked well for small-screen mobile, tablet, and desktop devices. Something we did not look into was handling screen orientation. While you are fully able to design sites by using `min-width` and similar media queries, you can also use the `orientation` media query to change the styles on your site.

By including `orientation: portrait` or `orientation: landscape` you can create new sets of styles that are applied only when the device reports back the requested orientation.

Let's take a look at Listing 15.5 where the contents of media_orientation.html are shown.

LISTING 15.5   Applying Styles Based on Device Orientation

```
 1: <!DOCTYPE html>
 2: <html>
 3:   <head>
 4:     <title>Developing with jQuery Mobile</title>
 5:     <meta name="viewport" content="width=device-width, initial-scale=1">
 6:     <link rel="stylesheet"
href="http://code.jquery.com/mobile/1.1.0/jquery.mobile-1.1.0.min.css" />
 7:     <script src="http://code.jquery.com/jquery-1.7.1.min.js"></script>
 8:     <script
src="http://code.jquery.com/mobile/1.1.0/jquery.mobile-1.1.0.min.js"></script>
 9:     <style type="text/css" media="screen">
10:       .box {width: 140px;height: 120px;padding: 10px 0;margin: 10px;
text-align: center;}
11:       @media all and (orientation: portrait){
12:         .box {color: #fff;background: #333;}
13:       }
14:       @media all and (orientation: landscape) {
15:         .box {color: #333;background: # AAD4FF;float: left;}
16:       }
17:     </style>
18:   </head>
19:   <body>
20:     <div data-role="page">
21:       <div data-role="header"><h1>Orientation Changing</h1></div>
22:       <div data-role="content">
23:         <div class="box">Box 1</div>
24:         <div class="box">Box 2</div>
25:         <div class="box">Box 3</div>
26:       </div>
27:     </div>
28:   </div>
29:   </body>
30: </html>
```

Lines 1-8 show the required setup for using jQuery Mobile, and line 9 begins a `style` element that contains the media queries we want to use. Line 10 shows the styles that will be applied on all elements that contain an attribute of `class="box"`. These are the base styles that will be applied no matter what orientation the device is currently in. Line 11 shows the media query that will be applied when the device is being viewed in portrait. This media query is applied in the same manner that was used to apply the media queries based on `min-width`; by adding `orientation: portrait` to the media query the browser will report what layout the screen is currently in and possibly trigger the media query. Line 12 shows the styles that will be applied when the media query for portrait is active. Line 13 closes the styles block for our portrait media query. Line 14 shows the media query for landscape mode. This is done just like the previous media queries; by adding `orientation: landscape`, the media query will trigger when the browser reports that the device is currently being viewed in landscape. Line 15 shows the styles that will be applied when the landscape media query is triggered. Line 16 closes the block for the styles that will be applied when the landscape media query is triggered. Line 17 closes the `style` element that contains our styles and media queries. Lines 20-28 show the page that our styles will be running on. Lines 23-25 show the elements that contain the attribute of `class="box"` that our media queries will affect.

You should have a pretty good idea of what is going to happen when this page is viewed on a mobile device in both portrait and landscape mode. Just to make sure you are correct, take a look at Figures 15.7 and 15.8 where the page is viewed in both portrait and landscape on a mobile browser.

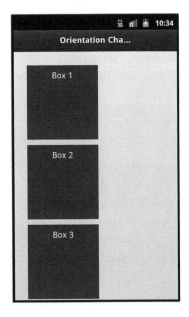

FIGURE 15.7
A page with elements styled from a media query triggered from portrait

Not all browsers support the orientation media query; however, most modern mobile browsers do. If you find that users are not getting the styles to work when they browse the site, you can try triggering layout changes with JavaScript, or you can include various libraries like css3-media-queries.js (http://code.google.com/p/css3-mediaqueries-js/) that add support for CSS3 media queries when using older browsers. Remember that anything extra you throw on top of your original project can add performance issues and download time. Choose carefully before you opt to add another library to your site.

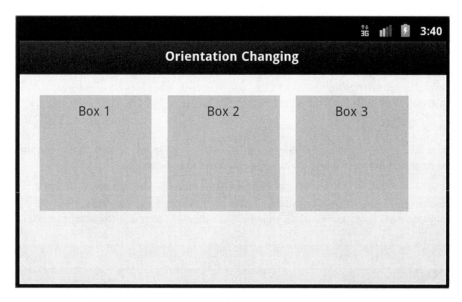

FIGURE 15.8
A page with elements styled from a media query triggered from landscape

Finally, I will again point out that if you design the site with a mobile first approach and plan ahead using `min-width`, you will not have to rely much on using the `orientation` media query, but it is always good to know that it is an available option.

Summary

In this hour you just learned about media queries and how they can be leveraged to create sites that maximize the available screen resolution of the device viewing them. You learned how to design from the mobile up, and how doing this saves on extra CSS code and makes your site easy to extend. You also learned about using device orientation and how it can be used as a media query to help adjust layout based on how a user is using a device to view your site.

Q&A

Q. Do I really have to use media queries or can I just use default styles?

A. You only have to use media queries if you want to. They are a tool to help designers and developers create new experiences that are easily tailored to the browser the user is using to view your site. You are more than welcome to use any style or even use a little JavaScript to dynamically change your site.

Q. Can I mix and match more than two media queries to get a little more specific on the exact resolution of devices I want to have certain styles?

A. Remember that not all browsers respect the `orientation` property of media queries, but yes you can. Here is a query you can use that specifically targets mobile devices that have a resolution of 480×800: `@media all and (min-device-width: 480px) and (max-device-width: 800px) and (orientation: portrait) {/*Styles here*/}`.

Q. I've heard a little about combining CSS3 transitions with media queries. Does that mean that the entire page can animate itself whenever screen orientation changes?

A. Sort of. Elements that are not styled with positioning or floats can be transitioned and it actually looks fairly cool. However, if you used the portfolio page example from this hour you'd really only notice the `#app-name` element animating or using any transitions at all.

Workshop

The workshop contains a quiz and some exercises to help you check your comprehension and understanding.

Quiz

1. What version of CSS are media queries in?

2. What is the difference between `min-device-width` and `min-width`?

3. True or False: When using a media query you cannot link to styles included in external CSS files.

4. True or False: The `orientation` property of media queries is compatible will all browsers.

5. True or False: When using responsive layout you should use a grid system or percentages for widths.

Answers

1. Media queries were introduced as part of the CSS3 specification.

2. `min-device-width` uses the actual device resolution for width, where `min-width` uses viewable space of the browser window.

3. False. You can run a media query that links to an external CSS file for all of the styles. For example you could use: `<link rel="stylesheet" media="screen and (min-width: 800px) and (max-width: 1280px)" href="css/tablet.css" />`.

4. False. While the `orientation` property is compatible with most mobile device browsers, it is not supported by all browsers (including desktop browsers).

5. True. For best results you should always use a grid system or percentages for styling. This is part of what makes the site responsive and able to adapt to the browser it is being viewed in. You can always add an element to wrap the content portion in to control how wide the site gets.

Exercises

1. Open the portfolio_desktop.html file and modify the existing styles to play with the site layout. Think of a different way to display the site and change the sections around using CSS only.

2. Modify the portfolio site to have another media query. You could change the site to adjust styles at 480 or 512 instead of 800. This would allow you to change the display for older generation smartphones.

3. Using either a sketch pad or program, create your own wireframes for a mobile, tablet, and desktop design and then create it using media queries.

Rolling Your Own Theme with ThemeRoller

What You'll Learn in This Hour:

▸ What the jQuery Mobile ThemeRoller is us ed for

▸ How to use ThemeRoller to create your own theme

▸ How to import themes into ThemeRoller for editing

▸ How to include a ThemeRoller theme in your site

You already know that you can create your own theme by modifying an existing swatch or using a little cut-and-paste action. While you are still more than welcome to create your swatches and themes that way, there is another tool that was highly anticipated and is now yours to use and enjoy. The tool is called ThemeRoller, and if you are not already familiar with it, the time has finally come to start using it.

Introduction to ThemeRoller

There are a few different offerings from the jQuery family. For instance there is the standard jQuery library, the jQuery UI library, and the jQuery Mobile library. While the original library is used to help extend and make using JavaScript faster and easier, the jQuery UI library was introduced to help developers create widgets and a common style that could be used to create a cross-browser experience. Developers who have used the jQuery UI library have undoubtedly at least heard of, if not dabbled with, the ThemeRoller system that was originally created for that library. The jQuery UI ThemeRoller (http://jqueryui.com/themeroller/) is similar to the jQuery Mobile ThemeRoller (http://jquerymobile.com/themeroller/). Both show the basic page elements and include an area to change the styles.

The version of ThemeRoller available at the time of this writing is compatible with jQuery Mobile only up to version 1.0. The new ThemeRoller that will be released alongside the final release of jQuery Mobile 1.1 will have a utility to convert previously generated themes to be compatible with the 1.1 release of jQuery Mobile.

The jQuery Mobile ThemeRoller was developed with help from Adobe and features kuler (http://kuler.adobe.com/) integration. This means that you can load color swatches or even search for your own publicly shared color swatches.

While it's great talking up such a fantastic tool, let's get into the nuts and bolts of actually using it.

Creating a Theme with ThemeRoller

Using the jQuery Mobile ThemeRoller is simple. When you load the ThemeRoller page in your browser you are greeted with a simple welcome message telling you that you can create up to 26 swatches and that it is recommended that you create at least 3 swatches for your theme. After acknowledging the message, you are dropped on a page that has a menu bar on the left and three separate swatch sections on the right. Figure 16.1 shows the default page after the welcome message has been acknowledged.

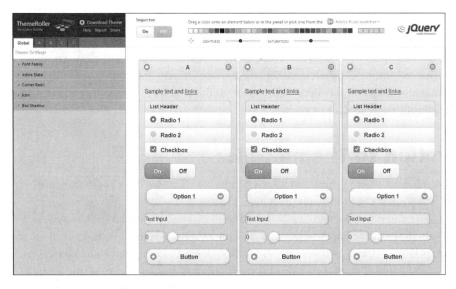

FIGURE 16.1
ThemeRoller is ready to be used for theme creation.

There are three ways to get started creating your swatch. You can use the color palette at the top of the page to drag and drop colors onto the theme-swatch areas below, you can use the inspector tool to select the portion of the swatch you want to edit, or you can just use the menu bar on the left to manually change any and all facets of the entire theme. Let's take a deeper look at each of the three methods.

Using the Color Palette for Adjustments

Along the top of the ThemeRoller page is a color palette that is stretched out into a single line. You can use this palette line to click-and-drag a single color from the palette to a swatch area below. Depending on where you drag and drop the palette color, the swatch changes based on the color. For example, if you drag a color to the header element of a swatch below, the header for that swatch changes to that color.

You are not limited to the initial colors displayed on the color palette. Two sliders below them allow you to adjust the lightness and saturation of the colors. By adjusting the lightness you can easily slide between the entire color spectrum of dark and moody to washed out pastels. Changing the saturation level changes the intensity of the color. This gives you the option of getting those eye-piercing neon colors and emergency reds as well as faded tones with just a shred of color left in them. The slider method gives you a quick and easy way to move around available colors.

There is no reset button on the lightness and saturation sliders, so if you see a color or two that you want to use click on them, before you make adjustments. Doing so saves them to a set of color palette spots to the right of the main palette. These saved or recently used colors can be dragged and dropped just like the other palette colors so you can map out a quick color scheme before you drag and drop if you want, and then change colors on the fly after that. Figure 16.2 shows a screenshot of the color palette area including the adjustment sliders and recently used colors section.

FIGURE 16.2
The color palette is used to drag and drop colors to adjust your swatch colors.

As can be seen in Figure 16.2, there is also the option of getting color schemes from the Adobe Kuler website. Clicking on the link opens a modal window that contains the newest additions to the Kuler website. To create your own you must register on the Kuler website (http://kuler.adobe.com) and create a public swatch. You can then use the search feature to find your swatch. For those who prefer not to jump through any registration hoops, I find that changing the display options in the Kuler modal to "Search Colors" and typing in a color you want (red, blue, gray, and so on) returns a great set of possible palettes to use. This even works on colors that you might not normally consider such as "carbon," "ultraviolet," and "predator."

Using the color palette is a fast and efficient way to get your custom theme started, but it doesn't give you the full control that you may want. To learn how to fine-tune your theme, let's take a look at the using the inspector tool.

Using the Inspector Tool for Adjustments

The inspector tool works similarly to the common inspection tools found in many of today's modern browsers. You simply click the On button and then as you hover over a portion of swatch it will be outlined. When you have the exact element you want to edit outlined, click your mouse to select it. When an element has been selected, the properties area on the left side of the ThemeRoller site automatically opens to the style properties of the selected element.

Let's walk through an example of using the inspector to change some values on a swatch. We're going to change the header color of the A swatch from the default gray to something a little more colorful. To start, make sure the inspector is currently enabled by clicking on the On button. Next move your cursor down over the header section of the A swatch. You'll know that you are in the right area when the entire header section is outlined.

When the header is correctly outlined, click your mouse, and the Header/Footer Bar properties of the A swatch opens for editing on the left side of the ThemeRoller site. Note that the inspector will still be on, so as you move your mouse over the swatch on the way to edit the properties, any swatch elements you pass over will be outlined. While this may be a little confusing at first, it actually comes in handy when you accidentally select an element you didn't mean to select the first time.

With the properties for the Header/Footer Bar open, you can see that you can change the TEXT COLOR, TEXT SHADOW, BACKGROUND, and BORDER color. The colors can be changed using standard RGB hex color codes, or you can click on them to open a color wheel to help you select the color you want. While RGBA values can be used with ThemeRoller, the tool is a little buggy with them. The values must not have spaces between them, and the input text field and the text color may turn white. The TEXT SHADOW has four boxes used for adjustments. The first box adjusts the x-axis of the shadow, the second box adjusts the y-axis of the shadow, the third box controls the spread or dithering of the shadow, and the fourth box controls the shadow color.

TIP

Shadows Are Not Black

While your mind may play tricks on you and tell you that shadows are pure black, they most definitely are not. To try this out for yourself, grab a flashlight and head toward a wall. Turn on the flashlight and then put your hand in front of it. While this does enable you to make some killer shadow puppets, you should notice that the shadow on the wall is not pure black. Rather your shadow is generally either a different shade of the color of the wall it's being projected on, or a different shade of the light being projected out of the flashlight or light source you are using. I'm not saying you can't use #000000 for your shadow color, just that it isn't the real color of a shadow.

The BACKGROUND section is another property that contains some extra options you can use to fine-tune the settings. Next to the base color property is a slider that adjusts the gradient level of the selected color. Moving the slider to the right adds a gradient that moves from light at the top to dark at the bottom. The opposite is true for adjusting the slider to the left. If you change the base color from the default setting of #e9eaeb to another color, say #f7931e, then the slider adjusts for various shades of orange to be applied. If you click the little + box next to the slider, then START and END properties appear, and you can manually change the gradient that is applied. You can also watch the values in these boxes change by dragging the slider around. I've found this particular piece of ThemeRoller to be useful on occasion to use as a gradient tool when I am away from my design software.

Figure 16.3 shows the properties changed by use of the inspector.

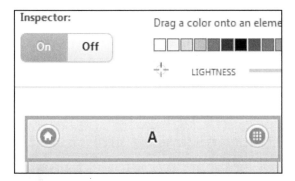

FIGURE 16.3
The inspector tool makes it easy to find the exact element you want to edit.

As you may have already noticed, when using the inspector tool to select a header, the properties for the swatch you clicked on were opened. If you didn't notice, use the inspector to change the settings for the header of the B swatch. Notice how when the header is selected the properties are opened for only the B swatch. While this is expected behavior, there are some elements that are part of the Global swatch.

To change the Global swatch settings make sure that you have the inspector enabled by clicking on the large On button. Next, move your cursor down over the icon in the header that looks like a house of any of the open swatches. When your mouse is hovering over the home icon it should have a box outline surrounding it. Click your mouse to select it for editing. Notice how the properties editing area is not opened to the settings of a particular swatch letter but is instead being automatically opened for editing the Global swatch. This is because some elements are shared between all swatches. This includes the icons used on your site, as well as the radio button colors, the check marks, and the active state for some sliders and select boxes.

Now that we know how to use the inspector to quickly get an idea of where properties are and how to adjust them in various swatches, let's take a look at adjusting the properties manually.

Manually Adjusting the Swatches

When you have the time or want to really fine-tune your theme, you can manually set all the properties. This is similar to using the inspector, but instead of using the inspector to find the elements you want to edit, you only use the properties section. The benefit to this is that you can use your mouse to test the elements in your swatch. For example, when the inspector tool is turned to Off, you can click on the Option 1 button on any swatch. This makes a select box appear above the swatch that allows you to see what your properties changes have done.

If you have just loaded the ThemeRoller page and have not changed any settings, you should notice that the properties section starts with the Global properties selected. By default three swatches named A, B, and C appear as navigation tabs. Each of these navigation tabs has submenus that you can expand to change the properties below.

The General tab contains:

- ▶ Font Family

- ▶ Active State

- ▶ Corner Radii

- ▶ Icon

- ▶ Box Shadow

Figure 16.4 shows the Global tab with collapsed submenus.

FIGURE 16.4
These settings apply to all swatches.

The Font Family submenu contains only the FONT property to edit. Remember that themes are CSS driven; the value for this property can be any valid web font or font. The default setting is Helvetica, Arial, sans-serif.

The Active State submenu contains four properties that you can edit, TEXT COLOR, TEXT SHADOW, BACKGROUND, and BORDER. These all contain fairly standard CSS values and can accept some shorthand CSS values such as #CCC instead of typing in #CCCCCC. The TEXT COLOR allows you to pick what color you want your default text to be and is set by default to a value of #FFFFFF. If you are not familiar with using shadows, they are written out as shadow color, x-offset, y-offset, and spread. The boxes for the TEXT SHADOW property section are set up in the same order with default values being set at 0px, -1px, 1px, and #145072. The BACKGROUND property contains a single color and a slider that adds a gradient depending on which way it is moved. Clicking on the + box expands another submenu that allows you to adjust the colors the gradient uses. The default value is set at #6CA6D4. The BORDER property allows you to change what color the border appears in; the default value is set to #155678. The Active State affects the selected option for the flip toggle switch, and the selected option in a select button for all swatches.

The Corner Radii submenu contains two properties for editing, GROUP and BUTTONS. The GROUP property affects any element that uses the `.ui-control-group` class; this includes the elements with an attribute of `data-role="controlgroup"`. It is set with a default value of .6em and can be adjusted by typing in a value or using the slider. Note that even though this property can take any em value typed in, it will not display any value greater than 2em or less than .1em. The BUTTONS property works similarly, allowing you to adjust how rounded the buttons appear. With a default value of 1em, you may adjust the value from .1em to 2em. Note that this value not only affects the appearance of buttons but also the appearance of the handle on input sliders. Some settings here may seem a little confusing as sliders appear in the same positions but have drastically different ranges. This is especially apparent when loading the page. As there is always the chance of bugs in this tool, make sure that you double-check your settings before and after you generate your file.

The Icon submenu contains three properties that you can edit, DEFAULT ICON, DISC COLOR, and DISC OPACITY. The DEFALT ICON contains two select boxes; the first allows you to change which icon color set is used. The options are either White or Black, with a default option of White. The second select box allows you to toggle between With disc and W/O disc. The disc is used to add contrast to any icons used. That being said, with the correct color scheme you can create some beautiful minimalistic swatches when not using the disc. The default value is With disc. Changing the DISC COLOR does exactly what you think it will. Again, this is used to enhance the appearance of your icons and is completely ignored if the disc is not used. The default disc color is #000000. The DISC OPACITY changes how transparent the disc is. If you want the disc to blend in with the colors behind it, try lowering the opacity. If you want the disc to use more of the currently set color, set the opacity to a high number. The default value is 25, but can be changed from 0 to 100. While you can put higher or lower values in, they are ignored if not in that range.

The Box Shadow submenu has three properties that you can change, COLOR, OPACITY, and SIZE. These settings affect anything that uses the `.ui-shadow` class, including dialog windows. Changing the COLOR value makes the shadow use the specified value instead of the default value of #000000. The OPACITY value changes how transparent the shadow is, and ranges in value from 0 to 100 with a default value of 25. Finally, the SIZE property changes the spread of the shadow. The default value is 4px, but can be changed to just about any pixel value. If you change the value to a negative value the shadow will not be seen.

Now that the Global settings are covered, let's take a look at the submenus available for use with individual swatches.

All swatch tabs contain:

▶ Header/Footer Bar

▶ Content Body

▶ Button: Normal

▶ Button: Hover

▶ Button: Pressed

Figure 16.5 shows the A swatch tab with collapsed submenus.

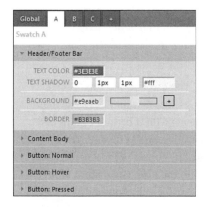

FIGURE 16.5
These settings apply only to the A swatch.

The Header/Footer Bar submenu contains four properties that can be edited, TEXT COLOR, TEXT SHADOW, BACKGROUND, and BORDER. We already covered changing these settings when using the inspector tool, so you should be familiar with these properties.

The Content Body submenu contains five properties that can be edited, LINK COLOR, TEXT COLOR, TEXT SHADOW, BACKGROUND, and BORDER. The LINK COLOR has a default setting of #2489CE and can be changed using any hex color. This of course changes the color of any a elements or links using this swatch. The TEXT COLOR property has a default setting of #333333 and controls the color of the text that is used with this swatch. This can also be changed to any hex color. The TEXT SHADOW property works exactly the same as it does with the Active State submenu on the Global tab. The difference here is that the default values are 0, 1px, 0, and #fff. The BACKGROUND property also works the same here as it does in the Active State submenu of the Global tab. The default setting is different on the swatches, however, as it is set at #f0f0f0 and can be changed to any hex color value. The BORDER property is used to add a border to the element that contains an attribute of `data-role="content"`. The default setting is #B3B3B3, and can be changed to any hex color value.

The Button: Normal submenu contains four properties that are used to change the appearance of a button when in a normal state. The normal state is reached when the button is not being clicked, pressed, or hovered over. The properties that can be edited are TEXT COLOR, TEXT SHADOW, BACKGROUND, and BORDER. The TEXT COLOR changes the text that appears on the button. The default value is #2F3E46 and can be changed to any hex color value. The TEXT SHADOW property works the same way as it does in the Content Body submenu, with the default values being 0, 1px, 1px, and #f6f6f6. The BACKGROUND property contains a default hex color value of #eee and is used to change the color of the button. It contains a familiar slider that is used to adjust or apply a gradient to the button. Using the + box drops down two hex color values that can be used to adjust the gradient. The BORDER property adjusts the color of the border that is applied to the button. The default value is a hex color value of #ccc and can be changed to any other hex color value.

The Button: Hover submenu contains the exact same properties as the Button: Normal submenu and is used to change button appearance when hovered over. This has limited application for touchscreen devices but is always triggered when a cursor or mouse is used to interact with the button. The only difference in the properties between Button: Normal and Button: Hover is the default property values. The default TEXT COLOR is still the same with a value of #2F3E46. The default values for TEXT SHADOW are 0, 1px, 1px, and #fff. The default value for BACKGROUND is #dadada. The default value for the BORDER is #bbbbbb. All these properties can be changed in the same way they can be changed on the Button: Normal submenu.

The Button: Pressed submenu works just like Button: Hover does. It contains the exact same properties but does contain slightly different default values that can be changed to new ones. The default value for TEXT COLOR is #2F3E46. The default values for TEXT SHADOW are 0, 1px, 1px, #ffffff. The default value for BACKGROUND is #fdfdfd. The default value for BORDER is #808080. The Button: Pressed styles are applied when the screen is tapped or clicked.

All the swatch tabs have these same submenus and properties. The difference is that what is changed on the A swatch will not be applied to the B swatch and so on. If you need more than the three default swatches default you can click on the + tab that is next to the C swatch tab and a D tab will appear. You can continue to do this until you have swatches A-Z.

When you are finished making your theme, it is time to save the swatch so you can start using it. Let's take a look at doing just that.

Working with a Custom Theme

Now that you have created your theme, you may just want to get started right away using it. We start by covering how to download your theme, and then we cover importing it back into ThemeRoller. This comes in handy when you want to add another swatch or change a value that you missed. Finally we add a custom theme to a page.

Downloading Your Theme

ThemeRoller makes it easy to download and start using your theme immediately. There is a Download Theme link on the upper-left side of the main ThemeRoller page. By clicking on this link a modal window appears and asks you to name the theme as well as gives you some brief instructions on how to include the theme in your jQuery Mobile pages. After you name your theme, click on the Download Zip button to begin your theme download.

The zip file that you download contains an index.html file as well as a themes folder. The file gives you a brief example of how your theme looks and gives you the instructions for including your theme on a page.

Inside the themes folder that is inside your downloaded zip file, you find two CSS files. They have whatever name you happened to give your theme when you downloaded it. One of them contains the uncompressed full version of your theme, and the other contains a compressed or minified version of your theme. I recommend that you use your minified version in production and keep your uncompressed version around for editing. There also is an images folder that contains the icons needed by your theme. These are the same image files used by the default jQuery Mobile styles. Before we get to adding your custom theme to a page, let's look at one last portion that I find useful, the ability to import an existing theme and work on it.

Importing a Theme into ThemeRoller

Occasionally you may run into a problem with a style that you had missed or overlooked, or you may need to add an additional swatch to your custom theme. Rather than resort to using hack-and-slash or cut-and-paste methods of adding swatches to your theme, you can actually upload or import your existing custom theme into ThemeRoller and modify it there.

To import your custom theme and continue working with it you need the uncompressed version of your theme. Open that in a text editor, select all the text, and copy it to your system clipboard (usually done through Command+C or Ctrl+C). Next open your browser back up to http://jquerymobile.com/themeroller/ and click on the Import link just below the Download Theme link. When you do that, a modal window appears and asks you to paste your code into the text area. Paste your code into the text area (usually done with the Command+V or Ctrl+V keys) and click the Import button in the modal window. As soon as you click the button, your theme is applied and your styled swatches appear.

Please note that the import function does not work with themes that you created yourself, but only with themes generated with ThemeRoller. The import feature does have one other feature that makes it easy to extend the default theme that comes with jQuery Mobile. This is useful for when you are upgrading a legacy app, or when you have built a site using the default styles and want to customize the original swatch. To import the original jQuery Mobile styles, click on the Import button. When the modal window opens, instead of pasting in your CSS code. click on the Import Default Theme link on the top-right of the modal. This automatically puts the styles into the text area. After it has loaded, click the Import button to finish the process. As soon as the import is finished, you should see the familiar swatches appear.

Now that we know how to download our custom theme, and how to import it back into ThemeRoller for more modification, let's learn how to include our custom theme in our page.

Including a Custom Theme

When you download your theme, you are shown a snippet of code that enables you to use your custom theme. While the sample code does use a bold style to highlight the inclusion of your custom theme, it is easy to overlook the other style that is being used.

When using a custom theme instead of using the standard jQuery Mobile styles you need to use just the structure. This may feel a little vague so let me give you an example.

Instead of using this standard styles reference:

```
<link rel="stylesheet"
href="http://code.jquery.com/mobile/1.0/jquery.mobile-1.0.min.css" />
```

Use this line:

```
<link rel="stylesheet"
href="http://code.jquery.com/mobile/1.0/jquery.mobile.structure-1.0.min.css" />
```

The major difference may appear to be the filename, but the files are actually quite different. The file jquery.mobile.structure-1.0.min.css contains only the pieces necessary for the layout or structure of jQuery Mobile. It does not contain any swatch information. This helps cut down on the file size, and more importantly prevents the default jQuery Mobile styles from overwriting your custom theme styles. You can load this style either using one of the jQuery Mobile Content

Delivery Network (CDN) locations, or by downloading the file and referencing it locally. Listing 16.1 shows the contents of custom_theme.html, which is a page that includes a custom theme.

LISTING 16.1 **A Page Using a Custom Theme**

```
 1: <!DOCTYPE html>
 2: <html>
 3:   <head>
 4:     <title>Developing with jQuery Mobile</title>
 5:     <meta name="viewport" content="width=device-width, initial-scale=1">
 6:     <link rel="stylesheet" href="css/myTheme.min.css" />
 7:     <link rel="stylesheet"
href="http://code.jquery.com/mobile/1.0/jquery.mobile.structure-1.0.min.css" />
 8:     <script src="http://code.jquery.com/jquery-1.6.4.min.js"></script>
 9:     <script src="http://code.jquery.com/mobile/1.0/jquery.mobile-1.0.min.js">
</script>
10:   </head>
11:   <body>
12:     <div data-role="page" data-theme="a">
13:       <div data-role="header" data-theme="b"><h1>Custom Theme Page</h1></div>
14:       <div data-role="content">
15:         <p>Below is a button using the b theme</p>
16:         <a href="#" data-role="button">Button text</a>
17:         <ul data-role="listview" data-inset="true">
18:           <li data-role="list-divider">Check out this list</li>
19:           <li>This is a list item</li>
20:           <li>This is another list item</li>
21:         </ul>
22:         <div data-role="collapsible" data-collapsed="false"
data-content-theme="c">
23:           <h3>Collapsible container</h3>
24:           <p>Content inside of the collapsible area using theme c</p>
25:         </div>
26:       </div>
27:     </div>
28:   </body>
29: </html>
```

The file starts out normally enough, but you can see the difference between this page and a page that doesn't include a custom theme on line 6. This line shows a custom theme being included from a local resource location. Line 7 shows the modified jQuery Mobile style sheet being included through a CDN location. The custom theme file should be loaded before any of the other jQuery Mobile styles. Continuing down the file, line 12 shows that we are changing the default theme to use the A swatch. This is done by using the attribute data-theme="a". Line 13 shows the default theme for the header being changed to use the B swatch; this is done in the same fashion as line 12 with an attribute of data-theme="b". Lines 14-27 finish out the sample page demonstrating various page elements being included so that you get an idea of how the custom theme looks. Figure 16.6 shows the page being viewed in a mobile browser.

FIGURE 16.6
A page using a custom theme generated through ThemeRoller viewed on a mobile browser

Summary

In this hour you learned what the jQuery Mobile ThemeRoller is and how to access it. You learned how to use the color palette to drag and drop colors onto color swatches to change styles. By using the inspector tool you can figure out exactly what element and property you need to edit to get the customization you want. You also learned how to download your theme when finished, import it back into ThemeRoller to make changes, and implement your custom theme into your page.

Q&A

Q. When reading about adjusting the properties for the various Global and swatch styles, why are some of the default values inconsistent in the way they are presented?

A. I'm not entirely sure why the values in the tool do not follow a preset guideline for presentation or entry. For example, the Button: Hover submenu has a property for TEXT SHADOW that is set at #fff while the Button: Pressed contains the same submenu and TEXT SHADOW property, but contains a default setting of #ffffff. The good news is that both values are actually the same; one is just written in shorthand. This also applies to hex values that use capital or lowercase letters. Even though the values do not appear quite the same, you do not have to worry about the values being interpreted incorrectly by the browser viewing your theme.

Q. Can I include more than one custom theme CSS file?

A. Sort of, but in all honesty you should avoid it. Each theme can have up to 26 swatches, and then you can mix and match the styles inside them to create even more custom styles. So if you are asking whether you can combine two CSS files to create a theme with 52 swatches instead of 26, the answer is a solid no. If you mean that you want to include one file with swatches A-E and another file with swatches F-Z, then yes you can technically do that, but it will cost you an extra HTTP request and make managing your styles much more difficult.

Q. Do I have to use the compressed version of the CSS file? I tried opening it and it doesn't appear human-readable.

A. Whether you use the compressed or minified version of your styles is completely up to you; however, the minified version of your theme is included because it reduces file-size and makes the file download faster to the client browser.

Workshop

The workshop contains a quiz and some exercises to help you check your comprehension and understanding.

Quiz

1. Where do you go to access the jQuery Mobile ThemeRoller?

2. What files are included inside the downloaded theme zip file?

3. True or False: You can import any CSS files into ThemeRoller and they will work.

4. True or False: The A swatch settings in ThemeRoller affect all styles regardless of whether they are in the A swatch.

5. What jQuery Mobile CSS file should you be including when you use a custom theme?

Answers

1. http://jquerymobile.com/themeroller/ is the current online home of the jQuery Mobile ThemeRoller.

2. An example index.html file, a themes folder, your custom compressed and uncompressed theme CSS files, the icon image files, and loader image are all included in the downloaded theme zip file.

3. False. You may only copy CSS that is generated with ThemeRoller originally, and it must be the uncompressed version.

4. False. The Global properties affect all swatches, but any changes made to the A swatch affect only the A swatch.

5. When using a custom theme, you should include the jquery.mobile.structure-1.0.min.css file as you most likely do not need the jQuery Mobile default styles overwriting your custom ones.

Exercises

1. Open the ThemeRoller site and create your own swatch. Get familiar with all the ways to create your own swatches.

2. Register with Adobe Kuler and create a public color scheme (make sure it's public or you won't be able to find it). Go to the ThemeRoller website and use the Adobe Kuler swatches menu to search for your color scheme and create a theme using the drag-and-drop palette.

3. Using the included theme file myTheme.css, import it into ThemeRoller and change the property settings and add two more swatches. When finished, download your customized version and use it in the included custom_theme.html file.

HOUR 17
Detecting Mobile Devices

What You'll Learn in This Hour:

- ▶ Why developers choose to use mobile detection
- ▶ Various methods of detecting mobile devices
- ▶ How to redirect a mobile device after detection
- ▶ Pros and cons of mobile detection methods

You may have noticed that when you visit some websites on your mobile device you are automatically redirected to a mobile version of the site. While this may seem like Internet black magic, there is a much simpler explanation for the events that happen behind the scenes. Before we get to the magic, let's take a moment and learn why mobile detection is important.

Learning the Importance of Mobile Detection

Over the last decade we have enjoyed progressively faster and faster connection speeds. Companies have raced to wire every home with broadband connections, satellite service has improved and expanded to remote users, and wireless technology has taken leaps forward in providing service to users on the move. As the connection speed of users has increased developers have continued to cram more and more data down the pipe. The benefit to the amount of data that a developer can send to the user is the ability to create rich user experiences and websites that act like fully installed applications. The downside is that heavy websites bring slow connections to a crawl and force users to watch loading screens while data is painfully pulled down to the client.

You may remember back when you would type in an address for a site and a page would appear asking if you would like the high-bandwidth or low-bandwidth version of the site. The high-bandwidth version often contained animated images, Flash content, and for a while every site had to have music playing. On the other hand, if you chose the low-bandwidth alternative, you were treated to possibly one or two pictures and a screen full of text. This is where mobile detection comes into use.

Mobile detection gives developers the ability to create a lighter experience that can either be made generic or custom tailored to the device requesting the data. In this respect you can choose whether you want to force a large media-filled experience down to a user or trade it out for a minimalistic design. It also allows you to decide to include full size images and backgrounds or to include smaller images and a solid color background instead. Knowing when a mobile device is viewing your site is also important as it gives clues to the audience that is viewing your content and can help you make changes that benefit the main users of your site.

Detecting mobile devices has shifted over the last few years as mobile devices continue to blur the line between desktop browsers and mobile browsers. Methods that used to be valid and indispensible are now flawed and not recommended for filtering traffic from one version of your site to another. One method previously used to determine which devices were mobile was to detect JavaScript support. A test could be run on the client browser and if the JavaScript could not be run then it would run the mobile version of the page. While this worked to some degree, it left large gaps and holes on who would see the mobile page. As smartphones crossed into using browsers with JavaScript support, this method quickly fell from prominent use and is now used for feature detection and fallbacks for browser support.

Today there are methods that still let some devices through but have a greater chance of catching the majority of mobile devices. Let's take a look at using some server configuration files to find out what device is browsing our network.

Using the .htaccess File

Those familiar with using the Apache web server already know that using .htaccess files can come in handy for a variety of different uses. These files allow you to create server configurations that apply to the folder they are placed in. Configuration changes can range anywhere from redirects to cookie creation to even placing files under authentication. It just so happens that they can also be used to help direct mobile visitors to a different site or page when used.

To use the .htaccess file as a means to redirect traffic you need to learn a little about what a mobile browser reports to the web server. Each mobile browser has a specific string it passes to the server when it requests a file. This is known as the User Agent (UA). By checking the UA when a page is requested you can determine whether the page should be delivered as is, or whether it should tell the browser requesting the page to go to a different directory, domain, or file.

Take a look at the following UA and see whether you can tell where they came from:

▶ "Mozilla/5.0 (iPhone Simulator; CPU iPhone OS 5_0 like Mac OS X) AppleWebKit/534.46 (KHTML, like Gecko) Version/5.1 Mobile/9A334 Safari/7534.48.3"

▶ "Mozilla/5.0 (Linux; U; Android 2.3.3; en-us; sdk Build/ GRI34) AppleWebKit/533.1 (KHTML, like Gecko) Version/4.0 Mobile Safari/533.1"

▶ "Mozilla/5.0 (iPod; CPU iPhone OS 5_0_1 like Mac OS X) AppleWebKit/534.46 (KHTML, like Gecko) Version/5.1 Mobile/9A405 Safari/7534.48.3"

▶ "GET /favicon.ico HTTP/1.1" 404 209 "http://192.168.0.9/" "Mozilla/5.0 (Linux; U; Android 2.3.5; en-us; YP-G70 Build/ GINGERBREAD) AppleWebKit/533.1 (KHTML, like Gecko) Version/4.0 Mobile Safari/533.1"

The preceding examples are from both emulators and actual devices. I used both so that you would have an example of how the UA can vary even when it's coming from an emulator that should be mimicking the actual device you are trying to use. The first two listed above are emulators, an iOS emulator and an Android emulator. The third and forth are actual mobile devices—an iPod Touch running iOS 5.0.1 and a Galaxy Player 5.0 running Gingerbread 2.3.5.

Taking a closer look at these UA strings you can see they have a few similar elements. For example, both the iOS emulator and the iPod have the word iPhone in the UA. For the other two examples, both the emulator and the Galaxy Player have the word Android in them. Knowing this, we can build a simple regular expression (regex) based on finding these keywords in the UA when a page is requested. Listing 17.1 shows a simple .htaccess file used to find iPhone and Android devices.

LISTING 17.1 Using regex and .htaccess to Filter Mobile Devices

```
1: Options +FollowSymlinks
2: RewriteEngine On
3: RewriteCond %{HTTP_USER_AGENT} "android|iphone" [NC]
4: RewriteRule ^(.*)$ http://localhost/mobile/ [L,R=302]
```

Line 1 shows a statement that is needed by the Apache server to enable the rewrite to work. I have read that if this line is already included in your server configuration it may cause your page to error. While I have not run into this particular problem myself, if you are getting an Error 500 page when this runs, try removing line 1. Line 2 shows the RewriteEngine being enabled. The RewriteEngine is part of the server magic that makes this all run; it enables the server to read the request from the client browser and rewrite it to something else. One other common use for rewriting the request is for blog engines to make the URLs more human readable. Line 3 is where we start using a regex to determine a RewriteCond that checks the UA for the words android and iphone. If you are wondering why I didn't type "Android" and "iPhone" inside the regex, it is because that particular line has [NC] at the end. The [NC] means "No Case", meaning that it will ignore the case of the characters in the regex. Line 4 shows what happens when the condition from line 3 is met. The URL that is listed should be where you want the mobile user to go. The [L,R=302] means two things actually; the L means that it is the last rule that should be processed by the RewriteEngine, and the R=302 means that the browser will be told that the original page has been temporarily moved.

While this is a great start, this regex will not work for all mobile devices. In fact, if you crack open a different mobile device, say a BlackBerry, and browse to where the .htaccess file is running, it will not trigger the mobile redirect and you will be treated to the original site. To accurately create your perfect regex you should look at your server access logs and view the different UA strings of users viewing your site and add entries to your regex based on that data. Several catchall scripts and regex strings are available as search results from your favorite search engine as well that you can try. Keep in mind before you push one into your production environment that every script should be looked over carefully and still compared with your server logs to see whether it is needed.

To get a summary of using the .htaccess file for detecting and redirecting mobile devices let's take a look at the pros and cons.

The pros to using the .htaccess file for mobile detection are

- Fairly easy to manage
- Works at the server level without reliance on client capability
- Does not require any other server-side languages

The cons to using using the .htaccess files for mobile detection are

- Can be a strain on the server
- Can create possible redirect loops
- Does not natively work with all web servers

If you have access to your server configuration file (usually a file named httpd.conf), you can do all your rewriting inside that file. This has the added benefit of loading into memory rather than being evaluated on every request.

For those who do not want to mess with any type of configuration file, but still want the server to handle the detection and redirection of mobile devices, you can use server-side languages to get the job done. Let's take a look at doing this with PHP.

Playing Device Detective with PHP

You have seen how you can use an .htaccess file to rewrite the requests coming from mobile browsers to direct them to a mobile section or page of your site. While using that method works, more developers seem to have a deeper knowledge of using PHP than they have of working with .htaccess files. PHP is an excellent language to start with because it is readily available on most web host providers, and it runs with most servers that you can download and use on your own system.

While it is impossible for me to cover everything that you can do with PHP in a couple of pages, I can show you how to detect the UA with PHP. To get started let's take a look at a built-in PHP variable named $_SERVER.

The $_SERVER variable is actually an array and contains many elements that you can use to find out information about the server itself as well as some information about the client visiting it. It is important to note that when using the $_SERVER variable, it may not always return values. This is because some servers are configured not to pass some data to the PHP variable. Listing 17.2 shows the content of detect.php, a simple PHP file that is being used to display some information using the $_SERVER variable.

LISTING 17.2   Using the PHP $_SERVER Variable

```
 1: <!DOCTYPE html>
 2: <html>
 3:    <head>
 4:      <title>UA with PHP</title>
 5:    </head>
 6:    <body>
 7:      <h1>Using PHP to detect UA</h1>
 8:      <p>The UA viewing this page is:</p>
 9:      <p><?php echo $_SERVER['HTTP_USER_AGENT']; ?></p>
10:    </body>
11: </html>
```

The file is really very simple; it starts off on line 1 declaring the HTML5 DOCTYPE and continues setting up the page. In the body element of the file we can see that we have a few elements that are telling us what the page is for, and what the UA of the device viewing the page will be. Line 9 shows the PHP script used to actually get the UA. In PHP, echo outputs whatever is after it to the screen. By using the $_SERVER array object and passing HTTP_USER_AGENT into it we are able to retrieve the value that has been stored there. Depending on the browser we use when we view the page, the information displayed changes. Figure 17.1 and Figure 17.2 show the results of the page being viewed through a desktop browser and on an iPhone simulator.

FIGURE 17.1
The page viewed in a desktop browser

FIGURE 17.2
The page viewed from the iOS simulator

Now that we know how to get the UA with PHP, let's look at actually redirecting the page when a mobile device is detected. Listing 17.3 shows a PHP script that redirects the browser based on the UA.

LISTING 17.3   Redirecting a Mobile Device with PHP

```
1: <?php
2: $ua = $_SERVER['HTTP_USER_AGENT'];
3: if(stripos($ua,'iphone') !== false) {
4:    header('Location: http://localhost/mobile');
5:    exit();
6: }
7: ?>
```

This script should be placed at or near the top of your PHP file so that it executes before the rest of the page is rendered. Line 1 is the standard opening for running PHP. When that is not there, any PHP code will not run. Line 2 shows a variable named $ua being created. This variable contains the UA of the browser viewing the page by being set to $_SERVER['HTTP_USER_AGENT']. Line 3 is a little interesting, but to sum it up it is checking for the existence of the string 'iphone' within the $ua variable. You do not have to worry about case because the PHP stripos method ignores the case of the variable it is checking. When found it executes line 4, which informs the browser viewing the page to redirect the browser to a different location. Line 5 simply stops further execution of the script. Line 6 closes the if block, and line 7 closes our PHP script.

This script can be modified to include more strings to look for either in the current if block, or if you wanted to redirect to different pages or locations based on device type by including an else and/or else if block.

As a summary of using PHP for detecting and redirecting mobile devices let's take a look at the pros and cons.

The pros to using PHP for mobile detection are

- ▸ Cleaner than using and managing .htaccess files

- ▸ Compatible with any server that can run PHP

- ▸ Not dependent on client-side logic to run

The cons of using PHP for mobile detection are

- ▸ Can still be spoofed by modified UA strings.

- ▸ Needs to match a string exactly.

▶ The `if` block must be updated for new devices.

▶ May still suffer from redirect issues.

To learn more about other elements and data that you can get out of the $_SERVER variable, visit the PHP manual at http://www.php.net/manual/en/reserved.variables.server.php.

While we have covered two methods of detecting mobile devices from the server, you can also use JavaScript to detect and redirect a browser from the client.

Using JavaScript as a Detection Method

JavaScript can be used in nearly the same manner as using PHP or a .htaccess file. While it does have some rather obvious differences, it is still a method that you may at times want to employ. When using JavaScript you can still get the UA by calling the userAgent property of the navigator object. Listing 17.4 shows the contents of detect_js.html.

LISTING 17.4   Displaying the UA with JavaScript

```
 1: <!DOCTYPE html>
 2: <html>
 3:   <head>
 4:     <title>UA with JS</title>
 5:   </head>
 6:   <body>
 7:     <h1>Detecting the UA with JavaScript</h1>
 8:     <p>Click the button below to view your device UA.</p>
 9:     <button type="button" onclick="getUA()">View UA</button>
10:     <script>
11:       function getUA() {
12:         alert(navigator.userAgent);
13:       }
14:     </script>
15:   </body>
16: </html>
```

The code here looks like some standard test page boilerplate, and it is, so we'll start on line 9. Line 9 shows a button that calls the getUA() function when clicked. This function is defined inside the script element that starts on line 10. The function is declared on line 11. Line 12 shows an alert() function being called that displays the value of navigator.userAgent when run. Line 13 closes the getUA() function, and line 14 closes the script element.

This shows similar results to what we saw with the PHP tests. Figure 17.3 shows the test being run from a desktop browser, and Figure 17.4 shows it running in an iOS simulator.

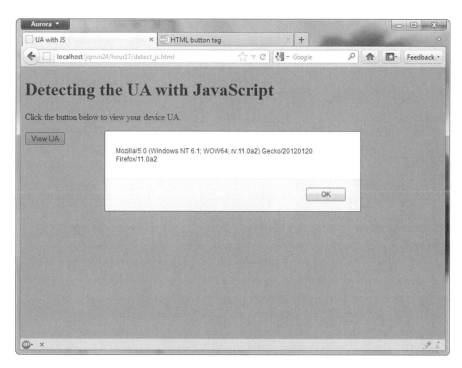

FIGURE 17.3
Testing the UA with JavaScript on a desktop

FIGURE 17.4
Testing the UA with JavaScript on the iOS simulator

Now that we know how to get the UA with JavaScript, let's parse it and redirect the device to another location on page load. Listing 17.5 shows a script that redirects some mobile devices to another page when loaded.

LISTING 17.5 Redirecting the Mobile Browser with JavaScript

```
1: <script>
2:     var ua = navigator.userAgent;
3:     if ((ua.match(/iPhone/i)) || (ua.match(/Android/i))) {
4:         location.replace("http://localhost/mobile");
5:     }
6: </script>
```

Line 1 begins the `script` element. Line 2 shows a variable being set up to contain the UA by use of the `navigator.userAgent`. This variable is important especially if you are going to be doing more than one check because the value will not change, so it can be stored in memory once instead of forcing the browser to grab it and compare it over and over again. Line 3 shows an `if` block that is using the `.match()` function on the ua variable. The `.match()` function takes a regex that it then compares to the string it is attached to, which in this case is the ua variable. The trailing `/i` on both the `iPhone` and the `Andoid` regex strings represents case-insensitivity. If you prefer, you may leave those off and change the ua variable setup to contain the `.toLowerCase()` function. Before you do that, though, keep in mind that using a regex is about 50% faster than using the `.toLowerCase()` function on the ua variable. Line 4 shows that when the `if` block is found to be `true`, it redirects the browser by using the `.replace()` function on the `location` object. Line 5 closes the `if` block, and line 6 closes the `script` element.

While this method does a great job of mimicking the server-side versions, you can also use this method to dynamically include different files. Listing 17.6 shows the contents of include_js.html, which gives an example of some JavaScript that includes another JavaScript file (external_script.js) when it detects either an iPhone or Android device.

LISTING 17.6 Using JavaScript to Include Files Based on Mobile Detection

```
 1: <!DOCTYPE html>
 2: <html>
 3:   <head>
 4:     <title>UA with JS</title>
 5:     <script src="http://code.jquery.com/jquery-1.7.1.min.js"></script>
 6:     <script>
 7:       window.onload = function() {
 8:         var ua = navigator.userAgent;
 9:         if ((ua.match(/iPhone/i) || ua.match(/Android/i))) {
10:           $.getScript('external_script.js');
11:         }
```

```
12:       }
13:    </script>
14:  </head>
15:  <body>
16:    <h1>Including files based on UA with JavaScript</h1>
17:    <p>If an alert is displayed, you are using an iPhone or Android device</p>
18:  </body>
19: </html>
```

The file begins as a standard HTML file, but on line 5 we have included the jQuery library. Line 6 then begins a `script` element. Line 7 shows that we are going to run an anonymous function as soon as the page is loaded. Note that since we are using jQuery you could switch this code to run inside the `$(document).ready()`. Line 8 shows the setup of a variable named `ua` that contains the UA. Line 9 shows an `if` block starting and the `ua` variable being used with the `.match()` function to look for certain strings using regex. Line 10 shows an interesting jQuery function. This is a shorthand version of an AJAX call to an external script file. It pulls the external_script.js file into the DOM and executes it as soon as the load is complete. To learn more about the `$.getScript()` method, visit the official jQuery docs at http://api.jquery.com/jQuery.getScript/. Line 11 closes the `if` block. Line 12 closes the anonymous function that is running on page load. The rest of the file is mainly some description, so that it can be tested on other devices, or on a desktop. Figure 17.5 shows the results of running this page in the iPhone simulator.

FIGURE 17.5
The iPhone simulator matches the regex and loads the external JavaScript file.

Using this method you can include extra functions or libraries that you may want to run only on a mobile device. This is especially useful for libraries focused on touch events only.

To summarize the use of JavaScript for detecting and redirecting mobile devices let's take a look at the pros and cons.

The pros to using JavaScript for mobile detection are

- ▶ The client does all the work.

- ▶ Can be combined with AJAX to include files dynamically.

- ▶ Not dependent on server technology to run.

The cons to using JavaScript for mobile detection are

- ▶ Can be ignored by turning off JavaScript on the client.

- ▶ Code is visible in the page source.

- ▶ Due to connection speeds a page may render before a script has finished executing causing possible site inconsistency for the user.

Now that you know about using the server and client to detect a mobile device, let's look at a completely different way of handling mobile devices.

Non-Detection Solutions

The future of mobile browsing is changing rapidly, and the very definition of a mobile device is being challenged as the devices we take with us become more powerful and capable. Techniques that were used to detect mobile devices either do not work, or are working on the wrong devices. Another complication is the ability of some mobile browsers to alter the UA that they send to the server. This makes UA-only detecting methods fail, or obsolete.

While there are still some great solutions such as the Wireless Universal Resource FiLe (http:// wurfl.sourceforge.net/) that keep an expanding list of mobile devices and provide an API you can use for mobile device detection, you should consider some existing solutions to help combat mobile devices.

Using Responsive Design

Creating a site that changes based on the viewing capabilities of the client certainly seems like best approach. It is comfortable to users because they get an experience that feels like it has been tailored to fit their device. It has been gaining in popularity as more and more sites are taking this approach in handling mobile devices.

Current mobile devices tend to have browsers that support most HTML5 and CSS3 features, making them ideal for use with a responsive design. Devices that have these browsers generally have a big enough processor in them to handle a fair amount of images as well as JavaScript processing. This is important to consider when handling mobile devices.

Device overload is becoming less of a problem, but it wasn't all that long ago that I built a site that would routinely crash the mobile Safari browser. It was an elusive problem, and it wouldn't happen every time the site was viewed. The problem turned out to be a couple of sprite images that were too large to be stored in memory and then referenced repeatedly when some elements were injected into the DOM. While this may not happen on current generation devices, older phones may be prone to problems similar to this.

Unless you are planning your site or app to work only with a specific list of devices, you need to rely on the use of analytics to give you clues as to how you should change your site. Many analytics packages are available including some open-source ones that you can compile and run on your own server. For ease of use, I recommend setting up a Google Analytics (http://www.google.com/analytics) account and using it to get a feel for what your users are using to view your site, and how they arrive on your site. With this information you can make a more informed decision on what dimensions your site should be designed for.

Another option you may need to consider with a responsive design is that some users may not want the responsive version of your site. While that may sound a little strange, there is one site in particular that whenever I visit, I instantly click on the View Full Site link. I do this because the mobile version of the site actually leaves out not only the navigation menu I want, but also an entire section of the site. While I may be in the minority, the idea of visiting the full version of the site is something left out of most responsive designs.

To summarize using a responsive design for handling mobile devices let's take a look at the pros and cons.

The pros to using a responsive design are

- ▶ No dependence on the client UA

- ▶ Create an experience that fits a wide gamut of device resolutions

- ▶ Does not require the use of a separate site to maintain

- ▶ Does not require extra views, pages, or directories specifically for mobile users

The cons to using a responsive design are

- ▶ May not work with legacy or "dumb" phone browsers.

- ▶ The browser on the device must have either CSS3 support to run media queries, or it must be able to run JavaScript and a compatibility script.

▶ Creating a successful responsive design can take a lot of time and planning.

▶ Giving the user an option to view the full site is not generally offered and may need to be considered.

Now that we've discussed using a responsive design, let's look at another way to handle mobile detection, without the detection.

Using jQuery Mobile

Why bother checking for a mobile device at all when you can use a framework that handles mobile devices as well as desktops? The jQuery Mobile library makes a fabulous choice when it comes to dealing with cross-platform and cross-device browsers. Only a handful of frameworks allow you to create and manage a mobile site that behaves the same way on a desktop. With jQuery Mobile you know that you are getting a well-tested, community-driven, and proven framework that is already included in everything from blogs to native applications.

jQuery Mobile is an ideal solution because not only does it work on most platforms, it contains a large amount of fallback support for legacy devices. That means that when someone browses your site with a legacy device, they can still use it. While it's true that site functionality decreases, it does not leave them without a means of navigating. Another reason that makes jQuery Mobile an ideal solution is that it can be blended with custom CSS and JavaScript allowing you to customize your site exactly how you want. You can still use a responsive design with jQuery Mobile, and you can include other plug-ins to extend functionality.

To quickly summarize the use of jQuery Mobile as a method for handling both desktop and mobile devices, let's take a look at some pros and cons.

The pros of using jQuery Mobile are

▶ No mobile detection needed, works on most devices.

▶ Other utilities, plug-ins, and design methods can be combined with jQuery Mobile.

▶ Part of the jQuery family.

The cons of using jQuery Mobile are

▶ The framework requires a download of assets including the jQuery library.

▶ The AJAX navigation model can get a bit complicated when used with template engines.

▶ Some elements may look a little out of place when viewed on high-resolution screens.

Summary

In this hour you learned not only why mobile detection should be considered, but also how to detect and redirect mobile devices on the server using a .htaccess file and PHP. It is also possible to use JavaScript to do some client-side mobile detection and redirection. These methods are all accomplished by reading the UA of the browser making the request to view the site. While the UA may be spoofed, it does give you a place to start with filtering any mobile devices.

Finally you learned that sometimes it may be better not to direct a user to a special mobile page or site, but instead to leverage a responsive design or just use jQuery Mobile to handle all site visitors.

Q&A

Q. How often do legacy devices really browse websites?

A. Smartphones may seem to be everywhere, but there are still many phones that are text-only or that use the Wireless Application Protocol (WAP). This all comes back to your own site analytics; you really will not know the frequency of legacy devices until you start tracking them.

Q. When can UA detection fail?

A. UA detection can fail when you are trying to target a specific browser. Many browsers have the same name in the mobile version as they use in the desktop version. This has happened in the past when attempting to target Gecko based browsers (Firefox). When creating the regex strings you are going to use, try to be as specific to the mobile device as possible. Even then you may run into trouble, so you need to test with as many devices as you can (both actual devices and emulators), and you need to do periodic updates to the regex strings you are using.

Q. I do not run an Apache server; can I still use a .htaccess file?

A. A few servers support the use of .htaccess files, but for the most part they work only on Apache servers. You can, however, with a little work copy the settings from .htaccess files into your current server config. For IIS v7+ users you can actually do most things you would do in a .htaccess file inside your Web.config file. Other servers such as nginx have support for a module that can be used to perform redirection (http://wiki.nginx.org/HttpRewriteModule). Take a look at your server guide and see whether there is a configuration file or module that works on your server.

Workshop

The workshop contains a quiz and some exercises to help you check your comprehension and understanding.

Quiz

1. What can a .htaccess file be used for?

2. What is a User Agent?

3. Why does using a test for JavaScript support make for an inconsistent detection method?

4. What gives you the best idea of what visitors view your site and on what devices?

5. What makes using jQuery Mobile so ideal for even legacy devices?

Answers

1. A .htaccess file can be used to control file access, read and write cookies, create redirects, and other things that would normally only be configured in server configuration files.

2. The User Agent is a string passed in the HTTP header request of a browser. This contains information about the browser and device that is doing the requesting.

3. While WAP devices will fail the JavaScript check and be directed to the proper page, most smartphones will pass the test and not be redirected.

4. An analytics package gives you a look at how a user found your site, what they came looking at it with, and how long they stayed. This is valuable information that can be used to help you optimize the mobile experience you are trying to convey.

5. Fallback support. Even when a user browses your site on a device that doesn't provide all the bells and whistles that a newer device gets, they are still able to use the site and to browse it fully.

Exercises

1. Create your own .htaccess file and regex and experiment with using it. Try to redirect the mobile device to another page or site.

2. Using either a server-side method or JavaScript, create a couple of entries using a regex file that will direct different types of devices to different pages. For example, try redirecting tablet users to one page and small-screen devices to a different page.

3. Create a page that uses JavaScript to display the UA of the device viewing the page. If you want to get a little extra fancy, add a second section that uses some PHP to output the same information. Test with your JavaScript processing turned on and off and compare the results between the two methods.

PART IV

Extending the Mobile Experience

Embedding Video Playback for Mobile

Whether you are piecing together a group site or a trying to create a tutorial site, there will probably be a time when you will want to add some video content. Even if you do not have the resources to host your own video, there are other service providers that you can leverage to handle the video for you. Let's learn about them and how we can embed video into our mobile site.

Understanding Video Playback

Videos are a fantastic medium that can be leveraged to help express ideas, show tutorials, and present information in a controlled fashion. Displaying content through video is a good choice, as you already know exactly what the user is going to be looking at. Many sites have come into existence simply because of their ability to display and share video content. With more people getting mobile devices capable of video playback and sharing content socially, you should consider adding a little video content to your site.

Playing back videos on mobile devices can be tricky. Although some devices can play back and even stream crystal-clear 1080p video, other devices can barely stream back 480p video at 15 frames per second. Another concern is network bandwidth. Few things are worse than trying to start a video that is 45 seconds long, but buffers for more than 5 minutes. With these concerns in mind, there are several websites or services that specialize in hosting and sharing videos that you can leverage to overcome or at least alleviate some of these obstacles.

Let's start by taking a look at the ever-popular YouTube.

Embedding a Video with YouTube

YouTube (http://www.youtube.com) is a fantastic site that allows users to create unique content and then share it with friends, coworkers, and users. It also allows users to interact with each other, and as a content creator gives some valuable insight into the analytics of users watching your content.

Currently when you create a YouTube account you can upload videos and edit them from within the site. Videos are uploaded to YouTube with a resolution usually somewhere between 240p (426×240) to 1080p (1920×1080). Users can, however, upload video up to 4k (4096×3072) in resolution. Videos may vary in length, but all users are allowed 15 minutes per video. Longer videos may be played, but must go through a verification process. Keep in mind, though, that for most mobile sites, if you can't get your message out in 15 minutes or less, you may need to rethink the message you are trying to deliver.

The easiest way to get a YouTube video into your mobile site is by using the embed code. Let's take the profile site we worked on earlier and add a link to a videos page that has an embedded video from YouTube on it. Listing 18.1 shows the contents of portfolio.html, which shows our profile page with a link added to view the embedded video.

LISTING 18.1   Adding a Link to portfolio.html

```
 1: <!DOCTYPE html>
 2: <html>
 3:   <head>
 4:     <title>Developing with jQuery Mobile</title>
 5:     <meta name="viewport" content="width=device-width, initial-scale=1">
 6:     <link rel="stylesheet"
href="http://code.jquery.com/mobile/1.1.0-rc.1/jquery.mobile-1.1.0-rc.1.min.css"/>
 7:     <script src="http://code.jquery.com/jquery-1.7.1.min.js"></script>
 8:     <script
src="http://code.jquery.com/mobile/1.1.0-rc.1/jquery.mobile-1.1.0-rc.1.min.js">
</script>
 9:     <script src="jquery.fitvids.js"></script>
10:     <script src="scripts.js"></script>
11:   </head>
12:   <body>
13:     <div data-role="page" id="home">
14:       <div data-role="header"><h1>My Portfolio</h1></div>
15:       <div data-role="content">
16:         <div class="ui-grid-a">
17:           <div class="ui-block-a"><img src="pd_logo.gif" alt="My logo" />
</div>
18:           <div class="ui-block-b"><h2>Portfolio Developer</h2></div>
19:         </div>
```

```
20:           <ul data-role="listview" data-theme="d" data-divider-theme="a"
data-inset="true">
21:             <li data-role="list-divider">Contact Information</li>
22:             <li>
23:               <h3>Phone number</h3>
24:               <p>Office: 555-555-5555 ext. 512</p>
25:               <p>GVoice: 555-555-5551</p>
26:             </li>
27:             <li>
28:               <h3>Email</h3>
29:               <p>developer@emailaddress.com</p>
30:             </li>
31:             <li>
32:               <h3>Websites</h3>
33:               <p>http://www.mywebsite.com</p>
34:               <p>http://www.myotherwebsite.com</p>
35:             </li>
36:             <li data-role="list-divider">My Videos</li>
37:             <li data-theme="e">
38:               <a href="videos.html">
39:                 <h3>View my videos</h3>
40:                 <p>Check out my latest work</p>
41:               </a>
42:             </li>
43:             <li data-role="list-divider">My Experience</li>
44:             <li>
45:               <h3>Famous Company</h3>
46:               <p>Developed an entirely new way to parse and process.</p>
47:             </li>
48:             <li>
49:               <h3>Start-up</h3>
50:               <p>Lead a small team to success through innovation.</p>
51:             </li>
52:             <li>
53:               <h3>Meh Incorporated</h3>
54:               <p>Engineered and designed a revolutionary new mobile app.</p>
55:             </li>
56:             <li data-role="list-divider">My Interests</li>
57:             <li>Mobile Development</li>
58:             <li>Technology</li>
59:             <li>Media</li>
60:           </ul>
61:           <ul data-role="listview" data-theme="d" data-divider-theme="b"
data-inset="true">
62:             <li data-role="list-divider">My Social Links</li>
63:             <li>
64:               <a href="http://twitter.com/!#/userprofilename"
data-rel="external">
```

```
65:                     <img class="ui-li-icon" src="twitter.png" alt="Twitter icon" />
66:                     Follow me on Twitter
67:                 </a>
68:             </li>
69:             <li>
70:                 <a rel="author" href="https://profiles.google.com/userprofilelink"
data-rel="external">
71:                     <img class="ui-li-icon"
src="http://ssl.gstatic.com/images/icons/gplus-16.png">
72:                     Find me on Google+
73:                 </a>
74:             </li>
75:             <li>
76:                 <a href="http://www.facebook.com/userprofilename"
data-rel="external">
77:                     <img class="ui-li-icon" src="fb.png" alt="Facebook icon" />
78:                     Friend me on Facebook
79:                 </a>
80:             </li>
81:         </ul>
82:       </div>
83:     </div>
84:   </body>
85: </html>
```

The last time we saw this code was when we where building a profile with a responsive design. Before you get too excited and dismiss this code thinking that you've already seen it. I simplified the example to only use jQuery Mobile for styling and combined several of the areas together. With that in mind, let's start at line 9 where an external JavaScript file is being included. The file jquery.fitvids.js is a jQuery plug-in that can be used to make embedded videos responsive. The plug-in contains a method called fitVids() that does some styling and adds a wrapper around any embedded video code. This plug-in is compatible with jQuery Mobile and can be found at http://fitvidsjs.com/. While we won't be able to see exactly what this does until we load a video, it needs to be included on this page due to the AJAX model that is used with jQuery Mobile. Line 10 shows a call to a second external JavaScript file. This file contains the following few lines of code:

```
$(document).delegate("#videos","pageinit", function() {
  $(".video").fitVids();
});
```

This is simply a pageinit event binding that runs when the page with an id of videos is loaded. The code then finds any elements with a class equal to video and applies the fitVids() method to them. Continuing down the code to line 13 you can see that we are creating a page on a div element with an attribute of id="home". Line 14 shows the header for the page being created, and line 15 shows the start of the `div` element that will be used as the content area. Lines 16-19 show a grid being set up and used that contains an image and a name. The image and name should be familiar from the original portfolio we created before. Lines 20-35 show the creation of an unordered list and a few list item elements that contain some basic content information. Line 36 shows another list item that is being used as a list divider with the text of "My Videos" in it. Line 37 contains another list item element, but it contains the attribute of `data-theme="e"`; this changes the color of the section to help make this particular list item stand out from the other list items. On line 38 a link is being set up that points to a file named `videos.html`. Line 39 shows an `h3` element that is inside the link and will be used as a descriptive title for the link. The `p` element on line 40 is the text that appears as a subtitle or description of what the link will do. Line 41 closes the `a` element, and line 42 closes the list element. Lines 43-60 show a few more list elements that display some various sample data that may be found on a portfolio site. The last time we used this sample code each section had been broken out into a separate section so it could be moved around the page with CSS. Since we are not using a different design based on the device browsing the site, I put these sections together. The exception to this is the second unordered list that starts on line 61 and ends on 81. I changed the code here as well to make each list item contain a link, an icon, and a description to where the link would go.

Figure 18.1 shows what the page looks like on a tablet browser.

FIGURE 18.1
The portfolio site viewed on a tablet browser

Now that we've seen how the profile page looks, let's take a look at the video page that we included the link to. Listing 18.2 shows the contents of videos.html.

LISTING 18.2   Embedding a YouTube Video

```
 1: <!DOCTYPE html>
 2: <html>
 3:   <head>
 4:     <title>Developing with jQuery Mobile</title>
 5:     <meta name="viewport" content="width=device-width, initial-scale=1">
 6:     <link rel="stylesheet"
href="http://code.jquery.com/mobile/1.1.0/jquery.mobile-1.1.0.min.css" />
 7:     <script src="http://code.jquery.com/jquery-1.7.1.min.js"></script>
 8:     <script
src="http://code.jquery.com/mobile/1.1.0/jquery.mobile-1.1.0.min.js"></script>
 9:     <script src="jquery.fitvids.js"></script>
10:     <script src="scripts.js"></script>
11:   </head>
12:   <body>
13:     <div data-role="page" id="videos">
14:       <div data-role="header">
<a href="portfolio.html" data-rel="back">Back</a><h1>Videos</h1></div>
15:       <div data-role="content">
16:         <div class="video" data-role="collapsible" data-collapsed="false"
data-content-theme="a">
17:           <h3>YouTube</h3>
18:           <iframe width="400" height="225"
src="http://www.youtube.com/embed/vG-9nNDwr84" frameborder="0" allowfullscreen>
</iframe>
19:           <p>My ascent on an airplane - hosted on YouTube</p>
20:           <p><a href="#" rel="external">View my YouTube channel</a></p>
21:         </div>
22:         <a href="portfolio.html" data-rel="back" data-theme="b"
data-role="button" data-icon="arrow-l">Go Back</a>
23:       </div>
24:     </div>
25:   </body>
26: </html>
```

The page starts out the same as portfolio.html, including the references to JavaScript files. Under normal user behavior, the contents of this page would be inserted into the DOM through an AJAX call and these files would be skipped, but if a user manually refreshes this page and the JavaScript files are not included, then any scripts would fail. Moving down to line 13 you can see the div element that contains our page. Line 14 shows the header section of the page, and line 15 uses another `div` element to create the content area. On line 16 you can see a `div` element that contains several attributes. The attribute `class="video"` is what the `fitVids()` method will use as a selector to run. The attributes `data-role="collapsible"`, `data-collapsed="false"`, and `data-content-theme="a"` create a collapsible container, leave it open, and then style it with the a swatch. The `h3` element on line 17 will be used as the title for the collapsible area. Line 18 shows the embed code generated by YouTube. The code uses an `iframe` element with five attributes. The `width` and `height` attributes are optional, but I have set them at a value that works with most mobile devices. It is worth noting that the these values will be ignored or overwritten when you are using the `fitVids()` method. The `src` attribute contains the link to the actual page that will be embedded. The attribute `frameborder="0"` turns off any added borders that would be present on the `iframe`. The last attribute, `allowfullscreen`, is used as a Boolean attribute for the YouTube player. This attribute may not always be needed, or even supported by the browser, but it is good to add as a fallback. Lines 19 and 20 are some descriptive text and a link that can be used to point to a page on YouTube. Line 21 ends the collapsible container by closing the `div` element. Line 22 is an a element that will be styled as a button that links back to the first page. Even though it contains the attribute `data-rel="back"` and will move the user one page back in the browser history, the `href` attribute has been given the value of what page to go to. This is done for accessibility and fallback support. Lines 23-26 close the remaining elements that are still open.

NOTE

Full-Screen Playback

Not all devices handle videos the way you think they might. Several devices automatically play the video in full-screen mode as soon as the play button is clicked. Other devices may even default to the built-in video player of the device. Even the behavior at the end of playback may vary. Some devices leave you on the video screen in case you want to watch it again, while others return you to the page that contains the video. When you are not expecting this behavior, you may think that your site is broken.

Figure 18.2 shows the page being rendered on a mobile browser.

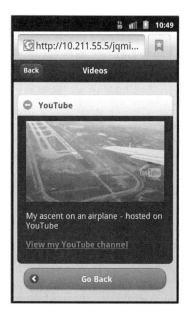

FIGURE 18.2
The embedded video is ready to be played back.

Another popular video hosting service, named Vimeo, also allows embedded video playback. Let's take a look at how to get started with Vimeo.

Embedding a Video with Vimeo

Vimeo is another service that allows users to sign up and upload videos that may be shared with others. Vimeo offers three different types of accounts ranging from free to business users. The free account is similar to the YouTube account offering, but it does not limit you to a specific time. Instead you are limited by the bandwidth you may upload each week and the content quality. For those starting out with a video service, Vimeo is a great place, as it allows you to get a good feel of the service before diving into a subscription.

Videos supported on Vimeo are similar to those supported by YouTube. They recommend uploading videos with a resolution of 640×480 for Standard Definition and 1280×720 for High Definition. They do support 1920×1080, but for the limits on your free account that will burn up your weekly upload allowance very quickly.

Vimeo allows users to embedded video content on their blogs, sites, and apps. Let's continue to build on the page we already created and add a video from Vimeo to it. Listing 18.3 shows a snippet of code that can be added to videos.html to add an embedded video hosted on Vimeo.

LISTING 18.3   Embedding Video from Vimeo

```
1: <div class="video" data-role="collapsible" data-content-theme="a">
2:    <h3>Vimeo</h3>
3:    <iframe src="http://player.vimeo.com/video/35734163?title=0&amp;byline=0&amp;
portrait=0&amp;autoplay=0" width="400" height="225" frameborder="0"
webkitAllowFullScreen mozallowfullscreen allowFullScreen></iframe>
4:    <p><a href="http://vimeo.com/35734163">Airplane Ascent</a> from
<a href="http://vimeo.com/user10166318">Phil Dutson</a> on
<a href="http://vimeo.com">Vimeo</a>.</p>
5:    <p>My ascent on an airplane - hosted on Vimeo</p>
6: </div>
```

The snippet starts out with line 1 using a `div` element to create a collapsible container that will be collapsed on page load. Line 2 shows the `h3` element that used as the title for the collapsed content area. Line 3 shows the video embed code generated from Vimeo. Similar to the embed code from YouTube, Vimeo also uses an `iframe` element. In fact the only difference is the value in the `src` attribute, the capitalization difference of `allowFullScreen`, and the additions of `webkitAllowFullScreen` and `mozallowfullscreen` attributes. The three full-screen attributes act as Boolean attributes that can be used to allow full-screen playback. Line 4 is some simple content that describes the video content and gives links to the video hosted at Vimeo, to my user on Vimeo, and to the Vimeo home page. This code is actually generated by Vimeo when requesting embedding links. Line 5 is some redundant text that can either be removed or replaced as an added description for the video. Line 6 closes out the `div` element that is being used as a collapsible container.

If you were to copy this snippet and place it in the videos.html file under the collapsible `div` element for the YouTube video you would be able to tap it open and watch the video. Something to keep in mind when using Vimeo is that free users are not allowed to have mobile videos generated for them. Unless the video is uploaded in a format that will already play back on a mobile device, when viewing the embedded video you will see an error message that the browser does not support the video or that Flash must be installed. Figure 18.3 shows what the videos page looks like with the code from Listing 18.3 added to it.

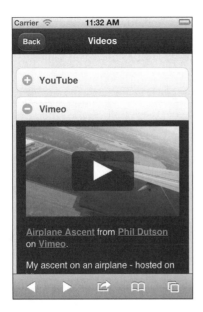

FIGURE 18.3
The Vimeo section and video have been added to the page as viewed in the iOS simulator as an iPhone4 (with Retina™ enabled).

Now that we've seen how to add some embedded videos using popular video hosting and sharing sites, let's take a look at how to add your own video.

Embedding Your Own Video

If you prefer to have total control over your video files, you can always host the files yourself. This of course means that you'll have to monitor your own bandwidth, and you'll need to provide your own playback method. Luckily, HTML5 can help with the playback method.

Video playback has always been something wanted on websites. Unfortunately, early HTML standards left out the means needed for browsers to properly deal with video files. This in turn led developers to start seeking elsewhere for video playback. Flash was quick to dominate the Web, and several programs were developed to leverage some of the Flash code to allow users to view videos. Videos were encoded into `flv` (flash video) files and could be referenced through an `swf` object loader. Support for mp4 files was added to Flash in version 9. While that was and still continues to work well for desktops, some mobile devices do not include Flash compatible browsers or even allow Flash to run on the mobile platform at all. This is where HTML5 comes in.

NOTE

Flash for Mobile

Adobe announced in November 2011 that mobile versions of Flash would no longer be developed. This means that the last version of Flash available on a mobile device is version 11.1. Security updates will still be maintained, but Adobe has shifted focus to pursuing HTML5 technology. Keep in mind that Flash is not completely dead in the mobile scene as it may still be used for developing mobile Adobe AIR applications. You can learn more by reading the blog post from Adobe located at http://blogs.adobe.com/conversations/2011/11/flash-focus.html.

The HTML5 standard has support for video playback and can be used to embed video files into web pages. While a war is still waging on the file types supported for videos in each browser, HTML5 has provided a way to skirt the issue. Listing 18.4 shows a snippet of HTML5 code used to load and play back a video.

LISTING 18.4   Using HTML5 to Play Back a Video

```
 1: <video class="localvideo" controls>
 2:   <source id="mp4_src"
 3:       src="ascent.mp4"
 4:       type='video/mp4; codecs="avc1.42E01E, mp4a.40.2"'>
 5:   </source>
 6:   <source id="ogg_src"
 7:       src="ascent.ogv"
 8:       type='video/ogg; codecs="theora, vorbis"'>
 9:   </source>
10: </video>
```

Line 1 shows the use of the HTML5 `video` element with an attribute of `class="localvideo"` and a Boolean attribute of `controls`. The `class` attribute can be used for styling or to help with selecting the element, and the `controls` attribute is used to include play, pause, scrub, and audio controls when the video element is rendered in a browser. If you choose to omit the `controls` attribute you will have to build your own player controls. Lines 2 through 5 can actually be placed on the same line, but I have broken them out so that they are easier to read and understand. Line 2 shows the opening tag of a `source` element. The attributes stored in this element are what the browser will use to prepare the proper playback codecs to play the video. The `id` attribute works the same way on the `source` element as it does on other HTML elements, so no change or surprise there. Line 3 shows the `src` attribute, which is used to give a path to the video that will be played back. In this instance the file is in the same directory as the HTML file and is named `ascent.mp4`. Line 4 shows a rather complex `type` attribute. This attribute actually supports attributes passed inside it, so you will notice that it uses a mix of single and double quotes to get all the data it needs passed through. The first part of data passed is the MIME type for the file. The codec attribute is then passed and contains some strings that will tell the browser what codec it should be using to decode the video file. Whenever mp4 files are used, you must use avc1.42E01E, mp4a.40.2 as the value for the codec attribute. Line 5 simply closes the source element.

Now for a twist; not all browsers are compatible with mp4 playback. Firefox, for example, shows an area on the screen where the video should go, but gives you an error message that it doesn't know what to do with the file. This means that you need to include another source element with the correct setup for another video file. Line 6-9 shows another source element being created for an ogv file. Line 6 opens up the source element and contains an id attribute. Line 7 displays the path to the file named ascent.ogv. Line 8 gives the MIME type settings as well as the codecs attribute populated with the value of theora, vorbis. Line 9 then closes the source element.

If you were to include the code in Listing 18.4 in the video.html file, and had the referenced video files in the same directory, the video would be added to the page. However, you would notice that the video does not act responsively with the size like the embedded YouTube and Vimeo videos do. To fix that, we need to use an iframe as well as modify the JavaScript call we are using to initialize the fitVids() method.

You can start by creating an HTML file that contains the video element from Listing 18.4 (you can also reference video_iframe.html) and then modify the JavaScript method call to the fit-Vids plug-in to appear as follows:

```
$(".video").fitVids({ customSelector: "iframe[src^='http://youraddresshere']"});
```

Make certain that you change the http://youraddresshere portion of the code to either your IP address or your domain address. Failure to do so will cause the fitVids() method to fail on your iframe video. For reference you can look at scripts.js. After you have done that, the only thing left to do is to add the container that is holding your embedded video to your HTML file. Listing 18.5 shows the snippet you need to add.

LISTING 18.5   **Embedding a Self-Hosted Video**

```
1: <div class="video" data-role="collapsible" data-content-theme="a">
2:    <h3>Self Hosted</h3>
3:      <iframe src="http://localhost/hour18/video_iframe.html"
width="400" height="255" frameborder="0" webkitAllowFullScreen
mozallowfullscreen allowFullScreen></iframe>
4:    <p>My ascent on an airplane - Self-hosted (locally in this case)</p>
5: </div>
```

This example should be a little more than familiar now as it follows the same basic structure that we used for both the YouTube and Vimeo embedded videos. It starts by setting up a collapsible container and adds a title. Line 3 shows the iframe element with the path to the HTML file that was created that contains the code from Listing 18.4. Make sure that you change the `src` attribute to point to where your actual file is located, or this will not work. Just like in the Vimeo embedded video code, this `iframe` element also contains the `width`, `height`, `frameborder`, `webkitAllowFullScreen`, `mozallowfullscreen`, and `allowFullScreen` attributes. Line 4 then shows a `p` element that contains some descriptive text about the video. Line 5 closes the `div` element that is being used as the collapsible container.

Figure 18.4 shows what our videos page looks like with the collapsible container added and open.

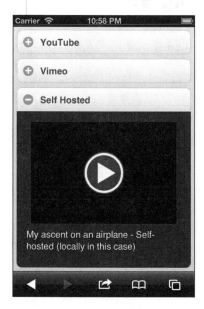

FIGURE 18.4
Our custom embedded video is visible and ready to be watched.

CAUTION

Emulation Failure

Not all device emulators actually come with full codec support for videos built in. If you are running into issues when testing video playback, or are receiving error messages about being unable to play video, try to use an actual device instead of an emulator. This is also good practice, as users that visit your site will not be using emulators to do so.

In case things are not working out quite the way they should be, take a look at videos_complete. html. This file shows the YouTube, Vimeo, and self-hosted videos all on the same page.

Our video has been added and is ready to be watched. While we now know that this is possible and how to do it, keep in mind the extra steps you need to take when preparing your own embedded code. While other video services handle the player for various devices and choose the correct video to play back (flash versus mp4 versus ogv and so forth), when you code your own you are responsible for handling the playback on all device types. That may be something that you are looking forward to doing, but for others it is a little more convenient to let someone else handle the playback while you handle the site or application.

Exploring Other Video Embedding Services

There are other services and hosts that you may be interested in looking into or using for your next video project. The following is a list of video hosting and sharing sites:

- YouTube (http://www.youtube.com)

- Vimeo (http://www.vimeo.com)

- Blip.tv (http://blip.tv/)

- Viddler (http://viddler.com/)

- Metacafe (http://www.metacafe.com/)

If you need more control or an enterprise solution, some good choices are available that usually features integration with a Content Delivery Network to help get your videos to your viewers with minimum routing delays. Although these services come with a price attached, when you need guaranteed performance and control, they are worth looking into:

- Brightcove (http://www.brightcove.com)

- Limelight Networks (http://www.limelight.com/media-web-publishing/)

- Akamai (http://www.akamai.com/html/solutions/media_delivery.html)

- Amazon CloudFront (http://aws.amazon.com/cloudfront/)

No matter what service you pick, make sure that you are catering to your users. No matter how great you think your video appears or looks on your device it doesn't matter if 90% of your visitors can't see it or use it. Managing video integration may be challenging, but when done correctly the payoff is always worth it.

Summary

In this hour you learned how to embed video code from YouTube and Vimeo and add them to your mobile site. You can also use plug-ins such as fitVids.js to help the videos dynamically respond in size to the device viewing them.

You also learned how to embed videos that are hosted on your own server by using HTML5. You learned a little about how HTML5 `video` elements work, and that not all browsers support all video types. This was overcome by including `source` elements that contained attributes that the browser could use to find a supported video and codec to play back the video.

Finally, you learned that more sites are available that can get you started with using, sharing, and/or hosting video files. You also were given a list of enterprise sites that you could check into for content hosting and delivery.

Q&A

Q. **Do I need to sign up for an API key with YouTube to use embedded video?**

A. Not necessarily. Signing up for an API key allows you to build your own video playlist and controls, but if you are using the embedding code, then you do not need to get one.

Q. **When using a Content Delivery Network, do I need to use any special links to my video?**

A. It completely depends on your provider. Most Content Delivery Networks that I have used have you set up one base URL to use for your content and then they handle the transmission of the media back. This is a question that your provider should be able to answer.

Q. **How much should I be worried about bandwidth when I use embedded videos?**

A. When you use YouTube or Vimeo, the bandwidth is all handled on their end. If you are worried about the user experience, make sure you are embedding the non-HD version of your video. Doing so allows a faster download of the video to the mobile device and ensures a smoother playback experience.

Workshop

The workshop contains a quiz and some exercises to help you check your comprehension and understanding.

Quiz

1. True or False: All mobile devices are capable of video playback.
2. True or False: When self-hosting a video you only need to worry about using an mp4 file.

3. When using the HTML5 `source` element, what is required in the `type` attribute?

4. Why is Flash generally not considered for video playback on mobile devices?

5. What possible problems can be alleviated by using a hosted video site?

Answers

1. False. Some mobile devices such as eReaders are capable of surfing the Internet, but cannot play back video files.

2. False. While most mobile devices are capable of playing back an `mp4` file, not every browser can. Opera and Firefox require that you use `ogv` or `webm` files.

3. The `type` attribute must contain the MIME type as well as the codec needed to decode the video.

4. Many mobile devices lack support for Flash. Flash support for mobile also stopped in 2011, with only security releases continuing into the future.

5. Not all mobile devices support HD video. By using a video host you can start with a lower quality file and allow devices that support higher quality playback the option of using the higher quality file. You also do not have to worry about transcoding multiple files for cross-browser support.

Exercises

1. Create a YouTube account and upload your own video. Then using the embed code from YouTube, add it to the profile site.

2. Create a page that contains a list of embedded videos with links to them. Experiment with the site on different devices including a desktop computer. Notice when the embedded videos play back in a Flash player instead of an HTML5 one.

3. To get a better feel for how each video sharing or hosting site works, take a few minutes and visit some of the video hosting sites mentioned in the hour. Get familiar with the terms of service agreements and what types of video files can be shared. Try browsing the different sites for a video licensed under Creative Commons and experiment embedding the video on your own site to get a feel for how videos hosted on that service play back and function.

Encoding Your Own Video for Mobile

What You'll Learn in This Hour:

▶ What a video container is

▶ What popular codecs are available for mobile playback

▶ Codec support on mobile devices

▶ The settings to use to encode a video for mobile playback

▶ Options available for delivering the video

Last hour we learned about how to get an embedded video to play back in our application. Although we learned how to embed our own video, we did not see how to create the video that we used. This is what we cover in this hour.

Learning the Basics of Video Encoding

Every time you open or watch a video file you are setting into motion a complex process of file parsing and processing. To get started, let me give you a quick high-level view of how a video works.

Each video file is made up of at least one video stream and can be accompanied by several audio streams. When you watch a video file, the player must open the file and determine what data is available and how to display the video content on the screen and the audio content through your sound system. To make matters worse, video files can contain only audio, and they can contain only video. Let's take a closer look at why this is possible by learning about the video container.

Video Containers

When most people talk about video files they seem to leave off what the file actually is. While techies obsess over the actual extension and container used, people in general have no idea what goes into a video, and what it does. To put it plainly, a container is exactly that—a file that can contain data. You can think of a container as a box that has room inside to hold or contain audio and video data. Figure 19.1 gives a diagram of a container.

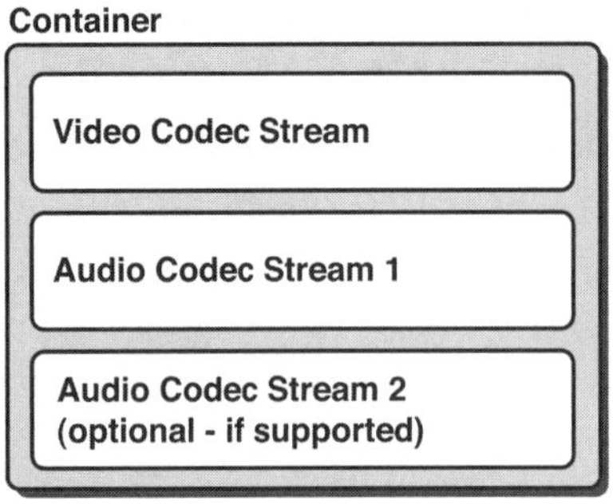

Container

Video Codec Stream
Audio Codec Stream 1
Audio Codec Stream 2 (optional - if supported)

FIGURE 19.1
A diagram of a basic container

Now before you start trying to stuff all sorts of video and audio files into a text file under the idea that is a suitable container, each container has limitations on what and how much it is allowed to hold.

If you are familiar with Windows, you may have heard about or even used .avi files. This file type was extremely common, and although it has now seen better days, can still be found today. A file with an extension of .avi is an Audio Video Interleaved, which is a generic description of what the file contains—a video stream and an audio stream. The default standard in Windows has changed to use the .wmv container, which stands for Windows Media Video.

Macintosh users are no doubt familiar with the QuickTime .mov container. This container is still in common use today and can be played back on other systems when QuickTime or another suitable player is installed.

WebM is a video container created specifically for web videos and can be used with HTML5 video on Opera, Firefox, and Chrome. Internet Explorer supports it when a plug-in has been installed. Other popular containers are Ogg and Matroska (.mkv), which are similar to the MPEG-4 container but usually contain different codecs. Speaking of codecs, let's take a few minutes and talk about what they are, and why you need them.

Codecs

When videos are encoded, they use a coder/decoder or *codec* to store the data. Both video and audio streams have different codecs that they can use to achieve a mixture of compression ratio and quality. Some codecs use a better compression method and can achieve a higher quality picture and sound than other codecs, but then often require more processing power to decode the stream. This can create stuttering or frame skipping on the video when it is being watched. On the other hand, if you encode a video with very little compression you may end up with a file that is likely too big to stream or too pixelated if you cut back on your quality.

When dealing with mobile devices you have a limited number of codecs that are supported, and even fewer that are compatible among all devices. Let's start by looking at the available codecs for audio.

Audio Codecs

Most videos have an audio track that is played back in sync with the video. Quite a few codecs are available that can be used to encode the audio to be played back from a container. Keep in mind that many audio codecs are available, and this list is just of the most common that are compatible with mobile devices.

WAV

WAV files are generally uncompressed audio files and are popular both because of how long they have been around and because they can be used with Windows, Macintosh, and Linux systems. Due to the uncompressed nature of this codec, files are extremely large. While you can use a WAV file for playback on mobile devices, you really should avoid using them in any video you plan on streaming due to bandwidth constraints.

WAV codec summary:

- ▶ Stored as `.wav` files.

- ▶ One to two channels at 8000-44100Hz with 4-16 bits per sample.

- ▶ Files must be less than 4GB each.

MP3

A format that became extremely popular in the 1990s is the MPEG-1/2 Audio Layer III or MP3 codec. This codec is the audio compression used with MPEG-2 files. MP3 files are highly favored as their compression is great for storing files, and allows easy portability. Not all MP3 files are created equal; some use a different bitrate than others. The bitrate controls the amount of compression used and the amount of room in the spectrum to contain the audio frequencies. Lower bitrates often sound distorted on some frequencies (most notably during cymbal crashes). Most MP3 files are encoded at a Constant Bit Rate that gives a dedicated amount of space to the audio that limits how much space is available. Variable Bit Rate encoding allows space to be shuffled from frequencies that are not currently in use to ones that are in an attempt to make the file stay small while allowing a more dynamic range of music to be heard. Regardless of some of the possible quality concerns, many online music stores including Google Music and Amazon MP3 use this format to distribute audio files. Due to the amount of mobile devices that support this codec, you should consider using it to encode your audio.

MP3 codec summary:

▶ Stored as .mp3 files.

▶ 1 to 5.1 multichannel at 16000-48000Hz at 32-320kbps.

▶ Can be encoded in either a Constant Bit Rate or a Variable Bit Rate.

▶ MP3 files do not contain Digital Rights Management.

Ogg Vorbis

Another audio format similar to MP3 is known as Ogg Vorbis. This codec is copyright free and endorsed by both Opera and Firefox as being the preferred audio codec in HTML5 videos. Ogg Vorbis is occasionally referenced as just Vorbis. This is because Ogg is a container and Vorbis is the actual codec used inside the container. The Ogg Vorbis codec is versatile and can encode files at a bitrate anywhere from 45kbps to 500kbps. It can also handle samples from 8kHz to 192kHz and can even handle up to 255 discrete channels. When encoding, the quality levels range from -2 to 10. This can make encoding somewhat of a chore as you may need to encode a file multiple times to make sure you are getting the quality you want. However, a quality level of 5 is generally a good value for use when streaming a file. As with all audio, though, your mileage may vary, and you may be able to get by with a lower quality encoding.

Ogg Vorbis codec summary:

▶ Files are encoded by quality level.

▶ The codec to use for video files played back in HTML5 on Opera and Firefox.

▶ Capable of being encoded at higher bitrates than MP3.

▶ Free from licensing and patent issues.

AAC

Anyone familiar with iTunes or devices running iOS have used the AAC codec. The Advanced Audio Coding or AAC codec is a popular audio codec that can compress audio with more quality than that of an MP3 file of the same size. AAC files are versatile and can have Digital Rights Management solutions embedded into them. AAC files can be encoded in Constant Bit Rate or by Average Bit Rate, which is similar to the Variable Bit Rate that MP3 files use. AAC files can also be encoded in different profiles such as AAC-LC (Low Complexity), HE-AAC (High Efficiency), and HE-AAC v2. Each of these profiles has a different amount of support and features in relation to compression, spectrum, and channel support. Of the three of these mentioned profiles, HE-AAC v2 is the newest and allows a very high rate of compression; unfortunately this and the HE-AAC codec are not compatible with most mobile devices. AAC-LC, however, is not only compatible with most mobile devices, but is highly recommended for use as the audio codec used in videos you want to stream.

AAC codec summary:

- ▶ Newer than the MP3 codec.

- ▶ Ability to compress with greater quality than other lossy codecs.

- ▶ Contains multiple encoding profiles.

- ▶ The AAC-LC profiles should be used for maximum compatibility.

- ▶ Can contain Digital Rights Management.

NOTE

Lossy Listening

The term "lossy" refers to compression methods that remove data to reduce file size. Because this data is deleted, it can never be returned and is a loss. Codecs that use this data loss are called lossy codecs for this reason. Audio codecs that retain all data are referred to as lossless codecs. These include FLAC, APE, Apple Lossless Audio Codec, and others.

Now that we've covered a few of the codecs that can be used, let's take a look at some of the video codecs available.

Video Codecs

Just like audio, video also has codecs that are used for compression. The following is a list of video codecs that can be used with HTML5 and mobile device playback.

VP8

VP8 is a relatively new codec on the field that is used with the WebM container with a Vorbis encoded audio stream. VP8 was acquired by Google and pushed as a replacement codec to the somewhat-legally challenged H.264 codec. VP8 is free to use as it is released from Google under a free patent license. The quality of VP8 is comparable to the existing H.264 codec. There is no official maximum bitrate, but keep in mind that the higher your bitrate, the more bandwidth it needs. Encoding with VP8 can be done in Variable Bitrate (VBR), Constant Bitrate (CBR), and Constrained Quality (CQ). VBR works like it does with some of the audio codecs. Sections of video with fast movement or color changes will be allocated more data bits, while sections that remain mostly still will receive less data bits. Encoding your video with a CBR setting does not actually keep the bitrate constant all the time, but instead offers slight fluctuations in the data bit distribution. Encoding with the CQ setting is similar to VBR, but places a limit on how much data can be spent in one section. When using the CQ setting, encoding the video with a two-pass system is highly recommended.

VP8 codec summary:

▶ Similar to H.264

▶ Supports VBR, CBR, and CQ encoding modes

▶ Capable of multipass encoding

▶ Compatible with Opera 10.60+, Firefox 4+, Chrome 6+, and IE9 (with WebM MF plug-in installed)

Theora

Theora is the video codec support by the Ogg container. This means that it is license free and can be used with any project or video distribution. Oddly enough, Theora is a spinoff of the VP3 codec (which continued on to become the VP8 codec). In relation to quality and compression, it falls in the middle of the current offering of video codecs. It is currently a well-supported video codec when it comes to use with HTML5 video as it is supported by many modern browsers. While other codecs focus on the bitrate to use, Theora uses a quality setting to adjust the bitrate as needed. When starting out with Theora, it is a good idea to make a few different files at various quality settings and choose the one that has the best balance of quality and file size for Internet delivery.

Theora codec summary:

▶ Similar to both H.264 and VP8

▶ Encoding based on quality instead of bitrate

▶ Compatible with Firefox 3.5+, Opera 10.50+, and Chrome 3.0+

H.264

H.264 actually has a few names. It can also be referred to as MPEG-4 Part 10 and AVC (Advanced Video Coding). I have been guilty on occasion of just referring to the codec as the container it is usually stored in, which is mp4. The H.264 codec is extremely popular, and you can find support for it on most mobile devices including the Sony PSP and iPod Touch. Because the codec can also be used on Blu-ray discs, there are profiles that devices can certify at to guarantee playback. Most mobile devices cannot play anything higher than the Baseline profile. While there are roughly 18 different profile settings, the three commonly found in encoders are Baseline, Main, and High. Each profile determines what features of the codec can be used. In addition to the profiles, you can also use levels to adjust the data available for encoding. The levels currently range from 1 to 5.2; however, most mobile devices do not support any level higher than 3.0. H.264 is a licensed codec, but it has been given a status of being free for encoding and decoding video over the Internet. This license may, however, be changed in the next few years as the license is up for renewal every five years. Depending on the program you use to encode, you may do multipass, CBR, and VBR encoded videos. Note that even though some programs offer this, it may not work and also may affect the playback functionality of your video.

H.264 codec summary:

▶ Very common codec, used in many commercial products

▶ Currently license free for videos distributed over the Internet

▶ Profile and level based encoding

▶ Supported by Internet Explorer 9+ and Safari 4+

Comparing Video Codecs and Mobile Devices

Video playback is important on today's mobile devices. Users expect to be able to watch movies, news, and entertainment. Because of this, most devices have built-in support for many video types. The following sections provide a handy reference list of devices and relevant specs for video playback. This list is important to know as it can be used to help you determine what you should be aiming for when creating videos for end users.

Android

Android has good support for common video formats as well as a wide range of audio file support. Something that should be noted with devices running Android is that some codec support can be added by custom builds and by third-party manufacturers. For example, the Samsung Galaxy Player 5.0 has support for FLAC audio files even though it runs Android version 2.3.5.

▶ Native resolution: Varies on make and model of device

▶ Video codecs: H.263, H.264 AVC, MPEG-4 Baseline Profile, VP8 (Android 2.3.3+)

▶ Audio codecs: AAC LC 0-160kbps 8-48 kHz, HE-AACv1 0-160kbps 8-48kHz, HE-AACv2 0-160kbps 8-48kHz, AMR-NB 4.75-12.2kbps sampled @ 8kHz, AMR-WB 9 rates from 6.60-23.85kbit/s @ 16kHz, MP3 8-320kbps CBR/VBR, FLAC (Android 3.1+) recommended sample at 44.1 kHz but supports up to 48kHz, 16-bit recommended but support for 24-bit

▶ Video containers: `.3gp`, `.mp4`, `.webm`, `.mkv`

▶ Visit http://developer.android.com/guide/appendix/media-formats.html for changes in support

A challenge that you may encounter with Android devices is the wide resolution differeces between devices. This can be somewhat overcome by choosing a resolution for video that fits most devices. There will still be a problem on high resolution devices that may get either a small video playing back on their device or a video that is pixelated.

BlackBerry

BlackBerry has stepped up its media support game since the v6 of the BlackBerry OS. Devices running a previous OS have varied support for both audio and video codecs. For media content on your site, you can start by using the media that works on OS 6+ devices and then use device analytics and user feedback to adjust content to your consumer.

▸ Native resolution: Varies per device and OS

▸ Video codecs (v6 OS): Varies, but `.3gp`, `.avi`, `.asf`, `.mp4`, `.mov`, `.wmv`

▸ Audio codecs (v6 OS): `.aac`, `.amr`, `.flac`, `.mp4`, `.m4a`, `.ogg`, `.wma`, `.wav`

Similar to Android, the resolution of each device varies. This means you need to adopt a similar strategy for video playback. BlackBerry recently changed the way it lists supported audio and video codec for each device. Visit http://docs.blackberry.com/en/smartphone_users/?userType=1 and search for "media types". This should return a few links to a current `.pdf` file for smartphones and another for tablets that contain the supported codecs for current devices. You may also use the navigtion menu on the page to find a link to Supported Media under the Tablets section, and also under the Smartphones an entry for BlackBerry Smartphones.

iPhone 4S

The iOS system that runs on the iPhone 4S allows some advanced playback features. While the original iPhone was limited on the encoding of the H.264 video it would play back, the current OS offers greater support and playback options.

▸ Native resolution: 640×960

▸ Video: H.264 Main Profile Level 3.1 - MPEG-4 2.5Mbps 640×480, 15/23.9/30 fps, 2 Simple Profile - also supports MJPEG

▸ Audio: AAC (8 to 320 Kbps), HE-AAC, MP3 (8 to 320 Kbps), MP3 VBR, Audible (formats 2, 3, 4, Audible Enhanced Audio, AAX, and AAX+), Apple Lossless, AIFF, and WAV

▸ Video containers: `.m4v`, `.mp4`, `.mov`

▸ Visit http://www.apple.com/iphone/specs.html for changes in support

While the iPhone 4S runs at a set resolution of 640×960, remember that the previous iPhone models prior to the iPhone 4 run with a resolution of 320×480. To complicate this a touch more, the iPad and iPad2 both have a resolution of 1024×768 while the new iPad contains a resolution of 2048×1536.

Windows Phone 7

The Windows Phone system currently runs with a set resolution for all devices. This makes designing for them nice as all screens display things in the same proportion. This may change shortly, but for now you can skip worrying too much about how the video is going to play back on all devices.

▶ Native resolution: 480×800

▶ Video codecs: WMV Simple, Main, and Advanced profile, MPEG-4 Part 2 Simple and Advanced profile, MPEG-4 Part 10 (H.264, AVC) Baseline, Main, and High Profile Level 3.0, and H.263

▶ Audio codecs: AAC-LC, HE-ACC v1 (AAC+), HE-ACC v2 (eAAC+)

▶ Video containers: `.wmv`, `.3gp`, `.3g2`, `.mp4`, `.m4v`, `.amr`

▶ Visit http://msdn.microsoft.com/en-us/library/ and search for media formats to learn about the latest media support

With the release of tablets and mobile devices pending, the support level for media playback may change soon. Microsoft has shown strong support for H.264 in HTML5 video playback, so with that in mind video support on mobile devices should stay near whatever can be played back in Internet Explorer.

Now that we have a list of what common mobile devices are capable of, let's learn about the tools and settings used to encode videos for playback.

Encoding Video for Mobile Playback

If you've never encoded video before, it's common to think that you need to use the absolute highest quality possible. While getting the highest quality possible may sound like the best idea, it will result in either a file size that is unacceptable for mobile delivery or a file that is unable to be played back on mobile devices. Luckily there are some tools you can use to help you learn how to create the perfect video. Sometimes the best way to learn is through a little investigation, and some slight reverse engineering. Let's take a look at some tools to find out how videos are encoded.

Discovering Inspection Tools

Inspection tools work as analyzers that open a container file and tell you about the video and audio stream information. This is similar to the Get Info option in OSX and like viewing properties of a file in Windows. The biggest difference is that when using an inspector program you get a lot more detail. Figure 19.2 shows what is returned when using Get Info on OSX and viewing file properties in Windows.

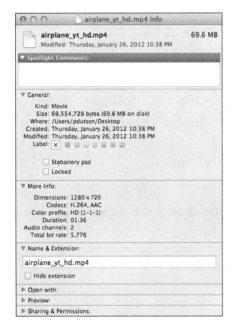

FIGURE 19.2
Details about the video container are shown.

While the details given are relevant, such as file size and resolution, in Windows they do not tell you the bitrate used or even what codecs are used for each stream in the file. On OSX you see some basic information, but you are not shown the bitrate for the individual audio and video streams but instead are shown a combined total bitrate. You also are not shown extra codec features such as the level the video was encoded at. For that we need to use some other tools.

My absolute favorite video inspection tool is called MediaInfo and is available for Windows, Mac, and Linux users. It is available as a free, GPL licensed download on sourceforge at http://mediainfo.sourceforge.net/en/Download. Once you have downloaded and installed the application, you are ready to start inspecting files. When MediaInfo is opened, it presents an empty window divided into sections. To inspect a file, either use the program menu to select a file, or drag-and-drop the file into the program window. Once a file has been dropped, the window populates the sections with data from the file. Figure 19.3 shows the program inspecting a video.

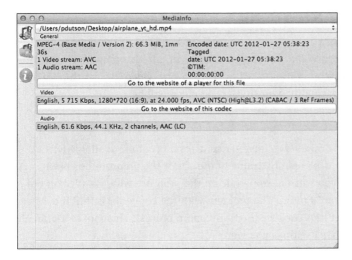

FIGURE 19.3
MediaInfo inspecting a file

As you can see from Figure 19.3, the file in use has one video stream, and one audio stream. The video codec used was AVC, and the audio codec was AAC. In the sections below you can get more detailed information. The video section shows the bitrate the video was encoded at, the resolution of the video along with ratio, how many frames-per-second, and the actual codec along with applicable profile and level. Other encoding features also are shown when detected. The audio section displays the bitrate, sample rate, channels, and codec used.

While this is the best standalone solution for Windows users, other inspection tools available are as follows:

OSX

▶ Media Inspector—Available in the AppStore

▶ Invisor and Invisor Lite—Available in the AppStore

▶ VideoSpec—Available at http://videospec.free.fr/english/

▶ iMediaHUD—Available at http://www.iffmpeg.com/styled-6/index.html

Linux

▶ Themonospot—Available at http://www.integrazioneweb.com/themonospot/

Now that you know how to determine what is in a video file, you use this information to encode a video. Let's look at some programs that you can use to encode your video.

Exploring Transcoding Programs

Many programs are available to help you encode your mobile video. Most of these programs work through a process known as transcoding. This process takes an already prepared video and changes the settings including codecs and bitrate used to create a new video file. The higher the quality of your source file, the higher quality your transcoded video will be.

MiroVideoConverter

The MiroVideoConverter (http://www.mirovideoconverter.com/) is a program available for free to Windows and Macintosh users. It is incredibly simple to use. Once the program has been opened, you drag and drop the file you want to transcode on the program window, pick an output format, and then click the Convert! button. The problem with the converter is that it does not give you any control over the settings used for the transcoding process. This makes it difficult to fine-tune your video files to the exact settings you want.

HandBrake

HandBrake (http://handbrake.fr/) is another open-source video transcoding program available for Windows, Macintosh, and Linux users. While the primary function of the program is more along the lines of creating personal DVD backup files, it can be used to create both .mp4 and .mkv files. Once the program has been installed, you open the file you want to transcode and then make adjustments to the output by using the Video, Audio, Subtitle, Advanced, and Chapter sections at the bottom of the program window.

MediaCoder

MediaCoder (http://www.mediacoderhq.com/) is a program that has gone through a bit of change in the last few years. When it first appeared it was an all-in-one solution, but it has since branched out into specialized versions. It is a Windows program, but the author mentions that by using an emulator it can be used on Linux and on Macintosh systems. MediaCoder is a transcoding program compatible with most format containers and codecs. It may occasionally throw an error when you attempt to create a file with incompatible codecs together. I have found that for Windows transcoders, this particular program gives you a considerable amount of flexibility and options. The program is built with a wizard to walk you through file creation, or you may adjust everything manually. If you are using the manual settings you can drag and drop the file or files you want transcoded into the program and then use the Settings tabs at the bottom to adjust the output type and format.

MPEG Streamclip

The last encoding/transcoding program we are going to cover is MPEG Streamclip (http://www.squared5.com/). It is available for both Macintosh and Windows systems. It contains a player and editor, and of course the ability to transcode files from one format into another. The program works similarly to the others listed. Once you have opened the program, you can drag and drop a video onto it. You can then use the File menu to view information about the streams contained in the video, and to export the video to another format.

Encoding a Video

Regardless of the program you end up using, if you want to support the widest number of devices possible there are some rules you need to follow:

▶ Encode with an .mp4 container.

While it is true that some browsers do not support .mp4 for HTML5 video playback, almost every mobile device supports the .mp4 container for native playback.

▶ Keep your bitrate low between 400-800 kbps.

The bitrate does affect how clear or pixelated your video is; however, it is also a key factor in file size and CPU load when decoding the video. If you can keep it in that range, you should be able to get acceptable quality and file size.

▶ Encode your audio with AAC-LC.

Of the AAC codecs this is the lowest in quality, but it is the most supported. Don't worry too much about it; even at 48kbps it still sounds fairly good. Most encoders allow you to use a quality setting that creates a variable bitrate file that gives a good balance between file size and sound.

▶ Encode your video with H.264, Baseline, level 3.0, no B-Frames.

This should be pretty straightforward. Use AVC or H.264 and then if your encoding program allows you to choose a profile and level, choose Baseline and 3.0. If your encoding program does not allow these options, then turn off any extra options such as B-Frames.

▶ Unless you absolutely need HD video, use a resolution near 480×360 (4:3) or 480×270 (16:9).

The maximum resolution supported with level 3.0 is 720×576 when playing back at 24 frames per second. This really means that you will not be able to provide a true HD file anyway unless you use a file with a different level or container. While this is changing, legacy devices will continue to be an issue for several years.

If you follow those rules, the videos you create will play back on most smartphones, personal media players, and tablets.

To get an idea of how the settings should look let's take a look at some figures. Figure 19.4 shows the export to MPEG-4 setting screen from MPEG Streamclip with the settings for mobile video. Figure 19.5 and Figure 19.6 show the Video and Advanced settings tab configurations needed when using HandBrake for transcoding mobile video.

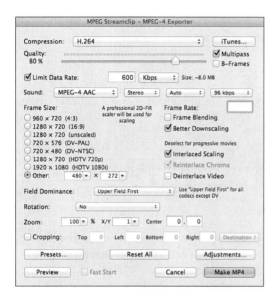

FIGURE 19.4
The export screen of MPEG Streamclip using mobile-safe settings

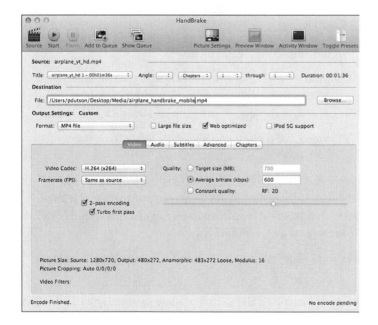

FIGURE 19.5
The settings used on the Video tab for mobile-safe encoding

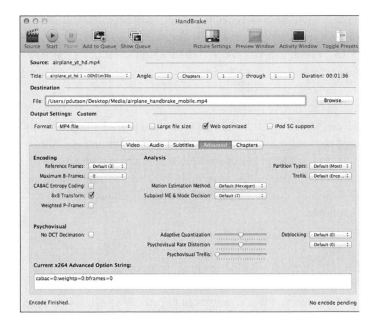

FIGURE 19.6
The settings used on the Advanced tab for mobile-safe encoding

Now that you can encode or transcode your video content, let's look at how to get it to play back on mobile devices.

Delivering Video Content

When displaying video content on a mobile device you have a few options. You can use HTML5 video tags to display and control your video, you can use various JavaScript plug-ins, or you can link directly to the file allowing the device to play the file back in the native device player. Since we have already covered using the HTML5 `video` element, let's take a look at some common plug-ins to help handle our mobile videos.

Using Plug-Ins and Players

Before you get too excited about the prospects of using a plug-in or player to handle all your video needs, there is one thing you need to do first. It doesn't matter what web server you are running, but you must configure your MIME types or some of these plug-ins may not work. Either modify your server configuration file or if using an Apache server, add the following to an .htaccess file:

```
AddType video/ogg .ogv
AddType video/mp4 .mp4
AddType video/webm .webm
```

Many of the video plug-ins available for use are a clever collection of JavaScript and CSS allowing skinning support and device detection. Some players even allow fallback support to Flash for browsers that do not support HTML5. Several players on the Web today do not support mobile devices at all, so we're going to take a look at the ones that do.

Projekktor

Projekktor (http://www.projekktor.com/) was one of the first HTML5 video players that I actually heard about. It is a fully featured player and can be tailored to suit almost anything you need. Projekktor is released under the GPL, so it is free to use in your projects. If you get stuck or need some support you have several options from free (in the form of an FAQ and document listing) to paid support. For nonmobile devices that browse this plug-in that do not support HTML5 video, a Flash fallback option is available.

MediaElement.js

MediaElement.js (http://mediaelementjs.com/) is quickly becoming the popular choice for guaranteed video playback regardless of browser and device type. It even allows you do decide how much support you want to give. This means that if you only want to provide one H.264 encoded video, then that is all you need to do. By doing so you limit older browsers, but it does save you a few lines of code and makes prototyping or testing a snap as you can always go back and add extra support later. It also has some built-in plug-ins that add a little extra functionality and/or eye candy to the player. The license is either GPL v2 or MIT, so you can feel free to use this in your web projects.

JPlayer

JPlayer (http://jplayer.org/) is another player that sports some excellent ideas. It can be used as both a video player and as an audio player. Just like the other players, it contains fallback support to Flash. Similar to MediaElement.js, you can get by with just an `.mp4` file; however, for full compatibility you need to generate an `.ogg` and `.webm` file as well. It is licensed as GPL or MIT so you are free to include it in your web projects.

Video.js

Video.js (http://videojs.com/) is another option that provides a player with a common skin that works cross-browser. It also features integration with either Flash or Silverlight for fallback support. Unlike some of the previous players, it does not rely on including the jQuery library and can be run as a standalone or with others. Video.js is one of the easier players to use as you can include the required files from their CDN, and then create the HTML5 video `element` as you normally would with a few extra classes and a custom data attribute named `data-setup`. The license is a variant on the GPL known as the Lesser GPL, which allows you to use it on your site as long any improvements you make are contributed back to the Video.js team.

While there are always times when you would like use a specific interface that a player brings, occasionally it is better to just let the device handle the video. This is where using the native video player comes in.

Using the Native Player

The native video player varies on each mobile device; however, on most iOS and Android devices the player is a simple one that allows the playback of `.mp4` files. To trigger one from your site, you can simply create a link directly to your video file as follows:

```
<a href="videos/demo.mp4">Watch a demo</a>
```

When the link is clicked, the browser should detect that it is a video file and ask what to do with the file, or it launches the native player for the device. When viewing is finished, the user is usually returned to the page that called the file.

Sometimes, however, this method can be a little unpredictable. While most iOS and Android devices play the `.mp4` file when linked from a website, some devices and browsers download the file instead, which in turn forces the user to find the file and load it into the native player themselves. With my own testing I've found that by declaring the MIME types mentioned earlier, most devices play the video or at least ask whether you want to play the video before just downloading and storing the file. Another problem with using this method is that a user is shifted to the video screen and then forced to wait until the file has been downloaded enough to begin playback. This can be a little strange for users who are not expecting the transition, or the possibly long wait time.

Summary

In this hour you learned what video containers are and what they are capable of holding. You learned about the various codecs available for both video and audio streams and what the current specs are for several mobile devices in regards to video and audio playback capability.

You learned about some tools available for the inspection and creation of videos. This included learning about the basic rules of encoding a video with an almost guaranteed setting for playback on all video-capable mobile devices.

You also learned about some plug-ins available to integrate HTML5 video into your site that work with mobile devices. When plug-ins are not desired, you can link directly to a video file and have the device play the file inside the native player.

Q&A

Q. Are there any other video inspectors or encoders?

A. Yes, there are quite a few. I chose to cover the ones that either I have used personally or would fit the budget of a user just starting out. Many commercial programs such as Adobe Premiere and Final Cut have the capability to produce videos with the same constraints on them. There are also specialized encoders such as Firefogg that creates .ogg files for video playback.

Q. How do these videos work with jQuery Mobile?

A. Using jQuery Mobile doesn't change the way any of the plug-ins are used, although you may have to change the load to the `pageinit` event.

Q. What happens if I try to view a video on a device that does not support HTML5, Flash, or any other fallback?

A. Generally when this happens you either get an error message about a failure to play back the video or get a direct link to download the video. As a developer what the end user sees is completely up to you.

Workshop

The workshop contains a quiz and some exercises to help you check your comprehension and understanding.

Quiz

1. What is the profile you should use for H.264 to maximize device compatibility?

2. What is the video codec used with an .ogg container?

3. What is a benefit to using a plug-in for video playback?

4. What version of the AAC codec should be used with mobile devices?

5. How can you use the native player from your site?

Answers

1. A profile of 3.0 allows maximum compatibility with mobile devices.

2. The Theora codec is used inside the .ogg container.

3. Plug-ins supply customization, ease of use, support for legacy browsers, and fallback support for other video delivery systems like Flash and Silverlight.

4. AAC-LC works on almost all mobile devices and as such should be used whenever possible.

5. If supported, the native player is triggered when direct link is used to the video file.

Exercises

1. Download MediaInfo and use it to analyze some video files on your computer. Compare the codec settings with what we learned this hour.

2. Create a video, or use the one from the previous exercise, and transcode the file into one that works on your device. Copy the file to your device and see whether it will play back. Take this a step further and create a simple HTML page with a direct link to the file. Use your mobile device to see whether the video will play in the native player.

3. Experiment with one of the player plug-ins and compare how it functions on various browsers and systems. If you have multiple devices available, examine the playback experience between them.

Creating QR and Tag Codes

What You'll Learn in This Hour:

▶ How QR and Tag codes are used

▶ Programs that can be used to read them

▶ How to create and customize QR and Tag codes

▶ Ways that QR and Tag codes can be used

Unless you've managed to avoid social websites, newspapers, flyers, billboards, and the advertising market in general, you have seen a QR and/or Tag code before. This hour you learn what they are and how you can use them.

Delving into QR and Tag Codes

Barcodes are heavily used in inventory tracking. When you want to buy an item at a store, a barcode is usually scanned at the register, displays how much the product costs, and makes a mark in the store inventory that the item was sold. The entire transaction is facilitated by the few characters of information held in the barcode on the item. This same principle of containing data also works on Quick Response (QR) codes and Tag codes.

Standard barcodes are read along a single axis; this makes them known as 1D or one-dimensional codes. This single axis of data limits the amount of data available but makes the code easily read by a scanner. QR codes are read along the X and Y axis, making them 2D or two-dimensional codes. This allows more data to be stored inside the same area as a barcode. Due to the complexity of the layout, some scanning devices may not scan the code correctly as it may be too small to be read. Microsoft Tag codes work in a similar but proprietary fashion. The Tag is read by a scanner and then referenced against an online database to deliver data back to the scanning application.

QR and Tag codes are found today in a variety of places. You can find them on billboards, magazines, catalogs, TV and Internet ads, business cards, conference tickets, and in many more places. The use of QR codes is gaining traction as more users take advantage of the experience that can be created by using them. Some businesses have even integrated the codes into an online shopping cart allowing users to scan and purchase an item directly from a catalog or ad.

NOTE
QR Code
The term QR Code is registered trademark of DENSO WAVE INCORPORATED (http://www.densowave.com/en/adcd/).

Scanning QR Codes

Most mobile devices do not come with a barcode scanner built in; however, as long as the device has access to an application store, you can download an app that allows you to scan codes. The following sections provide a list of applications and what platform they work on.

Scan

Scan aims to be as simple as possible. There are no buttons to press, no extra frills, just a simple scanner that also keeps track of the codes that you've scanned. Many iOS users prefer Scan due to the scanning speed. I did run into issues while using this on an Android device where the image was backwards, making it awkward to get the code to line up to be scanned—but it still worked as advertised. Scan is available for iOS and Android devices. You can learn more at http://scan.me/.

RedLaser

RedLaser is a scanning application created by eBay. It is a ridiculously detailed app in what it offers for features. It ties in with an online database for scanning results that makes it a fantastic tool for using on standard barcodes. If you want an all-in-one scanner that can be used for price checking as well as reading QR codes, this is one of the apps to look at. It is available for iOS, Android, and Windows Phone. You can learn more by visiting http://www.redlaser.com/.

ShopSavvy

This was the second scanner I ever installed, and it still remains one of my favorites. ShopSavvy works like RedLaser; for someone who only wants to scan QR codes and follow the links or read the messages, it is serious overkill. However, it is well-designed, keeps a history of previous scans, and worked on everything I attempted to scan with it. It is available on iOS, Android, and Windows Phone. You can learn more by visiting http://shopsavvy.com/.

ScanLife

ScanLife is another full-featured scanning app similar to RedLaser and ShopSavvy. ScanLife boasts support for a surprisingly large number of mobile devices. A unique feature included in the app is a live stream that lets you see what other people are scanning and allows you to tap on them and view information about the product that was scanned. ScanLife is available for iOS, Blackberry, Android, Windows Phone, and Nokia. To learn more, visit http://www.scanlife. com.

Barcode Scanner

The same team behind the ZXing library also released an app to go with it. This is a simple, no-frills app that allows you to scan barcodes and view the data contained in them. It does not hook into a database and return shopping results, price matches, or social options. Of course, it doesn't hit any third-party servers to collect your scanning information, either. Instead, it is a dead-simple scanner that I use as my main tool for scanning QR codes. It is available for Android (by ZXing Team) and iOS (by Romain Pechayre). You can stay up to date on app releases by visiting http://code.google.com/p/zxing/wiki/GetTheReader.

Microsoft Tag

The Microsoft Tag reader works with QR codes as well as Tag codes. It is an easy-to-use application that keeps a tidy history of the codes you scan. The history does not seem to keep track of text-only QR codes, but it does keep track of ones that direct you to view a web page. It is available for Windows Phone, Windows Mobile, iOS, Android, Blackberry, Symbian, and J2ME phones. Learn more by visiting http://tag.microsoft.com/download.aspx.

Let's take a deeper look at QR codes and how to create them.

Rendering Quick Response Codes

QR codes are not only useful, they can be used in many different ways. QR codes currently can be used to distribute contact information, appointments, SMS messages, text, websites, and more. Some QR codes require an Internet connection to be used while others contain purely text or information avoiding the need for a connection. To illustrate this, Figure 20.1 shows a QR code that contains only text, and Figure 20.2 shows a QR code with a URL.

FIGURE 20.1
This QR code displays "QR Codes are pretty cool" when scanned.

FIGURE 20.2
This QR code contains the URL http://www.jquerymobilein24.com/qrexample/.

QR codes do have some limitations you must be aware of to maximize their effectiveness. First of all, size matters—the bigger the code, the higher the compatibility of devices that can scan them. It is recommended that you use a code that measures 1.25"x 1.25". I have done a bit of experimenting and found that a 1"x1" code works; however, using a larger code allows the scanner to read the code faster and from a greater distance. The farther away your scanner is from the object, the larger your code needs to be.

Another limitation to keep in mind is that these codes generally are meant for mobile devices. That means you should plan on handling them accordingly. If you are creating QR codes for your website, you had better have a mobile site or at least a responsive layout done to accommodate these devices.

Lighting conditions also matter. This is just like trying to focus your camera in the dark, only worse. Most phones have a camera that will not allow the use of a manual focus when used with a scanning application. This means that your camera may drive itself nuts trying to focus on a blurry code over and over again due to poor lighting. Printing your code on a glossy surface may also affect the readability of your code. If you can print it on a matte sheet of paper, or in a location with minimal glare, your code will be easier to scan and process.

While there are some style tweaks that you can do with QR codes, you should use a solid background color that has a high contrast with the squares or dots of your code. You should never use a gradient as the background image.

QR code Do's:

▶ Make the code as large as possible for your campaign.

▶ When printing codes, try to use a matte finish rather than glossy.

▶ Make sure you are planning for mobile devices to be using your codes.

▶ When possible, use good lighting where your code is displayed.

QR code Don'ts:

▶ Use codes smaller than 1"x1".

▶ Direct mobile users to a full desktop site.

▶ Use noncontrasting colors or a gradient on the background.

Now that we know a little about QR codes, let's take a look at generating them.

Third-Party QR Generation

Many websites are available that will generate your QR codes for you. Some of these websites are free to use in both commercial and personal settings, while others have license restrictions. Some sites also have free and paid plans that add extra options and analytics packages to your code. The following sections outline sites available for use and what features you can expect to find when using them.

ZXing

The ZXing (Zebra Crossing) project created by Google provides a scanning library that can be used in both Android and Java projects. They also feature a QR code generator that can be found at http://zxing.appspot.com/generator/. The generator is a straightforward application that allows you to pick the type of data you want to store in the QR code and then generates the code for you as well as gives you a link that you can use to replicate the image using the Google Chart Tools.

Kaywa

Kaywa provides a QR code generator found at http://qrcode.kaywa.com/ that is free for noncommercial use. They also make a scanning app that is available in the Android Market. The generator allows the creation of URL, text, phone number, and SMS QR codes. The images may be sampled on the site and then downloaded for use on your noncommercial site.

QRStuff

QRStuff is a service that offers both free and commercial services that can be found at http://www.qrstuff.com/. This service allows many different types of data to be embedded into QR codes and uses its own algorithm to create QR codes rather than relying on third-party API services. QRStuff offers a commercial account that allows the use of a URL shortener that enables you to build QR codes that point to a short link which can then be repointed at any time to make a pseudo-dynamic QR code. This service also allows some analytic tracking so that you can get some data on the amount of scans your code has received.

Delivr

Delivr is another service that allows both free and registered member services for QR code generation. You can visit http://delivr.com/qr-code-generator to get started creating your own QR codes. To differentiate itself from the competition, Delivr offers code generation for various app stores, social media links, affiliate links, and analytics campaign links. Signing up for the service gives you access to code analytics, short-link URLs, and statistics.

BeQRious

BeQRious is another provider that offers a well-designed QR code generator which also gives tracking and profile perks to registered members. BeQRious also offers design services that bring a unique and personalized appearance to your QR code. You can check out the generator by visiting http://beqrious.com/qr-code-generator/.

SPARQCode

SPARQCode offers a full suite of services, including its own scanner, a generator, and an API that can easily be tapped to create QR codes. The SPARQCode experience is a good place to start for anyone who wants to eventually go commercial. The services include a free trial that allows for 250 tracked scans so that you can decide whether you want to jump in and go for a full package. Check out the QR generator and learn more by visiting http://www.sparqcode.com/static/maestro.

Now that you know where to go to get codes, let's take a look at how to create your own codes.

Generating Your QR Codes

The easiest way to get started generating your own code is to use the Google Chart Tools. By utilizing the Google Chart Tools, you can create codes instantly that will appear in your browser when you visit a parameterized URL. To begin generating QR codes, you need to use this base URL:

```
https://chart.googleapis.com/chart?cht=qr
```

Once you have that, you can then add some extra URL parameters to finish the code creation. By adding `chs=300x300` you get back an image 300x300 pixels in size. You can change this value to change the dimension of the code returned. The current maximum size that you can request is 547x547 pixels.

To add the text or data you want to encode, you need to add a parameter of `chl=yourtexthere`. You should change the value of `"yourtexthere"` to whatever you want the QR code to contain. An important detail here is that whatever values you decide to put into the code must be URL encoded. This means that the text `I am awesome` would become `I%20 am%20awesome` when encoded.

That is all the data required to create a QR code, but you may want to consider passing the `chld=` parameter for the error correction level. The error correction level affects how much of the embedded data is made redundant. Redundant information allows more compatibility and allows some of the QR code to be altered, missing, or destroyed and still maintain readability. By default the value is set at `L`, which allows for up to 7% of the code to be lost but still readable. You may choose to use `M` allowing up to 15%, `Q` allowing up to 25%, or `H` allowing up to 30%. Remember that data redundancy requires more space to write out the information, so you cannot put as much data into a QR code with a value of `H` as you can with one set at `L`.

Let's take a look at a full URL that generates a QR code for us using the parameters we just learned about. Type the following URL into your browser:

```
https://chart.googleapis.com/chart?cht=qr&chs=300x300
&chl=I%27ve%20generated%20my%20own%20QR%20code&chld=H
```

Figure 20.3 shows the resulting QR code from running that URL in a browser.

FIGURE 20.3
This QR code reads: "I've generated my own QR code."

If you find that you are using this method a lot to generate codes for websites you are visiting or for assets available online, you can use a handy little bookmarklet to generate the QR code for you. A *bookmarklet* is a self-contained bit of JavaScript that can be saved and executed from your bookmark menu in your browser. You can use Google Chart Tools with a bookmarklet to create a QR code for the page you are currently on. The following is an example of a bookmarklet:

```
javascript:void(location.href="https://chart.googleapis.com/chart?cht=qr
&chs=300x300&chl="+encodeURIComponent(location.href)+"&chld=H");
```

When executed, the bookmarklet forwards you to the generated QR code that contains a link to the website you were at. By taking a look at the code inside the bookmarklet, you can see that it is going to return a QR code that is 300x300px and uses a redundancy level of H. You can take the preceding code snippet and create multiple bookmarklets with different settings based on what you'd prefer to have returned.

To learn more about using the Google Chart Tools for QR code generation, visit http://code.google.com/apis/chart/infographics/docs/qr_codes.html.

If using Google Chart Tools isn't something you'd like to pursue, you can still create your own codes by implementing the Java library available from ZXing, or you can use some other libraries such as JSQR—JavaScript QR Code Encoder Library (http://www.jsqr.de/home.html)—or the d-project (http://www.d-project.com/qrcode/) libraries for ActionScript3, Java, JavaScript, and PHP.

Now that we can create QR codes, let's look at what we can do with them to make them a little more personalized.

Stylizing QR Codes

Even though most scanners work better with a simple black-and-white QR code, you may actually get a better customer response if you stylize your code and give it a little personality. This can be done a few ways. You can adjust the color and size, and include some custom imagery inside it. Let's start with adjusting the color of the code.

Adjusting the Color

The safest change you can make as far as color goes is to the foreground color. This can be done either by the generator or by processing the image in an image manipulation program by colorizing or selectively replacing the color. Figure 20.4 shows a QR code that has a red foreground color and a white background. For those who are reading the black and white version of this hour, the figures can be viewed in color at http://jquerymobilein24.com/qr.

FIGURE 20.4
The code will still be readable when enough contrast is available.

You can also use a gradient on the foreground image to change the style as well. Figure 20.5 shows a QR code with a diagonal gradient, which starts with orange in the top left and transitions to black at the bottom right and is applied to the foreground color with a white background.

FIGURE 20.5
Gradients must still contain a high contrast to be scanned.

If you decide to change the background color, you must remember to keep a high contrast between the foreground and background colors. Even with a high contrast, you cannot use white or any color that would appear lighter in contrast to the color behind it. A yellow background with a black foreground will work well, but a blue background with a white foreground will fail spectacularly. Figures 20.6 and 20.7 show two QR codes with color backgrounds and foregrounds.

FIGURE 20.6
Using yellow and black provides enough contrast to be scanned.

FIGURE 20.7
Using a dark background and a white or light foreground causes the QR code to fail.

Experiment to find color combinations that work when mixing background and foreground colors. Sometimes odd combinations, such as a lime-green background and a blue foreground, will work as shown in Figure 20.8.

FIGURE 20.8
Green and blue work as they create a high enough contrast to be scanned.

Another option you have for customizing the QR code is to change the image or include others inside the code. Let's take a look at what you can do.

Custom Images

When creating codes with data redundancy or a high level of error correction, you can mess up the image on purpose to make something more unique and brand fitting. When modifying the QR code, it is important that you pay attention to the four location boxes. Three of them are black boxes with a white inner border and then a black square. These are located in the top-right, top-left, and bottom-left. On the bottom-right is the fourth box. It is similar but contains fewer pixels or boxes. These boxes help the scanner orient itself to the code, so if you can avoid covering them, it helps. You can still place or stylize them a little, but stay away from covering them completely. You also need to stay away from a line that exists between the top-left and top-right boxes, as well as another line between the top-left and bottom-left box. These lines extend between the closest inside corners of the boxes. Figure 20.9 shows a guide you can use for areas that you should avoid.

FIGURE 20.9
Areas to avoid when modifying QR codes

By looking at the guide, the light gray frame that borders the entire figure is called the quiet zone. The quiet zone helps the scanner find the area where the QR code is. The dark gray areas near the three large black squares are where the information about the QR code structure is stored. If you edit these areas, your code may fail to scan at all. The other boxes can be slightly modified, but other than changing the color, you may not want to modify them too heavily. For an exact detail of areas that are safe for editing, visit the entry for QR code at Wikipedia (http://en.wikipedia.org/wiki/QR_Code).

Figures 20.10 and 20.11 show a couple of QR codes that have been altered to display custom images. When using custom images inside a QR code, they can be color or black and white.

FIGURE 20.10
The logo inside the QR code still allows the code to be scanned.

FIGURE 20.11
The stylized QR code still works even with rounded edges.

Remember that not everyone uses the same software to scan your codes, so it is best to test with as many devices and scanners as possible. Now that we know about generating and styling QR codes, let's take a look at creating Microsoft Tag codes.

Generating Microsoft Tag Codes

Microsoft created a unique code of its own that can be used to serve content to mobile devices just like QR codes do. Currently the only thing you need to get started is a Windows Live ID account. As soon as you create one, you can start generating codes and distributing them.

The benefits of using a Tag over a QR code include the ability to edit the Tag at any time. This is especially helpful when you find you have generated a QR code that has a typo encoded into it, when a link no longer points to a correct domain, and even when contact information has changed.

Let's take a short walk through creating a Tag code.

Generating a Tag

The easiest way to start generating your own Tags is to go to http://tag.microsoft.com and click on the Sign In link. Either create a Windows Live ID, or sign in with an existing one. After you have signed in, you will be at the Tag Manager screen. From here you can manage all your Tags and create new ones. Find the Create a Tag button and click it. This takes you to a new screen where you can choose the details of the Tag that you are generating. On this screen you can type in a Tag Title that will be shown when the Tag is scanned as well as displayed in the history section of the Tag app. You can also choose the type of Tag you want to generate. The following is a list of the types of Tags you can create:

- ▶ **URL**—This launches the URL in the mobile browser when scanned.

- ▶ **App Download**—This allows you to create a URL that is opened based on the device that scans the Tag. If the device is not supported, a default link is used instead. This is handy for creating links to files or marketplaces for installation.

- ▶ **Free Text**—This works just like a plain text encoding inside a QR code. The maximum size for text storage inside a Tag is 1,000 characters.

- ▶ **vCard**—This points to a vCard that can be imported into the mobile address book. Inside the editor you are given the option of uploading a vCard or typing all your details in and having it generate one for you.

- ▶ **Dialer**—This creates a prompt that allows the device that scans it to call a phone number embedded in the Tag.

After choosing your type, you then have the option of putting some notes in that help you organize your Tags or remind you what the Tag was created for. After the notes you can upload an image. This is actually a cool feature. When your Tag is scanned the picture you uploaded is downloaded to the device and shows in the user's history. This helps the user remember your brand, name, or content. The next feature allows you to change the start and end dates of your Tag. That's right, you can actually schedule your Tags' available date. This allows you to get Tags printed and distributed without worry that someone is going to see your campaign before you want them to, and allows you to schedule the end of the campaign as well.

Depending on the type you picked, the fields below allow you to fill out the details to finish your Tag. When done click the Save button and you are taken back to the management screen. From here you can download the Tag that you just created. When you choose to download your image you are given some options on how you want the code to be generated. Let's look at the options and how to maximize them for your project.

Downloading a Tag

When you download your tag, you are given the option of downloading a Tag Barcode (with a colorful triangle pattern drawn on it), a Custom Tag Barcode (uses colored dots instead of triangles), a QR code, or a Near Field Communication (NFC) URL. The default download option is to generate a Tag Barcode that will also add some help text with a link to download a scanner. It will also be generated in color, but you have the option of generating it in black and white only. Figure 20.12 shows a Tag generated with the default options.

Get the free mobile app at
http://gettag.mobi

FIGURE 20.12
A Tag with help text and generated in color

A Tag downloaded this way can be saved as a .pdf, .wmf, .jpeg, .png, .gif, .tiff, .tag, or URL (as a .txt file). The format options allow you to easily move the work to a graphics editing program such as Adobe Illustrator to get the Tag ready for print.

The option of downloading a Custom Tag Barcode has the same basic options as the standard Custom Tag Barcode; however, you can only download a .pdf, .wmf, .tag, or URL (as a .txt file). When the file is downloaded, it contains colored or black-and-white dots instead of triangles. Using a graphics editing program or even PowerPoint, you can then embed an image into the code. Figure 20.13 shows an example of a Custom Tag.

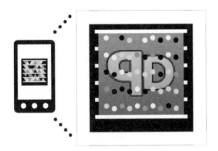

Get the free mobile app for your phone
http://gettag.mobi

FIGURE 20.13
A Tag that has been customized

The interesting part about customizing a Tag is that you don't need to worry about using the same color as the dots. You can blend into them and create some truly unique Tags and they still function. When creating a custom tag, you need to make sure that you leave the top and bottom white bars as well as the sidebars. If you save the file as a .wmf, you can actually import the file into PowerPoint and overlay it on another image. This makes generating custom codes a quick and easy process, provided you have PowerPoint. You can learn more and see some examples by visiting http://tag.microsoft.com/what-is-tag/custom-tags.aspx.

The option to generate a QR code allows you to download the code in .pdf, .wmf, .jpeg, .png, .gif, .tiff, and URL (as a .txt file) format. Oddly enough, it works just like a QR code, so there isn't much to cover that we haven't gone over already.

The last option to download an NFC URL allows you to download only a .txt file that contains the information needed for an NFC chip to be encoded with the data required to make the chip detectable with NFC.

After you download the file, you can then start using it just like you would with a QR code. One of the cool things is that the management page has a Reports link that takes you to an analytics page where you can view different stats about your Tags and how they are doing over a given timeframe.

Summary

In this hour you learned that there are many third-party vendors and tools that allow you to create QR codes and embed various data in them. You also learned how to create your own QR codes by leveraging Google Chart Tools as well as how to modify them for a unique experience. This is possible by using a parameterized URL that returns an image. You also learned about how a bookmarklet could be used to access the service. Some QR scanners were also covered so that you have an idea of the popular scanners available today and what devices they are compatible with.

You also learned about Microsoft Tag codes and how they are different from QR codes. Tag codes are similar to QR codes; however, they are managed by using a Windows Live ID account. Tag codes also use a code that can either be color or black-and-white with either triangles or dots. You also learned how to generate a Tag and about the types of data that can be contained in them.

Q&A

Q. If I generate a Microsoft Tag, will the service be around in the next five years?

A. Microsoft has stated that they will keep the codes working until at least 2015, and they will give a two-year notice to all users with a free account that the service is either being terminated or moving to a pay model.

Q. I've generated a QR code that was .75"x.75" and it worked fine on my phone. Do I really need to generate them at a 1.25"x1.25" size?

A. That depends. Are you sure that everyone who is going to scan your code has the same phone as you? Can you guarantee that even if they have the same phone they will be scanning your code under the same lighting conditions and medium? If you can, then by all means, create a .75"x.75" code; otherwise, you may want to use a larger code to increase your compatibility.

Q. You listed a few QR scanners but not any Tag scanners. Are any Tag readers available or just the one from Microsoft?

A. Currently the Tag scanner from Microsoft is the only Tag scanner available that can read Tags. It was listed under the QR scanner section because it also works with QR codes. If you are working with both codes, it's not a bad app to have installed.

Workshop

The workshop contains a quiz and some exercises to help you check your comprehension and understanding.

Quiz

1. When the highest level of error correction or redundancy is in effect on a QR code, what is the maximum percentage of the code that can be wrong and still work?

2. What does QR stand for?

3. What is the recommended display size for a QR code and why?

4. True or False: Custom images cannot be used inside QR codes.

5. How do custom images work inside Tag codes?

Answers

1. Depending on the level of error correction in the QR code, up to 30% of the code can be missing, lost, edited, or destroyed and the QR code will still work.

2. QR stands for Quick Response.

3. 1.25"x1.25" is the recommended size. At this size more than 90% of devices capable of scanning a QR code should work.

4. False. You can use custom images as long as they stay out of certain areas within the QR code, and as long as they do not exceed the 30% error correction limit of the code.

5. Custom images must be used with a custom Tag. The image is embedded behind the code itself. In a Tag image, the custom image can cover the dots used in the image, but not the white lines at the top and bottom or the sidebars.

Exercises

1. Use a few of the mentioned services to generate your own QR codes. Try using the bookmarklet, or create your own. After you have generated some codes, open one in an image manipulation program and experiment with changing the color of the QR code. Try removing a few sections of the code to test the readability of the code with errors present.

2. Download and try out a few of the scanning apps. Check your device to see whether any of the programs function better than others. If you have access to multiple devices, give them a try as well.

3. Either with an existing or new Windows Live ID account, create a Tag code. After you have created your first code, go back and create a custom Tag and use a custom image with it.

HOUR 21
Learning to Minify Everything

What You'll Learn in This Hour:

▶ The importance of minifying your files
▶ How to minify JavaScript and CSS files
▶ How to compress images
▶ Enabling server compression

When creating a website you may not put much thought into the little details like overall file size, URL requests, or the amount of JavaScript, CSS, and images used, but these details can really make or break your site. This hour we learn how to compress or minify as many of the assets of your site as possible to create a lighter and fast-loading site.

Compressing Code

You may have noticed that jQuery Mobile comes with two versions of each JavaScript and CSS file it provides. The first file is usually named something close to jquery.mobile-1.0.1.js, while the second is named jquery.mobile-1.0.1.min.js. You may not notice the difference in the file names right off, but the second contains the word min. Whenever min is present, it means that the file has been minified. A file that has been minified will have all the trailing spaces removed, including hard returns, tabs, and spaces. It will also have some of the variables renamed so that they are shorter as well as all comments removed from the file. This may not seem like it would save too much room, but in the case of the previously mentioned jQuery Mobile files, the savings is actually 138KB, or just about 62%. With that in mind, why wouldn't you want to compress all your JavaScript and CSS files? Let's learn about how we can get started minifying files.

Using the YUI Compressor

Although a few JavaScript compressors were available, the team of web specialists from Yahoo! that are the developers of the Yahoo! User Interface (YUI) library found problems that they didn't like, and so they created their own compressor. They then took things a step further and added the ability to minify CSS files as well. The YUI Compressor requires Java (at least version 1.4) to be installed on your system.

To use the YUI Compressor you first need to download it from http://yuilibrary.com/download/ yuicompressor/. The YUI Compressor is open-source, so when you unzip the file do not be surprised by all the build folders. If you do not want to make any modifications you can find the ready-to-use .jar file in the build directory. You can run the .jar file from that location, or you can move it somewhere else. I recommend copying the .jar file out to another folder in an easy to remember location. I usually put mine in a folder called "compression." Once you have the .jar file where you want, it is time to get the script you want compressed moved or copied into the same directory. If you are comfortable with the command line you can leave your files where they are and change the following command to use the path to the files you want to compress. Otherwise, once your file has been copied there you need to drop to either terminal or command line and run the following command:

```
java -jar yuicompressor-2.4.7.jar filetobecompressed.js -o stdout.js
```

In the preceding line we use version 2.4.7 of the YUI Compressor; be sure to change the numbers to match the version you are currently running. The file we are compressing in the example is named filetobecompressed.js. Make sure to specify the actual name of your file. By adding the -o stdout.js we specified what the output file should be named. If you do not specify an output file, then the compressed output appears onscreen only.

To see the results of minifying JavaScript, Listing 21.1 shows a sample JavaScript file before compression, and Listing 21.2 shows the minified file.

LISTING 21.1 A Simple JavaScript Function

```
1: // This function will display the value passed to it
2: function popUp(value) {
3:   if (value == undefined) {
4:     // No value was passed
5:     alert("There was no value passed");
6:   } else {
7:     alert("Value passed: "+value);
8:   }
9: }
```

LISTING 21.2 The Minified Version of the Simple JavaScript Function

```
1: function popUp(a){if(a==undefined){alert("There was no value passed")}
else{alert("Value passed: "+a)}};
```

The first difference you probably noticed between the two files is the number of lines used. Listing 21.1 is nine lines while line 21.2 is actually just one long line. Continuing to compare them, you can see that on line 2 of Listing 21.1 there is a variable named `value`. This was renamed to a in Listing 21.2. This will happen with most variables and values you use when you minify your JavaScript. The last major difference between the two files is that the comments have been completely stripped out of the minified version. So how much difference do these little changes make in file size? The file in Listing 21.1 is 222 bytes. The compressed file in Listing 21.2 is 103 bytes. That shrinks the file down to roughly 46% of what it was before. Granted this was a simple example with an extra line of comments, but this is still an exciting result.

The process of minifying your CSS is the same. In the command line call, just replace the `filetobecompressed.js` with `filetobecompressed.css` and `stdout.js` with `stdout.css` and you should be set. To see an example of how CSS compression works when minified, Listing 21.3 shows a CSS file before compression and Listing 21.4 shows the file after compression.

LISTING 21.3 A Sample CSS File

```
 1: body {
 2:     font-family: Helvetica, Arial, sans-serif;
 3:     font-size: 1em;
 4:     margin: 0;
 5:     padding: 0;
 6: }
 7:
 8: #header {
 9:     height: 90px;
10:     padding-left: 15px;
11:     margin-bottom: 10px;
12: }
13:
14: #content {
15:     padding: 5px;
16:     width: 950px;
17: }
18:
19: #footer {
20:     height: 30px;
21:     font-size: 80%;
22:     text-align: center;
23: }
```

LISTING 21.4 **The Minified Version of the Sample CSS File**

```
1: body{font-family:Helvetica,Arial,sans-serif;font-size:1em;margin:0;padding:0}
#header{height:90px;padding-left:15px;margin-bottom:10px}#content{padding:5px;
width:950px}#footer{height:30px;font-size:80%;text-align:center}
```

For Listing 21.3 I wrote out the CSS in the easy to read, pretty-print, or paragraph-style format. When comparing to Listing 21.4, the immediate difference is that the CSS has been compressed down to one line instead of 23. The second difference that you may have missed is that the last semicolon has been removed from each section, and the space between property and value has been removed to help save space. The changes are relatively small, but they do make a difference. The file from Listing 21.3 is 297 bytes, while the file from Listing 21.4 is 219 bytes. This comes out as a file that is about 74% of the original file, or a savings of about 26%. To learn more about how CSS is minified by the YUI Compressor, visit http://developer.yahoo.com/yui/compressor/css.html.

The YUI Compressor is an excellent choice to start with for compressing your JavaScript and CSS. While we are looking at compressing code, there is a similar compiler called the Closure Compiler. Let's take a look at this compiler and how it works.

Using Closure Compiler

Google also has a project aimed at minifying JavaScript. The Closure Compiler also analyzes your JavaScript, and if there is code that is never used or is impossible to get to, it removes it during the compile. It also checks for code efficiency and changes your existing code into a more efficient version if needed.

Just like the YUI Compressor, the Closure Compiler is available as a `.jar` file that can be run from command line or terminal. If you do not have Java installed, a web UI is available that you can use to copy and paste your code into for compilation. If that isn't enough an API also can be used to build your own page that can be used to compile code.

Let's take a quick walk through using each of these methods. Starting with the `.jar` file, the following line can be executed to compile your JavaScript:

```
java -jar compiler.jar --js filetobecompiled.js --js_output_file compiledfile.js
```

In the preceding line you can see that the `compiler.jar` file is used with the first argument or option being a `--js`, yes it is a double-dash, and this specifies what the input file is. In this example our input file is called `filetobecompiled.js`. If you have more than one JavaScript file that you want compiled and put into the same output, you can specify another `--js` option. Just be careful about the order you are feeding the scripts into the compiler or they may fail to run due to dependency problems. The `--js_output_file` specifies what the output file should be named.

NOTE

Closure Compiler Version

When you download Closure Compiler, the latest version is always included in the `.zip` file. However, the `.jar` file included will be named `compiler.jar`. If you are ever in doubt about what version of the Closure Compiler you are using, type `java -jar compiler.jar --version` into a command line or terminal window to find out what version you have (you may have to press Ctrl+C after executing the script to exit interactive mode). Of course if knowing what version you have doesn't help with knowing whether you are running the latest version, then go and grab the latest copy from http://closure-compiler.googlecode.com/files/compiler-latest.zip.

The second method of using the Closure Compiler is to use the web UI. To get to the web UI, visit http://closure-compiler.appspot.com/. Figure 21.1 shows what the page looks like when you first visit the site.

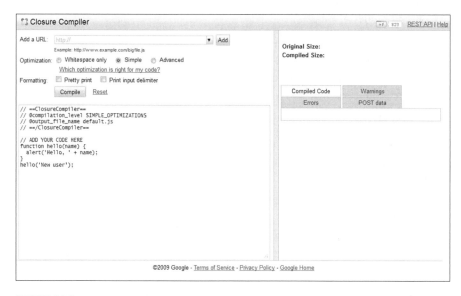

FIGURE 21.1
The Closure Compiler web UI

There are several options that you can adjust in the upper-left of the site. There are options to include some popular JavaScript libraries, as well as what level of optimization you would prefer, and how you want your code delimited.

CAUTION

Out of Date Libraries

While the Closure Compiler is a fantastic online resource to compile your JavaScript files, it may not be up to date with the current versions of JavaScript libraries. Make sure when using the option to include a library from the drop-down menu that you check the version number of the included library before you compile your code. You can always fix the version number by correcting the version that is inserted or even the address where the code is included.

After selecting your options, you can paste in the code that you want compiled into the window below. Clicking the Compile button then sends your code to be compiled on the server. When finished your code is returned in the window on the right. This can then be copied out and pasted into a local JavaScript file, or you can reference the link to default.js that is built when you compile the file. You may also look over potential problems by viewing the Warnings tab and the Errors tab. The POST Data tab shows how you could replicate the request yourself by leveraging the Closure Compiler API.

To create your own page that uses the API, visit http://code.google.com/closure/compiler/docs/gettingstarted_api.html and follow the tutorial. This gives a great starting point into how easy it is to use the API. To learn more about the Closure Compiler and all the options it provides visit http://code.google.com/closure/compiler/.

Another code compressor uses a completely different algorithm to compress your JavaScript. Let's take a look at using PACKER.

Using PACKER

While minifying code has lately been the champion of choice for JavaScript compression, at times you need a different form of compression. This is where using the Dean Edwards PACKER comes very well into play. We know that minifying code removes white space, clears out comments, and does some light sprucing up to your code. When you use PACKER your code is obfuscated and packed into a nice little self-compiling piece of JavaScript.

JavaScript files that contain .pack.js in the name usually indicate that the file was packed instead of minified. You can think of the PACKER method as applying a zip-like algorithm to your JavaScript, thereby decreasing your file size considerably. For example, I have a JavaScript file that is 18.1KB without any compression applied. When I run this through the YUI Compressor I get the file minified down to 5.0KB. However, when I put this file into PACKER with the Base62 Encode and Shrink Variables options enabled, I can reduce the file size down to 4.4KB. While it may not appear to be a substantial savings, the fact that it can compress more than half a KB off than the minified version is impressive.

To get started using PACKER on your JavaScript files, head over to http://dean.edwards.name/packer/ and paste the code you want packed into the window at the top. Choose the options you want, click on the Pack button, and your PACKED code appears in the box below. Using Base62 encoding wraps your code in a JavaScript `eval` function and also makes your code not very human readable.

So if this method helps obfuscate your code and compresses smaller than the minify process, why didn't I start talking about it first? Well, that's where we throw a curve ball into the mix. When you use PACKER on your JavaScript, you cannot add any extra compression onto it. This means that when I enable gzip or deflate on my web server I do not see any benefit on my packed files. However, minified files are compressible meaning that my original file that was 5.0KB when minified will become 1.8KB when gzipped by the web server. So why even mention PACKER? Simple, many web hosts do not allow you to enable gzip or deflate. This is because it uses the server CPU to do the compression. Since many shared hosts need as much CPU as possible to keep all their servers running, they do not want to allow all their users to drain CPU without paying for it. In an instance where you cannot enable server compression, using PACKER is definitely an option that should be considered.

Note that when using Base62 encoding your script will be wrapped in an `eval` function that on any browser may cause significant lag while the code is read into memory and then compiled. This may not be an issue on modern phone and tablet devices as it is dependent on the size and processing required to uncompress your PACKED JavaScript. When using PACKED scripts always test on as many devices as possible before launching straight into production with them. One last thing to consider is that even though a minified file is larger, by the time it is downloaded and processed it may actually be done faster overall than a PACKED file would be when processed. I strongly recommend against using PACKER on large JavaScript files such as the jQuery and jQuery Mobile framework files; use the minified version of these files instead.

If talking about gzip and deflate made you feel a little lost, don't worry; we're going to take a look at what they are all about next.

Using Gzip and Deflate

Two server-side compression methods that you use almost everyday without realizing it are gzip and deflate. Just like a text file can be made smaller when zipped, the same thing can be done with HTML, JavaScript, and CSS files. The server wraps them up in a compressed container and then sends them to the browser. When the browser receives them it unpacks the container and allows you to see the results. While this seems like it would slow down your browsing, this is all done in milliseconds and the payoff of data compression to time spent compressing is usually more than worth it.

While there are differences between both gzip and deflate, each is highly compatible with many web servers and can usually be enabled by including a module or configuration file.

NOTE

Browser Support for Compression

Not all browsers are compatible with compression. Any browser that does not support at least HTTP 1.1 encoding will not work with gzip or deflate compression. Most modern browsers support HTTP 1.1, but some proxies and even antivirus software can force the browser to support only HTTP 1.0, making the browser incompatible with server-side compression methods.

The good news about handling compression on the server is that if the client asking for content cannot handle compression, the server will not send it compressed. This allows you to not worry so much about keeping separate configurations, or even files based on compressed or uncompressed versions.

Let's take a look at configuring server-side compression on a couple of popular servers.

Configuring Your Apache Server

Some servers come preconfigured to use server-side compression (such as IIS v7+). For an example of how to configure your web server, we walk through the ever-popular open source Apache server and the Deflate module.

Apache can be configured in two ways. You can use an .htaccess file, or you can change the configuration of the server itself to always have compression turned on. To get started with either method, you first need to make sure you have the correct module enabled. The easiest way to see whether you have the module is to open your httpd.conf file and search for an entry of

```
#LoadModule deflate_module modules/mod_deflate.so
```

If you have that line, you need to remove the # that is commenting out the line. While you have this file open, you can enable compression to always be on by moving to a section of the file where MIME types can be set. If you do not already have a section, add an entry at the bottom of the file. When you find a suitable location, add the following:

```
<files *.js>
  SetOutputFilter DEFLATE
</files>
```

Once you have done that, save the file and then restart your server. When the server comes back up it will start using server-side compression automatically.

Now that you have compression working, you may want to clean up what actually gets compressed. Movies, images, music, and already-compressed files will not benefit from any added compression and will just use up CPU that could be used elsewhere. So to take care of that, go back into your httpd.conf file and change the line you previously entered in a files element so that it appears as follows:

```
AddOutputFilterByType DEFLATE text/html text/css application/javascript
```

Using the preceding code applies compression to only HTML, CSS, and JavaScript files that are served.

Another way you can control what files are compressed is to manage it at the directory level by using a .htaccess file. To manage files this way the only modification you need to make to the httpd.conf file is to uncomment the line containing the `LoadModule` entry. After that you just need to create the .htaccess file and make sure it contains the following:

```
AddOutputFilterByType DEFLATE text/html
AddOutputFilterByType DEFLATE text/css
AddOutputFilterByType DEFLATE application/javascript
```

This method works just like the other method, but allows you to control what folders have compression applied. You'll notice that only files that contain text are being compressed. This is because movies, images, and audio files are already using a form of compression that is either not supported, redundant, or will actually become inflated when server-side compression is turned on for these file types.

That really is all there is to enabling server-side compression for Apache. Let's shift our attention now to getting the most out of image compression.

Compressing Images

Image compression can be a little confusing, especially because many people believe that all images are JPEG files. This stems from the fact that point-and-shoot cameras as well as most mobile phones all take pictures that are saved as JPEG files. While it is true that many pictures on the Web are served as JPEG files, there are benefits and drawbacks to using different types of image files to get the compression you want. Since we've already started talking about JPEG files, let's start there and then move on to some other image types.

Using JPEG Image Compression

JPEG comes from the Joint Photographic Experts Group who created this particular type of image compression. It is generally used as a lossy form of image compression, so what goes in does not always come out. The idea behind using JPEG compression is finding a balance between file size and image distortion or pixelation. Depending on the program you use to save the image, you have several options for compression. Some save images on a quality scale that ranges from 0 to 100, while others use another scale that goes from 0 to 12, and as you can probably guess, the lower the quality, the smaller the file. JPEG files also contain a large color palette, supporting up to 16.7 million colors.

To illustrate the quality levels of JPEG compression, Figure 21.2 shows a series of an image saved at different quality levels.

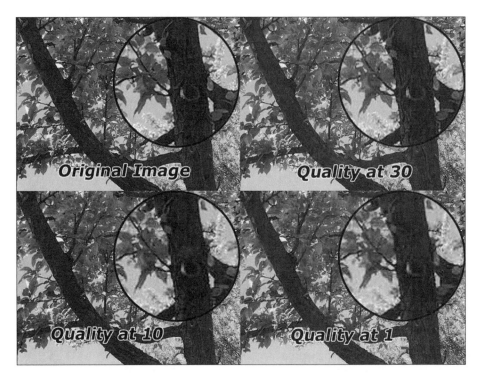

FIGURE 21.2
As the quality decreases, the pixelation and blur increase.

As you can see in Figure 21.2, some areas do not seem to be affected terribly by the lower compression, while other areas become a blurred mess of square pixels.

As far as using JPEG compression goes, it is generally a safe bet as it is compatible with almost every browser. It is generally also the format of choice for large images or pictures. In a few situations, however, it should be avoided—for example, when you need edges without distortion, images with fewer than 256 colors in them, and transparency. For those times, you should probably look at using a GIF image.

Using GIF Image Compression

The Graphics Interchange Format (GIF) image compression has been around since 1987 and boasts some very usable features. While it is limited to a 256-color pallet, it supports transparency and animation. It uses a lossless compression codec that makes it the perfect choice for logos, text, and drawings.

You should stay away from attempting to save photographs as GIF files as the color palette makes the image appear textured, noisy, or dithered. For the images that you do want to save in the GIF format, many graphics programs create a modified color palette containing as many colors and shades as needed to match the image you are compressing, as well as drop any unneeded colors to compress your file more. If you have a high number of colors, or just are not sure what colors you may need, you can default to a web-safe color palette.

Transparency is supported with GIF files; however, the support is somewhat limited. For the best results adding an outline or stroke to the portion of the image shown that contains the same color as the background it will be placed on will have the greatest effect. Failing to do so may give you an image that appears jagged or rough. Figure 21.3 shows an example of the jagged edge that can occur with text or other images that do not match the background color.

FIGURE 21.3
Images with many edges, such as text become jagged when transparent.

While images compressed as GIF files are still in use today, another format was built to eventually replace GIF images. Let's take a look at using PNG compression.

Using PNG Image Compression

PNG files were created with the intention of improving on the original GIF compression. PNG image compression was also created to sidestep a possible royalty payment when the compression algorithm used in GIF was patented. PNG files are similar to GIF files in that they are fantastic for use as logos, text, and drawings. While PNG files can be used for photos, the compression ratio is not as forgiving as JPEG. This means your image will look good, but the file size will be huge, and as such should be avoided.

PNG files are not limited to a 256-color palette (8-bit) but can instead use up to 281,474,976,710,656 colors (48-bit). Keep in mind that just because the format supports that many colors, user hardware may not. If you were to compare a file with the same color palette as a GIF file, though, you would find that you can usually get a smaller file with PNG compression instead of GIF compression. Figure 21.4 shows a GIF and a PNG file that contain the same color palette.

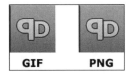

FIGURE 21.4
The GIF file is 6KB, and the PNG file is 5KB.

Another improvement over GIF is the use of an alpha channel for transparency. This means that you do not have to apply an outline or stroke to your image to keep corners looking smooth.

With all the benefits of PNG images, you may wonder why they have not already taken over as the format of choice for images and graphics. This is mostly due to lack of browser support. Until recently not all browsers supported PNG files, or all the features that the PNG format brings. The lack of animation support has also been a concern to those who like a little movement in their images. When considering these from a mobile perspective, PNG files make sense to be used as most mobile devices have browsers that support the PNG format.

Now that we've covered the basic formats that can be used for image compression, let's look at some tools that can squeeze them a little more.

Tools for Further Image Compression

Programs are not always perfect. Sometimes you may save a file and think that it will automatically generate the best file available in regards to quality and file size. Unless you know specifically what you are doing, using another program or tool to optimize your images is a good idea. The following sections discuss tools that you can use to get the most out of your images. For testing the following tools, I used a sample JPEG photo and PNG logo file.

Smush.it

Smush.it is another compression tool by Yahoo! that allows you to upload images or even paste the URL where your image is hosted to be analyzed for compression. When the file has been analyzed, the web app tells you how much space can be saved on the image and gives you a zip file containing the compressed images. Smush.it works with JPEG, GIF, and PNG files. That being said, if you upload a GIF file, it will be converted to a PNG file automatically. If you are not expecting this, you may think the tool is broken. Also you should know that you can only upload files around 1MB in size. This is a great free service that you should look into using. Visit http://www.smushit.com/ysmush.it/ to get started with the program. Using my test JPEG file, it managed to squish the file down an extra 108KB of the original 1.1MB. My PNG file faired a little better by getting almost an extra 1KB out of the file, reducing it from 4.8KB to 3.8KB.

JPEGmini

This is another web app that can be used to considerably shrink the size of your JPEG images. It uses a custom compression algorithm that works similarly to how our eyes work when looking at images. Although that makes it work differently on different images, if you use a lot of JPEG images, you may want to look into using the service. It is currently free, although to use a batch process you need to sign up for an account. They are working on a downloadable program to compress images on your desktop, but there is no current launch date. Visit http://www.jpeg-mini.com/main/home to try it out for yourself. JPEGMini was extremely impressive with my test JPEG file. It compressed it down to 446KB of the original 1.1MB. Results vary, but a file that is more than two times smaller with no visible difference is quite the feat.

PunyPNG

PunyPNG is another image compression web app that allows you to upload JPEG, PNG, and GIF files. As PunyPNG is geared more toward PNG files, the upload file size is limited to 150KB. If that is too small for your needs, PunyPNG does offer a paid plan that allows you to upload images up to 500KB in size. To get started compressing your images, visit http://punypng.com/. In my test I uploaded my PNG file, and the end result was a file that was 122 bytes smaller.

ImageOptim

For OSX users who would rather compress files locally, you can use ImageOptim. ImageOptim is a freeware download available from http://imageoptim.pornel.net/. The magic of ImageOptim is that it is a front end for the popular command-line image processors PNGCrush, OptiPNG, AdvPng, PNGOUT, jpegtran, and Jpegoptim. Due to some license restrictions, to use PNGOUT, you must download it separately to be used in the program. Using ImageOptim is as simple as opening the program and dragging your image files directly to it. Using ImageOptim I was able to compress my test JPEG file down about 10% to 1.0MB, and my test PNG file was compressed about 20% to 3.9KB. As far as compressing images in OSX, this is my favorite tool and well worth the few minutes it takes to download.

PNGGuantlet

Windows users who want a program to optimize their images can use PNGGuantlet, a free download available at http://pnggauntlet.com/. It does require an installation of .NET 4.0 before it can run, but once installed the program opens up and allows you to drag and drop images into it for compression. My test PNG file came out compressed with a 26% savings at 3.6KB. The difference here may be that I was able to use PNGOUT with PNGGuantlet where I did not opt to use it with ImageOptim.

Photoshop

Yes, Adobe Photoshop has the ability to compress your images in a very fine manner. The trick is to not save the image as you normally would, but instead to use the Save for Web & Devices menu option. When you use Save for Web & Devices, a few options are automatically set that help keep the file size down. For example, PNG files are automatically saved with 8 bits per channel instead of 24. The other nice thing about saving for the Web is the interface that you are shown when saving. You can see exactly what your quality changes do to the image. Running my test files through this method I was able to get my JPEG image compressed down to 633KB with minimal distortion and my PNG test file down to 3.5KB.

Picasa

Picasa is a free offering from Google that runs on Windows and OSX. This imaging software allows you to edit and group photos as well as export them as compressed JPEG images. Linux users can also get the program installed by using WINE.

Now that we've covered image compression, let's take a look at an experimental Apache module that provides an all-in-one compression solution.

Using mod_pagespeed on Your Apache Server

For those running Apache 2.2+ for your web server, you should look into running Google's mod_pagespeed. This is an open-source Apache module that uses a set of rewrite filters that help with compression and HTTP request limiting. It even has some of the previously mentioned image compression techniques built in to help compress your images for delivery. I like to think of it as a magic pill for improving the Web experience.

It works in a fairly simple manner. Instead of responding to every HTTP request that comes in, it accepts all requests first and then prioritizes them as well as groups similar files together. These files are then treated with server-side compression and sent to the client requesting the resources.

For an example of how files are bundled together, let's say your website has a base.css and a category.css file that are called on the same page. Instead of using two requests and responses to get both files to the browser, it accepts both requests, and then appends both CSS files together and minifies them for return so that only one HTTP response is used. This works the same way for JavaScript files. If you combine this with a caching policy, the savings can really start to add up.

Some sites may not see much of an improvement, while others can see a speed increase of around 40%. As always, your mileage will vary, but if you have a Debian or RPM-based Linux distribution, go to http://code.google.com/speed/page-speed/docs/module.html and get started with optimizing your server.

Summary

In this hour you learned that compression matters as it helps to minimize the bandwidth needed for a user to experience the site. You have several options for minifying JavaScript by using the YUI Compressor, the Closure Compiler, or the PACKER. Compressing CSS files is also possible and should be considered.

You learned about server-side compression through the use of the gzip and deflate methods. Deflate can be enabled in the server settings of Apache or in a more restricted approach by using .htaccess files.

You learned about image compression and what type of image compression should be applied depending on the needs of the image being compressed. Not all images are fully compressed when originally saved and may see improved compression by using either an image optimization service or program.

Finally, you learned that an Apache module is available that aims to tackle everything from minified code and compressed images, to combined and zipped files.

Q&A

Q. Why didn't you mention WebP for image compression?

A. WebP is an up-and-coming format that does have some serious potential as a mainstay for images used on the Web. However, it is currently supported natively only in Opera and Chrome. While techniques do exist to make WebP images work in other browsers, I wanted to mention only types currently supported by the vast majority of browsers.

Q. So is there anything I can do if my web host does not allow gzip and/or deflate to be used?

A. Yes and No. Some people have had luck using a PHP script to attempt forced compression. The best thing to do is to contact your hosting company and ask them whether if they support server-side compression and how to enable it. Most hosting companies already have a policy in place and will work with you when asked. Support for gzip in web browsers is nearly universal now as it has been supported since IE4, so some developers are uploading only gzipped code. This forces browsers without support for gzip to not display gzipped content, so if you take this approach your mileage may vary.

Q. Does the size of my images really matter and is 20KB or 30KB really a big deal with broadband speeds as fast as they are?

A. I would love to tell you that speed doesn't matter. I would also love to tell you that everyone has a fiber broadband connection. Unfortunately, though, neither of those is true. When dealing with mobile devices it gets even worse since network latency and connection speed can vary even in the same room. Search engines have also started ranking websites based on loading times. This means that if you cannot figure out how to deliver your site in 1 to 3 seconds, your search ranking may slide. Every KB of size you can shave off your site helps.

Workshop

The workshop contains a quiz and some exercises to help you check your comprehension and understanding.

Quiz

1. True or False: Minified files can also be compressed with server-side compression.

2. True or False: PACKED files should be used whenever server-side compression is not available.

3. When should JPEG image compression be used?

4. Why was PNG image compression not very popular?

5. What is the maximum number of colors supported in a PNG file?

Answers

1. True. Files that run through the YUI Compressor or Closure Compiler can be further reduced in size through the use of gzip or deflate on the server.

2. True. PACKED files do not get any extra compression from gzip or deflate, but when neither is available, PACKED files will become smaller than their minified counter parts.

3. Whenever you are using a large image or picture you should use JPEG compression.

4. Until recently, the PNG format was not fully supported in all browsers. Because GIF was widely supported there was no big push for developers and designers to start using PNG files.

5. The maximum amount of colors that can be used in a PNG file is 281,474,976,710,656 (48-bit).

Exercises

1. Download or use one of the online code tools to minify your code. Compare the size of your original to the minified version. If you can, enable server-side compression and then compare the size of your original file, the minified one, and the compressed one.

2. Use one or more of the image compressing programs on some of your own images. If you have access to Photoshop, do a comparison between the Save for Web & Devices option and the results of the other image compression tools.

3. Download and configure `mod_pagespeed`. If you do not have access to a web server, then download either CentOS or Ubuntu into a VM and set up an Apache server there to try it. Experiment by adjusting some of the filters for `mod_pagespeed` that can be found at http://www.modpagespeed.com/.

HOUR 22
Using Mobile Device Emulators

What You'll Learn in This Hour:

▶ Why you should use device emulators

▶ The weaknesses of device emulators

▶ Where to find device emulators

▶ How to use emulators with your site

Whether you are developing a website or a web application, considering the way it will display and handle on different devices is an issue that you must deal with. When you fail to plan ahead for different devices and browsers, you can leave some fairly embarrassing gaps in your site. While it is true that most smartphones either ship with or can run an HTML5 capable browser, there are still legacy devices and proprietary browsers that render your code differently. This is where using mobile device emulators come into play.

Turning to Mobile Device Emulators

If you've never used an emulator before, you can think of it as a virtual device or program that performs similarly to the actual device. Many emulators allow you to experience how the device will behave from startup to shutdown. Other emulators are application wrappers that allow you to use certain applications of the mobile device. When dealing with a mobile site, emulators give you an idea of how the site will be displayed and how the user will interact with what they are presented.

Using an emulator for mobile devices is especially important as mobile devices translate some events differently than desktop browsers. Another reason that you should use an emulator is to understand the wide array of screen resolutions available to mobile devices. While it's always good to test the theory of responsive design and site layout, until you have used either an emulator or an actual device it may be difficult to fully appreciate how your design and site layout handles on a tablet device instead of on a smartphone.

From a cost perspective, device emulators offer a great starting point for small shops, individual developers, and those who are only able to devote weekend-warrior status to development. Emulators are generally free or only require a short developer application to be filled out prior to download. This makes it easy for you to get started testing and creating websites and web applications that run as smoothly as possible on the actual device.

While using an emulator may sound like a developer's dream come true, there are actually several potential problems that you need to keep in mind. The biggest issue stems from emulators not giving a completely accurate portrayal of how the device works. Think about how most mobile devices work. Most tablets or smartphones use a touchscreen. When you use an emulator you are presented with a screen or image of the device or application. The problem then becomes manipulating the device. While the mouse does a fair job at acting out taps, some gestures or swipes are impossible to perform. Many emulators have found some assisted ways around this, adding some features that allow you to hold down a key on your keyboard while click-and-dragging to create gestures like pinching. Other emulators include special keyboard and mouse modes to help you navigate around them. Another problem you run into when using emulators is speed. Because most mobile devices run on different types of processors, the languages they use are translated differently to the processor. This means that for an emulator to function either it needs to be compiled in another language or it needs to convert all the input from the host machine into a native form that it can use to process. This takes a considerable amount of processor function, leaving you with a device that may not function at the same speed as an actual device. By that same token, there are occasions where the emulator actually runs faster and more responsively than the actual device does.

Another problem is application support. Many emulators come with a limited feature set and limited ability to add new programs. Since most emulators provide a browser this will not be too much of an inconvenience for testing websites or web applications, but it can be a little bit of a shock if you are not expecting it. You should also be aware that some emulators do not run inside another emulator. While that may sound like a no-brainer, let me explain it in a way that is more common for developers. If you are on OSX and are running a version of Windows in a VM, you will not be able to use the Windows Phone Emulator. You may be able to install it, but it will not function. On a similar note, the iOS simulator will not function on any OS except OSX. Some pseudo-emulators will skin either Safari or Chrome to act like iOS, but if you want the official emulator, you need to be running on hardware with OSX installed.

Following is a quick summary of the pros and cons to using device emulators:

Pros of using device emulators:

▶ Low cost alternative for development

▶ Properly displays device resolution

▶ Can be used to test responsive layouts between devices

▶ Easily test websites and applications inside native device browsers

Cons of using device emulators:

▶ Device input is emulated and may not be completely accurate.

▶ Device operating speed may be incorrect.

▶ Some emulators may not run on your current OS.

▶ Lack of full device feature support.

Now that you know why you should use emulators, and some of the common pitfalls that come with them, let's look at the process of acquiring them and running them on your system.

Finding Emulators for Testing

Getting your hands on an emulator is usually a straightforward process. Visiting the developer section of almost any mobile OS website usually results in a link to sign up for development tools or the Software Development Kit (SDK). Some sites make getting the emulator easy, while others require you to sign up as a developer. Once you have jumped through the correct hoops and filled out the required forms you are given the link to the files that contain the emulator.

Android

The emulator for Android is part of the Android SDK, which is available for download at http://developer.android.com/sdk/index.html. The download does not require any signup or registration and is available for Windows, OSX, and Linux systems. Once you have downloaded and either unpacked or installed the Android SDK, you can use the Android Virtual Device (AVD) Manager to create emulators for different Android devices. Unlike other emulation software, the AVD Manager allows you to create multiple emulators that run different versions of the Android OS. To create emulators with different versions of Android, you need to first use the included SDK Manager to download the versions that you want for your emulator. While the base Android API versions can be downloaded without any developer registration, some of the API versions require registration. You may choose to sign up, or skip downloading the specialized API versions. Once you have downloaded the API versions that you are going to use, you can open the AVD Manager and click on the New button. From there you are presented with a virtual device creation screen. Figure 22.1 shows the screen with some settings filled out.

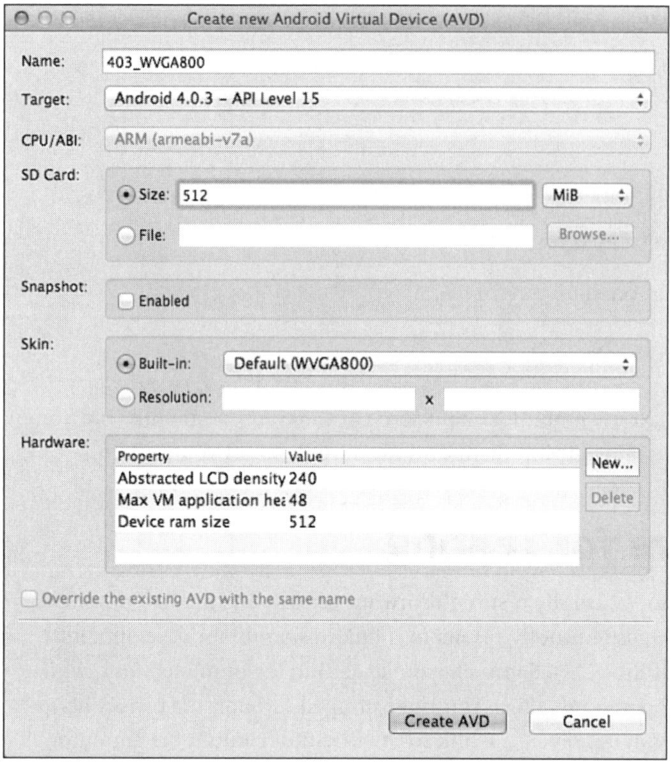

FIGURE 22.1
Creating an AVD

To create the AVD you need to name it, select a version or target version of the OS, select the amount of memory available, choose to enable snapshots of your AVD, and choose a resolution. Once you have filled out these options you can click "Create AVD" to finished creating your AVD.

After you have created your AVD, you can then start or boot the device by selecting it and clicking the Start button. When you do a new window appears, and the device begins the boot sequence. When finished you are presented with the lock screen of whatever version of Android you picked to boot. Figure 22.2 and Figure 22.3 show the lock screen of a smartphone running Ice Cream Sandwich (4.0.3) and a tablet running on Honeycomb (3.2).

FIGURE 22.2
The lock screen of Android version 4.0.3 on a smartphone

FIGURE 22.3
The lock screen of Android version 3.2 on a tablet

Once you have unlocked the device you are presented with the home screen. From there you either have an icon that gets you the built-in web browser, or an option to launch the app from the application menu. Once you have opened the browser, you can then navigate to anywhere on the Internet, or on your local network. If you are trying to connect to a server running on the computer that you are running the AVD from, then you need to reference the site by IP of the computer instead of by using `localhost`. When the site loads you can see how it responds just as it would on an actual device. When you want to interact with the site you have to use your mouse and use a click and drag to simulate swiping. By clicking your mouse you initiate a tap event. In case you wondered about changing the orientation of the device in the emulator, pressing the Ctrl+F11 and Ctrl+F12 keys on your keyboard will do this.

When developing with jQuery Mobile, I tend to use at least two AVDs, one for a smartphone and one for a tablet. This is not only because of the difference in screen size, but because the built-in browser is different on both platforms. Once again, before you go creating an AVD for every version and every screen size, you should always check the analytics and needs of your site. If you are starting a new site and want to try to target the most popular Android devices, visit http://developer.android.com/resources/dashboard/platform-versions.html. This data is taken from Android devices that have used Google Play, so the data may be a bit skewed as it does not include devices such as the Kindle Fire. However, if you do not have any data to go off of, this gives you a good idea of what the common OS is for Android users. To learn more about developing for Android, visit http://developer.android.com/.

iOS

iOS is the OS that runs the iPod Touch, iPhone, and iPad devices. Getting your hands on the iOS Simulator requires that you be running OSX and have access to the App Store. This means that there is not a version available for Windows or Linux users. To install the iOS Simulator you need to log in to the App Store and download a program called Xcode. When Xcode has been installed, you can then use Spotlight to launch the iOS Simulator. You can also launch the iOS Simulator from inside Xcode, or by using Finder and moving through your local file system to /Developer/Platforms/iPhoneSimulator.platform/Developer/Applications/iOS Simulator. When launched for the first time an iPhone will appear on your desktop as shown in Figure 22.4.

FIGURE 22.4
The iOS Simulator emulating an iPhone

While a few stock applications are installed, you'll want to tap to launch the Safari app and start testing. Similar to the Android emulator, you may load links on the Internet, your host machine, or on any other reachable computer on your network. I've even been able to load an Apache server in a VM on the host computer and reach it from the iOS Simulator.

The iOS Simulator also allows you to load an iPad and the iPhone with a retina display. If you use the iPhone with the retina display, be prepared to see a huge iPhone appear on your screen. You may also worry about the iPad taking up a large portion of your screen. This can be scaled down, however, by using the either the Window, Scale menu, or by using a hotkey combination. Some hotkeys that you may be interested in using are

▶ Command+1 changes the device scale to 100% (iPad only).

▶ Command+2 changes the device scale to 75% (iPad only).

▶ Command+3 changes the device scale to 50% (iPad only).

▶ Hold down the option key and use a click-and-drag to perform a pinch.

▶ Command+left-arrow rotates the device orientation to the left.

▶ Command+right-arrow rotates the device orientation to the right.

▶ Command+S saves a screenshot to the desktop as a PNG file.

To learn more about iOS development visit https://developer.apple.com/programs/ios/.

Windows Phone

While the adoption rate of Windows Phone devices has not been as fast as iOS or Android, a partnership with Nokia aims to change that. Windows Phone features a streamlined and modern OS that is simple to use with a good-looking UI. The Windows Phone SDK comes with everything you need to get started developing, including the Windows Phone Emulator. The SDK installs only on computers running at least Windows Vista SP2. Note that the Windows Phone Emulator will not run in an installation of Windows that is running inside an emulator. This means that those running VMWare Fusion, Paralells Desktop, and VirtualBox will be able to install the SDK, but not be able to use emulator for testing. That means that developers on Linux or Macintosh systems need to dual- or tri-boot their system with a Windows installation to use the Windows Phone Emulator.

While the Windows Phone Emulator is aimed at loading and testing applications developed for the OS, it comes with Internet Explorer Mobile installed. This is perfect for testing websites and web applications built on jQuery Mobile. Figure 22.5 shows the home screen of the Windows Phone Emulator.

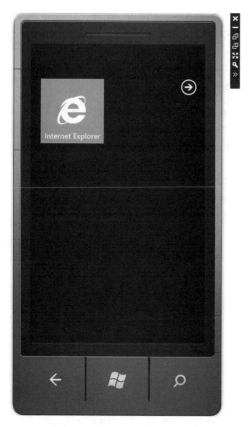

FIGURE 22.5
The Windows Phone Emulator running Internet Explorer

Similar to both the AVD emulator and the iOS Simulator, you can rotate the device orientation. This is done by clicking on one of the rotation icons in the device toolbar. You can also take screenshots from the emulator that will be saved as 480x800 PNG files. To do this use the expand button in the toolbar and choose the Screenshot tab. Clicking the Capture button grabs the current frame from the emulator. If you like what is displayed, click on the Save button and a dialog window appears asking where you want to save the image. To learn more about developing for the Windows Phone OS, visit the APP HUB at http://create.msdn.com/en-US/.

BlackBerry

The BlackBerry OS has seen quite a few changes over the last several releases. The latest versions include an HTML5 browser that works very well with jQuery Mobile.

The BlackBerry OS has also released a tablet version as well as the smartphone version of the OS. Luckily, they provide emulators for both. The emulators covered so far require the installation of the SDK to get the device emulator; however, with BlackBerry it's a little different. The emulators are provided on a per-device basis, with the Playbook Simulator available as a VMWare image that can be played back in either VMPlayer for Windows or VMWare Fusion for OSX users. The smartphone simulators run on the Windows platform. By visiting http://us.BlackBerry.com/developers/resources/simulators.jsp you can download the simulator you want to use.

For the smartphones, if you need to support multiple devices you should download each one you want and install them. When you want to start using the BlackBerry Simulator, you should find the file fledgelauncher.exe (in the folder where you installed your BlackBerry simulator[s]) and open it. You are presented with a screen that allows you to select the model of device you want to launch. After launching the device you then can watch it boot the OS in a large window that shows the screen of the device. Figure 22.6 shows a BlackBerry 9930 simulator running the web browser.

FIGURE 22.6
The browser on recent BlackBerry devices is a WebKit-based browser that offers users a modern web browsing experience.

The smartphone simulator has many advanced features that can be used such as device tilt, rotation, and two types of screenshots (one with the body of the device, and the other only saving the screen).

For the PlayBook you need to download the VMware image and then have it added to the VMPlayer (for Windows) or VMWare Fusion (for OSX). When you start the VMWare image, the device boots and you are deposited at a desktop with only a browser installed. From here you can open the browser and begin using the simulator to test your website or web application. Figure 22.7 shows the home screen of the PlayBook.

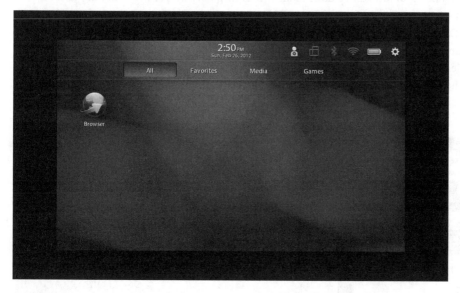

FIGURE 22.7
The PlayBook Simulator comes with only a web browser installed, which is perfect for testing websites and applications.

The browser included on the PlayBook is based on WebKit and has support for many HTML5 features. The features of the browser make it a great addition to testing along with the Android Emulator with a Tablet AVD and the iOS Simulator running an iPad.

Application Emulators

While the device emulators are great for allowing you to test applications and give you an idea of how the device will behave with your site, you can also grab emulators that allow you to test other browsers that may be supported on the device. Both Opera and Mozilla have a browser that can be installed on many mobile devices that gives a different approach to web browsing than the stock browser installed on the device. Another application called Ripple also can be used to help debug HTML5 web applications as it acts like the stock browser of many popular devices.

Opera Mobile

Opera Mobile is an application available for devices running Android, Symbian, Maemo, and MeeGo. It is a nice alternative browser for those familiar with Opera, and for those who are using cellular connections that want to use the extra compression that comes from using the Opera browser.

The Opera Mobile Emulator can be downloaded from http://www.opera.com/developer/tools/ mobile/ and allows you to test how the Opera Mobile application will behave on a specific device. The Opera Mobile Emulator is available for Windows, OSX, and Linux. When the application is launched you are presented with a window allowing you to choose what device, resolution, pixel density, and input type you want to emulate. After you have made your choices, a window of the Opera Mobile application appears. Figure 22.8 shows the Opera Mobile Emulator running.

FIGURE 22.8
The emulator changes size based on the options you choose. This displays a common smartphone size.

The Opera Mobile Emulator is a fast and capable emulator. While it may initially lack developer tools to help you debug your code, it can be connected to an open Opera browser that has Opera

Dragonfly installed. When combined you get a similar tool to Firebug and the Developer Tools from Webkit-based browsers that allows you do remote debugging. You can learn more about Opera Dragonfly by visiting http://www.opera.com/dragonfly/.

Fennec/Firefox Mobile

The Mozilla team originally started with project Fennec as their solution to the mobile browser market. Since then it has been renamed Firefox Mobile and released for devices running Android 2.1 or above. The emulator for Firefox Mobile runs on Windows, OSX, and Linux and can be found under Developer Tools at http://www.mozilla.org/en-US/mobile/.

After you download the application, running it brings up a window displaying a welcome screen. Do not be too surprised if you still see the Fennec name on the emulator, as it uses the same base rendering engine as the Android version of Firefox. Figure 22.9 shows the welcome screen when the emulator is launched.

FIGURE 22.9
The Fennec/Firefox Mobile emulator being run for the first time in OSX

The emulator works just like Firefox Mobile does; this means that you'll have some options by swiping (or clicking and dragging) to the left or the right. Clicking on the location bar brings up the menu options for pages you have visited, your bookmarks, your history, and the options to sync tabs and bookmarks with your desktop.

Ripple Emulator

Another option for browser testing is the Ripple emulator that is now part of BlackBerrys HTML5 WebWorks. Ripple allows you to choose from a variety of mobile devices and simulate the resolution and browser experience. It even changes the User Agent (UA) to the device it is emulating so that you can perform logic based on the device viewing your site. Due to some of the features, such as Geo Location and Accelerometer, Ripple makes a decent tool for use with frameworks such as PhoneGap for mobile application development. The one minor problem I have found with Ripple is that screen navigation must be done with the arrow keys, or with a touchpad instead of a click and drag method. The Ripple emulator is available for download on computers running Windows or OSX from https://bdsc.webapps.blackberry.com/html5/download/ripple. Figure 22.10 shows the Ripple emulator in action. Note that when the option panels are visible they overlap the middle section of the application. This can make the option panels a little tricky to see and differentiate from the testing window.

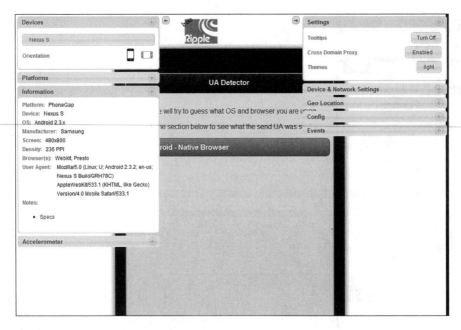

FIGURE 22.10
The Ripple interface using the light theme with option panels visible overlapping the testing window

In the case of Figure 22.10 the screen area is cramped with the options panels out. Luckily there are buttons that look like arrows that will collapse the panel and make room for the emulator. For more information on Ripple, visit https://bdsc.webapps.blackberry.com/html5/.

Using Emulators for Testing

When you want to use an emulator to test your website or application, all you really need to do is open the emulator, find the browser, and type in the address of your site. When the site appears you can begin to test it using the capabilities of the emulator. When you are satisfied that it works the way you want it to, the best thing to do is to find someone who has an actual device and test with it. If that is not something you can do, you can always watch the analytics of your site, or even use a survey to get user feedback.

Generally when using an emulator you are testing how the site is rendered on your screen and how the user interaction and user experience work. Depending on your site or project you may want to route users with certain devices to different sections of your site. Emulators will transmit a different UA allowing you to display different content based on the device. To give an example of how emulators display the UA, let's build a simple page using jQuery Mobile that you can then load in an emulator that will display the device that is viewing the site based on the UA information passed from the emulator. Listing 22.1 shows an excerpt of the JavaScript detection method used in ua_detector.html.

LISTING 22.1   Simple UA Detection with JavaScript

```
 1: <script>
 2:   $(document).on("pagecreate","#ua-detector", function() {
 3:     var ua = navigator.userAgent;
 4:     var uaOS = "", uaString = "";
 5:     if (ua.match(/Windows/i)) {
 6:       uaOS = "Windows";
 7:       if(ua.match(/Windows Phone/i)) {
 8:         uaOS = "Windows Mobile";
 9:       }
10:     } else if (ua.match(/Macintosh/i)) {
11:       uaOS = "Macintosh";
12:     } else if (ua.match(/iPad/i) || ua.match(/iPhone/i)) {
13:       uaOS = "iOS";
14:     } else if (ua.match(/Android/i)) {
15:       uaOS = "Android";
16:     } else if (ua.match(/RIM/i) || ua.match(/BlackBerry/i)) {
17:       uaOS = "BlackBerry";
18:     } else if (ua.match(/Linux/i)) {
19:       uaOS = "Linux";
20:     } else {
21:       uaOS = "Totally Stumped";
22:     }
23:     if (ua.match(/Chrome/i)) {
24:       uaString = "Chrome";
25:     } else if (ua.match(/Firefox/i)) {
26:       uaString = "Firefox";
```

```
27:        if (ua.match(/Fennec/i)) {
28:          uaString = "Mobile FireFox/Fennec";
29:        }
30:      } else if (ua.match(/MSIE/i)) {
31:        uaString = "Internet Explorer";
32:        if (ua.match(/IEMobile/i)) {
33:          uaString = "IE Mobile";
34:        }
35:      } else if (ua.match(/Opera/i)) {
36:        uaString = "Opera";
37:        if (ua.match(/Opera Mobi/i)) {
38:          uaString = "Opera Mobile";
39:        }
40:      } else if (ua.match(/Safari/i)) {
41:        uaString = "Safari";
42:        if (ua.match(/Mobile/i)) {
43:          uaString = "Mobile Safari";
44:          if (uaOS == 'Android' || uaOS == 'BlackBerry') {
45:            uaString = "Native Browser";
46:          }
47:        }
48:      }
49:      uaString = uaOS +" - "+uaString;
50:      $("#guess").text(uaString).trigger("create");
51:      $("#ua").text(ua);
52:    });
53: </script>
```

The script in this listing is not the most efficient way of parsing out devices, but it is an easy-to-read example of how to parse out the OS and the browser of the device loading the script. Starting at line 2 you can see that we use some jQuery to bind to the pagecreate event. We use the pagecreate event so that when the script modifies the text of the page, it will still be rendered correctly by jQuery Mobile. If you were to use the pageinit event, then parts of the page would break when loaded. Line 3 shows the setup of a variable named ua. This variable contains the UA as passed from the browser viewing the page and will be used for determining the final values of the variables created on line 4. Lines 5-22 show an if statement with many else if statements used to determine the OS of the device viewing the page. Note that the order of the else if statements does matter. For example, if you were to move the clause on line 18 that searches for Linux devices above the clause on line 15 that searches for Android devices, then all Android devices would report as Linux devices. This is because the UA of Android devices reports Linux as part of the string, so if Linux is checked for first it will exit the loop and continue down the code. Moving down to lines 24-48 you can see the check for browser type.

Some of these sections, such as the one for Firefox starting on line 25 have another `if` statement that does a second check for the presence of a mobile browser name or type. Line 27 checks for the word `Fennec` inside the `ua` variable and when found will change the browser to say `Mobile Firefox/Fennec`. This process is repeated in the following clauses to make sure that mobile devices do not get flagged as being desktop browsers. Line 49 sets up the string that will display on the page after the variables have been populated. Line 50 and 51 populate elements that are present on the ua_detection.html page with the values returned from the script.

The following figures show the page being loaded on various emulators. Figure 22.11 shows the Windows Phone Emulator, Figure 22.12 shows a BlackBerry Emulator, and Figure 22.13 shows the iOS Simulator viewing ua_detection.html.

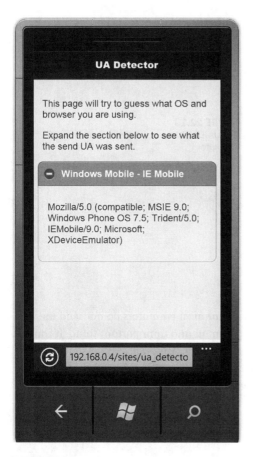

FIGURE 22.11
The UA Detection page running on the Windows Phone Emulator

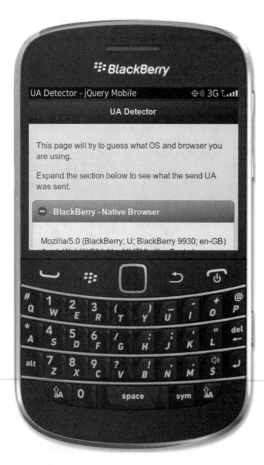

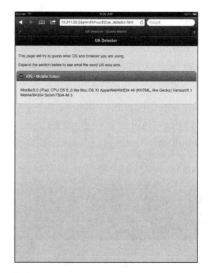

FIGURE 22.13
The UA Detection page running on the iOS Simulator

FIGURE 22.12
The UA Detection page running on a BlackBerry Emulator

Something you may want to pay a little attention to is that most emulators do not send the same UA as the actual device. While this is a seemingly small and unimportant thing, it can be a potential problem if you are trying to handle a specific device. Although it is possible to trip up the detection script by modifying your UA in the browser (when allowed or supported), this should give you a good example of how emulators work.

Summary

With mobile emulators it is possible to be better prepared to handle different devices and know how your site will work and appear on them. In this hour you learned how to acquire some mobile device simulators and what platforms they run on. You also learned that not all emulators are full device emulators but are applications that simulate a browser that can be installed on some mobile devices.

Mobile emulators are not perfect; you should test with actual hardware as often as possible. This is due to the emulation of hardware and software running on a different chipset and platform.

You also learned that by using a UA detection script with mobile emulators you can detect mobile devices and plan ahead for them.

Q&A

Q. What about an emulator for Opera Mini?

A. Oddly enough the main difference between Opera Mobile and Opera Mini is how the data is handled. In Opera Mini every request is sent to the Opera backend servers for compressed data. This results in smaller downloads and less bandwidth used, while the Opera Mobile application skips this step when connected to Wi-Fi. So in short, testing with Opera Mobile should get you close enough to Opera Mini to work.

Q. Should I be concerned if I don't use a remote debugging utility like Opera Dragonfly on my iOS or Android development?

A. Yes and No. If the page loads and functions as planned, then I'd say you are most likely in the clear. However, both default browsers for iOS and Android run WebKit, so to be safe, fire up Safari and Chrome and use the Developer Tools to look for errors and fix them on your desktop. After you have fixed any errors, try loading the site on your device or emulator again. If it's still broken, you can resort to some good old alert debugging or similar visual debug tool. iOS devices also allow you to turn on a Debug Console in the system preferences that will show you errors that occur on pages you are working on.

Q. If jQuery Mobile handles issues including fallback support for legacy devices, why should I even bother with emulators?

A. Using emulators is mostly a personal preference, and jQuery Mobile does a fantastic job of making your website work on legacy devices. However, unless you really want to be that developer that passes a site off because it works on your mobile device, you should always test on as many devices as possible. What may work for you in your chosen browser might not work for someone else.

Workshop

The workshop contains a quiz and some exercises to help you check your comprehension and understanding.

Quiz

1. What platform can you install the iOS Simulator on?

2. What is required to create and Android Virtual Device?

3. What is Fennec?

4. What makes emulating BlackBerry devices a little different from other devices?

5. True or False: You can run the Windows Phone Emulator on a copy of Windows running inside a VM.

Answers

1. iOS comes with Xcode and only runs on computers running OSX.

2. You need to download the Android SDK and any APIs that you want to use.

3. Fennec was the codename for Firefox Mobile. The UA for Firefox Mobile still contains Fennec, and the emulator still displays Fennec as the application name.

4. BlackBerry offers emulators on a per-device situation. This allows you to get the emulator for the device you want to test.

5. False. The Windows Phone Emulator will not function inside a VM. It will only run from a standard Windows installation.

Exercises

1. Download at least one of the mentioned emulators and install it on your system. Use it to start surfing some websites and see which ones direct you to the mobile version of their site.

2. Take the ua_detector.html file and either modify it or copy out the detection script and use it on your own page or site to do something else when a certain mobile device is detected. You could do something as simple as changing a background or including an image on your page.

3. Get the emulator for a device or browser you have installed on your mobile. Compare them side-by-side on the same site. Note any differences and see whether you can find out why things are displayed differently. Load the ua_detector.html file on both devices and note any differences in the UA string.

Building an App with PhoneGap and jQuery Mobile

What You'll Learn in This Hour

▶ Why PhoneGap is ideal for web developers

▶ The difference between native and web apps

▶ How to create an Android project with PhoneGap

▶ How to import a jQuery Mobile project into a PhoneGap project

There has been some debate about building native applications or using web applications and while both sides have valid points, there are times when a web application either isn't feasible or just doesn't provide the device permissions needed to allow the application to function properly. This hour we spend some time looking at a project that helps bridge the gap between native and web applications.

Getting Started with PhoneGap

PhoneGap started out as a project aimed at taking HTML5 web applications and making them available on mobile devices without requiring web developers to learn new languages to create native applications. PhoneGap currently supports features of the iOS, Android, Windows Phone, BlackBerry, webOS, Symbian, and bada platforms. For a list of currently supported features for each platform, visit http://phonegap.com/about/features. At the Adobe MAX Conference in 2011 it was announced that PhoneGap would be acquired by Adobe. Adobe recently donated the original codebase of PhoneGap to the Apache Software Foundation where it has become the Apache Cordova project (http://incubator.apache.org/cordova). That being said, PhoneGap can be thought of as a project powered by Apache Cordova, or a distribution of Apache Cordova. PhoneGap is a framework that allows you create native applications. Let's learn more about native applications, how to install PhoneGap, and how to create a project.

Going Native

Native applications are built to run as standalone applications on the device. This means that they have been compiled and optimized for the device OS. Native applications are put into a different sandbox of security restrictions and allowed access to different layers of the hardware inside the machine. For example, a native application is granted access to the device storage, accelerometer, camera, and hardware keys. Another positive of native applications is that they may not require an Internet connection or a cached version to function. Not all applications use device features, and some may not use any features at all. Applications that are utilities generally do not use extra device features, although some check for and use an available data connection to push updates to the application.

When creating a native application it is important to know the capabilities of each device you are planning to build for and to plan for them. Not all devices will have a compass, accelerometer, or camera. They may also contain different screen resolutions and file system partitions. Some of these issues can be dealt with by the nature of your application, while others, such as layout concerns, can be handled with responsive layouts and by using frameworks such as jQuery Mobile.

Installing PhoneGap

PhoneGap is itself a framework, which means that the installation process is as easy as including it in your project. The downside to this is that depending on what platform you are programming for you need to change how you include PhoneGap. To get started we need to first download the current version of PhoneGap, which is available at http://phonegap.com/download-thankyou. Once you have the compressed file downloaded, you can start installing the other prerequisites. Each platform has a list of requirements that must be met to develop for that platform. For our sample work in this hour we are going to use PhoneGap with an Android project. We use Android because the Android SDK runs on Windows, OSX, and Linux, allowing anyone to create a sample project and test it. To develop with the Android SDK, you need to download the Android SDK as well as install Eclipse.

Downloading the Android SDK

To start with the Android SDK, following these steps:

1. Open a browser to http://developer.android.com/sdk/index.html and download the version of the SDK for your system. If you download a compressed file you only need to uncompress the file on your file system and then run the `android` script or batch file.

2. When the script or batch file is executed, the Android SDK Manager should appear and allow you to start downloading the pieces of the SDK that you want to develop with.

3. For testing across the most common Android devices you will probably want to download Android 2.3.3 (API 10 – Gingerbread), Android 3.2 (API 13 – Honeycomb), and Android 4.0.3 (API 15 – Ice Cream Sandwich). As we learned before, to use an Android Virtual Device (AVD), you need to have at least one of these APIs downloaded.

4. When you have finished downloading the files you want, open the Android Virtual Device Manager and create at least one AVD by clicking the New button and then walking through the values to create your device.

Once you have the device created you are ready to download Eclipse.

NOTE

Java for Eclipse

Windows and Linux users may need to install a Java Runtime Environment to use Eclipse; head over to http://java.com/ to download and install Java.

Downloading Eclipse

To download Eclipse, follow these steps:

1. Open a browser and go to http://eclipse.org/downloads/. On this page find the installation package for Eclipse Classic and download either the 32- or 64-bit version (depending on the OS and hardware of your computer).

   If you are unsure of what version to run, you should be safe downloading the 32-bit version. The file comes down as a compressed file that can be uncompressed to any folder in your file system. OSX users may want to uncompress the file in the Applications folder, while Windows users may feel more comfortable uncompressing the file in their Program Files folder.

2. Once you have the file uncompressed you can open Eclipse by launching the eclipse application or executable file. When launched you are prompted for a workspace location. This is where all your project files will be created and saved. While the defaults are generally fine for most, if you are meticulous about where files are stored on your system, this is where you will want to change it. If you do not want to be prompted for your workspace location every time you open Eclipse, you can check the box asking to make this workspace your default.

3. After you have chosen your workspace location you are then shown the welcome screen. To get out of this screen and onto your workspace, an arrow icon in the top-right takes you to the workbench. You are now ready to install the Android Developer Tools (ADT) plug-in into Eclipse.

   The ADT plug-in allows Eclipse to interface with the Android SDK that you downloaded previously.

4. To install the latest version of the ADT plug-in, click on the Help menu and then click on Install New Software. This brings up a new Install window that is used to install new software and plug-ins that work with Eclipse.

5. On the right side of the Install window click on the Add button. This brings up the Add Repository window that asks for the name and location of the plug-in. For the Name field type in **ADT Plugin**. For the Location field type in **https://dl-ssl.google.com/android/ eclipse/**. Figure 23.1 shows the Install and Add Repository windows with the repository information filled out.

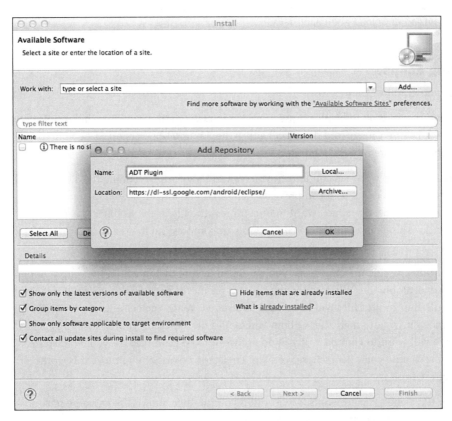

FIGURE 23.1
Adding the site for the ADT plug-in

6. After clicking OK, the files that are available to be installed appear in the Install window under Developer Tools with several entries below it. Click the Developer Tools check box and then click the Next button. The file dependencies will then be automatically checked, and either you will be shown errors with a description of what caused the error, or you will be able to click Next. After clicking Next you are shown the licenses for the files you are going to download. After giving them a thorough reading, click on I Accept the Terms of the License Agreements and click the Finish button.

7. During the installation process you may be shown a window telling you that the software you are downloading contains unsigned content. As this is an official plug-in from Google, as long as you are certain you typed in the address correctly, this can be noted and then safely ignored. Clicking OK dismisses the message and continues the installation process.

8. After the files have been downloaded you are asked to restart Eclipse. Click on Restart Now and wait while Eclipse shuts down and then restarts with the ADT plug-in installed. Now that the ADT plug-in is installed we need to make one more adjustment to make sure that it works with the Android SDK.

9. Open the Preferences window (press Command+, in OSX, or click on the Window menu and then select Preferences in Windows). Look on the right side of the Preferences window for an entry titled Android. Clicking on the Android entry shows the options for the ADT on the right side of the Preferences window. Make sure that the path to your uncompressed SDK is in the SDK Location field. If the field is empty or has an incorrect entry listed, click on the Browse button and navigate to the correct folder. When finished selecting the correct folder, click OK to save the setting.

Once that has been completed, you are now ready to start developing an Android project using PhoneGap. Let's walk through setting up and compiling a project.

Creating an Android Project

To create a new project, follow these steps:

1. Click on the File menu and select New, Android Project. If you do not see Android Project, click on Project and a New Project window appears asking you to Select a Wizard. Many different types of projects are shown in the lower section of the window that can be created. In the lower section find the entry for Android in the list and expand it to show the option for Android Project. Select Android Project and click Next.

2. On the next page you need to give your project a name in the Project Name field. For our project, let's type in **WebCalc**; the rest of the settings can be left at default. Figure 23.2 shows the screen for reference.

FIGURE 23.2
Initial setup page of a new Android project

3. Clicking Next moves the New Project Wizard to the Build Target section. In this section you have the option of choosing the API level your project will use. Unless you are specifically targeting a known version of the Android API, you should pick the highest version of the API level available.

TIP

Choosing an API Level

While you may be tempted to pick a low version of the API, you should always try to choose the highest API level available and allow Android to handle degradation. If you are worried about older devices running your application, you will be allowed to choose a minimum API level in your configuration file that limits legacy devices.

4. After selecting your build level, click Next to move the New Android Project Wizard to the Application Info section. On this page the Application Name should already be filled out, and the Package Name should be highlighted and ready to be changed. If you already have a namespace it can be typed here.

If you are unsure of what a namespace is, you can think of it as a kind of reverse domain name with the project name on the end. For example, `com.phonegap.webcalc` would be an acceptable namespace, although for your own projects you should change it to reflect your name or your company name. For the example code I chose a namespace of `com.dutsonpa.webcalc`.

5. After you have given your project a namespace, make sure that Create Activity is checked. You can change the Minimum SDK setting if you want, but by default it should be at the build level that you selected during step 3.

6. When you are happy with your project settings, click Finish.

Adding the PhoneGap Resources

Your base project will be generated and almost ready for use. To add PhoneGap there are three folders we need to add to your project:

1. Right-click on your project folder and choose New and then Folder from the expanded menu. In the New Folder window that appears select your base project for the Enter or Select the Parent Folder section. In the Folder Name field, type **libs** and click Finish.

2. After creating that folder, right-click on your project folder again and again choose New and then Folder from the expanded menu. When the New Folder window appears, expand the WebCalc folder in the Enter or Select the Parent Folder section and select the folder named assets. In the Folder Name field type **www** and click Finish.

   Once these folders have been created, copy the PhoneGap assets into them.

3. Find the zip file you downloaded earlier from the PhoneGap website and unzip it. Inside there should be a folder named Android. This folder contains several files and subfolders. Find the file cordova-1.5.0.jar (where 1.5.0 is the version number) and either drag-and-drop the cordova-1.5.0.jar file or copy it to the libs folder that you created in your project during step 1.

4. After dragging or copying that file over, right-click on it and look at the context menu that appears for the Build Path option; then select Add to Build Path in the expanded menu.

   This then adds the file to the Referenced Libraries section of the project.

5. Once you are finished adding the phonegap-1.5.0.jar file to the build path, copy the cordova-1.5.0.js file to the www folder that you created in the assets folder of your project during step 2.

6. Copy the entire xml folder from your extracted PhoneGap directory to the existing res folder in your project.

Figure 23.3 shows what your project structure should look like with the files copied into the project.

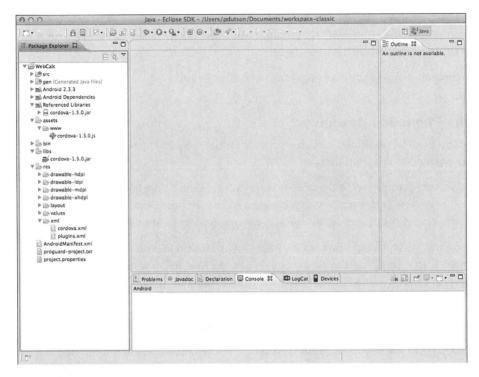

FIGURE 23.3
The basic project structure with PhoneGap resources added

The last things that we need to do to finish our project setup is make some modifications to the main Java file for the project and to the AndroidManifest.xml file.

Modifying WebCalcActivity.java and AndroidManifest.xml

The Java file can be found under the src folder inside our namespace package. It should be named after your project. In the example files it can be located at src/com.dutsonpa.webcalc/WebCalcActivity.java. Open the file by either double-clicking on it or by right-clicking on the file and choosing Open. When the file has opened in the editor look near the top of the file for some import statements. You may need to click on a little plus icon to expand the section and see them completely. First, you need to delete the first import statement `import android.app.Activity`. Next you need to add the following on the line after the `import android.os.Bundle;` statement:

```
import org.apache.cordova.*;
```

Move down to line 6, find the text that says extends Activity, and change it to say extends DroidGap. After that move down to line 11 and replace the line that says setContentView(R. layout.main); with super.loadUrl("file:///android_asset/www/index.html");.

To double-check the changes needed in the file refer to Listing 23.1 that shows the complete WebCalcActivity.java file with the changes made.

LISTING 23.1   The Edited WebCalcActivity.java File

```
 1: package com.dutsonpa.webcalc;
 2:
 3: import android.os.Bundle;
 4: import org.apache.cordova.*;
 5:
 6: public class WebCalcActivity extends DroidGap {
 7:    /** Called when the activity is first created. */
 8:    @Override
 9:    public void onCreate(Bundle savedInstanceState) {
10:       super.onCreate(savedInstanceState);
11:       super.loadUrl("file:///android_asset/www/index.html");
12:    }
13: }
```

If you used a different namespace in your project you should see it reflected in the package shown on line 1. Lines 3 and 4 show the default import used with an Android project and the import needed to use PhoneGap. Line 6 shows the change from Activity to DroidGap, and line 11 shows the new entry that will launch the index.html file when the application is launched. We add the index.html file in the next section, but before we do that let's make a change to the AndroidManifest.xml file.

The AndroidManifest.xml file is located in the root of your project. This file holds many of the application settings crucial to the application being compiled and running properly. For our project we are going to add screen size support, a few device permissions, and an orientation activity.

We start by adding the following chunk of code to the AndroidManifest.xml file on line 7:

```
<supports-screens
  android:largeScreens="true"
  android:normalScreens="true"
  android:smallScreens="true"
  android:xlargeScreens="true"
  android:resizeable="true"
   android:anyDensity="true"
/>
```

Adding in the screen support section allows our application to work on various sized screens instead of working only on large, normal, or small screens. After this, we insert the following permissions making them lines 15 and 16:

```
<uses-permission android:name="android.permission.INTERNET" />
<uses-permission android:name="android.permission.READ_PHONE_STATE" />
```

While many different types of permissions can be used with PhoneGap, two permissions are required for your PhoneGap projects. These are the READ_PHONE_STATE and INTERNET permissions.

NOTE

Application Permissions

Your project may require several permissions to function properly. The following is a list of available permissions in your PhoneGap project:

- ▶ android.permission.CAMERA
- ▶ android.permission.VIBRATE
- ▶ android.permission.ACCESS_COARSE_LOCATION
- ▶ android.permission.ACCESS_FINE_LOCATION
- ▶ android.permission.ACCESS_LOCATION_EXTRA_COMMANDS
- ▶ android.permission.READ_PHONE_STATE
- ▶ android.permission.INTERNET
- ▶ android.permission.RECEIVE_SMS
- ▶ android.permission.RECORD_AUDIO
- ▶ android.permission.MODIFY_AUDIO_SETTINGS
- ▶ android.permission.READ_CONTACTS
- ▶ android.permission.WRITE_CONTACTS
- ▶ android.permission.WRITE_EXTERNAL_STORAGE
- ▶ android.permission.ACCESS_NETWORK_STATE
- ▶ android.permission.GET_ACCOUNTS
- ▶ android.permission.BROADCAST_STICKY

After the permissions have been added we then need to add the following extra property to the activity element:

```
android:configChanges="orientation|keyboardHidden"
```

After adding the preceding property to the existing activity element, we need to add a new activity element below the existing activity element:

```
<activity android:name="org.apache.cordova.DroidGap"
    android:label="@string/app_name"
    android:configChanges="orientation|keyboardHidden">
    <intent-filter></intent-filter>
</activity>
```

Listing 23.2 shows what the AndroidManifest.xml file should look like with the changes applied.

LISTING 23.2   The Edited AndroidManifest.xml File

```
 1: <?xml version="1.0" encoding="utf-8"?>
 2: <manifest xmlns:android="http://schemas.android.com/apk/res/android"
 3:     package="com.dutsonpa.webcalc"
 4:     android:versionCode="1"
 5:     android:versionName="1.0" >
 6:
 7:     <supports-screens
 8:         android:largeScreens="true"
 9:         android:normalScreens="true"
10:         android:smallScreens="true"
11:         android:resizeable="true"
12:         android:anyDensity="true"
13:      />
14:
15:     <uses-permission android:name="android.permission.INTERNET" />
16:     <uses-permission android:name="android.permission.READ_PHONE_STATE" />
17:
18:     <uses-sdk android:minSdkVersion="10" />
19:
20:     <application
21:         android:icon="@drawable/ic_launcher"
22:         android:label="@string/app_name" >
23:         <activity
24:             android:name=".WebCalcActivity"
25:             android:label="@string/app_name"
26:             android:configChanges="orientation|keyboardHidden">
27:             <intent-filter>
28:                 <action android:name="android.intent.action.MAIN" />
29:
30:                 <category android:name="android.intent.category.LAUNCHER" />
31:             </intent-filter>
32:         </activity>
33:         <activity android:name="org.apache.cordova.DroidGap"
34:             android:label="@string/app_name"
35:             android:configChanges="orientation|keyboardHidden">
36:             <intent-filter></intent-filter>
37:         </activity>
38:     </application>
39:
40: </manifest>
```

For the most part it is okay if your file doesn't match up line for line with the preceding code, but it does matter if your XML is malformed. Make sure when you create elements that you properly close them and that they are named correctly. Eclipse will parse your file and underline in red elements or attributes that it believes are errors. Make sure to correct these problems and you should be all set. Now that we have all the base configuration set up, let's add some assets that use jQuery Mobile to the project.

Including jQuery Mobile in Your Project

While it is possible to port just about any web app that currently uses jQuery Mobile to PhoneGap, the integration process depends heavily on how the web application behaves. For the sake of simplicity we are going to port a simple calculator that works as a web application into the PhoneGap project. The calculator is made up of three pages and uses jQuery Mobile for function and style. Listing 23.3 shows the index.html file that we will use.

LISTING 23.3   The Ratio Calculator and Starting Page

```
 1: <!DOCTYPE html>
 2: <html>
 3:   <head>
 4:     <title>WebCalc</title>
 5:     <meta name="viewport" content="width=device-width, initial-scale=1">
 6:     <link rel="stylesheet" href="css/jquery.mobile-1.1.0-rc.1.min.css" />
 7:     <link rel="stylesheet" href="css/styles.css" />
 8:     <script src="cordova-1.5.0.js"></script>
 9:     <script src="javascript/jquery-1.7.1.min.js"></script>
10:     <script src="javascript/scripts.js"></script>
11:     <script src="javascript/jquery.mobile-1.1.0-rc.1.min.js"></script>
12:   </head>
13:   <body>
14:     <div data-role="page" id="ratio">
15:       <div data-role="header" data-id="header-nav">
16:         <h1>WebCalc - Ratio</h1>
17:         <div data-role="navbar">
18:           <ul>
19:             <li><a href="phi.html" data-direction="reverse"
data-transition="flow">Phi</a></li>
20:             <li><a href="index.html" class="ui-btn-active
ui-state-persist">Ratio</a></li>
21:             <li><a href="divisible.html" data-transition="flow">Divisible</a>
</li>
22:           </ul>
23:         </div>
24:       </div>
25:       <div data-role="content">
26:         <h3 class="center">Ratio Calculator</h3>
27:         <p><em>Width x Height = Aspect Ratio</em></p>
```

```
28:            <div data-role="fieldcontain" class="ui-hide-label">
29:              <div class="ui-grid-c">
30:                <div class="ui-block-a">
31:                  <label for="ratio-width">Width:</label>
32:                  <input type="text" name="ratio-width" id="ratio-width"
placeholder="Width" />
33:                </div>
34:                <div class="ui-block-b center lh-two-em">x</div>
35:                <div class="ui-block-c">
36:                  <label for="ratio-height">Height:</label>
37:                  <input type="text" name="ratio-height" id="ratio-height"
placeholder="Height"/>
38:                </div>
39:                <div class="ui-block-d"> </div>
40:              </div>
41:              <div class="lh-two-em bold">
42:                Ratio (Aspect) = <span class="ratio-aspect">0</span>
43:              </div>
44:            </div>
45:            <hr />
46:            <p><em>Calculated ratio based on original values</em></p>
47:            <div>
48:              <div data-role="fieldcontain" class="ui-hide-label">
49:                <div class="ui-grid-c">
50:                  <div class="ui-block-a">
51:                    <label for="ratio-cWidth">Width:</label>
52:                    <input type="text" name="ratio-cWidth" id="ratio-cWidth"
placeholder="Width" />
53:                  </div>
54:                  <div class="ui-block-b center lh-two-em">x</div>
55:                  <div class="ui-block-c lh-two-em bold" id="ratio-cHeight">?
</div>
56:                  <div class="ui-block-d"> </div>
57:                </div>
58:                <div class="lh-two-em">Ratio (Ascpect) = <span
class="ratio-aspect">0</span></div>
59:              </div>
60:            </div>
61:            <hr />
62:            <input type="button" name="ratio-btn-reset" id="ratio-btn-reset"
value="Reset Values" />
63:          </div>
64:        </div>
65:    </body>
66: </html>
```

By looking at Listing 23.3 you can see that we are using the basic setup needed for a site using jQuery Mobile. We used the HTML5 DOCTYPE on line 1, the meta element for viewport sizing on line 5, and our includes for the jQuery Mobile assets on lines 6, 9, and 11. The PhoneGap required JavaScript file is included on line 8. Continuing down the page to line 14 you can see the div element has been given an attribute of id="ratio". This id will be used with the navigation bar to move between the three calculators of the site. Line 15 shows the header of the site being defined, and it also contains an attribute of data-id="nav-header". This attribute is used to create a static header that should stay in place even during page transitions. To accomplish this, the same attribute must be on the page that the one will link or transition to. Lines 17-23 show the navigation bar that links to the other two pages. Lines 25-63 show the actual bulk of the page. These lines contain some basic layout styling as well as two grids used to help format the data for the user. The page contains three input areas that allow the user to input dimensional data that will then be calculated and returned so that the user can find a given ratio. The ratio can then be used to figure out the height of another element when given the width of the element. There also is an included reset button that clears all three input fields. Figure 23.4 shows what the ratio calculation page looks like in a browser.

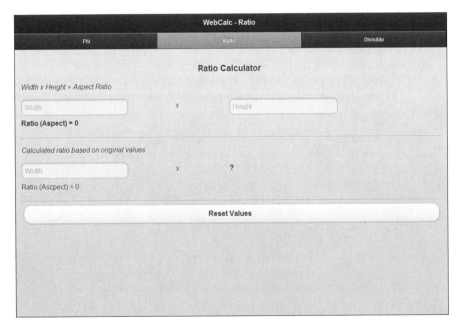

FIGURE 23.4
The ratio calculator rendered as a web application

According to the navigation bar at the top of the page, there is a page to the right of this page called Divisible. This is actually a link to the file divisible.html. The page section of this file is shown in Listing 23.4.

LISTING 23.4 The Page of the Calculator for Divisible Calculation

```
 1: <div data-role="page" id="divisible">
 2:   <div data-role="header" data-id="header-nav">
 3:     <h1>WebCalc - Divisible</h1>
 4:     <div data-role="navbar">
 5:       <ul>
 6:         <li><a href="phi.html" data-direction="reverse"
data-transition="flow">Phi</a></li>
 7:         <li><a href="index.html" data-direction="reverse"
data-transition="flow">Ratio</a></li>
 8:         <li><a href="divisible.html" class="ui-btn-active ui-state-persist">
Divisible</a></li>
 9:       </ul>
10:     </div>
11:   </div>
12:   <div data-role="content">
13:     <h3 class="center">Divisible Calculator</h3>
14:     <p>Enter a number to see what it is divisible by. This is useful when
calculating grid and column sizes for layouts.</p>
15:     <hr />
16:     <div data-role="fieldcontain">
17:       <label for="dbl-base">Base Number:</label>
18:       <input type="text" name="dbl-base" id="dbl-base" />
19:     </div>
20:     <div class="ui-grid-b" id="dbl-results">
21:       <div class="ui-block-a"> </div>
22:       <div class="ui-block-b" id="left-col">
23:         <div id="result2">2: <span></span></div>
24:         <div id="result3">3: <span></span></div>
25:         <div id="result4">4: <span></span></div>
26:         <div id="result5">5: <span></span></div>
27:         <div id="result6">6: <span></span></div>
28:         <div id="result7">7: <span></span></div>
29:         <div id="result8">8: <span></span></div>
30:         <div id="result9">9: <span></span></div>
31:         <div id="result10">10: <span></span></div>
32:         <div id="result11">11: <span></span></div>
33:       </div>
34:       <div class="ui-block-c" id="right-col">
35:         <div id="result12">12: <span></span></div>
36:         <div id="result13">13: <span></span></div>
37:         <div id="result14">14: <span></span></div>
```

```
38:              <div id="result15">15: <span></span></div>
39:              <div id="result16">16: <span></span></div>
40:              <div id="result17">17: <span></span></div>
41:              <div id="result18">18: <span></span></div>
42:              <div id="result19">19: <span></span></div>
43:              <div id="result20">20: <span></span></div>
44:           </div>
45:        </div>
46:     </div>
47: </div>
```

Line 1 sets up the page section and has a property of `id="divisible"`. Lines 4–10 show the navigation bar that was on the first page, although with some slight differences as to which button contains the property of `class="ui-btn-active ui-state-persist"`. These classes make the element they are attached to appear in the active state and allow it to keep the active state when transitioned to and from the page. Another difference in this section is the use of the `data-transition="flow"` property as well as the `data-direction="reverse"` property that is being used. These have been added to help give a visual flow to the application. Lines 12-46 show the content section of the page. This section holds the setup for the calculator. You can see from the description that this section contains an input that allows the user to enter a number and then see in a list what the number is divisible by and how many times that particular number will go into the base number. This is a useful calculator when dealing with grids and layouts as you can do quick calculations and see the results in the `div` elements displayed in the content section. The calculations will be displayed in the empty `span` elements in JavaScript. Figure 23.5 shows what the divisible calculation page looks like in a browser.

The third page of the calculator is used to calculate phi or the Golden Ratio. Listing 23.5 shows the page section of phi.html.

LISTING 23.5 The Page of the Calculator for Phi Calculation

```
 1: <div data-role="page" id="phi">
 2:    <div data-role="header" data-id="header-nav">
 3:       <h1>WebCalc - Phi</h1>
 4:       <div data-role="navbar">
 5:          <ul>
 6:             <li><a href="phi.html" class="ui-btn-active ui-state-persist">Phi</a>
</li>
 7:             <li><a href="index.html" data-transition="flow">Ratio</a></li>
 8:             <li><a href="divisible.html" data-transition="flow">Divisible</a>
</li>
 9:          </ul>
10:       </div>
11:    </div>
```

```
12:    <div data-role="content">
13:       <h3 class="center">Phi Calculator</h3>
14:       <p>
15:          The Golden Ratio, or phi, is used in nature, and also in design. This
16:          calculator will help you create two columns split by the Golden Ratio.
17:       </p>
18:       <hr />
19:       <div data-role="fieldcontain">
20:          <label for="phi-base">Base Number:</label>
21:          <input type="text" name="phi-base" id="phi-base" />
22:       </div>
23:       <div class="ui-grid-c">
24:          <div class="ui-block-a"> </div>
25:          <div class="ui-block-b center">
26:             <div id="phi-a" class="bold">a: <span></span></div>
27:          </div>
28:          <div class="ui-block-c center">
29:             <div id="phi-b" class="bold">b: <span></span></div>
30:          </div>
31:          <div class="ui-block-d"> </div>
32:       </div>
33:    </div>
34: </div>
```

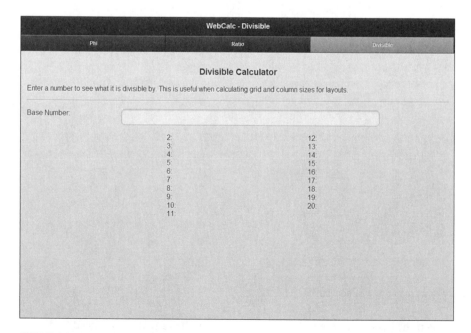

FIGURE 23.5
The divisible calculator rendered as a web application

Just like the previous pages, this page has been given an id and shares the same navigation bar that is on lines 4-10. The property of `class="ui-btn-active ui-state-persist"` has also been moved, and the `data-transition="flow"` properties have been applied. The other difference here is that none of the links contain the `data-direction="reverse"` property. This is because this page is located on the far left of the viewable area and should only transition to the right, which is the default direction of the transition. The content area is contained in lines 12-33, and as indicated by the `h3` element on line 13, contains the input and display for the Phi Calculator. This calculator is useful when designing to the Golden Ratio or Phi ratio. The next time you visit a blog site, look to see whether they are using two or three columns. If they are, there is a good chance that one of the columns is just over one and half times as wide as either the second or the second and third columns combined. When that is the case, the site has most likely been calculated using the Golden Ratio. To figure this ratio out, line 21 shows an input field where the user can enter a base value. Lines 23-32 show a grid system that will display the first and second columns or sections of the layout. Once again the empty `span` elements will be populated using JavaScript. Figure 23.6 shows what the phi calculation page looks like in a browser.

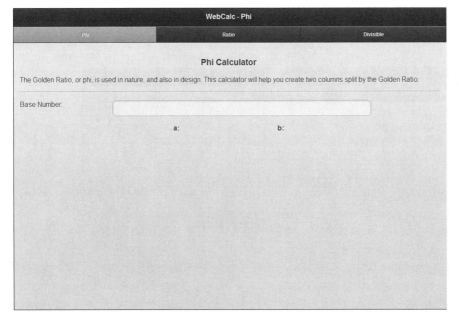

FIGURE 23.6
The phi calculator rendered as a web application

Now that we've seen the pages that are part of the application, the only thing we need to do is take all the files (including the CSS and JavaScript files) and drop them into their existing structure into the assets/www folder of our webcalc project in Eclipse. This can be done either by using the file system on your computer or by moving files into the project by using drag-and-drop. If you decide to drag and drop the files, a dialog window may appear asking whether you want to copy the files or link to them. I strongly recommend that you copy the files into the project, as this will protect you from accidental deletion or even from moving files and breaking your project later. Figure 23.7 shows what the project should look like with all the assets copied into the application.

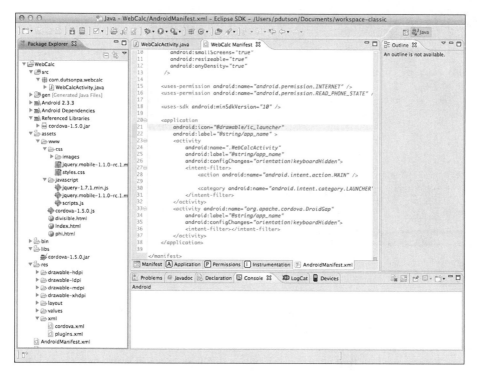

FIGURE 23.7
With all the assets moved into the project, it is ready for testing.

Once you have copied all the asset files into the project you are ready to test and compile your application.

Compiling the Application

The easiest way to test the application is to right-click on the project name, find the Run As option in the context menu, and then select 1 Android Application. If you already have an AVD created, it will automatically launch and install the application on the device. If you do not have an AVD created, or if you have one that was created on an incompatible API level, an error will be thrown and you will be prompted to create a new AVD that is compatible with your application.

When the AVD launches you have to unlock it, and the application should launch automatically. Figure 23.8 shows the application running inside an AVD.

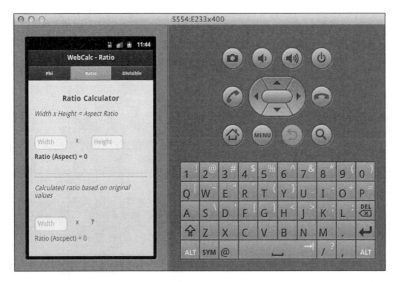

FIGURE 23.8
The application is ready to be tested in the AVD.

Before you start your final testing you should know that not all the page transitions are supported when using PhoneGap and jQuery 1.1RC1. When a transition is not supported the default transition used is the "fade" transition, which causes the screen to "blink" between pages. Currently the "flow" transition that we are using in this application is not supported by Android devices running Gingerbread (Android 2.3). If you decide to change the transition to "none" it will not display a transition, but will introduce a slight lag between button press and page load. Issues with page transitions will hopefully be fixed by the 1.1 final release. If this is a major setback for your application, you can fall back to jQuery Mobile 1.0 where the basic transitions are supported.

With page transition behavior aside remember that when using an emulator you may get some odd behavior. Some delay, blinking between screens, and even occasional failure to reorient the screen are all problems that may occur when using an AVD. If available, using at least one actual Android device for testing is ideal. To test with your Android device, put the device into USB debugging mode. This setting is located in either the Settings -> Applications -> Development or Settings -> Developer Options menu on your device. Once enabled plug the USB cable into your device and into your computer and then choose to run the project as an Android Application.

NOTE

Drivers for Debugging

Depending on your OS you may need to download some drivers. If you have trouble connecting your device to Eclipse and running the application, visit http://developer.android.com/guide/developing/device.html and follow the steps to set up your hardware. Also remember to read the fine print and ignore setting the `android:debuggable="true"` in your AndroidManifest.xml file.

When you are satisfied that your application is working properly you can prepare it for deployment by right-clicking on the project and choosing Android Tools and then Export Signed Application Package from the submenu. This opens a window that checks your project for errors. If none are found, you can then click the Next button. If you have already created an Android application before, then you should already have keystore, which you can use to sign your application. If you have never created one, you need to create a self-signed certificate by clicking on the CreateXXXX radio button and clicking Next. Follow the menu as it helps you generate a certificate. For more information on Android and certificates, visit http://developer.android.com/guide/publishing/app-signing.html. After you have used or created your certificate you are prompted to save the APK file to your file system. This is the file that contains your application, so make sure you know exactly where you are putting it. Once you have chosen a location, click on Finish to start the export process.

When the file has been exported, you are returned to your project. From there you can email, copy, or move the APK file onto your Android device and install it. Remember that when installing APK files in this manner you must go into your device settings and enable Unknown Sources in the Applications section. If you have a developer account to publish your app in Google Play, you can upload the exported APK directly to your account. To register as a Google Play developer, visit https://play.google.com/apps/publish/signup.

NOTE

Default Icon

When you create an application in Eclipse a default icon is used with your application. If you want to customize your icon, follow the icon guidelines found at http://developer.android.com/guide/practices/ui_guidelines/icon_design.html.

Once created, copy the images into your project into the appropriate res/drawable- folders.

That is really all there is to quickly creating an app using PhoneGap and jQuery Mobile. If you want to port your application to another platform such as iOS or BlackBerry, you can follow the guides at http://phonegap.com/start, or you could use the PhoneGap Build service (https://build.phonegap.com/). Using PhoneGap Build you only need to upload a zip of your HTML, CSS, and JavaScript files and it automatically generates application store ready files. PhoneGap is a useful framework that could be covered in a book by itself, but hopefully you have seen how it can be easily leveraged to quickly create or port applications from the Web to a mobile device.

Summary

In this hour you learned how to use PhoneGap and jQuery Mobile to create an application that can be used on the Android platform. You learned what tools are needed and how to create a project. By using PhoneGap, it is possible to port simple web applications to mobile devices in a short amount of time, and by using jQuery Mobile the layout of your application appears just like it does on a website. This allows you to use styling that you are already familiar with and provides a comfortable cross-platform experience.

Q&A

Q. It seems way too simple to include a jQuery Mobile project; is that really all it takes?

A. The difficulty level depends on the project. You can create some very complex and awesome applications by including backbone.js and using some web service calls. Doing so increases the possible difficulty level of your application. If you tie into the native hardware system it also increases the complexity level of your app. For example, the project sample in this hour did not include access to the camera. The application created in this hour was to give you a taste of using PhoneGap with a simple jQuery Mobile project.

Q. When using PhoneGap can I make the device make noises or take pictures?

A. Absolutely, just remember that when users install your application they are shown what permissions the application needs. If someone downloads an app that wants to use the camera and doesn't explain why, the user may not complete the install.

Q. Is the app from this hour available in the Android section of Google Play?

A. Yes, this app is published and available for free download.

Workshop

The workshop contains a quiz and some exercises to help you check your comprehension and understanding.

Quiz

1. What platforms does PhoneGap work on?

2. True or False: PhoneGap is a standalone application.

3. What Android permissions must be included when using PhoneGap?

4. What file controls the application settings in your Android project?

5. What is required to test your application from Eclipse?

Answers

1. PhoneGap works with iOS, Android, Windows Phone, BlackBerry, webOS, Symbian, and bada.

2. False. PhoneGap is a framework that allows web applications to interface with mobile hardware allowing web developers to create applications with native capabilities.

3. At a minimum you must include `android.permission.INTERNET` and `android.permission.READ_PHONE_STATE`.

4. The AndroidManifest.xml file controls everything from the devices that are compatible with your application to the permissions your application needs to run.

5. Either an Android device in USB Debugging mode or an AVD created at a compatible API level must be created to run and test your application.

Exercises

1. Modify the project to be compatible with a different range of devices. The default included in the example project is API 10. Try lowering it and see how it handles on your AVD or on an actual device.

2. Check out the documentation at PhoneGap (http://docs.phonegap.com/) and add sound playback or even a vibration control when a reset button is pushed or when a calculation is run.

3. Create a new project in Eclipse; try porting one of your own web applications onto the Android platform.

Including jQuery Mobile with WordPress

What You'll Learn in This Hour:

▶ An overview of WordPress

▶ How themes work with WordPress

▶ How to include jQuery Mobile in a theme

WordPress is an extremely popular framework used by thousands of people and companies to serve up dynamic content and even drive ecommerce sites. WordPress is an impressive and extensible framework, and while I would love to cover it more in depth, this hour we cover the basics and then get a theme ready using jQuery Mobile.

Introducing the WordPress CMS

Static websites are great for use as tools or for information sharing, but they lack the ability for live updates. The power behind a dynamic website is an integral part of a website's capability to attract visitors and even to get better rankings on search engines. While it is true that you could edit your site manually every time you have an update or change, this soon becomes monotonous work that increases the chance for errors with every update. This is where a Content Management System (CMS) comes into play. By using a CMS you can control what appears on a page and easily add content to different sections of a page.

Two types of sites run using a CMS that you are already familiar with: social sites and ecommerce sites. Let's start with social sites; they give you a tool that allows you to update content and change visible content. This is dynamic content generated by the user, and the site displays your data in a given field. Whether it is a social system that records and displays 140 characters or a blog that one of your friends updates with his collected works on the migratory habits of rocks in Death Valley, they are all a CMS to one extent or another.

Ecommerce sites are simply CMS sites that use a utility to import product data, including descriptions, prices, pictures, reviews, and more, that are then compiled and displayed to the user visiting the site. Can you imagine how difficult it would be to manually update and edit a site by hand as well as organize product placement, layout, and images? These reasons are why WordPress exists.

WordPress has been around for years, and while it is generally billed as simple blogging software, it is an extremely flexible and capable system that can be used as a full-blown CMS solution. You may ask why you should even bother with WordPress when other solutions such as Textpattern, Pixie, or even Anchor CMS are available. WordPress may not be the end-all solution for your CMS needs, but it is one of the most popular systems on the Internet. It is so popular that most web hosts offer one-click installs of the platform. WordPress also has one of the largest community followings on the Internet and carries almost 19,000 plug-ins hosted in the plug-in repository. This gives you options, extensibility, and a place to go to when you need help. Let's take a look at how to get and install WordPress.

Installing WordPress

WordPress is available in two versions, a hosted version that can be found at http://www.WordPress.com, and a version for developers that can be downloaded and installed on their own server. This version can be found at http://www.WordPress.org. While the hosted version of the platform is great for most standard users, we are more interested in downloading our own copy of WordPress and installing it on our own server. By opening http://WordPress.org/download/ in your browser you are taken to the download page for the current version of WordPress. This allows you to download two different versions of the software. There is a .zip file and a .tar file. Both files contain the same files, but the .tar file is a bit smaller. Windows users should opt for the .zip download, while Linux and OSX users can grab the .tar download. After you download the file, you are ready to start the installation process. WordPress comes with a "famous 5-minute installation" that can be found at http://codex.WordPress.org/Installing_WordPress. This page includes a section on how to install WordPress on your own computer. If you require some extra resources, you can try the links listed at http://codex.wordpress.org/WordPress_Installation_Techniques#Installing_WordPress_Locally. If you already have a web host with a MySQL version 5.0+ database and PHP version 5.2.4+, you can upload the files from the compressed download you grabbed earlier and start there. If you are developing locally on your computer you need to install PHP, MySQL, and a web server. Common all-in-one solutions for this are XAMPP and Ampps. Once you have WordPress installed and running, it is time to start using a theme.

Creating a Custom Theme for WordPress

Themes in WordPress are collections of various PHP, JavaScript, and CSS files bundled together that control the display and functionality of the site. They can be used to radically change the way the site functions and help to extend the capability of WordPress to be just about anything. Hundreds of themes are available for download, and some are even available through purchase. Many online theme libraries offer themes by color, layout, and cost. In recent versions of WordPress, a theme library can be searched and themes can be installed from inside the administration area.

So what do you do when you want to create a theme? You have a few options. You can grab an existing theme and change it to suit your purposes, you can find a "starter" or "blank" theme, or you can visit the codex on theme creation (http://codex.WordPress.org/Theme_Development) and build your theme from scratch. No matter what option you choose, you should be familiar with the basic structure of a theme which is as follows:

- ▶ Header
- ▶ Loop
- ▶ Sidebar
- ▶ Footer

Each of these sections is controlled by at least one file. For example, the header section is controlled by header.php, while the loop section works like a content area that can be controlled by files like index.php, single.php, and page.php.

To better show how this works, let's download a blank theme and set our blog to use it. Several blank themes are absolutely perfect for starting a new theme with. You could start with the HTML5Reset theme (html5reset.org), or you could start with another empty theme like Starkers. The Starkers theme was created in 2008 and has been updated to be kept contemporary with WordPress releases. Recently the Starkers theme is being rebuilt and has been rebranded under the Viewport Industries name. When completed, it will be available at http://viewportindustries.com/. For this hour we use the previously released version 3.0 of the Starkers theme, which is released under the GPL and is available at http://jquerymobilein24.com/starkersor on GitHub at https://github.com/viewportindustries/Starkers. Visit the website and download the theme. When the file has finished downloading, unzip the file and then copy or FTP the Starkers folder to your themes folder, which is found at *wordpressInstallationDirectory*/wp-content/themes (where *wordpressInstallationDirectory* is the name of the folder where you originally set up your WordPress install). Once the copy or transfer is complete you need to make it the active theme. To do this, open up your WordPress site in a browser and click on the Log In link (on the default installation this is on the right sidebar under the Meta category). When logged in you should see a navigation menu on the left side of the screen. Look down the list for the Appearance section and hover your mouse over it. A subnavigation menu appears allowing you to select Themes. Figure 24.1 shows the menu as shown in WordPress version 3.3.1.

FIGURE 24.1
All themes are managed this subsection.

After you have loaded the Themes page, you should see the active theme at the top of the page and the newly copied or transferred theme down below in the Available Themes section. All you need to do now is scroll down the page and click on the Activate link under the Starkers theme. Once you have done that the page should reload, and Starkers should be listed as the Current Theme. With the new theme active, your blog should now look something like Figure 24.2.

Now that we have the theme installed and running as our active theme, it's time to add jQuery Mobile to it.

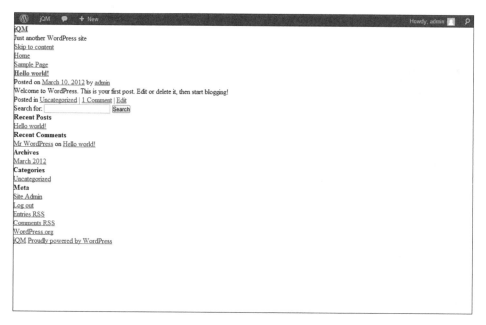

FIGURE 24.2
The Starkers theme lives up to the name.

Adding jQuery Mobile to Your Theme

Modifying a theme for jQuery takes some work, and while you may at first think that everything is done and picture perfect, there are bound to be some flaws. Although the way we are about to add jQuery Mobile to a theme does work, there will always be something that was missed or no longer supported as new versions roll out. Some plug-ins also break the functionality of a theme, so be sure to fully test them before adding them to your live blog. Just like plug-ins, some widgets can also cause undesirable effects to occur including some formatting issues. To avoid some of these issues now, open the administration section of the blog and find the Widgets subnav under the Appearance section and remove both the Search and Recent Comments widgets from the Primary Widget Area. This can be done by either clicking and dragging the widget to the left or expanding the widget and clicking on the Delete link. With those widgets gone, we are ready to start adding jQuery Mobile to the theme.

Let's start by editing the header.php file. A lot of code and included files go into this file, and it is included on every page. While I could tell you every line to replace or add, the easiest way to display this is to show the header.php file with the comments removed and the new code applied.

Listing 24.1 shows the header.php file with all the comments removed and some formatting applied.

LISTING 24.1   The header.php File with jQuery Mobile Added

```
 1: <!DOCTYPE html>
 2: <html <?php language_attributes(); ?>>
 3:   <head>
 4:     <meta charset="<?php bloginfo( 'charset' ); ?>" />
 5:     <meta name="viewport" content="width=device-width, initial-scale=1">
 6:     <title><?php wp_title( '|', true, 'right' );?></title>
 7:     <link rel="profile" href="http://gmpg.org/xfn/11" />
 8:     <link rel="stylesheet" type="text/css" media="all" href="
<?php bloginfo( 'stylesheet_url' ); ?>" />
 9:     <link rel="pingback" href="<?php bloginfo( 'pingback_url' ); ?>" />
10:     <link rel="stylesheet"
href="http://code.jquery.com/mobile/1.1.0-rc.1/jquery.mobile-1.1.0-rc.1.min.css"/>
11:     <script src="http://code.jquery.com/jquery-1.7.1.min.js"></script>
12:     <script>
13:       $(document).delegate("#jqm-page","pageinit", function() {
14:         $.mobile.ajaxEnabled=false;
15:       });
16:     </script>
17:     <script
src="http://code.jquery.com/mobile/1.1.0-rc.1/jquery.mobile-1.1.0-rc.1.min.js">
</script>
18:     <?php
19:       if ( is_singular() && get_option( 'thread_comments' ) )
20:         wp_enqueue_script( 'comment-reply' );
21:       wp_head();
22:     ?>
23:   </head>
24:
25:   <body <?php body_class(); ?>>
26:     <div data-role="page" id="jqm-page">
27:       <div data-role="header" data-position="inline">
28:         <h1><?php bloginfo( 'name' ); ?> -
<?php bloginfo( 'description' ); ?></h1>
29:         <a href="<?php echo home_url( '/' ); ?>" title="
<?php echo esc_attr( get_bloginfo( 'name', 'display' ) ); ?>" rel="home"
data-icon="home" class="ui-btn-right">Home</a>
30:       </div>
31:       <div id="access" role="navigation" data-role="navbar">
32:         <?php wp_nav_menu( array( 'container_class' => 'menu-header',
 'theme_location' => 'primary' ) ); ?>
33:       </div>
34:       <div data-role="content">
```

There are quite a few differences here compared to the base file so let's start at the top and work down through the differences. The first change is the addition on line 5 of the `meta` element that jQuery Mobile requires. The next additions are found on lines 10-17. Line 10 is the include for the jQuery Mobile styles, line 11 is the include for the jQuery library, and lines 12-16 are a custom script. The script is used to disable the automatic AJAX navigation that jQuery Mobile uses. This has been disabled due to administrative users getting errors and browser-lock whenever they try to transition to the administration area with AJAX enabled. If you are experienced with WordPress development, you may override some of the link-building functions to insert a `rel="external"` attribute on links that transition into the admin area. For those new to WordPress development disabling the AJAX allows you to get up and running immediately.

Line 17 shows the include for the jQuery Mobile library. Continuing down the file, the next change is on line 26 where a `div` element was added containing the properties of `data-role="page"` to make it a page, and `id="jqm-page"` so that we could tie events to the page in our JavaScript. Line 27 was also added to create the header section of the page by using a `div` element with the properties of `data-role="header"` and `data-position="inline"`. The inline style was used due to the button included in the header. Line 28 shows some modification to the way the blog name and description are shown. Line 29 shows a button added to the header to give another visible cue for users to return to the home page. Line 31 shows that the `data-role="navbar"` property added to help style the section through jQuery Mobile. Also the line that contained the link for Skip to Content was removed as it becomes useless when the styling and structure are completed. The last major change is line 34, which probably appears a bit out of place. The opening of the `div` element was added because it will wrap everything after the header down to the footer, so it is opened in the header.php file and closed in the footer.php file.

Now that we have modified the header.php file to use jQuery Mobile, Figure 24.3 shows what the changes have done to the site.

The site is coming along quite nicely as we now have a styled header in place and a small navigation section. We do still, however, have that broken `div` that was on the last line in header. php. Let's fix that by opening up footer.php and making some changes there. Listing 24.2 shows the completed footer.php file with the comments removed.

LISTING 24.2 The Completed footer.php File

```
1:         </div><!-- /data-role="content" -->
2:         <div data-role="footer">
3:         <?php get_sidebar( 'footer' ); ?>
4:             <a href="<?php echo home_url( '/' ) ?>" title="
<?php echo esc_attr( get_bloginfo( 'name', 'display' ) ); ?>" rel="home">
<?php bloginfo( 'name' ); ?></a>
5:             <a href="http://wordpress.org/"
title="Semantic Personal Publishing Platform"
```

```
rel="generator">Proudly powered by WordPress </a>
 6:         </div><!-- /data-role="footer" -->
 7:        </div><!-- /#jqm-page -->
 8:       <?php
 9:           wp_footer();
10:      ?>
11:    </body>
12: </html>
```

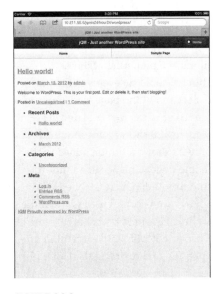

FIGURE 24.3
Even small changes make the site look more presentable.

Line 1 shows the closing `div` element that was started in the header.php file. Line 2 shows a new `div` element with the `data-role="footer"` property applied that adds the jQuery Mobile footer section. The footer section is then closed on line 6, and the page section that was also started in header.php is closed on line 7. It is closed before the PHP function `wp_footer()` due to some plug-ins requiring that function being the last call in the file. Figure 24.4 shows what the page looks like with the edited footer.php file in place.

The next file we need to change is index.php as this will be the main page users are shown when they visit the blog. Listing 24.3 shows the edited version of the file with comments removed.

FIGURE 24.4
The change is still subtle but frames the page nicely.

LISTING 24.3 The Edited index.php File

```
1: <?php get_header(); ?>
2: <div id="main">
3:     <h1>Lastest Posts</h1>
4:     <?php get_template_part( 'loop', 'index' ); ?>
5: </div><!-- /#main -->
6: <div id="sidebar">
7:     <?php get_sidebar(); ?>
8: </div>
9: <?php get_footer(); ?>
```

The header.php file is included by the PHP function `get_header()` that is called on line 1. Line 2 shows a `div` element that was added and given a property of `id="main"`. Line 3 shows an `h1` element that was added for display purposes. Line 4 loads the loop, which is part of the WordPress framework that grabs blog posts and displays information from them. Line 5 closes the `div` started on line 2, and line 6 starts another `div` element with a property of `id="sidebar"`. This `div` element contains the sidebar elements that will be displayed on the site and is closed on line 8. Line 9 then loads the bottom half of the file by calling the PHP `get_footer()` function. Because this page calls the loop and the sidebar, there isn't much of a difference to be seen yet, so lets open up loop.php and make some modifications to it. Listing 24.4 shows the edited loop.php file with the comments removed.

LISTING 24.4   The Edited loop.php File

```
1: <ul data-role="listview" data-inset="true" data-theme="a">
2:   <?php if (have_posts()) : while (have_posts()) : the_post(); ?>
3:       <li><a href="<?php the_permalink() ?>"><?php the_title(); ?></a></li>
4:     <?php endwhile;endif ?>
5: </ul>
6: <?php if (  $wp_query->max_num_pages > 1 ) : ?>
7:     <?php next_posts_link( __( '&larr; Older posts', 'twentyten' ) ); ?>
8:     <?php previous_posts_link( __( 'Newer posts &rarr;', 'twentyten' ) ); ?>
9: <?php endif; ?>
```

That really is the way the file is supposed to look now. The file has been gutted down to the base use of rendering the link and title of the blog entry. Line 1 shows that we added a `ul` element with the properties of `data-role="listview"`, `data-inset="true"`, and `data-theme="a"`. This is done to style the posts into a list, which is why opening and closing `li` element tags were added to line 3. The list is closed on line 5. With this file changed the site is starting to come together a bit more. Some of the PHP functions may be a little confusing as they pass around variables named `twentyten`. This variable is part of the theme functions and allows customization that mostly takes place in the functions.php file. To learn more about using functions and how to customize them in WordPress visit the Function Reference in the codex at http://codex. wordpress.org/Function_Reference.

Figure 24.5 shows the site with the modified loop in place.

The next portion of the site that needs adjustment is the sidebar. Listing 24.5 shows the edited sidebar.php file with some formatting changes and the comments removed.

LISTING 24.5   The Edited sidebar.php File

```
 1:        <div data-role="navbar">
 2:          <?php get_search_form(); ?>
 3:        </div>
 4:        <ul data-role="listview" data-inset="true" class="xoxo">
 5:          <?php
 6:            if ( ! dynamic_sidebar( 'primary-widget-area' ) ) : ?>
 7:            <li>
 8:              <h3><?php _e( 'Archives', 'twentyten' ); ?></h3>
 9:              <ul>
10:                <?php wp_get_archives( 'type=monthly' ); ?>
11:              </ul>
12:            </li>
13:            <li>
14:              <h3><?php _e( 'Meta', 'twentyten' ); ?></h3>
15:              <ul>
16:                <?php wp_register(); ?>
```

```
17:                 <li><?php wp_loginout(); ?></li>
18:                 <?php wp_meta(); ?>
19:               </ul>
20:             </li>
21:           <?php endif; // end primary widget area ?>
22:         </ul>
23: <?php
24:   if ( is_active_sidebar( 'secondary-widget-area' ) ) : ?>
25:       <ul class="xoxo" data-role="listview data-inset="true">
26:          <?php dynamic_sidebar( 'secondary-widget-area' ); ?>
27:       </ul>
28: <?php endif; ?>
```

FIGURE 24.5
The modified loop now displays the post title.

The first change here is that we moved the search bar out of the ul element to a div element above it. This was done to fix a formatting problem that occurred with the Search widget being enabled. The div element with the property of data-role="navbar" is used to help format the search. Line 4 shows that the original ul element has been given additional properties of data-role="listview" and data-inset="true". This affects the presentation of the list. The only other new change was the same properties being added to the list on line 25.

Even with the search being moved out of the list, WordPress will format it as a list element and will break formatting, so we need to create a new file called searchform.php and include it in the theme folder on the file system. The file is simple and needs to contain only the following lines:

```
<form action="<?php bloginfo('siteurl'); ?>" id="searchform" method="get">
    <div data-role="fieldcontain">
        <input type="search" id="s" name="s" value="" placeholder="Search" />
    </div>
</form>
```

After creating the file and saving it to your theme folder, WordPress automatically looks in the theme folder on the file system for it and uses it when found. With the file in place and with the changes we just made to the sidebar.php file, the site is now starting to look like a jQuery Mobile designed site. Figure 24.6 shows the site as it appears on an iPad.

FIGURE 24.6
The theme is really coming together with our changes.

We still have a few more PHP files to tweak, but let's take a break and adjust the styles to make the site a little user-friendlier for those on tablet devices. Listing 24.6 shows the edited style.css file with some comments removed.

LISTING 24.6   The style.css File Edited with Media Queries

```
 1: /* Not needed with jQM
 2: @import "css/reset.css";
 3: */
 4: @import "css/typography.css";
 5: @import "css/layout.css";
 6:
 7: img {max-width: 100%;}
 8: .center {text-align: center;}
 9: .comment-body .ui-li-desc {white-space: normal;}
10:
11: /* media queries for jQM*/
12: @media all and (min-width: 650px){
13:     #sidebar {width: 34%;margin-left:65%;}
14:     #main {width: 63%;float:left;}
15: }
16: @media all and (max-width:649px) {
17:     #sidebar {border-top: 2px solid #999;}
18: }
```

CAUTION

Theme Information

Every theme used in WordPress contains important data in the comments at the top of the styles. css file. These comments are used to display the name, version, and description of the theme in the administration area of WordPress. While it is fine to modify the data, make sure you do not delete it and leave it empty!

Lines 1-3 are a comment and import of the reset.css file. Because jQuery Mobile already provides a reset, this file does not need to be called, so it can be safely commented out. Lines 4 and 5 show the other included imports for other styles. Line 7 shows the image style we want applied to help resize images for different mobile devices, and line 8 shows a class that was added for some page formatting. Line 9 shows a class file that will overwrite some of the included jQuery Mobile styles that we'll be using later. Line 11 is a comment to let you know that the area below is media queries. Line 12 shows a media query that will run on all devices that support media queries and have a minimum screen width of 650px. Lines 13 and 14 show the styles that will be applied on these devices. Line 16 shows a media query that will be run on all devices that support media queries and have a maximum screen size of 649px.

With those few changes, let's see what has happened to our site. Figure 24.7 shows the site viewed on a tablet, and Figure 24.8 shows the site viewed on a smaller screen device.

FIGURE 24.7
The media queries shift the sidebar to the right side of the screen.

FIGURE 24.8
The sidebar drops below and adds a border on top.

Now that the page is properly styled for different screen resolutions, let's continue to edit the other pages and use the styles where applicable. Listing 24.7 shows the edited single.php file with the comments removed and some formatting done. This file is used to display individual posts.

LISTING 24.7   The Edited single.php File

```php
1: <?php get_header(); ?>
2: <div id="main">
3: <?php if ( have_posts() ) while ( have_posts() ) : the_post(); ?>
4:    <h1><?php the_title(); ?></h1>
5:    <?php twentyten_posted_on(); ?>
6:    <?php the_content(); ?>
7:    <?php wp_link_pages( array( 'before' => '' . __( 'Pages:', 'twentyten' ),
'after' => '' ) ); ?>
8:    <?php if ( get_the_author_meta( 'description' ) ) : ?>
9:       <?php echo get_avatar( get_the_author_meta( 'user_email' ),
apply_filters( 'twentyten_author_bio_avatar_size', 60 ) ); ?>
10:      <h2><?php printf( esc_attr__( 'About %s', 'twentyten' ),
get_the_author() ); ?></h2>
11:      <?php the_author_meta( 'description' ); ?>
12:      <a href="
<?php echo get_author_posts_url( get_the_author_meta( 'ID' ) ); ?>">
13:
14:         <?php printf( __( 'View all posts by %s &rarr;', 'twentyten' ),
get_the_author() ); ?>
15:      </a>
16:   <?php endif; ?>
17:   <p><?php twentyten_posted_in(); ?></p>
18:   <p><?php edit_post_link( __( 'Edit this post', 'twentyten' ), '', '' ); ?></p>
19:   <div class="ui-grid-a">
20:      <div class="ui-block-a center">
21:         <strong>Previous Post:</strong><br />
22:         <?php previous_post_link( '%link', '' . _x( '&larr;',
'Previous post link', 'twentyten' ) . ' %title' ); ?>
23:      </div>
24:      <div class="ui-block-b center">
25:         <strong>Next Post:</strong><br />
26:         <?php next_post_link( '%link', '%title ' . _x( '&rarr;',
'Next post link', 'twentyten' ) . '' ); ?>
27:      </div>
28:   </div>
29:   <?php comments_template( '', true ); ?>
30:
31: <?php endwhile; // end of the loop. ?>
32: </div><!-- /#main-->
```

```
33: <div id="sidebar">
34:    <?php get_sidebar(); ?>
35: </div>
36: <?php get_footer(); ?>
```

The first change between this file and the original file is shown on line 2 where a `div` element with the `id="main"` property has been added. This `div` wraps all the way down to line 32. The next change in the file is the removal of two lines of code that should have been on lines 4 and 5. These were navigation links that felt a little redundant for a mobile theme and so were removed. Continuing down the page we did change the formatting on the lower navigation links by inserting a grid that starts on line 19 and continues down to line 28. This is a two-column grid that contains a previous post and next post link. Text was also added inside `strong` elements on lines 21 and 25 to help describe what the links are for. These links will only populate when you have a next and/or previous post to show. The last change added to this file is the `div` element with the `id="sidebar"` property that has been added on line 33.

Before we look at the page, let's make one quick change to the comments.php file.

This is a single-element, two-line change, so instead of listing out the entire file I just want you to open the comments.php file in an editor and find the opening `ol` element that should be on or near line 43. Replace the line with the following code:

```
<ul data-role="listview" data-inset="true">
```

Now replace the closing `ol` element with a closing `ul` element and save the file. Figure 24.9 shows what the changes to single.php and comments.php have done. To view the changes you need to view either a post you have created, or the default post included with the WordPress install. If you are developing on localhost, the URL to view the changes should be similar to http://localhost/jqmin24/hour24/wordpress/?p=1.

As you can see in Figure 24.9, some broken styles still appear in the new comment list. The formatting of the date and the comment look crammed together and would look a bit nicer if some spacing were added. We can also change the size of the avatar image as well as move it into the corner. Oddly enough, the formatting for this section is managed in the functions.php file. The functions.php file controls the custom logic that is used in your theme and can be used to overload existing functions in the WordPress framework. This file is rather large, and we need to replace only one function, so open the functions.php file and perform a search for the following:

```
function twentyten_comment( $comment, $args, $depth ) {
```

That is the beginning of the `twentyten_comment` function, and inside it should be a `div` element with a property of `class="comment-author vcard"`.

FIGURE 24.9
The post is now reformatted and comments appear in a styled list.

This `div` element should be deleted, but the contents of this `div` element need to be moved up above the preceding `div` element that contains the property of `id="comment-<?php comment_ID(); ?>"` before you delete it. This moves the avatar image out from within the comments and lets it float to the left of the comment. Another change you will want to do is to modify the `get_avatar()` function you just moved so that the number `40` is changed to `72`. This changes the size of the avatar image from 40x40 to 72x72 pixels.

The last thing you need to do is to wrap the second line you moved in an h3 element and save the file. This may sound more complicated than it really is, so refer to the functions.php file in the theme folder to make sure that you have made the correct edits.

Only three more files need to have any editing done to them, and they all need to have the exact same code added. The following edits set up a `div` element to wrap areas together. These areas then allow us to adjust the page through a responsive layout. Open the following files in your favorite text editor page.php, archive.php, and search.php. Each one of these files should contain the following line:

```
get_header(); ?>
```

On the next line add the following element:

```
<div id="main">
```

Then find the following:

```
<?php get_sidebar(); ?>
```

Above that line add the following:

```
</div><!-- /#main -->
<div id="sidebar">
```

Immediately after the line you found, add a closing `div` element to close the `div` element you started above it. This adds the formatting for the main content area and the sidebar. To view the changes made to page.php, click on the Sample Page link in the navbar at the top of the page. To view the changes to archive.php, click on the Archives link in the sidebar, and then click on a listed month to view the page. To view the changes to search.php, just use the Search box to find something on the blog. Figures 24.10, 24.11, and 24.12 show each of these pages loaded into a tablet browser with the changes applied.

With those changes applied, the theme is ready to be turned live. To move the theme to production, the only thing you need to do is to copy the entire theme folder from the current location on your development setup to the same location on your production installation of WordPress. This is the exact same process you used when you moved the original theme to begin editing and viewing the theme. If you were already working on the theme on your production environment, you don't actually have to do anything since it's already live.

FIGURE 24.10
The archive.php page rendered on a tablet

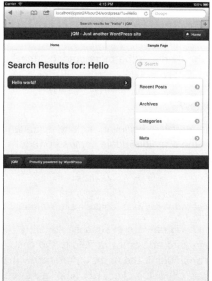

FIGURE 24.11
The search.php page rendered on a tablet

FIGURE 24.12
The page.php page rendered on a tablet

Remember that not all themes are the same, and implementing jQuery Mobile into them is different on every theme. That doesn't mean that it will be any more difficult, but it will be different. You may also be considering a mobile plug-in that does device detection and then directs mobile users to a mobile theme. WordPress is a wonderfully customizable platform that can do some amazing things with a little PHP know-how and determination. When combined with jQuery Mobile you get a truly dynamic site that works for everyone who visits.

Summary

In this hour you learned about the WordPress framework and how it is used as a publishing platform from CMS systems to ecommerce sites. WordPress uses themes to change appearance and function. These themes can be customized, and other frameworks can be included inside them.

You also learned that jQuery Mobile can be included in a theme and used to provide the styles and functionality for a theme used in WordPress. While integration of jQuery Mobile does touch quite a few files, it can be done fairly easily and still provide a rich user experience to your publishing platform.

Q&A

Q. Can I add jQuery Mobile to any theme?

A. Absolutely, but remember that the more customized the theme is the more potential the theme has for running into issues with the addition of jQuery Mobile.

Q. What will happen to my theme when WordPress updates?

A. Chances are usually good that you will not have to do anything; however, nothing is guaranteed to work in future releases. I suggest that every time a major update comes down for WordPress you grab it and throw it on a development blog and check your theme for functionality and appearance.

Q. I downloaded a plug-in for WordPress and when I activated it my site looks like it exploded!

A. I completely understand what you are going through. I have run into this issue with an antispam commenting system. The system was designed to add an extra field to the comments section making it difficult for robots to fill out and submit the form. Unfortunately the styles were hard coded and it made the comments section look broken. Not all plug-ins are compatible with all themes, and some are not even compatible with the current version of WordPress. The best thing to do in this instance is to see whether you can code around the issue, or modify the source code of the plug-in to play nice with jQuery Mobile. If that still doesn't work, try searching for a fork or port of the original plug-in.

Workshop

The workshop contains a quiz and some exercises to help you check your comprehension and understanding.

Quiz

1. What is WordPress?

2. What are themes in regards to WordPress?

3. True or False: Other frameworks can be included in theme files.

4. True or False: When adding jQuery Mobile to a theme it will work with all plug-ins automatically.

5. When adding jQuery Mobile into a WordPress theme, what feature may break access to the admin area?

Answers

1. WordPress is a popular framework that can be used to publish dynamic content.

2. Themes are bundles of PHP, JavaScript, CSS, and image files combined to provide functionality and style unique to the theme.

3. True. Plug-ins, widgets, JavaScript libraries, and more can be combined into themes.

4. False. jQuery Mobile may not even appear to be working when first applied to the theme. It may also break your widgets, plug-ins, and theme until properly integrated.

5. The AJAX Navigation system of jQuery Mobile may break your ability to enter the admin area, and even to edit posts and comments. This can be overcome by disabling the feature.

Exercises

1. Use ThemeRoller to add some custom color to the theme.

2. Try changing the comments section to use the original `ol` element and edit the functions. php file to change the display to something new.

3. Try customizing another WordPress theme to use jQuery Mobile and test and see how your implementation works.

Index

collapsible content, 127-129

color of QR codes

adjusting, 371-373

color palette (ThemeRoller), 295

commercial sources for icons, 258

commercial stock images, 260

compiling applications, 437-440

component bars, 237-238

configuring, server-side compression on Apache servers, 388-389

content

aligning with grid system, 122-126

collapsible content, 127-129

HTML, 24-27

video

delivering, 358-360

embedding with Vimeo, 334-336

embedding with YouTube, 328-334

hosting your own file, 336-340

playback, 327

plug-ins, 358-359

content area, mobile site structure, 80

content blocks, 237-239

counts, adding to standard lists, 195-196

creating

buttons, link-based, 153-154

collapsible content, 127-129

lists

inset lists, 192

numbered lists, 194

split lists, 199-201

standard lists, 191-192

mobile sites, 65-67

swatches, 241-245

Creative Commons license, 256

CSS (Cascading Style Sheets), 21, 27-31

@font-face, 266-268

custom themes, applying, 234-235

external CSS files, 29-30

inline styles, 31

jQuery Mobile framework, adding to web pages, 57

media queries, 275-276

single-line hierarchy, 28

style tags, 28-29

swatches, 240-241

creating, 241-245

custom swatches, 245-246

custom animation

adding, 54-58

placement of, 57

custom fonts, 265, 266-268

@font-face, 266-268

Google Web Fonts, 269-271

custom icons, 164-167

custom images, displaying with QR codes, 373-375

custom swatches, 245-246

custom themes, 234-235

in ThemeRoller, 302-303

for WordPress

creating, 445-446

jQuery Mobile, adding, 447-461

D

data attributes, 63-65

default theme

static file images, 229-231

swatches, 67, 230-234

delivering video content, 358-360

native video player, 359-360

plug-ins, 358-359

Delivr, 368

desktop layout, 284-286

desktops, support for jQuery Mobile, 10

development

Android

project, creating, 423-430

SDK, downloading, 420-421

application, compiling, 437-440

IDE, 13

jQuery Mobile, including in your project, 430-437

Linux applications, 16-17

OSX applications, 15-16

programming language support, 12

How can we make this index more useful? Email us at indexes@samspublishing.com

X–Y–Z

W

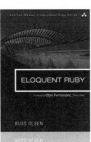
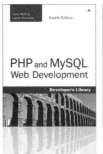

Where are the Companion Content Files?

Thank you for purchasing this digital version of:

Sams Teach Yourself jQuery Mobile in 24 Hours

Access to the sample code used in the book is available by following the steps below:

1. On your PC or MAC, open a web browser and go to this URL:
    www.informit.com/title/
    9780672335945
    Navigate to the Downloads tab and click on the "Sample Code" link.

2. Download the ZIP file (or files) from the web site to your hard drive.

3. Unzip the files and follow the directions for use in the READ ME included in the download.

Please note that many of our companion content files can be very large, especially image and video files.

If you are unable to locate the files for this title by following the steps above, please visit www.informit.com/about/contact_us and select "Digital Products Help" and supply the URL from step one within the Comments box. Our customer service representatives will assist you.

Note: The code is also available on the author's site at
http://jquerymobilein24.com

The Professional and Personal Technology Brands of Pearson

 Addison Wesley   Cisco Press   IBM Press.   InformIT   PEARSON IT Certification   PRENTICE HALL   QUE   SAMS   vmware PRESS

FREE
Online Edition

Your purchase of *Sams Teach Yourself jQuery Mobile in 24 Hours* includes access to a free online edition for 45 days through the **Safari Books Online** subscription service. Nearly every Sams book is available online through **Safari Books Online**, along with thousands of books and videos from publishers such as Addison-Wesley Professional, Cisco Press, Exam Cram, IBM Press, O'Reilly Media, Prentice Hall, Que, and VMware Press.

Safari Books Online is a digital library providing searchable, on-demand access to thousands of technology, digital media, and professional development books and videos from leading publishers. With one monthly or yearly subscription price, you get unlimited access to learning tools and information on topics including mobile app and software development, tips and tricks on using your favorite gadgets, networking, project management, graphic design, and much more.

Activate your FREE Online Edition at
informit.com/safarifree

STEP 1: Enter the coupon code: SAGRWBI.

STEP 2: New Safari users, complete the brief registration form. Safari subscribers, just log in.

If you have difficulty registering on Safari or accessing the online edition, please e-mail customer-service@safaribooksonline.com